D0867225

WITHDRAWN

The Unacknowledged
Legislator

The Unacknowledged Legislator

Shelley and Politics

P. M. S. DAWSON

Clarendon Press · Oxford
1980

Oxford University Press, Walton Street, Oxford OX2 6DP

OXFORD LONDON GLASGOW
NEW YORK TORONTO MELBOURNE WELLINGTON
KUALA LUMPUR SINGAPORE JAKARTA HONG KONG TOKYO
DELHI BOMBAY CALCUTTA MADRAS KARACHI
NAIROBI DAR ES SALAAM CAPE TOWN

Published in the United States by
Oxford University Press, New York

© *P.M.S. Dawson 1980*

British Library Cataloguing in Publication Data

Dawson, P M S
   The unacknowledged legislator
   1. Shelley, Percy Bysshe – Political and
  social views
   2. Politics in literature
   I. Title
821'.7   PR5442.P64   79-40843

ISBN 0-19-812095-8

Set, printed and bound in Great Britain by
Billing and Sons Limited and Kemp Hall Bindery
Guildford, London, Oxford, Worcester

Acknowledgements

I F ALL debts were paid in full, who would have a book left to call his own? My indebtedness to published sources will be apparent from the footnotes, though they cannot do justice to the less tangible contributions to my knowledge and awareness which have been made by the work of previous writers on the subjects dealt with in the following pages. A more personal debt is owing to the teachers, colleagues, and friends who by their instruction, advice, and conversation have helped me to understand Shelley and his works better: in particular, to John Beer, Richard Cronin, Paul Foot, Geoffrey Matthews, Roy Park, J. H. Prynne, R. T. H. Redpath, Claire Tomalin, and Timothy Webb. I would also like to thank Derek Beales, John Brewer, Arnold Harvey, and Leslie Mitchell for the patience and courtesy they have shown to a literary scholar in his attempts to get his bearings in the field of late eighteenth- and early nineteenth-century history. Particular thanks are due to Seamus Deane, who allowed me to see the chapter on Shelley from his forthcoming work on the influence of the Enlightenment on the English Romantic poets; to Roland Thorne of the History of Parliament Trust, who supplied me with information concerning the political activities of Shelley's father; and to Paula Feldman and Diana Pugh, who allowed me to see the typescript of their forthcoming edition of the Shelley journals.

I would also like to acknowledge the patient assistance given me in the course of my researches by the staff of the University Library in Cambridge, the British Library in London, and the Bodleian Library in Oxford. The Delegates of the Oxford University Press have granted permission for me to quote from the rich store of manuscripts by Shelley and his circle in the Bodleian; and the British Library, the Pierpont Morgan Library in New York, and the Library of Congress have kindly allowed me to quote from manuscript material in their possession. Lord Abinger has graciously allowed me to make use of his magnificent collection of material relating to Godwin, Shelley and their circle. In Chapter I I have made use of material from the Albery Manuscripts at Horsham Museum; in this connection I would like to thank Anthony

Windrum of the Horsham Museum Society for the courtesy and assistance he extended to me during my researches at Horsham, and Patricia Gill and the staff of the West Sussex Record Office for providing me with the revised references to this material. Finally, I would like to thank the staff of the Pforzheimer Collection in New York, of the Library of Texas Christian University, and of the Berg Collection of the New York Public Library for their prompt and helpful replies to my queries.

Parts of Chapters III and IV, with some material from other chapters, have appeared in the *Keats–Shelley Memorial Bulletin*, and I wish to thank the editor, Timothy Webb, for permission to reprint this material in the present work.

Contents

Abbreviated Titles

Journal	*Mary Shelley's Journal*, ed. F. L. Jones (Norman, Oklahoma, 1947).
K–SJ	*Keats–Shelley Journal*.
K–SMB	*Keats–Shelley Memorial Bulletin*.
Letters	*The Letters of Percy Bysshe Shelley*, ed. F. L. Jones (2 vols., Oxford, 1964).
Life	*The Life of Percy Bysshe Shelley as comprised in The Life of Shelley by Thomas Jefferson Hogg; The Recollections of Shelley and Byron by Edward John Trelawny; Memoirs of Shelley by Thomas Love Peacock*, ed. H. Wolfe (2 vols., 1933).
Medwin	Thomas Medwin, *The Life of Percy Bysshe Shelley* (1847), ed. H. B. Forman (1913).
Political Justice	William Godwin, *Enquiry concerning Political Justice and its Influence on Morals and Happiness* (1793; 3rd edn., 1798), ed. F. E. L. Priestley (3 vols., Toronto, 1946).
SC	*Shelley and His Circle 1773–1822*, Vols. i–iv ed. K. N. Cameron (1961–70), Vols. v–vi ed. D. H. Reiman (Cambridge, Mass., 1973).
Works	*The Complete Works of Percy Bysshe Shelley*, ed. R. Ingpen and W. E. Peck (1926–30; 10 vols., 1965).

Introduction

A GREAT Romantic poet once remarked to a visitor that 'although he was known to the world only as a poet, he had given twelve hours thought to the conditions and prospects of society, for one to poetry'.[1] No one would have a greater right to make such a claim than Shelley, who wrote to a friend: 'I consider Poetry very subordinate to moral & political science, & if I were well, certainly I should aspire to the latter.'[2] The poet in question was actually Wordsworth, and this fact should serve to remind us that Shelley's concern with politics was part of the 'spirit of the age'. No poet can stand outside his own history and that of the human community of which he is a part, but this involvement may be more urgent and more explicit at certain periods than at others. Such a period was that in which the Romantic poets lived, and the issues of contemporary politics were of the substance of their poetry, as Carl Woodring has shown.[3] This is hardly surprising, for the period between 1789 and 1832 was a momentous one in our history. The agricultural, aristocratic, and hierarchical society into which William Blake was born in 1757 was not the industrial, democratic, class-divided, and imperial nation in which William Wordsworth died in 1850. In history neat and summary divisions are impossible, and the change had begun before Blake's birth, and has continued since Wordsworth's death. What is most important about the period 1789–1832, especially for the literary historian, is not that the essential change occurred then, but that people became aware that it was occurring, and began to speculate on its nature, its significance, and the kind of world it was beginning to bring into being. This was the age that saw the emergence of seminal minds like Godwin, Burke, Bentham, Owen, Malthus, and Ricardo, to name only the most eminent and influential. The poets who came to maturity in this period were equally concerned with the social, economic, political, religious, and philosophical issues and problems

---

[1] Orville Dewey, *The Old World and the New* (1836), p. 90, quoted in F. M. Todd, *Politics and the Poet: A Study of Wordsworth* (1957), p. 11.

[2] *Letters*, ii. 71.

[3] *Politics in English Romantic Poetry* (Cambridge, Mass., 1970).

that faced society as a whole. Later in the nineteenth century men of letters like Wordsworth, Coleridge, Scott, Shelley, and Byron were to have influence that must be ascribed as much to their political and philosophical views as to their literary quality alone. A full understanding of their work can hardly be separated from an understanding of the historical situation in which they wrote.

It is a truism that all periods are periods of transition, but the period of Shelley's life is almost unique in being almost invariably studied as a period of transition. Historians have tended to treat it as an epilogue to the eighteenth century or a prologue to the Victorian age, to scrutinize it for signs of the aftermath of the French Revolution or for the roots of the First Reform Act. Valuable monographs and articles on particular aspects exist, but we still lack a satisfactory synthesis of the history of this period as a whole. This creates problems for the literary scholar seeking historical bearings in order to trace the connections between literature and the larger life of society, and all too often it imposes on him the obligation of rushing to judgement in areas where his historical colleagues have refrained from treading. I have tried to obtain the best lights available on the areas touched on in this study, and, where necessary, to supplement them with my own researches. The historians whom I have consulted on points of detail and interpretation have been invariably both sympathetic and helpful. It is my hope that this study might help to repay some of the debt I owe them. Historians understandably devote most of their attention to those figures whose actions demonstrably influence the course of events; however, an increasing amount of sympathetic attention is now being given to radical movements among those whose social status excluded them from the political nation, and whose historical importance, in the obvious sense, is questionable. Shelley, by choice rather than circumstance, was similarly excluded, and it might well be worth the while of historians to take into consideration the reactions to events of someone who, like most of us, had little control over them, but who possessed wider knowledge, greater sensitivity, and a more penetrating intelligence than most of us can lay claim to. The very fact that such a person should have renounced the possibilities of power that were the birthright of his class may well tell us more about his age than the successful political careers of others who shared his background and upbringing.

In recommending Shelley to the attention of historians I am implying a claim for his political sobriety and responsibility that may well raise eyebrows. Shelley is not notorious for such qualities. But the reader would be well advised to believe nothing of what he may have been told about Shelley, and (in view of the state of his text) only half of what he sees. The charge that Shelley evades the actual has all too frequently been made in ignorance of the actualities which he is asserted to have wished to evade. When his career is seen in the context of his age we shall be able to recognize that he struggled far more resolutely than is generally supposed with 'the difficult and unbending realities of actual life'.[4] We shall then be in a better position to appreciate *why* evasion was a temptation for him. What is often dismissed as facile escapism is in fact an integral and essential part of his political ideology. His politics was a politics of progress, resting on a demand for the total transformation of social life. The achievement of such a transformation depends on the ability to imagine an alternative. If you would not have what *is*, you must acknowledge that what you would have *is not*, or is not yet. This is the politics of the ideal, and to attempt to translate it into a practical programme is to reject the real and pursue an illusion. It is also to run the risks of escapism on the one hand and disillusion on the other. Shelley did not entirely escape either of these dangers, but neither did he escape the knowledge of the risks that he was running, and he would have held that they were not to be avoided. His Utopianism (though strictly speaking Shelley is not a Utopian) does indeed degenerate on occasion into a desire to retreat from the conditions of actual existence, but it more frequently includes within itself a sense of the pressures of the actual, and of the imperative need to bridge the gap between actual and ideal. Many of the charges of 'evasion' levelled against Shelley are based on that contradiction between what is and what ought to be that he himself was only too well aware of, but which his critics seem to think he overlooked. In none of his major works, however 'Utopian', are the pressures of reality absent or even softened, from the lurid melodrama of *Queen Mab* to the bleak appraisal of *The Triumph of Life*.

Merely to posit the contradictions between reality and desire would hardly be enough to repel the charge of political naïvety. There is also an obligation to provide a convincing account of the

[4] *Works*, vii. 43.

transition from the rejected present to the desired future. Shelley's problems here are the result not so much of any lack of practicality on his part as of the almost insuperable difficulties that face any politics so radical as to deserve the epithet 'millenarian'. Modern historians are beginning to regard these difficulties with some sympathy, especially when their own politics demand the transformation of society. As E. J. Hobsbawm notes,

The essence of millenarianism, the hope of a complete and radical change in the world which will be reflected in the millennium, a world shorn of all its present deficiencies, is not confined to primitivism. It is present, almost by definition, in all revolutionary movements of whatever kind, and 'millenarian' elements may therefore be discovered by the student in any of them, insofar as they have ideals.[5]

If we adopt this negative definition of 'millennium', Shelley is surely a millenarian; indeed, while his politics are far from primitive, the millenarian strain is unusually strong. Professor Hobsbawm is more than a little of a millenarian himself, and he speaks movingly of

that utopianism, or 'impossibilism' which the most primitive revolutionaries share with all but the most sophisticated, and which makes even very modern ones feel a sense of almost physical pain at the realization that the coming of Socialism will not eliminate *all* grief and sadness, unhappy love-affairs or mourning, and will not solve or make soluble *all* problems; a feeling reflected in the ample literature of revolutionary disillusionment. (p. 60)

Shelley would certainly understand this; he is in fact closer to Hobsbawm than to the primitive millenarian movements that the latter chronicles. He shares his ironic awareness of the limits of any possible transformation, and thus of the extent to which their millenarianism is a fiction, however necessary a one. In the conclusion to Act III of *Prometheus Unbound* Shelley acknowledges the limits of the Promethean transformation of the world, though he goes on to suggest that even the inescapable conditions of mortal existence are to be transcended in consciousness.

Hobsbawn's nostalgia for the millenarian spirit is significantly qualified by his awareness that its achievements can never match its aspirations, so that a reasoned defence of it must simultaneously

---

[5] *Primitive Rebels: Studies in Archaic Forms of Social Movement in the 19th and 20th Centuries* (1959; 2nd edn., Manchester, 1971), p. 57.

reveal it as a fiction. He argues that 'utopianism is probably a necessary social device for generating the superhuman efforts without which no major revolution is achieved', but goes on to add: 'It was essential for [the French and Russian revolutionaries] to believe that "the ultimate in human prosperity and liberty will appear after their victories". Obviously they will not, though the result of the revolution may nevertheless be very worth while' (pp. 60–1). It is the dilemma of the more sophisticated revolutionary that he has bitten into the apple of such knowledge. Shelley was very much aware that the achievement of even a limited degree of reform depends on a commitment to a far more radical transformation.

> Towards whatsoever we regard as perfect, undoubtedly it is no less our duty than it is our nature to press forward; this is the generous enthusiasm, which accomplishes not indeed the consummation after which it aspires, but one which approaches it in a degree far nearer, than if the whole powers had not been developed by a ⟨delusion⟩. (*Works*, vii. 46)

It cannot be easy to maintain the necessary commitment when one knows that it is to a 'delusion'. It was Shelley's achievement that he was able to do so and to resist the double temptation: either to relinquish his millenarian ideals and acquiesce in a more 'practical' politics, or to renounce the possibility of even limited progress in the real world and retreat into utopian fantasies. The most important task that faces the student of Shelley's politics is to trace the connection between his practical proposals for reform and his adherence to the millenarian dream.

The problem is the familiar one of ends and means. Hobsbawm's belief that progress can only come by revolution leads him to gloss over the point that revolutionary means may be incompatible with certain millenarian ends, though he is aware that millenarianism is not in itself revolutionary, however important the part it may play in the revolutionary psychology. He notes that 'millenarian movements share a fundamental vagueness about the actual way in which the new society will be brought about' (p. 58). Shelley of course is often accused of this kind of 'vagueness', and not entirely without reason, for his accounts of social transformation in terms of 'crisis' are not always convincing, and tend to appeal to a very primitive, even chiliastic millenarianism. Modern revolutionary movements cannot afford this kind of vagueness, and have, as

Hobsbawm says, 'certain fairly definite ideas on how the old society is to be replaced by the new, the most crucial of which concerns what we may call the "transfer of power" ' :

> The sort of thing revolutionaries do is, let us say, to organize a mass demonstration, throw up barricades, march on the town hall, run up the tricolour, proclaim the Republic one and indivisible, appoint a provisional government, and issue a call for a Constituent Assembly. (This, roughly, is the 'drill' which so many of them learned from the French Revolution. It is not, of course, the only possible procedure.) (p. 58)

This account puts the purposeful bustle of revolutionaries in a somewhat ironical light. Is this adaption of means to ends all that effective? Anyone who had lived through the aftermath of the French Revolution would have had ample reason to be sceptical concerning the value of the usual revolutionary 'drill'. As Hobsbawm goes on to point out, 'the "pure" millenarian movement operates quite differently, whether because of the inexperience of its members or the narrowness of their horizons, or because of the effect of millenarian ideologies and prescriptions. Its followers are not makers of revolution' (p. 58). It is unfortunate that the point about 'the effect of millenarian ideologies and prescriptions' is not elaborated upon. It was certainly Shelley's 'millenarianism' that prevented him from joining the 'makers of revolution', for there was a fundamental contradiction between the ends of the Godwinian anarchism to which he adhered, and the use of violence and the 'transfer of power' as means to effect social change. Again and again in his comments on the French Revolution he argued that the attempt to overthrow the old order by violent revolution merely perpetuated the spirit of that order, and *The Cenci* was written to prove just that point. Having seen how the (apparently) most effectual means only served to frustrate the only desirable end, Shelley well understood how it might seem that

> God made irreconcilable
> Good and the means of good. . .
> (*The Triumph of Life*, lines 230–1)

At this point the choice is between despair, and a retreat to less spectacular but ultimately more effective methods of change. It is in this perspective that we must view Shelley's gradualism and reformism. His reformist means are always directed to revolutionary ends, but he has accepted that the necessary transformation of society can only come about through the step-by-step purification and improvement of the old order, rather than by a single apocalyptic stroke. It was this decision that involved him in the daily activities of politics and in movements for limited reform, though, as we shall see, his thinking on those issues was always informed by his ultimate aims.

Shelley's close and active involvement with contemporary reform movements has led me to draw more heavily on the work of historians than on that of political philosophers. His politics are practical rather than theoretical, and in any case the study of political theory has in the past tended to ask questions that are not really relevant to his particular concerns. For example, political philosophy tends to centre on the problem of balancing and arbitrating between divergent interests. This is not a question that arises for Shelley, since he prefers to assume that there is a single 'general interest' that overrides all personal and sectional interests, or rather that subsumes the 'real' interest of all. Thus he assures even those who disagree with him that 'the endeavours of the truly virtuous necessarily converge to one point, though it be hidden from them what point that is: they all labour for one end' (*Works*, v. 267). The study of actual political institutions subjects any such assumption to enormous stress, but it was made by many philosophers, including Rousseau, Paine, Godwin, and even Bentham. It is an assumption that comes naturally to anyone who considers politics to be a branch of morals, since it would seem obvious that there must be one correct policy for a society in a given set of circumstances, just as there is one right course of action for the individual. The anarchism that Shelley derived from Godwin makes a particularly close connection between politics and ethics, and all anarchist philosophies have a moralistic slant to them that tends to make them openly apolitical. A philosophy that rejects politics as an activity and holds to millenarian aims is not easy for political philosophers to deal with. But at least one recent political philosopher has been willing to give serious attention to anarchism, and to argue in favour of speculations that go beyond the feasible.

One cannot know how satisfied we shall be with what we achieve among our feasible alternatives without knowing how far they diverge from our fantasied wishes: and it is only bringing such wishes, and their force, into the picture that we shall understand people's efforts towards expanding the range of their currently feasible alternatives. . . . I do not laugh at the content of our wishes that go not only beyond the actual and what we take to be feasible in the future, but even beyond the possible; nor do I wish to denigrate fantasy, or minimize the pangs of being limited to the possible.[6]

The examples that Nozick adduces from Fourier are strongly reminiscent of some of the speculations advanced by Shelley in *Queen Mab*. I shall have something to say about the value of such non-feasible speculation in talking about the political dimension of *Prometheus Unbound*, in Chapter III.

In the first three chapters of this study I attempt to expound the political ideology to which Shelley adhered, and to show how, and more important why, he came to adopt it. Chapter I, which deals with Shelley's attitude to the Whiggism of his family background, also serves to bring out those aspects of his political upbringing that left their permanent mark on him, often no doubt without his knowledge or intention. My account of the Foxite creed will not (I hope) strike historians as novel, but I have been able to add some details, from newspapers, parliamentary reports, and unpublished papers, to our knowledge of the political activities of Shelley's family. The second chapter, in which I argue that Shelley thought of himself as participating in a revolutionary movement which extended across the whole Western world and of which Tom Paine was the prophet, may strike many historians as heretical. I would stress that it is not necessary to accept the thesis of 'the democratic revolution' as a completely accurate historical account in order to agree that it was a powerful myth for Shelley and his contemporaries, and myth may be the concern of the historian as much as fact. In discussing Shelley's borrowings from and allusions to the works of Paine I adopt the perhaps rather risky course of contrasting Paine's ideas with those of Godwin, with which Shelley had probably become acquainted before his serious study of Paine. It may seem that I draw finer distinctions between the thinking of the two men than Shelley would have seen fit to make. Nevertheless there are distinctions to be made, and it seems to me important to stress that Shelley drew certain elements of his own political position from each that he would not have been able to find in the other. In Chapter III I attempt to expound the core of Shelley's political thinking, the 'philosophical anarchism'

[6] Robert Nozick, *Anarchy, State, and Utopia* (Oxford, 1974), p. 308.

that he derives from Godwin but develops with considerable intelligence and independence. Since drafting that chapter I have been able to consult John P. Clark's valuable and thorough study of Godwin.[7] I am not entirely in agreement with Clark's interpretations; in particular I think that he sees Godwin as a more consistent utilitarian than he really was. My own account focuses on the moral principles which are central to philosophical anarchism: Independence, Perfectibility, and Opinion. These are not necessarily the points that Godwin himself developed at most length, but then Godwin is not the most perspicuous or orderly of thinkers. Chapters IV and V consider Shelley's actual political activities in Ireland and on behalf of the movement for Parliamentary Reform. Since I have considered both Irish politics and the Reform movement mainly with reference to the periods at which Shelley was actively involved in them I see events in a rather different perspective from historians; but I hope that they would not find my interpretations too uninformed or wide of the mark. By relating Shelley's activities to what was going on around him I have tried to show that he engaged responsibly and intelligently with the issues of his day. I have also attempted to indicate the way in which his activities in promotion of local aims were connected with his wider goals. In considering Shelley's political ideology and activities I have naturally referred most frequently to his prose writings and letters, though wherever possible I have drawn illustrative material from his poetry. In Chapters III and V I also attempt to focus the political issues by readings of *Prometheus Unbound* and of the political verse of 1819–20. In Chapter VI I consider Shelley's attempts to reconcile his mission as a political reformer with his vocation as a poet. The central text here is *A Defence of Poetry*, but I also consider in some detail his moral writings, since it is by evolving a theory of the imagination as a moral power that Shelley finds the link between his political and poetic activities. Shelley managed to develop a theory of the imagination that is significantly different from that evolved by Coleridge, often taken to be *the* theorist of the Romantic Imagination. This theory of the imagination serves to illuminate aspects of *Adonais*. The last chapter is a reading of *The Triumph of Life*, Shelley's last and, I believe, his greatest poem, in which the central concerns of his idealist politics are focused and confronted.

[7] *The Philosophical Anarchism of William Godwin* (Princeton, 1977).

The unsatisfactory state of Shelley's text creates certain problems of reference. For the poems I have used the text of the Norton Critical Edition of *Shelley's Poetry and Prose*, edited by Donald H. Reiman and Sharon B. Powers; and for poems not included there (particularly *Laon and Cythna*) the text of the *Complete Works*, edited by Roger Ingpen and Walter E. Peck. Full references are given for poems quoted from other editions. For quotations from the prose works I give references to the *Works*, or to the appropriate source when not included in the *Works*, but the actual text has been derived by me from the most authoritative sources: from the original editions for works published by Shelley himself, from the original manuscripts for works of which the manuscript is in the Bodleian Library, from photostats of the original manuscripts held elsewhere, and from the careful transcriptions printed in *Shelley and his Circle* for manuscripts in the Pforzheimer Collection. Words in angle brackets were cancelled by Shelley, and words in square brackets have been supplied by the present author. In the course of my researches on the text of Shelley's prose works I have been able to arrive at reasonably accurate dates for these works, and I include an Appendix with a list of these works and the most precise date that it would be safe to assign them.

CHAPTER I

The Party of the People

AMONG HIS many revealing glimpses of the young Shelley, Hogg recorded the following.

Two or three Eton boys called another day, and begged their former schoolfellow to curse his father and the king, as he used occasionally to do at school. Shelley refused, and for some time persisted in his refusal, saying that he had left it off; but as they continued to urge him, by reason of their importunity he suddenly broke out, and delivered, with vehemence and animation, a string of execrations, greatly resembling in its absurdity a papal anathema; the fulmination soon terminated in a hearty laugh, in which we all joined.[1]

It is curious that commentators have not adduced this passage in discussing the Curse motif in *Prometheus Unbound*. The ironies surrounding Prometheus' curse and his 'recalling' of it are well enough understood, but it does not seem to have been appreciated that Shelley uses it to make a point that is of great relevance to his own political career. Christian La Cassagnère has made the pertinent observation that Prometheus, in cursing Jupiter, simultaneously curses himself and mankind.

> Be thy swift mischiefs sent
> To blast mankind, from yon etherial tower.
> Let thy malignant spirit move
> Its darkness over those I love:
> On me and mine I imprecate
> The utmost torture of thy hate
> And thus devote to sleepless agony
> This undeclining head while thou must reign on high.
> (1.274–81)[2]

All the evils that Prometheus attributes to Jupiter's reign were invoked by Prometheus himself in his Curse; there is present a

[1] *Life*, i. 92.
[2] See Christian La Cassagnère, *La Mystique du* Prometheus Unbound *de Shelley: Essai d'interprétation* (Paris, 1970), pp. 44–6.

subliminal pun, by which Jupiter is quite literally the curse of Prometheus – 'Sceptred Curse', as the Earth says (IV.338). Prometheus' motive for withdrawing the Curse – 'I wish no living thing to suffer pain' (I.305) – is less high-minded compassion for Jupiter (who is nearer to a figment of Prometheus' imagination than a 'living thing') than concern for those who were involved in its consequences. Prometheus is beginning to recognize that such concern can hardly express itself in the form of a curse, for a curse is a form of hatred, and hatred is one of the central aspects of Jupiter. To oppose Jupiter in this way is to help keep him in existence.

Shelley's point is clear: some kinds of uncompromising opposition actually work to support what they ostensibly oppose. It is into precisely this trap that the young Shelley, in his violent rejection of father, King, and God, actually fell, and his awareness of this is registered in a passage probably written in 1817.

None is indeed exempt from that species of influence which affects as it were the surface of his being, and gives the specific outline to his conduct. Almost all that which is ostensible submits to this legislature created by the general representation of the past feelings of mankind—imperfect as it is from a variety of causes as it exists in government, the religion, and the domestic habits ⟨of mankind. Those who do⟩ not nominally, yet actually submit to the same power. The external features of their conduct indeed can no more escape it, than the clouds can escape from the stream of the wind. And his opinions—which he often hopes he has dispassionately secured from all contagion of prejudice and vulgarity—would be found on examination to be the inevitable excrud[es]cence of the very usages from which he so vehemently dissents. (*Works*, vii. 82–3)

The change from third person plural to singular towards the end of this suggests that Shelley had his own case in mind. That Shelley recognizes the problem suggests that he will be able to make a productive effort to solve it. But even in his maturity Shelley could not entirely escape from the conditions of his age, though he was to be more successful in coming to terms with them. Traces of his early Whig upbringing can be found in *A Philosophical View of Reform* (1819), and even when he transcends it he will often be found to have extended and built upon Whig premises. It is virtually impossible to understand Shelley's mature political thinking without first investigating the Whiggism of his family background, and seeing what he rejected, and what he retained.

The Whig party of Shelley's day was hardly a party at all in the modern sense, though it had a rudimentary form of party organization, and a certain number of policies common to all who claimed the name Whig. It embraced a fairly wide spectrum of view, however, from the group headed by Lord Grenville, Pitt's cousin and a former supporter of the war with France and of domestic repression, to the 'mountain' of radical Whigs, who followed the lead of Samuel Whitbread, and flirted with the Reform policies of Sir Francis Burdett.[1] The politics of the Shelley family were determined by those of their patron, the Duke of Norfolk, who while hardly a radical was on the left of the Whig party. He had been a lieutenant of the charismatic Charles James Fox, whose hostility to the King and to the war with France had made him almost a symbol of opposition. Through the Duke of Norfolk the Foxite creed was passed on to the young Shelley, and it was to leave indelible marks on his thinking on politics.

Charles Howard, the eleventh Duke of Norfolk (1746–1815), was in many ways an unprepossessing figure. He was renowned for his consumption of food, beefsteaks for preference, and of wine, which he drank 'for quantity, not quality'. By the end of his life 'such was his size and breadth, that he seemed incapable of passing through a door of ordinary dimensions'.[2] Like Johnson, he had no passion for clean linen, and it was rumoured that he had to be washed by his servants when he was too drunk to know or care. His wearing a new coat was the occasion of a mild sensation in the House of Lords. He was, Lady Holland unsympathetically concluded, 'gross in everything'.[3] Such a man would hardly seem to have much in common with the intense and rather ascetic Shelley. Nevertheless, it would seem that the latter rather liked and respected the Duke – a considerable tribute to his personal qualities. At the height of his opposition to aristocracy as an institution Shelley conceded that the Duke 'wd. be very well as a man' (*Letters*, i. 199).

[1] See Austin Mitchell, *The Whigs in Opposition 1815–1830* (Oxford, 1967), pp. 1–6, 19–21.

[2] *The Journal of Elizabeth, Lady Holland (1791–1811)*, edited by the Earl of Ilchester (2 vols., 1908), ii. 10; *The Historical and the Posthumous Memoirs of Sir Nathaniel William Wraxall 1772–1784*, edited by H. B. Wheatley (5 vols., 1884), iii. 366.

[3] Wraxall, *Memoirs*, iii. 362; *Annual Biography and Obituary*, i (1817), 123–4; Lady Holland, *Journal*, ii. 10. Charles Pigott gives a lurid account of Norfolk's 'sordid filthy debauchery' in the first part of his *The Jockey Club: or a Sketch of the Manners of the Age* (1792), p. 121.

Even after he had rejected the Duke's offer of a career in politics he continued to solicit his mediation with his family.[1] No doubt he was both attracted and repelled by this larger-than-life Regency eccentric, and he must have felt a similar ambivalence about the Duke's politics, admiring his adherence to Foxite principles while deploring his somewhat cynical readiness to compromise them.

Norfolk had entered politics in 1780 as an opponent of the war with America, and soon gravitated to the group around Fox, 'A party which he always actively and zealously espoused to the last'. His support for Fox was vigorous, even to excess, and he performed for him 'such parliamentary commissions as required little delicacy or circumlocution'.[2] His services were rewarded by the Lord-Lieutenancy of the West Riding under the Rockingham administration of 1782, and by a seat on the Treasury Board under the Fox–North coalition in the following year. When he entered the Lords in 1786 he continued to support Fox, speaking on behalf of motions which paralleled those made by Fox in the Commons. When the Whig party split in 1794 over the French Revolution and the war with France Norfolk remained loyal to Fox, though both no doubt regretted the loss of those 'very valuable friends, a connection with whom both you & I should undoubtedly have preferred to any we may be obliged from circumstance to form'.[3] The 'friends' to whom Fox refers were the Rockingham Whigs, who, under the influence of Burke, had made common cause with Pitt's government; the undesirable connection at which he hints is with the radical Whig Friends of the People, which neither he nor Norfolk ever joined. As so often the Foxites found themselves caught in the middle between extremes of conservatism and radicalism. Their desire was to steer a middle course between the belligerent opposition to the French Revolution sponsored by Burke, and the fervent welcome given it by the radical societies and the followers of Paine; the Duke was careful to make it clear in the Lords that he thought Burke and Paine were equally wrong. This outspokenness drew a scathing attack from Burke in his *Letter to William Elliot, Esq.* (1795).[4]

---

[1] *Letters*, i. 158–9, 346–7.

[2] *Gentleman's Magazine*, lxxxvi, part i (Jan.–June 1816), 65; Wraxall, *Memoirs*, ii. 203, iv. 244.

[3] Fox to [Norfolk?], 2 Jan. [1795] (BL MS Add. 47569, fo. 56v).

[4] *The Parliamentary History of England* (36 vols., London, 1806–20), xxxi. 1496–1501 (8 May 1795); *The Works of the Right Honourable Edmund Burke* (6 vols., Bohn's Standard Library, 1854–6), v. 67–72.

Norfolk's support of Fox was often more vigorous than judicious, as in the case of his famous toast to 'Our Sovereign – the Majesty of the People!', and the accompanying remarks which compared Fox and his followers to Washington and the American rebels, delivered at a meeting to celebrate Fox's birthday on 24 January 1798.[1] The sentiment was intended more in the spirit of 1688 than in that of 1789, and one biographer of the Duke (possibly Thomas Taylor) called it an 'old Whig toast'.[2] But it sounded like advocacy of republicanism to the sensitive ears of men in the 1790s, and both the sympathetic Wraxall and the less sympathetic Pitt considered the toast 'not very remote from treason'.[3] Despite his protestations of loyalty Norfolk was dismissed from his Lord-Lieutenancy and his colonelcy of a West Riding regiment. When in 1806 Fox finally, if briefly, returned to office as Secretary of State for War in the Whig 'Ministry of All the Talents', Norfolk's services and sacrifices were repaid by the Lord-Lieutenancy of Sussex, where he had his main seat, Arundel Castle, and where he had already built up an important electoral interest. He was now in a position to reward a political client whose family had been helping him with his electoral designs by having his name put on one of the first lists of baronetcies created by the new government. On 3 March 1806 Bysshe Shelley, grandfather of the future poet, became Sir Bysshe Shelley of Castle Goring.[4]

With the death of Fox on 13 September 1806 Norfolk felt that 'his political marriage became dissolv'd',[5] and he largely transferred his allegiance to the Prince of Wales, a political associate of the Foxites, and a convivial companion of the Duke. But the Duke did not let this heavy investment in what was known as 'the reversionary interest' prejudice the 'manly independence of his character' or his reputation as 'a perfectly independent senator'.[6] During the

---

[1] *Annual Register* (1798), "Chronicle", pp. 5–6.

[2] *Public Characters of 1798–1799* (4th edn., 1803), p. 411. See also Fox to Norfolk 4 Feb. 1798 (BL MS Add. 47569, fo. 76).

[3] Wraxall, *Memoirs*, iii. 365.

[4] On 21 February 1806 the Duke applied to Lord Spencer for a baronetcy for Bysshe, adding that he was a friend of his, worth £10,000 a year in Sussex and Kent (information supplied by Mr Roland Thorne of the History of Parliament Trust).

[5] *The Correspondence of George, Prince of Wales, 1770–1812*, edited by A. Aspinall (8 vols., 1963–71), vii. 198.

[6] Wraxall, *Memoirs*, iii. 366; *Gentleman's Magazine*, lxxxv, part ii (July–Dec. 1815), 631.

scandal in 1809 over the involvement of the Prince's brother the Duke of York in the sale of army commissions, seven MPs sitting for boroughs controlled by the Duke (including Timothy Shelley) voted on three occasions against the Duke of York.[1] As we shall see, Norfolk also took a firm line over the Prince's desertion of the Roman Catholics, notwithstanding the offer of a coveted Garter – such was the 'tenacity of his political principles'.[2]

No doubt the Duke had his adherence to Foxite principles to thank for any political influence he may have been able to exercise over the young Shelley. Shelley, we may be sure, was attracted to Whig politics less as a mere party programme than as a set of idealistic and humanitarian concerns especially associated with the name of Fox, the 'man of the people' to his followers, 'that great and good man . . . the friend of freedom' in Shelley's estimation (*Works*, v. 227). In the years following his death Fox become a figure of legend for the Whigs, who saw him as the firm and con-sistent defender of liberty, and the staunch opponent of the arbitrary George III and his Tory ministers. Death had purged what was problematic about Fox: his early attacks on the liberty of the press, his all-too-opportune coalitions with former opponents like Lords North and Grenville, his serious political miscalculations, and the ambivalence of his support for Reform. It is hardly surpris-ing that a young man raised as Shelley was in a Whig household connected with a prominent Foxite should have felt a warm admira-tion for Fox, which was to outlive his disillusion with the actual policies of the Whigs. Before we condemn Shelley for being so naïve as to take Fox at the valuation of his supporters, we should remember that Shelley was able to transcend the politics of his family circle largely because he took seriously the ideals to which they paid lip service.

Fox's name was chiefly associated with five great causes: peace with France; the abolition of the slave trade; Parliamentary Reform; religious toleration; and the rights of juries in cases of

---

[1] *The Parliamentary Debates from the year 1803 to the present time* (1st series, 41 vols., 1812–20), xiii. 639–40, 708–9, 709–11. The MPs referred to were J. C. Curwen (Carlisle), Henry Howard (Gloucester), Robert Hurst (Steyning), J. M. Lloyd (Steyning), R. P. Scudamore (Hereford), Timothy Shelley (New Shoreham), T. P. Symonds (Hereford).

[2] *Morning Chronicle*, 29 Feb. 1812; Wraxall, *Memoirs*, iii. 366–7. See below, pp. 26–7.

seditious libel.[1] On all these issues Shelley adopted a basically
Foxite position, though it is often as interesting to see how he
extended such positions as to note what he retained unchanged.

It is hardly necessary to labour Shelley's distaste for war, a
distaste based on principle as much as on squeamishness. Still,
even Shelley could condone war under some circumstances, and
in 1821 he helped his wife to compose a 'Cry of war to the Greeks'.[2]
But he never approved of the war in Spain, though many others,
including Wordsworth, Coleridge, Southey, and Landor, saw it as
a war of national liberation. Even the 'official' Foxite party, led
by Fox's nephew Lord Holland, sympathized with the Spaniards.[3]
The Duke of Norfolk was virtually alone among the Whigs in
sticking to the old Whig line of deploring the war under all
circumstances, and he opposed 'the policy of assisting the Spaniards'
from 1808 on.[4] By 1811, before the tide turned in Wellington's
favour, he had been joined by the radical Whigs of the 'mountain',
and we can find the *Morning Chronicle* complaining that 'British
blood has been profusely shed, and British treasure prodigally
spent' for the sake of 'Barren military glory'.[5] The same rhetoric
can be heard in Shelley's attacks on 'that prodigal waste of human
blood to aggrandise the fame of Statesmen' (*Letters*, i. 208) and
denunciations of the 'barren victories of Spain' gained 'in behalf
of a bigotted and tyrannical Government' (*Works*, v. 239). Shelley
is clearly a shade more radical than even the extreme Whigs, but
it is only a matter of taking a few more steps along the same road.

The abolition of the slave trade was the great achievement of the
'Talents' ministry, and perhaps of Fox's career too, for he received
a possibly undue amount of the credit for it; it was called his
'death-bed Legacy of Liberty and Happiness to Africa'.[6] Shelley
was in his early teens when the agitation for abolition reached its
height, and the voters of Horsham, only two miles from Field

---

[1] Loren Reid, *Charles James Fox: A Man for the People* (1969), pp. 440–2.
[2] Bodl. MS Shelley adds. c. 5, fos. 91, 34. This work remains unpublished.
[3] See *Edinburgh Review*, xiii. 222–4 (Oct. 1808).
[4] Henry Fox, Lord Holland, *Further Memoirs of the Whig Party 1807–1821*, edited by Lord Stavordale (1905), p. 15. See *Parliamentary Debates*, xi. 1106–8, 1110–11, xii. 704, xiii. 797–8, xiv. 172, 712, xv. 357–8, 536.
[5] *Morning Chronicle*, 17 Sept. 1811, quoted by Coleridge in the *Courier*, 17 Sept. 1811 (Coleridge, *Essays on His Times in* The Morning Post *and* The Courier, edited by David V. Erdman (3 vols., 1978), ii. 295).
[6] [Samuel Parr], *Characters of the late Charles James Fox* (2 vols., 1809), i. 135.

Place, were strong abolitionists.[1] The Duke of Norfolk spoke on behalf of the Slave Trade Abolition Bill in the Lords.[2] This measure of course only abolished the *trade* – the slaves in the British colonies were not emancipated until 1833. It need cause no surprise that Shelley detested slavery, calling it 'the deepest stain upon civilized man' (*Works*, vii. 19). What is interesting is that Shelley adopts a very Whiggish attitude to the issue of final emancipation. Fox himself felt that 'It was possible for men to be slaves so long, as to make it dangerous all at once to give them their liberty'.[3] Shelley agreed, and in 1819 he praised 'the disinterested, yet necessarily cautious measures of the English Nation' in emancipating the slaves in the West Indies.[4] Like a true Whig, Shelley feared the oppressed, even while he desired to set them free.

The issue of Parliamentary Reform reveals most clearly both the conflicts between Whig theory and practice, and the tendency for Whig rhetoric to point to conclusions which the Whigs themselves would have rejected, but which Shelley was to embrace. No better example of Whig inconsistency could be found than the Duke of Norfolk himself, who was both an enthusiastic advocate of Reform, and a leading boroughmonger. Indeed, he was one of the leading boroughmongers of his day, controlling or influencing the return of no less than eleven MPs – more than any other private patron, and as many as the Treasury itself![5] Seven of these members sat for Sussex boroughs – Steyning, Arundel, Horsham, and New Shoreham – the Duke's influence in that county being based on his own extensive property, his position as Lord-Lieutenant, and the assistance of his political clients. It was as clients, helping the Duke to extend and consolidate his unconstitutional influence, that the Shelley family were connected with him. As the young poet drily commented, the Duke 'merely desires to gratify thro our family his own borough interest' (*Letters*, i. 246). The value of the Shelley connection to the Duke can be judged from the fact that

---

[1] William Albery, *A Parliamentary History of the Ancient Borough of Horsham 1295–1885* (1927), pp. 244–5.

[2] *Parliamentary Debates*, viii. 702, ix. 170.

[3] R. Fell, *Memoirs of the Public Life of the late Right Honourable Charles James Fox* (2 vols., 1808), ii. 71.

[4] *Works*, vii. 19. The MS reads 'causes' rather than 'cautious'.

[5] T. H. B. Oldfield, *The Representative History of Great Britain and Ireland* (6 vols., 1816), vi. 285.

in 1807 'Shelley's Int[eres]t' in the rape of Bramber alone was estimated to be 'upwards of 500' votes, all of whom could vote both at New Shoreham and in Sussex county elections.[1] In return the Shelleys got the kind of good things that depended on influence with the central government – like Bysshe Shelley's baronetcy. Medwin's statement that the baronetcy was a bribe for future services is misleading.[2] The Shelleys had been attached to the Duke's interest since the early 1790s at least, but the Whig exile from power had delayed the reward to which they had established a claim.

Although Bysshe got the baronetcy, his son Timothy seems to have done most of the work. In 1790 he had got himself returned for the borough of Horsham, proudly inviting his cousin T. C. Medwin (whose dubious tactics had a good deal to do with his election) to come and 'hear the Sussex Members' opinions upon the National Business'.[3] A petition by his opponents, however, soon deprived him of his place in the councils of the nation. The Irwin interest at Horsham being too strong for Norfolk's party it was not until 1806 that the contest there was renewed; in the end Norfolk had to buy the seats. Meanwhile Timothy Shelley had been elected for New Shoreham in 1802, where he sat until 1818. In so doing he was serving the Duke's interests, for since 1771 New Shoreham had been virtually reformed, and the Duke was only able to influence the return of one member.[4] Timothy was acceptable to the voters there, who asked him to stand in 1780, when he refused;[5] that he later decided to stand suggests that he was nursing the borough for the Duke. His election, as *The Times*

---

[1] Thomas Charles Medwin to Warden Sergison, May 1807 (Albery Collection, Horsham Museum, Horsham MS 139, fo. 14).

[2] Thomas Medwin, *The Life of Percy Bysshe Shelley* (1847), edited by H. Buxton Forman (1913), p. 10. In reading Medwin's comments on the Duke it is advisable to bear in mind that Medwin's father, Thomas Charles Medwin, had been dismissed from his job as Norfok's agent after he had complained that his services had not been properly rewarded (the relevant correspondence is in the Albery Collection, especially Horsham MS 255, fos. 2, 3, 8; the first of these is actually in the hand of the younger Thomas Medwin). The elder Medwin, a true professional, promptly offered his services to the opposing interest.

[3] 27 Nov. 1790 (Albery Collection, Horsham MS 5, fo. 27). See W. Albery, op. cit., pp. 139–91.

[4] T. H. B. Oldfield, op. cit. v. 26, vi. 285.

[5] Thomas W. Horsfield, *The History, Antiquities, and Topography of the County of Sussex* (2 vols., Lewes and London, 1835), Appendix III, "Parliamentary History", by W. D. Cooper, pp. 53–4.

noted, added 'another member to the great Parliamentary interest of the Duke of Norfolk'.[1]

Yet Norfolk was an active supporter of Reform. He had joined the agitation sparked off by the dispute with America, and was a representative at a general Reform meeting in the Guildhall. He also joined the Society for Constitutional Information.[2] His exertions in the Yorkshire Association, which gave the lead to the Reform agitation of the 1780s, earned the praise of the Revd Christopher Wyvill, and in the Commons he supported Pitt's motions for Reform.[3] His zeal outlasted his removal to the Lords, and he assured the King that, in making the notorious toast to 'the Majesty of the People', 'my only meaning was to express a wish to support Mr. Fox in his constitutional endeavours to obtain a reform in the representation of Parliament'.[4] As late as 1812 he became a member of the Reformist Hampden Club.[5] His contemporaries could hardly overlook the anomaly of a boroughmongering Reformer, and they were wont to lament that the Duke 'disgraced his character by a traffick in rotten boroughs'.[6] It laid him open to the most felicitous irony of Burke, who remarked, 'No peer has condescended to superintend with more vigilance the declining franchises of the poor Commons.'[7] The Duke's defence was that 'he would most willingly surrender all interests and pretensions of this kind, whenever a better system took place'.[8] He explained to the veteran Reformer Major John Cartwright that he intended to keep his parliamentary influence precisely in order to work more effectively for Reform, and Cartwright seems to have condoned this comfortable compromise between principle and prudence.[9] Shelley's comment on all this is rather refreshing: 'He desires and votes for reform tho' he has not virtue enough to begin it in his own person' (*Letters*, i. 246).

[1] *The Times*, 12 Apr. 1802 (reference supplied by Mr Roland Thorne).

[2] *Annual Biography*, i. 108; *The Life and Correspondence of Major Cartwright*, edited by F. D. Cartwright (2 vols., 1826), i. 134–5.

[3] See Christopher Wyvill, *Political Papers* (6 vols., York, [1794–1808]), i. 66–8, ii. 234, 383, 288–9, 302, 304, 305, 307–8, 323, iv. 195, 295; R. C. Wilton, 'Norfolk House: 1746–1815', *Dublin Review*, clxv (1919), 134–7; Wyvill, *Political Papers*, i. 424, 468, ii. 255, 443.

[4] *The Later Correspondence of George III*, edited by A. Aspinall (5 vols., Cambridge, 1962–70), iii. 17.

[5] Cartwright, *Life and Correspondence*, ii. 382.

[6] *Annual Biography*, i. 119.   [7] Burke, *Works*, v. 71.

[8] *Annual Biography*, i. 119.

[9] Cartwright, *Life and Correspondence*, ii. 185–6n.

Norfolk never made it clear exactly what kind of Reform he wanted, but it was clearly of the moderate brand. Wyvill reported, 'He is attached to our limited Monarchy and to the Rights of the People alike... he has uniformly supported Reform on the principles of moderation, and a due respect to the Laws'[1] — Norfolk's idea of Reform itself sounds like a compromise. Like a good Whig he believed in Reform 'from the top', carried out by the existing political classes, not by the masses; he commented on the French Revolution, 'when the people reformed for themselves, they reformed miserably'.[2] The Duke left it to Fox to formulate the details of a Whig Reform programme. Fox's position was in reality hardly more extreme than Norfolk's; but Fox had a knack of appearing more radical than he really was, and his rhetoric may well have helped to prepare Shelley for a kind of Reform far more thoroughgoing than the Whig brand.

Fox's commitment to Reform was exaggerated by his contemporaries. Coleridge declared that 'REFORM and FOX are political synonimes', and Oldfield called Reform 'the pillar on which the late Right Hon. Charles James Fox erected the standard of his popularity'.[3] There is a certain dryness about Oldfield's words that suggests that he realized the large measure of opportunism that entered into Fox's advocacy of Reform; it only interested him when he was in opposition, and his enthusiasm tended to vary in strict proportion to his need to gain support in the country as a whole.[4] Nevertheless, when it suited him to agitate for Reform, the rhetoric was very congenial to him. In Fox the traditional Whig distrust of the Crown was intensified to a 'passionate hatred for the King and [an] extravagant fear of the monarchy'.[5] Fox's view of the Constitution was a traditional one and he was equally opposed to absolute monarchy, absolute aristocracy, or absolute democracy.[6] But so long as he saw absolute monarchy as the imminent threat, he was very willing to present himself as 'a firm and decided supporter of that just weight which the people ought to have in the

[1] Wyvill, *Political Papers*, iv. 295–6n.
[2] *Parliamentary History*, xxxi. 1498.
[3] Coleridge, *Essays on His Times*, i. 17; Oldfield. *Representative History*, i. xvi.
[4] See J. R. Dinwiddy, 'Charles James Fox and the People', *History*, lv (1970), 347; Herbert Butterfield, 'Sincerity and Insincerity in Charles James Fox', *Proceedings of the British Academy*, lvii (1971), 237–8.
[5] Butterfield, loc. cit. 251.
[6] R. Fell, *Memoirs*, ii. 95. See also John W. Derry, *Charles James Fox* (1972), p. 22, 433.

scale of the constitution'.[1] Like Norfolk, Fox was always ready to appeal to 'Our Sovereign—the Majesty of the People!' and to cite Locke to the effect that 'government originated not only *for* but *from* the people, and that the people were the legitimate sovereign in every community'. Kings held their power in trust for the people, and in the last resort *'trust abused was revocable'*—the lesson of the Glorious Revolution of 1688. Taking this line of thought to its logical conclusion, Fox declared, 'If the king and the house of lords were unnecessary and useless branches of the constitution, let them be dismissed and abolished; for the people were not made for them, but they for the people.'[2] For Fox this is really no more than a speculative flourish of rhetoric; but we find the same position taken up by Shelley in true earnest. 'A man has no right to be a King or a Lord or a Bishop but so long as it is for the benefit of the People and so long as the People judge that it is for their benefit, that he should impersonate that character.' (*Works*, vii. 7) Fox would never have allowed 'the people' to be the judges of the utility of King or nobility—we have already seen the Whigs' distrust of Reform effected by 'the people', and Fox rejected Universal Suffrage as 'a wild and ridiculous idea'.[3] When the Whigs talked about strengthening the position of the people, they really meant strengthening the position of the Whigs, for they saw themselves as the natural guardians of the interests of 'the people'.[4] Moreover what they understood by 'the people' was rather different from what Shelley understood. 'The people' in Whig terms really meant the existing political classes, 'the sections of the electorate which had a real say in the choice of members of parliament, the patrons of those sections which did not, and any other members of the population . . . capable of wielding any political pressure'.[5] Burke estimated 'those who, in any political view are to be called the people' as 'about four hundred thousand'—out of a population of ten million.[6] When Shelley uses the word, however, he is thinking of 'the unrepresented multitude' which had previously had 'no

---

[1] R. Fell, *Memoirs*, ii. 577n. [2] Ibid. ii. 377, i. 288, ii. 375.
[3] Ibid. ii. 426.
[4] The Whig view of their own 'custodial' role is brought out by John Brewer, *Party ideology and popular politics at the accession of George III* (Cambridge, 1976), pp. 235–7.
[5] B. W. Hill, 'Fox and Burke: the Whig party and the question of principles, 1784–1789', *English Historical Review*, lxxxix (1974), 3.
[6] Burke, *Works*, v. 189–90.

constitutional presence in the state' (*Works*, vii. 23) Thus Shelley could mean something very different while still using the old rhetoric. Fox and the Whigs fundamentally held to 'a belief in aristocratic government on behalf, but only to a limited extent under the control, of the people'.[1] Shelley's opposition to this will be treated at length in Chapter II.

It should also be recognized that many Whig elements continue to be present in Shelley's later thinking on Reform, and may prove confusing to the reader who has not traced the development of Shelley's most radical ideas from their sources. Shelley's preference for gradual Reform reflects the extreme caution of Godwin, and also the views of Fox, who insisted on 'the danger of rash innovation, and the great advantage of temperate and slow reform'.[2] Fox, of course, hoped that a gradual Reform would purify and thus actually strengthen the old political order, as did the Whigs who passed the First Reform Act. Shelley, with rather more foresight, considered that a gradual Reform would transform and supersede the old order, and do so more effectively than a violent revolutionary overthrow.[3] If we bear this in mind we will find it easier to understand how Shelley could find a moderate Whig programme of Reform acceptable as late as 1819; he was always willing to unite his efforts with anyone who shared his goals, though well aware that large differences existed with respect to ultimate aims. The Whig tendency to adopt a populist rhetoric would in any case have made it difficult for Shelley to realize how large such differences were. The following comment by Fox is a remarkably Shelleyan pronouncement. 'In his opinion the greatest beauty of the English constitution was, that in its very principle it permitted of perpetual improvement.'[4] It is a remarkably open view for Fox to express, his usual praise of the Constitution being couched in terms of a static balance. Shelley was justifiably impatient of what he called 'political cant' (*Works*, v. 260) on the subject of the Constitution, but he would have had some sympathy for Fox's view. 'The excellence of the Constitution of Great Britain, appears to me, to be its indefiniteness and versatility, whereby it may be unresistingly accommodated to the progression of wisdom and virtue.' (*Works*, v. 244) Fox of course thought that the Constitution had other

---

[1] J. R. Dinwiddy, loc. cit. 356.

[2] R. Fell, *Memoirs*, ii. 377.

[3] See *Works*, vii. 40–1, 46.

[4] R. Fell, *Memoirs*, ii. 260.

virtues apart from its vagueness, and he and Shelley would hardly have agreed on the changes it should undergo.

Shelley's language on Reform, and on other subjects, frequently reflects his early Whig background.[1] Thus we find him referring to 'the Friends of Liberty', 'the Friends of Universal or of Limited Suffrage', 'the Friends of Reform', language inconceivable in, say, Cobbett, but reminiscent of Whig catch-phrases like 'the Friends of the People' or 'the Friends of Mr. Fox', which served to disguise political connection as personal attachment.[2] That Shelley did not believe in putting personal or party attachments before the dictates of justice only underlines how strong a hold Whig rhetoric had on him as late as 1817.

Shelley's activities in Ireland will be considered in detail in Chapter IV, but it will be useful to look at the background of the Irish problem, and at the related issue of religious toleration. Catholic Emancipation was one policy on which all the Whigs could agree, and it was their attempt to press it in 1807 that led to the fall of the 'Talents' ministry. But of all the Whigs perhaps none had more reason to be concerned for such issues than the Duke of Norfolk. Like all the Howards he had himself been brought up as a Catholic; in order to enter Parliament, to exercise the functions of Earl Marshal as deputy for his father (who remained a Catholic), and eventually to take his seat in the Lords, he had been obliged to renounce his religion.[3] He was naturally criticized for sacrificing his faith to his political career.[4] At the time his decision was 'attributed more to ambition, and the desire of performing a part in public life, or to irreligion, than to conviction'. 'Irreligion' is probably close to the mark, for Shelley assured Miss Hitchener, 'The D. is a Deist . . . he certainly is not attached to Catholicism'.[5] Nevertheless he had some sympathy for Catholics, and no doubt he resented what as a Whig he could only consider as unnecessary and dangerous interference by the civil power with the conscience

---

[1] Some examples of this are given by Kenneth Neill Cameron, *The Young Shelley: Genesis of a Radical* (1951), pp. 314–15.

[2] *Works*, vi. 65–7. 'Fox's whig party was more like a group of friends than a formal political organisation' (J. W. Derry, *Charles James Fox*, p. 435).

[3] *Annual Biography*, i. 106. He read his recantation before the Archbishop of Canterbury and received the sacrament on Sunday, 4 June 1780 (*Annual Register* (1780), "Chronicle", p. 215).

[4] Medwin, p. 101.

[5] Wraxall, *Memoirs*, iii. 364; *Letters*, i. 246.

of the individual. The leading political aim of his career was to obtain for the Catholics a concession that he himself no longer needed. He was resolutely opposed to the practice of 'excluding British subjects from their natural and political rights, merely on account of their religious opinion'. No doubt he had his own case in mind when in 1812 he pointed out that Catholics were still excluded from Parliament (by the exaction of an oath) while Protestant dissenters were virtually freed from the provisions of the Test and Corporation Acts by annual dispensing legislation.[1]

For the theoretical case for religious liberty we may turn to Fox, speaking for the repeal of the Test and Corporation Acts in 1789.

no human government had jurisdiction over opinions as such, and more particularly over religious opinions. It had no right to presume that it knew them, and much less to act upon that presumption. When opinions were productive of acts injurious to society, the law knew how and where to apply the remedy . . .[2]

Shelley argues from the same distinction between mere opinions and criminal acts in his *Letter to Lord Ellenborough* (1812), in which he defended Eaton for publishing Paine's Deist writings. 'Whom has he injured?' he demanded. 'What crime has he committed?' As a 'citizen unimpeached with crime' he could only be deprived of his 'rights as a citizen and a man' by what amounted to 'illegal and immoral violence'. Opinions, however erroneous, which do not issue in criminal acts are not amenable to law. In the case of a man who asserts what is 'demonstrably incorrect' on any subject, 'would he therefore deserve pillory and imprisonment? By no means; probably few would discharge more correctly the duties of a citizen and a man.' (*Works*, v. 283, 292–3) Shelley chooses to ignore the difference between professing a dissenting variety of Christianity and actively promulgating ideas subversive of Christianity itself; but this only serves to underline the similarity of his argument to Fox's. Shelley has taken a Whig position and extended it to areas where the Whigs never intended it to apply.

The abstract arguments were sharpened by urgent political considerations in the case of Ireland, where the majority of the population were excluded by their religion from sitting in Parliament, from staff positions in the armed forces, and from senior

[1] *Parliamentary Debates*, iv. 785, xxiv. 353.
[2] R. Fell, *Memoirs*, ii. 78.

positions in the government—an exclusion that the Whigs considered injurious both to the individuals excluded and to the society as a whole.[1] They could also point to the dangers of provoking discontent among the Irish during wartime; in 1798 the Irish had in fact rebelled, and called on the French to invade. When the British sent aid to Catholics in the Iberian Peninsula the refusal of full civil rights to their own subjects in Ireland took on an air of absurdity. 'Rebels in Cork are patriots at Madrid', as Thomas Moore pointed out.[2]

All the Whigs were committed to Catholic Emancipation, especially after having gone to the wall for it in 1807, but the Duke of Norfolk was virtually the Foxite spokesman on Irish affairs. Most of his speeches in the Lords were concerned with Catholic Emancipation, and his name was twice mentioned as the most likely choice for Lord-Lieutenant of Ireland under a Whig ministry.[3] The Whigs' main hope of achieving Emancipation lay in the sympathy which the Prince of Wales was believed to feel for the Irish, and this may explain why Norfolk attached himself to the Prince's interest. He certainly broke with the Prince over this issue. When the Prince came to power as Regent in 1811 the last thing he wanted to do was to touch the controversial and generally unpopular issue of Emancipation; he preferred to shelve the whole issue and concentrate on winning the war. Things came to a head while Shelley was actually in Dublin. The Regent finally made his long-awaited overture to the Whig leaders in February 1812, but he did it through the medium of the notoriously anti-Catholic Duke of York, and he made it clear that the Whigs who joined the administration could not expect any measure of Catholic Emancipation in return. On these terms the Whig leaders, Lords Grey and Grenville, refused to join the government, and the Duke of Norfolk, having seen the correspondence, endorsed their stand.[4] He not only refused the Garter he had been offered, but wrote an outspoken letter to the Regent affirming his agreement with Grey

---

[1] See *Edinburgh Review*, viii. 311–12.

[2] 'The Sceptic: A Philosophical Satire' (1809), line 58.

[3] *The Manuscripts of J. B. Fortescue, Esq., preserved at Dropmore* (10 vols., Historical Manuscripts Commission, 1892–1927), i. 400; R. C. Wilton, 'Norfolk House', 127.

[4] *Morning Chronicle*, 15, 17, 18, 19 Feb. 1812; *Manuscripts . . . preserved at Dropmore*, x. 224. See Michael Roberts, *The Whig Party 1807–1812* (1939), pp. 376–80.

and Grenville on 'the question of concession to the Catholicks of
Ireland & the danger of delay': 'Engrafting in the oath of allegiance,
a test of security to the Established Church; I hold it a measure of
justice, of right & even of safety to the Empire.' He went on to
remind the Regent that the Catholics expected his good offices on
their behalf. 'Permit me to call your attention to the feeling of the
Irish Catholicks, who to a man beleive they have your friendship
to their claims, & in the eagerness of their hopes, beleive they have
your assured protection.'[1] The Regent's apostasy on Emancipation
dashed the Whig hopes which had been growing throughout the
preceding winter. It was during this period that the Shelleys had
visited the Duke at Greystoke, and the conversation must often
have turned to the possibility of Emancipation. It has been suggested
that it was as a result of this visit that Shelley took his sudden
decision to go to Ireland.[2]

It is unlikely, however, that the Duke would have approved of
the plan, for Shelley's comments on the Irish situation show that
he had already moved beyond Whig orthodoxy. In the first place
Shelley expressed a perfectly justifiable scepticism concerning the
good intentions of the Regent. 'It is said that he has promised to
restore you to freedom . . . I hope he has pledged himself to this
act of justice, because there will then exist some obligation to bind
him to do right.' (*Works*, v. 227) Shelley admitted later that he had
hoped, as the Whigs had done, that with the removal of the restrictions on the Regency would have come 'a ministry less inimical to
the interests of liberty' (*Works*, v. 268), but I doubt that he was
very surprised to find that, as Lamb quipped,

> Some wind has blown the *wig* away,
> And left the *hair apparent*.[3]

But in any case Shelley relied more on the crisis of opinion in
Ireland than on the Prince's goodwill, and he hoped for more than

---

[1] *The Letters of King George IV 1812–1830*, edited by A. Aspinall (3 vols.,
Cambridge, 1938), i. 13–14.
[2] K. N. Cameron, *The Young Shelley*, p. 128; L. S. Boas, *Harriet Shelley:
Five Long Years* (1962), p. 71; Jean Overton Fuller, *Shelley: A Biography* (1968),
p. 114.
[3] These lines first appeared in the *Examiner*, 22 Mar. 1812; quoted from *The
Works in Prose and Verse of Charles and Mary Lamb*, edited by Thomas Hutchinson (2 vols., 1908), ii. 659.

a mere change of ministry.[1] He had become sceptical of the efficacy of the Whig panacea of Emancipation, which, he realized, would not alter the condition of the mass of the population in Ireland, however just and necessary it might be in itself. His language in putting this view is significantly anti-aristocratic.

It is my opinion that the claims of the Catholic inhabitants of Ireland, if gained tomorrow, would in a very small degree, aggrandise their liberty and happiness. The disqualifications principally affect the higher orders of the Catholic persuasion, these would principally be benefited by their removal. Power and wealth do not benefit, but injure the cause of virtue and freedom. (*Works*, v. 254)

The last sentence could almost be Shelley's epitaph for the Duke of Norfolk's political career. It is a clear disavowal of the central Whig belief in the natural 'influence of property' and the function of an aristocratic ruling class. Shelley continued to be concerned with the condition of Ireland, and to support Whig policies, as far as they went; but the Shelley who landed in Ireland was no longer a Whig.

Fox's name was especially associated with the attempt to make juries in cases of seditious libel judges both of the fact of publication and of the libellous nature of the work on trial. Previously the judge and the prosecutor (usually a government official) had decided that an obnoxious publication was in fact libellous, and the jury were restricted to deciding who was responsible for publishing it.[2] In 1791 Fox tried to remove this abuse by introducing two bills, which were blocked by Lord Chancellor Thurlow in the Lords; in 1792, however, the necessary legislation was finally passed.[3] It was known as Fox's Act, and was invoked by Shelley twenty years later in his *Letter to Lord Ellenborough* (*Works*, v. 284). Fox's Act 'ensured that the criterion of seditious libel would conform not to

[1] See below, pp. 147–9. The importance for Shelley of the Prince's attitude and changes of ministers seems to me to have been exaggerated by E. B. Murray, 'The Trial of Mr. Perry, Lord Eldon, and Shelley's *Address to the Irish*', *Studies in Romanticism*, xvii (1978), 42–6.

[2] Arthur Aspinall, *Politics and the Press c. 1780–1850* (1949), p. 37. The situation is succinctly described in the complaints of Junius (*The Letters of Junius*, edited by John Cannon (Oxford, 1978), pp. 15–20).

[3] R. Fell, *Memoirs*, ii. 172–91, 266–7. Professor Christie is inclined to deny Fox some of the credit usually given him for this measure (*Myth and Reality in Late-Eighteenth-Century Politics and Other Papers* (1970), p. 134).

the opinions of authority expressed by the judges but to those of the public from whom the juries came'.[1] Fox's intention was to vindicate 'the juridical power of *the people through the medium of juries*' as one of the two 'main springs upon which the constitution turned'—the other being representation in Parliament.[2] The quasi-political role that Fox assigns to the jury is of great interest in the light of William Godwin's proposal for government by juries. Fox's Act was actually passed while Godwin was working on *Political Justice*, and the debates on the Bills may have helped Godwin to define his own ideas. He had only recently parted company with the Whigs, and respect for the jury as an organ of public opinion was certainly a Whig tenet. Burke went so far as to say that the House of Commons was originally 'in the higher part of government what juries are in the lower'.[3]

Godwin went even further, arguing that juries could not only supersede codified law, but could also carry out all the necessary functions of government. As a thoroughgoing antinomian Godwin considered the operation of the individual judgement far superior to the application of a general law.

the inhabitants of a small parish, living with some degree of that simplicity which best corresponds to the real nature and wants of a human being, would soon be led to suspect that general laws were unnecessary and would adjudge the causes that came before them, not according to certain axioms previously written, but according to the circumstances and demand of each particular cause.[4]

Godwin hoped that government could be reduced to the scale of small autonomous parishes (as a prelude to its complete disappearance), and he saw the jury system as the obvious means of adminis-

---

[1] I. R. Christie, *Myth and Reality*, p. 328.

[2] R. Fell, *Memoirs*, ii. 190.

[3] Burke, *Works*, i. 347. 'It is to trial by jury, more than even by [*sic*] representation, (as it at present exists,) that the people owe the share they have in the government of the country' (Lord John Russell, *An Essay on the History of the English Government and Constitution* (1821; 2nd edn., 1823), p. 394). It should be remembered that Grand and Petty juries carried out many functions of local government at this period.

[4] *Enquiry concerning Political Justice and its influence on Morals and Happiness* (1793; 3rd edn., 1798), edited by F. E. L. Priestley (3 vols., Toronto, 1946), ii. 294. Godwin's distrust of general laws was shared by other writers in his circle; see Thomas Holcroft ,*The Adventures of Hugh Trevor* (1794–7), edited by Seamus Deane (1973), pp. 255–6, and Mary Wollstonecraft, *Posthumous Works*, edited by William Godwin (4 vols., 1798), ii. 154.

tering these local units—the jury, presumably, consisting of all who would be affected by the decision. 'It cannot reasonably be doubted, that the same expedient which is resorted to in our civil and criminal concerns, would, by plain and uninstructed mortals, be adopted in the assessment of taxes, in the deliberations of commerce, and in every other article in which their common interests were involved . . .' (*Political Justice*, ii. 32–3). Shelley shared Godwin's belief that a federation of small, autonomous republics was the most perfect form of government that could be envisaged as practicable. In the Preface to *Prometheus Unbound* he argued that 'If England were divided into forty republics, each equal in population and extent to Athens, there is no reason to suppose but that, under institutions not more perfect than those of Athens, each would produce philosophers and poets equal to those who (if we except Shakespeare) have never been surpassed'. In *A Philosophical View of Reform* he acknowledged the impossibility of direct democracy in large nations, and added that 'the most enlightened theorists have therefore proposed the dividing them into a great ⟨multiplicity⟩ of legitimate govern[ments,] federated republics' (*Works*, vii. 340). He also referred admiringly to 'The republics of Holland' (later altered to 'republic') and to 'The Republics of Switzerland',[1] and in referring to America he used Paine's federal title—'the United States of America', 'the Republic of the United States', 'the United States' (*Works*, vii. 11–13).

It is not clear whether Shelley would have followed Godwin in administering his autonomous republics by juries, but there is strong presumptive evidence. In 1833 Thomas Medwin published a fragment by Shelley under the title 'A System of Government by Juries' (*Works*, vi. 289–92). Since this fragment does not in fact deal with the governmental role of juries, it is unlikely that Medwin supplied the title; Shelley must have intended to treat this matter, but never completed the work. Shelley certainly follows Godwin as far as he goes, adopting a similar antinomian position, repudiating 'forms and superstitions' and asserting that law should be 'the apprehensions of individuals on the reasoning of a particular case'. It should not 'appeal from the common sense, or the enlightened minds of twelve contemporary *good and true men*, who should be the peers of the accused . . . to the obscure records of dark and barbarous epochs' (*Works*, vi. 291–2). It seems likely that this fragment

[1] See *SC* vi. 966.

was intended for *A Philosophical View*, in which Shelley actually declared, 'We would . . . extend the institution of juries to every possible occasion of jurisprudence' (*Works*, vii 34). It was probably written in March–April 1820, when Shelley reread *Political Justice*.[1]

Like Fox, Shelley aimed 'to give to public opinion its legitimate dominion' (*Works*, vi. 291). But Fox and Burke would have been horrified at the idea of reducing law to the *ad hoc* decisions of juries, or of making the jury an instrument of direct democracy. This issue reveals rather well what could happen to a germ of Whig orthodoxy when raised in the speculative hothouse of Godwin's philosophical anarchism. Shelley's background is important, not for what he preserved unchanged, but for what proved capable of translation into more radical terms. But to make use of what was valuable in his Foxite heritage Shelley had first to free himself from the inconsistencies and the cynicism of the actual political practice of his family milieu.

It is clear that by 1812 Shelley had rejected the Whigs as a party. Writing from Ireland he complained, 'Good principles are scarce here. The public papers are either oppositionist or ministerial; one is as contemptible and narrow as the other . . . I of course am hated by both of these parties' (*Letters*, i. 264). As he explained to the Irish, 'philanthropy is of no party' (*Works*, v. 258). To speak of the Whigs and Tories as 'oppositionists' and 'ministerialists' was to use the language of 'Ins' and 'Outs' favoured by the radical Reformers and other critics of the whole existing political structure, and to believe that the necessary changes must go beyond the musical chairs of party politics: 'Liberty gains nothing . . . from a change of Ministers in London' (*Works*, v. 247). In the 1790s Paine had satirized the party system as a kind of 'ride and tie' in which each party took its turn to ride 'the national purse', asserting that 'the *Outs* enjoy places and pensions as well as the *Ins*, and are as devoutly attached to the firm of the House'.[2] We have already seen how the Shelley family got their share of the pickings when their party was 'In'. In 1810, when the Whigs disowned Burdett's brand of Reform, Cobbett fulminated, 'we must now speak of the OUTS as being as much, if not more, enemies of Reform, than the INS are . . . there is no good to be expected from *a change of*

---

[1] *Journal*, pp. 130–1.
[2] *The Complete Writings of Thomas Paine*, edited by P. S. Foner (2 vols., New York, 1945), i. 283, ii. 472.

ministry'.[1] For many observers the 'other interest' was, in Byron's words, 'The same self-interest, with a different leaning'.[2] As we shall see, Shelley's first step away from the Whigs was towards the Reform programme of Burdett.

First we must look in a little detail at what it was that drove Shelley away from the Whigs. We have already seen enough of the way that Whig politicians compromised their own ideals in practice to see what Shelley meant by '*the time-servingness of temporizing reform*' (*Works*, v. 246). Shelley was never the kind of man to rest content when faced with a contradiction between standards of conduct and actual behaviour. This contradiction existed not only in the realm of politics, but even more immediately in the character and conduct of Shelley's father. It is not very surprising that Shelley broke with the Whigs at the same time as he broke with his family, for the family's plans for the young Shelley involved a career in politics; he was to take over his father's seat on coming of age, and enter Parliament in the interest of the Duke of Norfolk.[3] It was no doubt with a view to preparing him for this career that the Duke of Norfolk offered some friendly advice, Shelley's account of which has been preserved by Hogg. The conversation took place in the summer of 1810 before Shelley went up to Oxford. The Duke strongly recommended a career in politics, rather than the professions or literature, noting that politics was 'the proper career for a young man of ability and of your station in life. That course is the most advantageous, because it is a monopoly. A little success in that line goes far, since the number of competitors is limited . . .' (*Life*, i. 129). The limitation of the political nation to the aristocratic class into which Shelley had been born was the main grievance of the followers of the democratic revolution, as we shall see in Chapter II. Shelley, as can be imagined, did not care for the worldly, rather cynical advice of the Duke.

Hogg chose to interpret his distaste as a rejection of politics in general, but Hogg as usual misunderstands the nature of Shelley's attitude to public affairs, and underestimates its complexity. The terms that Shelley used to describe his father's colleagues— 'creatures', 'wretched beings', 'animals' (*Life*, i. 130)—express

---

[1] *Political Register*, 28 Apr. 1810, pp. 644, 646.

[2] *Don Juan*, XVI. lxx.

[3] Medwin, p. 101. Shelley's family may even have hoped that he would take the next step for the family by gaining a peerage.

personal distaste rather than political disillusion. The dislike he elsewhere expresses for Robert Hurst of Horsham Park, MP for Steyning, one of the managers of Norfolk's interests at Horsham, and a colleague of Timothy Shelley, is similarly personal.[1] Shelley's attitude is clarified by the anecdote he himself told Hogg in order to illustrate it.

A friend of mine, an Eton man, told me that his father once invited some corporation to dine at his house, and that he was present. When dinner was over and the gentlemen nearly drunk, they started up, he said, and swore they would all kiss his sisters. His father laughed, and did not forbid them; and the wretches would have done it; but his sisters heard of the infamous proposal, and ran upstairs, and locked themselves in their bedrooms. I asked him if he would not have knocked them down if they had attempted such an outrage in his presence. It seems to me that a man of spirit ought to have killed them if they effected their purpose. (*Life*, i. 130)

An absorbing glimpse into the domestic interior of the Shelley family, for the 'Eton man' was evidently Shelley himself, though it is not clear whether he or Hogg suppressed this fact, nor for what reason. Shelley had four sisters, aged between nine and sixteen in 1810. The 'corporation' would have been the corporation of Horsham, really a front for the Duke of Norfolk's election committee, of which Timothy Shelley, T. C. Medwin, and Robert Hurst were all members.

It is significant that Hogg chooses this point to quote (or rather misquote) Byron's dictum to the effect that 'Never did a more finished gentleman than Shelley step across a drawing-room!'[2] Not that Hurst and the rest of the sister-kissing corporation were plebeians; but Shelley's gentility involved an instinctive courtesy and regard for the feelings of others which seems to have been sadly lacking in the 'gentlemen' of Horsham. Timothy Shelley's circle were no worse than others of their class. The values of the English 'squirearchy' have never assigned a very high place to sensibility—nor, we might add, to excessive scruple in matters of conduct. As Leigh Hunt realized, it is here that we have the grounds of Shelley's quarrel with his family and his class.

---

[1] *Letters*, i. 58. For Hurst see W. Albery, op. cit., p. 123.
[2] *Life*, i. 130. See Byron, *Letters and Journals*, edited by R. E. Prothero (6 vols., 1898–1901), vi. 157.

To a man of genius, endowed with a metaphysical acuteness to discern truth and falsehood, and a strong sensibility to give way to his sense of it, such an origin, however respectable in the ordinary point of view, was not the very luckiest that could have happened for the purpose of keeping him within ordinary bounds. With what feelings is Truth to open its eyes upon this world among the most respectable of our mere party gentry? Among licensed contradictions of all sorts? among the Christian doctrines and the worldly practices? Among fox-hunters and their chaplains? among beneficed lawyers, rakish old gentlemen, and more startling young ones, who are old in the folly of *knowingness*? people not indeed bad in themselves . . . many excellent by nature, but spoilt by those professed demands of what is right and noble, and those inculcations, at the same time, of what is false and wrong . . .[1]

Shelley's own father is very much a case in point. Timothy's talent for inconsistency seemed close to hypocrisy to others beside Shelley. Medwin reports that he told his son 'that he would provide for as many natural children as he chose to get, but that he would never forgive his making a *mésalliance*: a sentiment which excited in Shelley anything but respect for his sire'. 'Licensed contradictions' indeed! Did Timothy remember this unfortunate announcement at the time of Shelley's elopement with Harriet? The initial break between Shelley and his father was caused by the latter's anger at his son's dissemination of unorthodox religious views; but Medwin considered that Timothy was far from active as a Christian, and that 'much of Percy Bysshe's scepticism may be traced to early example, if not to precept'.[2]

The question of Timothy's religious sentiments involves his political conduct too. While all the other MPs in the Duke of Norfolk's interest voted, as we would expect, for Catholic Emancipation, Timothy consistently voted *against* it.[3] No conclusion can be drawn from this as to his own feelings on the matter, since he was probably obliged to vote against the Catholics by his New Shoreham constituents. Emancipation was very unpopular in the country as a whole, and when Timothy addressed the voters before the general election of 1807 he was careful to stress his commitment

---

[1] *The Autobiography of Leigh Hunt*, edited by J. E. Morpurgo (1949), p. 262. This passage was first published in Hunt's *Lord Byron and Some of His Contemporaries* (1828).

[2] Medwin, p. 13.

[3] *Parliamentary Debates*, xxiii. 710–11, xxiv. 1076–8, xxvi. 361–3, xxxiv. 676–8, xxxvi. 438–42.

to 'the true principles of our most excellent Constitution, as now
established, in CHURCH AND STATE'.[1] There is some evidence to
suggest that his private sentiments were not illiberal, and that he
had some leanings to Unitarianism.[2] But the contradiction between
adherence to the Foxite Whigs, the party of religious freedom, and
votes cast against the Catholics was a glaring one. Does this not
help to explain his son's trip to Ireland to forward Emancipation?
Timothy himself had a shrewd suspicion that his son's individual
acts of rebellion were motivated by a systematic opposition to his
own values. 'To cast off all thoughts of his Maker, to abandon his
Parents, to wish to relinquish his Fortune, and to court Persecution
all seems to arise from the same source.'[3] What would he have said
had he known that within a year Shelley would add to the catalogue
of his 'sallies of Folly and Madness' a *mésalliance* and an attempt
to aid the Catholics?

Timothy's attempts to get his son to conform to what was
accepted were undercut by his own political rhetoric. In political
terms Timothy's contemporaries referred to him as a 'country
gentleman'.[4] The country gentlemen, possessed of their own landed
property, and (in theory) not tied to any party, were considered to
be the most 'independent' MPs, more influenced by public opinion
than by the hope of reward from the government. Notions of
'independence' were naturally attractive to the Whigs, and we find
Timothy Shelley's political circle making great play with the term.
Timothy praised his constituents for 'Independently' bestowing
their votes on him, and promised 'a faithful and Independent
Discharge of my Duty in parliament'.[5] Warden Sergison, one of
Timothy's political associates in Sussex, defined the kind of politics
his group liked to think of themselves as practising: 'I mean to be
independent of His Majesty's Ministers . . . I should give them my
Vote or if I did not perfectly agree with them I should vote against
them—if the Opposition brought forward any Propositions which

---

[1] *Sussex Weekly Advertiser*, 4 May 1807.
[2] See Newman Ivey White, *Shelley* (2 vols., 1947), i. 12.
[3] Timothy Shelley to William Whitton, 22 Apr. 1811 (in Roger Ingpen,
Shelley in England: New facts and letters from the Shelley–Whitton papers (1917),
p. 254).
[4] Medwin, p. 104; T. H. B. Oldfield, *Representative History*, v. 26.
[5] *Sussex Weekly Advertiser*, 27 Oct. 1806; draft of election address, dated 16
May 1807 (Albery Collection, Horsham MS 107, fo. 19; printed *Sussex Weekly
Advertiser*, 18 May 1807).

I approved they should have my Vote.'[1] Sergison presented himself as ' a MAN OF INDEPENDENCE, UNCONNECTED WITH PARTY', and his supporters boasted that he 'stands forward independent himself, and calls for the support of independent men'; his election song was called 'Independence and Sergison'.[2] 'Independence', of course, for all its fine overtones, was virtually a cant word for Opposition, and one of Sergison's associates wished, 'if he will not declare *decidedly* ag[ains]t the Ministry—that he will not speak so openly of his Independence'.[3] What the Whigs of Sussex paid lip-service to, the young Shelley took quite seriously. How could Timothy laud the virtues of Independence, and then expect his son to bow to the 'infamous concession' implied in his demand that he should renounce his opinions?[4]

It was Shelley's sensitivity about his independence that frustrated the Duke of Norfolk's well-meaning attempt to arrange a reconciliation. He invited Shelley and his father to dine at Norfolk House in the spring of 1811 'to talk over a plan for bringing him in as member for Horsham, and to induce him to exercise his talents in the pursuit of politics'. Such an arrangement would have suited the Duke very nicely, since he had just purchased the two seats at Horsham, and was in need of suitable nominees for the next general election, expected in 1813 or 1814, when Shelley would be of age. Shelley rejected the proposal, and his cousin remembered long after 'the indignation Bysshe expressed after that dinner at what he considered an effort made to shackle his mind, and introduce him into life as a mere follower of the Duke' (*Life*, ii. 156) Where Shelley felt that his independence was threatened his reaction was likely to be drastic and final.

Even before this final break Shelley had shown himself less interested in the official programme of the Whigs than in the activities of Sir Francis Burdett, who offered 'a new and active form of Whig creed and action'.[5] Burdett's Reform programme was

---

[1] Warden Sergison to Thomas Charles Medwin, 7 Feb. 1808 (Albery Collection, Horsham MS 148, fo. 21).

[2] *Sussex Weekly Advertiser*, 11, 18, 25 May 1807.

[3] Christopher Mayhew to T. C. Medwin, 22 Mar. 1808 (Albery Collection, Horsham MS 148, fo. 36).

[4] *Letters*, i. 198. As we shall see in Chapter III, 'independence' is a central concept in the theory of philosophical anarchism.

[5] Neville Rogers, in his edition of *The Complete Poetical Works of Percy Bysshe Shelley*, Vol. i (Oxford, 1972), 376.

based on Foxite principles, but went much farther than most Whigs were willing to go. But this 'aristocratic tribune of the people'[1] proved a very attractive hero for the young Shelley, devoted to liberty and the people, but distrustful of vulgar 'pothouse democracy' (*Letters*, i. 352). In 1810 Burdett became the centre of a political storm that brought himself and the Reform he advocated firmly before the attention of the public. The *affaire* Burdett, like the case of Peter Finnerty, grew out of the debate on the disastrous Walcheren expedition of 1809. Attempts were made during the debates in Parliament to prevent comments in the press. When the radical Reformer John Gale Jones attempted to canvass the issue of the freedom of the press in a placard for the British Forum debating society he was committed to Newgate for breach of parliamentary privilege.[2] Burdett denounced this unconstitutional infringement of the liberties of the subject in an open letter to his Westminster constituents which was published in Cobbett's *Political Register*. The Commons promptly voted to commit Burdett to the Tower, also for breach of privilege—a decision against which Timothy Shelley voted and the Duke of Norfolk spoke.[3] And to the Tower Burdett, after the employment of troops following several days of rioting that recalled the days of 'Wilkes and Liberty !', finally went on 9 April, to be automatically released when Parliament was prorogued on 21 June. All in all it was political martyrdom at a cheap rate, and Burdett's stand on behalf of the rights and liberties of Englishmen against the unjust usurpations of parliamentary privilege made him a popular hero. 'We may leave out the *Burdett*, for there is but one *Sir Francis* in England,' exulted Cobbett; 'he has been raised to a height of popular favour, which, perhaps, no man before him ever attained.'[4] While this scandal served to defuse the opposition's attack on the government's handling of the Walcheren expedition it also made 'Burdett's reformation' a topic of daily conversation in Sussex society, and the subject of a dozen petitions to Parliament.[5]

---

[1] M. W. Patterson, *Sir Francis Burdett and His Times (1770–1844)* (2 vols., 1931), i. 40.

[2] Shelley attended the British Forum and spoke there on at least one occasion (in the spring of 1811) (*Life*, i. 197).

[3] *Parliamentary Debates*, xvi. 547–8, xvii. 592.

[4] *Political Register*, 21 Apr. 1810, pp. 577, 584–5.

[5] M. Roberts, *The Whig Party*, pp. 267–8. The reference to 'Burdett's reformation' comes from a poem by Shelley's sister Elizabeth, dated 30 April, 1810 while Burdett was still in the Tower.

The real significance of Burdett's stand was that it was directed not against the King (as Wilkes's agitation had largely been), but against Parliament. In the view of the Reformers Parliament ought to be made more accountable to the people in a direct and immediate way. This was not Whig thinking, for the Whigs wished to strengthen Parliament against both the Crown and the people. Burdett's Reform has more in common with the aims of the democratic revolution, as we shall see in Chapter II.

When Shelley in the summer of 1810 dedicated his poem *The Wandering Jew* to Burdett 'In consideration of the active virtues by which both his public and private life is so eminently distinguished', it would seem that Reform was not the only issue that he had in mind. Burdett had associated himself with a variety of humanitarian causes, in the best tradition of Fox; between 1798 and 1800 he pressed for an investigation of the Cold Bath Fields Prison ('Burdett and no Bastille!'), and in 1811 he was to attack the use of *ex officio* informations to stifle the press, and the practice of flogging in the army. He also took a leading part in the campaign on behalf of the Irish journalist Peter Finnerty, in which Shelley involved himself while at Oxford, even publishing a poem (now lost) to raise money for Finnerty.[1] During his Irish expedition of the following year Shelley tried to organize a similar campaign around another persecuted Irishman, Redfern, an unwilling conscript into the English armies in Portugal. Shelley wrote to Elizabeth Hitchener, 'You will . . . soon hear of my or Sir F[rancis] Burdetts exertions in his favor' (*Letters*, i. 270). Shelley had probably invited Burdett to take up the case, for we know that he was sending letters to Burdett later in the year.[2] Shelley's own exertions appear to have included sending a letter to the *Sussex Weekly Advertiser* with an 'accompanying letter' which was probably the letter by Redfern that Shelley mentioned to Miss Hitchener.[3] The whole affair never

---

[1] For a detailed account of the Finnerty affair, and of Shelley's part in it, see Denis Florence MacCarthy, *Shelley's Early Life from Original Sources* (1872), pp. 77–106.

[2] See William Michael Rossetti, 'Shelley in 1812–13: An unpublished poem, and other particulars', *Fortnightly Review*, N.S. ix (1871), 68.

[3] The newpaper declined to participate, and suggested that 'a public exposure of the accused parties, however just, might irritate their minds and lead them to direct, with greater severity, the lash of *tyranny and oppression* against the object of his commiseration, who appears to be completely within their power' (*Sussex Weekly Advertiser*, 1 June 1812; see R. Ingpen, *Shelley in England*, pp. 383–4).

came to anything but it shows that Shelley's admiration for Burdett's 'active virtues' extended to emulation

Burdett's aggressive Reform programme had considerable attraction for several of the younger and more radical Whigs, such as Whitbread, Thomas Brand, and W. A. Madocks, who were trying to steer their party towards more active and popular policies.[1] Shelley was by no means the only Whig in the years after the collapse of the 'Talents' ministry to contemplate a complete break with the traditional party system in favour of Burdett's independent interpretation of the Foxite legacy. Thomas Moore, later to return to the Whig fold, exclaimed in 1809:

> Yet who, that looks to History's damning leaf,
> Where Whig and Tory, thief oppos'd to thief,
> On either side in lofty shame are seen,
> While Freedom's form hangs crucified between—
> Who, B-rd-tt, who such rival rogues can see,
> But flies from *both* to Honesty and thee?[2]

In 1813 the beautiful and charming Lady Oxford showed some interest in making Shelley's acquaintance (*Life*, ii. 8). Lady Oxford was Burdett's mistress and an active recruiter of supporters for her lover's programme, and David Erdman has suggested that she was making an attempt to enlist Shelley as she actually did enlist Byron.[3] If such an attempt was ever made it probably broke down because Shelley rejected the parliamentary career offered him by the Duke of Norfolk. But in any case his distrust for any kind of party politics must have been increased by his enthusiasm for the views presented by Leigh Hunt in his weekly *Examiner*.[4] Hunt supported Burdett but his support was for the measure rather than the man—he wanted 'Reform without party'.[5] To be a Burdettite was to sacrifice intellectual independence to party. Moreover at the root of Burdett's political philosophy was an almost Tory reverence

[1] M. Roberts, *The Whig Party*, pp. 354–5. Madocks's Reform connections may have had something to do with Shelley's decision to help his embankment project at Tremadoc; like Burdett, Madocks must have appeared to combine political liberalism with practical philanthropy.

[2] 'The Sceptic', lines 73–8.

[3] 'Lord Byron and the Genteel Reformers', *PMLA* lvi (1941), 1079n.

[4] Hunt, like Burdett, had suffered persecution for the cause, and Shelley admired him as 'one of the most fearless enlighteners of the public mind at the present time' (*Letters*, i. 54). Shelley made Hunt's acquaintance in May 1811.

[5] *Examiner*, 16 Apr. 1809, p. 242.

for the Crown, which he saw as the people's ally against the borough-mongers.[1] Shelley was to reject both the aristocratic bias of the Whigs and the latent monarchism of the Burdettite Reformers, and to attempt to build his own politics on the republicanism of Paine and the anarchism of Godwin. He was to attempt, in fact, to revive the principles and speculations of the 1790s in the far from congenial atmosphere of the 1810s.

---

[1] See M. Roberts, *The Whig Party*, pp. 231–2. Cobbett insisted that 'A reform in the Commons House of Parliament is as much the cause of the King and his family as it is the cause of the people' (*Political Register*, 5 June 1811, p. 1388). On the 'reactionary element' in Reform ideology, see A. D. Harvey, *Britain in the Early Nineteenth Century* (1978), pp. 227–9.

CHAPTER II

The Democratic Revolution

SHELLEY'S REJECTION of the Whig party and of a secure career in politics is intimately connected with his adherence to a far more radical political philosophy, that rejected the parliamentary power struggle and sought not just the remedy of specific abuses but the transformation of the whole structure of English society. In Shelley such demands were personal as well as theoretical, and one of his most uncompromising statements of his revolutionary aspirations was in fact made a propos of the way in which society corrupts the individual, and posits the transformation of society as necessary for the redemption of personal relationships.

The system of society as it exists at present must be overthrown from the foundations with all its superstructure of maxims & of forms before we shall find anything but dissapointment in our intercourse with any but a few select spirits. This remedy does not seem to be one of the easiest. But the generous few are not the less held to tend with all their efforts towards it. (*Letters*, ii. 191)

In the previous chapter we saw how uncompromising Shelley could be with respect to absolute standards, and it is hardly surprising that he adopted the revolutionary philosophy in its most extreme form, as expounded by William Godwin. But first we shall consider the theoretically less rigorous, though in practice far more aggressive, position of Thomas Paine, a rather more typical figure of the democratic revolution than Godwin, and a very attractive one for Shelley. Paine's influence can be traced behind all of Shelley's political activities, and behind a good deal of his early political theory too. But we should see both Paine and Shelley in the context of what I have chosen to call 'the democratic revolution'.

In what follows I am not concerned to supply an objective historical account but rather to describe the view that Shelley and many of his contemporaries held of their own immediate history. This view may have been largely a myth but historians are aware that even myths deserve serious study as the beliefs that motivate men's actions.[1] It is currently held by several modern historians, on whose accounts I shall draw, though it must be admitted that their interpretations have not gone uncriticized.[2] It is these historians who have coined the term 'the democratic revolution', though Shelley would have been quite familiar with the reality it was coined to describe. ⌐The democratic revolution was above all a movement of thought and opinion whose most notable historical manifestations were the revolt of the American colonies and the French Revolution. Shelley was proud to proclaim his adherence to this movement by declaring that his 'principles' had 'their origin from the discoveries in the science of politics and morals, which preceded and occasioned the revolutions of America and France' (*Works*, v. 263). For Shelley it seemed self-evident that these (and other) events were connected, and that the common source of them all lay in the realm of ideas. His hardest and most interesting thinking on politics was directed to English conditions, but he seems to have been convinced that progress there could only come as part of a general revolutionary movement. *A Philosophical View of Reform* was written to enforce the necessity of and explore the prospects of Reform in England, but Shelley prefaced this with a general survey of world history, and an examination of the revolutionary potential existing in Europe, South America, and Asia (*Works*, vii. 5–19). Like Paine Shelley believed that if liberty existed anywhere it must spread and propagate itself, like the forest-fire that begins with a single spark. This image often occurs in Shelley's poetry, as in his lament for Padua.

> In thine halls the lamp of learning,
> Padua, now no more is burning;
> Like a meteor, whose wild way
> Is lost over the grave of day,
> It gleams betrayed and to betray:
> Once remotest nations came

[1] See I. R. Christie, *Myth and Reality*, pp. 27–8.

[2] See R. R. Palmer, *The Age of the Democratic Revolution: A political history of Europe and America 1760–1800* (2 vols., Princeton, 1959–64), i. 4. See also Jacques Godechot, *France and the Atlantic Revolution of the Eighteenth Century 1770–1799*, translated by H. H. Rowen (New York and London, 1971). For criticisms of their approaches see George Rudé, *Revolutionary Europe 1783–1815* (1964), p. 7.

To adore that sacred flame,
When it lit not many a hearth
On this cold and gloomy earth:
Now new fires from antique light
Spring beneath the wide world's might;
But their spark lies dead in thee,
Trampled out by tyranny.
As the Norway woodman quells,
In the depth of piny dells,
One light flame among the brakes,
While the boundless forest shakes,
And its mighty trunks are torn
By the fire thus lowly born:
The spark beneath his feet is dead,
He starts to see the flames it fed
Howling through the darkened sky
With a myriad tongues victoriously,
And sinks down in fear: so thou,
O tyranny, beholdest now
Light around thee, and thou hearest
The loud flames ascend, and fearest . . .
('Lines written among the Euganean
   Hills' (1818), lines 256–82)[1]

This passage expresses Shelley's typical ambivalence about revolution. It, like fire, is purifying but also destructive and terrifying;
between lines 269 and 280 it is not quite clear that the seemingly
innocuous 'Norway woodman' does stand for tyranny, and in that
space we identify with his fear rather than the exultation of the
flames. The fire wins out, for it is both heat and light, and the
passage fuses the values of liberty and intellect. Shelley insists that
if the conflagration is political, the spark is thought, as it is elsewhere, most notably in the 'Ode to the West Wind' (1819).

Scatter, as from an unextinguished hearth
Ashes and sparks, my words among mankind!
(lines 66–7)[2]

[1] This passage was quoted by Leigh Hunt in the *Examiner* (30 July 1820, pp.
481–2) in anticipation of the spread of the constitutional revolution in Naples
to other countries.
[2] See also 'Sonnet: To a balloon, laden with Knowledge' (1812); *Adonais*
(1812), lines 408–9; and *The Triumph of Life* (1822), lines 206–7.

In fact Shelley prepared some very inflammatory sparks indeed in the shape of *The Mask of Anarchy* and other popular political poems shortly after writing these lines, and they were never scattered among mankind in Shelley's lifetime. The caution of his English friends is partly responsible, but a certain disinclination on Shelley's part to play with fire may have been responsible too.

A connected image in Shelley's poetry is that of the volcano. Volcanoes are equally ambivalent: their eruptions are immensely destructive, but the soil they leave behind is extraordinarily fertile (like the glacier in 'Mont Blanc' (1816) which both creates an uninhabitable wilderness and is the source of the river which is 'The breath and blood of distant lands' (line 124)). Volcanoes are an appropriate image in that they are subterraneously connected with each other, and one volcanic outbreak is the forerunner of others—just as all revolutions are connected in a single revolutionary movement, and one revolution serves to inspire others.

> England yet sleeps: was she not called of old?
>   Spain calls her now, as with its thrilling thunder
> Vesuvius awakens Ætna, and the cold
>   Snow-crags by its reply are cloven in sunder:
> ('Ode to Liberty' (1820), lines 181–4)[1]

The volcano which is still active but not actually erupting—like Vesuvius, which Shelley had seen while at Naples—is a telling image for the ominous period before the actual outbreak of revolution. 'In England', Shelley commented at the end of 1821, 'all bears for the moment the aspect of a sleeping Volcano' (*Letters*, ii. 371). In Shelley's usage volcanoes are generally regarded with favour, though as Geoffrey Matthews reminds us, they could just as easily be used as images of oppressive violence.[2] But to say that Shelley *approves* of volcanoes would sound rather odd, and would in fact miss what is perhaps the main point about his fondness for the image. Volcanic outbreaks, unlike fires, cannot be caused by human agency, and to view revolution under this image, as somehow inevitable and produced by impersonal forces, is to be relieved

---

[1] See G. M. Matthews, 'A Volcano's Voice in Shelley' (1957), in *Shelley: Modern Judgements*, edited by R. B. Woodings (1968), pp. 189–90. Volcanoes and revolution are connected in Shelley's poetry as early as February 1812 (see *Letters*, i. 253).

[2] G. M. Matthews, loc. cit., p. 187.

from responsibility for them. Shelley's ideals were revolutionary, but he doubted very much whether violent revolution was the right way to put them into action. If such a revolution had to come Shelley had no doubts about which side he would be on, but he preferred not to see himself as hastening its arrival.

We must now look at these ideals and their foundation in the nature of the social reality of Shelley's day. His version of the democratic revolution certainly included hopes and aspirations to which justice cannot be done in any summary formulation, and my attempt to define it is bound to seem inadequate to Shelley's fervour. Still, its general aims can be clarified by examining some of Shelley's pronouncements in the light of a modern summary. The historian who is most committed to the interpretation of the history of America and Europe in the late eighteenth century in terms of the 'democratic revolution' defines it as a movement in favour of 'democracy' and against 'aristocracy', terms which he glosses as follows:

Aristocracy meant the rule of certain constituted bodies, which claimed sovereignty for themselves, were self-perpetuating in a limited number of families, and denied the right of outside persons, or excluded classes, to have any influence on their policies or their personnel. The democratic movement, in one way or another . . . sought to broaden the basis of participation in political life, and to make the government accountable to some kind of a public . . .[1]

My own impression is that Shelley's contemporaries used 'democracy' and its cognates more freely and polemically than this account suggests,[2] while 'aristocracy' was used just as Professor Palmer claims, to refer to those classes by and for whom a country was governed. Thus James Mackintosh, in his radical youth, could distinguish three privileged 'Orders' or 'three Aristocracies' in pre-revolutionary France.[3] In England the main 'aristocratic' constituted body was Parliament (Lords and Commons together), responsible only to those classes from which their own members

---

[1] R. R. Palmer, op. cit. i. 365. For a fuller account see ibid. i. 22–3.

[2] 'Democratic' as late as 1830 'was still a term of abuse or condemnation among the ruling classes, and whigs as well as tories carefully dissociated themselves from its implications' (Norman Gash, *Politics in the Age of Peel* (1953; 2nd edn., Hassocks, Sussex, 1977), p. 4).

[3] *Vindiciae Gallicae* (3rd edn., 1791), p. 67. Mackintosh was referring to the Nobility, the Church, and the Parlements.

were recruited, as covered by the Whig definition of 'the people' considered above.[1] Indeed it was accepted that the Commons were not directly responsible even to those who elected them. In holding to this view the Whigs were every bit as 'aristocratic' as their opponents, and Burke vigorously repudiated the claim advanced by democratic reformers that an MP should be a mere 'delegate' of his constituents.[2]

Shelley's own background was eminently 'aristocratic'. He was to have been elected to Parliament thanks to family influence and connections, and he saw at first hand the machinations of his father, his uncle (T. C. Medwin), and the rest of the Horsham corporation, by which members of the Commons were made responsible not to a wider public but to a member of the Lords, the Duke of Norfolk.[3] Shelley was sceptical about the claim that the Commons allowed for the representation of the democratic element in the constitution. He saw Parliament as 'the aristocratical assemblies', and demanded, 'what conditions of democracy attach to an assembly one portion of which [is] imperfectly nominated by less than a twentieth part of the people, and another perfectly nominated by the nobles?' (*Works*, vii. 24) As he argued in a fragment on the Game Laws probably written in 1817, the Commons 'actually represent a deception and a shadow, virtually represent none but the powerful and the rich'.[4] Had Shelley followed the family plans he would have taken his seat in the Commons as the grandson of a baronet, the relative of several present and former MPs (including the Michelgrove Shelleys), an alumnus of Eton, and a graduate of Oxford. He would have been a typical member of the House. Out of the 5,034 MPs who sat between 1734 and 1832, 1,715 ended their careers with 'preferential social standing' as baronets or sons of peers; 2,813

[1] See above, p. 22.

[2] Betty Kemp, *King and Commons 1660–1832* (1957), pp. 43–5; Burke, *Works*, i. 446–8.

[3] In 1793 the Friends of the People claimed that no less than 170 MPs were returned by the influence of peers (*Annual Register* (1793), "Chronicle", pp. 94–5).

[4] Notebook of Mary Shelley now in the Percy B. Shelley Collection, Manuscript Division, Library of Congress, p. 11. My reading of this difficult passage differs from those given by F. L. Jones, 'Unpublished Fragments by Shelley and Mary', *Studies in Philology*, xlv (1948), 475, and by D. L. Clark in his edition of *Shelley's Prose; or, The Trumpet of a Prophecy* (Albuquerque, 1954), p. 342. Shelley is making ironic play with the claim that the Commons 'actually' represent their restricted electorate, but 'virtually' represent the whole community.

'had had a blood relative in the male line in the House before them'; 1,714 had been to a public school, 785 to Eton; 2,416 had been to a university, 1,286 to Oxford; about 75 per cent 'were mainly concerned with land rather than with other forms of wealth'; and 25 per cent entered the House at the age of twenty-five or under.[1] Shelley was very conscious that he had been born and bred to be one of the rulers, though he did not relish the prospect. 'I am one of these aristocrats,' he admitted to Merle in 1811. 'In me . . . the same machinery of oppression is preparing, in order that I also in my turn may become an oppressor.'[2]

To the end of his life Shelley could play the aristocrat when he chose, as his friends pointed out, intending a compliment which Shelley himself might not have appreciated.[3] Even his politics retain an aristocratic tinge, in that he believed that the existing ruling classes had to co-operate in reforming the existing system in order to avoid the horrors of revolution and civil war. '. . . the change should commence among the higher orders.' he assured Peacock in 1819, 'or anarchy will only be the last flash before despotism.' (*Letters*, ii. 115) But the moderation here is tactical; Shelley wants a radical and lasting change, and he fears anarchy because it is counter-productive and leads to despotism, as the Jacobins led to Napoleon. Shelley opposed revolution because he doubted its efficacy to promote his revolutionary ideals. But these ideals were totally revolutionary. He rejected the standards and ideals of his own class, and became what Professor Harold Perkin has called a 'social crank',[4] a self-appointed spokesman for the excluded classes. His aristocratic background gave him considerable critical insight into the way English society was structured by the power of the aristocracy.

As a Godwinian egalitarian Shelley saw this power as being economic as much as political. He lacked however the conceptual equipment to analyse the economic structure of his society, and his distaste for the study of political economy condemned his

[1] G. P. Judd, *Members of Parliament 1734–1832* (New Haven, 1955), pp. 31, 32, 37, 42, 71, 23. No less than five Shelleys sat for Sussex boroughs in the period 1734–1832 (ibid., pp. 332–3).

[2] [Joseph Gibbons Merle], 'A Newspaper Editor's Reminiscences. Chap. IV', *Fraser's Magazine*, xxiii (1841), 706.

[3] See Hogg, *Life*, i. 133, ii. 108; Medwin, p. 343; Leigh Hunt, *Lord Byron and Some of His Contemporaries* (1828), p. 49.

[4] *The Origins of Modern English Society 1780–1880* (1969), p. 220.

utterances on the subject to remain on the level of a callow moralism. Medwin records that 'Shelley frequently used to inveigh against the political economists; whose object is to stop the progress of mankind, and to keep up the *uti possedetis*'.[1] This judgement seems to have been based on the most slender of acquaintances with the works of the Classical Economists. The only evidence that he knew of Adam Smith is a sneering reference to the title of *The Wealth of Nations* (1776), probably the only part of the book that Shelley knew.

> The harmony and happiness of man
> Yields to the wealth of nations . . .
> (*Queen Mab*, v. 79–80)

Milton Millhauser has ingeniously argued that the anti-semitic passages in Act I, scene i of *Swellfoot the Tyrant* (1820) are in fact an attack on the Jewish-born political economist David Ricardo, whose *On the Principles of Political Economy, and Taxation* was published in 1817.[2] It is much more likely that Shelley had in mind the great Jewish financiers, particularly Rothschild; like every young man of his class Shelley knew only too well what 'going to the Jews' meant.[3] Ricardo was in fact a financier as well as a theorist, but there is no real reason to believe that Shelley had him or his *Principles* in mind. If he had read the book, he might have approved of some of the suggestions that Ricardo makes, including the recommendation that the National Debt be paid off by a capital levy. Shelley was certainly acquainted with Thomas Malthus's *An Essay on the Principle of Population* (1798, enlarged 1803), and his opposition to Malthus's ideas is notorious. But in fact Shelley did not dispute Malthus's economics, nor was he in a position to do so; what he objected to were the conclusions as to desirable social policies that Malthus drew. 'Malthus is a very clever man, & the world would be a great gainer if it would seriously take his lessons into consideration—if it were capable of attending seriously to any thing but mischief—but what on earth does he mean by some of his inferences!' (*Letters*, ii. 43) The 'inferences' to which

---

[1] Medwin, p. 345.

[2] 'Shelley: a reference to Ricardo in "Swellfoot the Tyrant" ', *N & Q*, 14 Jan. 1939, pp. 25–6.

[3] Leigh Hunt commented that anti-Jewish feeling had probably been stirred up by the activity of financiers like Rothschild in supplying money to the Holy Alliance (*Examiner*, 26 Sept. 1819, p. 616).

Shelley objects are, presumably, Malthus's contentions that Poor Relief should be abolished, and that the labouring poor should be discouraged from marrying. Shelley believed that he could avoid these conclusions, while accepting Malthus's economic reasonings, by the same manœuvre as that later adopted by the 'neo-Malthusians'. In a fragment headed 'Malthus', written in the same notebook as *A Philosophical View of Reform* and clearly intended as a footnote or addendum to that work, Shelley argued that

The sexual intercourse by no means presents as has been supposed the alternative of a being to be invested with existence for whom there is no subsistence, or the ⟨revolting⟩ expedients of infanticide and abortion. Every student of anatomy must be aware of an innocent, small and almost imperceptible precaution by which all consequences of this kind are precluded, and the ends of an union of two persons of opposite sexes in every other respect fulfilled—[1]

Shelley, it should be noted, is anticipating by over three years the first public advocacy of contraception as an answer to the Malthusian dilemma, by Francis Place and other Utilitarians.[2]

The writer on whom Shelley drew most deeply for his economic views was, unfortunately, William Cobbett.[3] Cobbett's no-nonsense analysis of the economic structure of English society was clearly far more congenial to Shelley than the complexities of the political economists. As early as 1811 he was aware of the existence of a new moneyed class existing alongside the old landed aristocracy. Between them these two classes composed the 500,000 'aristocrats' who lived 'in a state of ease' off the labour of the other 9,500,000 inhabitants.[4] By 1817 familiarity with Cobbett's ideas had confirmed him in the idea of a 'double aristocracy' (*Works*, vi. 78), which he saw in Cobbett's terms as the old 'boroughmongers' and the new 'fundholders'. As economic analysis this is hardly very sophisticated, and Shelley is much sharper in his comments on the political dimension. It was the political power of the aristocratic classes which had enabled them to create a National Debt (the main source of the new financial aristocracy) and to throw the burden

---

[1] MS in the Pierpont Morgan Library, New York. The 'precaution' referred to is probably the vaginal sponge.

[2] See Norman E. Himes, *Medical History of Contraception* (1936), pp. 214–17.

[3] For the injudicious extent of Shelley's borrowings from Cobbett see K. N. Cameron, 'Shelley, Cobbett and the National Debt', *JEGP* xlii (1943), 197–209.

[4] *Letters*, i. 132, 127. See also i. 151, 257.

of it, by indirect taxation, on to the unrepresented masses. Shelley condemns the class legislation by which the Commons '[loads?] the necessaries which the labouring poor consume with imposts, whilst the most productive as well as the most legitimate object of all taxation is spared, namely, vast accumulations of wealth, because it is the species of possession which its own members enjoy'.[1] He is concerned to demonstrate that the 'aristocratical system' is unjust, and to persuade its supporters that this injustice is so extensive and so beyond what is necessary that the system itself is threatened with violent destruction by its victims if it is not meliorated.[2]

In seeking to give effective warning Shelley often seems to defend one part of the system while he condemns another. He reserves his bitterest vituperation for the *nouveaux riches*, the commercial and financial aristocrats who have 'gained a right to the title of public creditors, either by gambling in the funds, or by subserviency to government, or some other villainous trade'.[3] He is considerably more generous towards his own class, the landed aristocracy, to whom he allowed positive moral qualities, admitting, 'my republicanism it is true would bear with an aristocracy of chivalry, & refinement, before an aristocracy of commerce and vulgarity'.[4] But it is clear that this approval is strictly relative. The chivalry and refinement is after all 'at bottom . . . all trick' to anyone who has grasped 'the base falshood upon which all inequality is founded' (*Works*, vii. 28). Shelley may temporarily 'acquiesce' in the existence of an aristocracy, so long as it is considered by society to be inseparably connected with 'the best practicable form of social order'.[5] But he cannot give it his positive approval, for in the final analysis any aristocracy consists of 'that class of persons who possess a right to the produce of the labour of others, without dedicating to the common service any labour in return'. These people are 'drones' and the less of them there are the better for society (*Works*,

---

[1] Mary Shelley Notebook in the Library of Congress, p. 11. My version again differs from those of F. L. Jones, 'Unpublished Fragments', 475, and D. L. Clark, *Shelley's Prose*, p. 342.

[2] *Works*, vi. 78–9, vii. 29–31.

[3] *Works*, vi. 78. See also vii. 28–9. As an example of what Shelley claims, journalists and other government supporters were often given slices of government loans as a reward for their services (see *The Autobiography of William Cobbett*, edited by W. Reitzel (1947), pp. 85–6).

[4] *Letters*, i. 352. See also *Works*, vi. 78, vii. 28–9.

[5] *Works*, vi. 79, vii. 28, 339.

vii. 27–8). In his popular poems of 1819 Shelley shows a fondness
for the metaphor of the social hive.

> Wherefore, Bees of England, forge
> Many a weapon, chain, and scourge,
> That these stingless drones may spoil
> The forced produce of your toil?
> ('Song to the Men of England', lines 9–12)

H. Buxton Forman managed to reconstruct a fragment in which
the same theme is treated even more elaborately.

> O Bees of England, that the idle drone
> Should have rebelled, & murdered on her throne
> Freedom, who was your Queen; the drone without a sting
> Who clogs with honey his inglorious wing
> And spoils what he consumes not, & defiles
> The happy hive, & breaks its garnered cells
> How beautiful might thine hive of wax . . .[1]

As Forman points out the trope is Virgilian, but it seems more
relevant to note that in Shelley's day it was used almost exclusively
by working-class socialists and radicals. Tom Paine complained
that the aristocracy 'when compared with the active world are the
drones, a seraglio of males, who neither collect the honey nor form
the hive, but exist only for lazy enjoyment'. Thomas Spence called
his bookshop 'The Hive of Liberty' and his famous 'plan' included
an allegory on the parish of the Bees with characters like Lord and
Lady Drone. Thomas Wooler rang a change on the metaphor in
denouncing 'the herd of locusts that prey upon the honey of the
hive, and think they do the bees a most essential service by robbing
them'.[2] A radical newspaper of the 1830s was called *The Bee*, and
one of the most famous labour newspapers was *The Bee-Hive* of
the 1860s and 1870s.[3] In addressing himself to a working-class
audience Shelley adopted the rhetoric of radicalism.

---

[1] *Note Books of Percy Bysshe Shelley from the Originals in the Library of
W. K. Bixby*, edited by H. Buxton Forman (3 vols., Boston, 1911), ii. 178.

[2] Paine, *Complete Writings*, i. 412; W. P. Hall, *British Radicalism 1791–1797*
(New York, 1912), p. 111; *Black Dwarf*, 20 Aug. 1817, quoted in *Class and
Conflict in Nineteenth-Century England 1815–1850*, edited by P. Hollis (1973),
p. 33. Hollis gives similar passages from *The Crisis* (17 May 1832) and Feargus
O'Connor's *Northern Star* (23 Jan. 1847) (pp. 162, 14).

[3] Patricia Hollis, *The Pauper Press* (1970), p. 319; Stephen Coltham, 'The

Shelley follows the more extreme theorists of the democratic revolution—Paine, Spence, and Godwin—in turning political demands into a claim for material equality. But our immediate concern is with Shelley's analysis of the political machinery by which the aristocracy ruled, as expounded in *A Philosophical View of Reform*. Shelley's account is by no means incompatible with modern views of the unreformed political system.

When it is said by political reasoners speaking of the interval between 1688 and the present time that the royal power progressively increased, they use an expression which suggests a very imperfect and partial idea.[1] The power which has increased is that entrusted with the administration of affairs, composed of men responsible to the aristocratical assemblies, or to the reigning party in those assemblies, and which represents those orders of the nation which are privileged and will retain power as long as it pleases them and must be divested of power as soon as it ceases to please them. The power which has increased therefore is the power of the rich. The name and the office of King is merely the mask of this power, and is a kind of stalking horse used to conceal these 'catchers of men' whilst they lay their nets—Monarchy is only the string which ties the robbers' bundle. Though less contumelious and abhorrent from the dignity of human nature than an absolute monarchy, an oligarchy of this nature exacts more of suffering from the people, because it reigns both by the opinion generated by imposture, and the force which that opinion places within its grasp.
(*Works*, vii. 24–5)[2]

The impression, gathered from a superficial reading of *Queen Mab* and *Laon and Cythna*, that Shelley's politics never went beyond a violent prejudice against kings hardly does justice to his mature thinking. He would certainly have agreed with Joel Barlow that 'The tyrannies of the world . . . are all aristocratical tyrannies': 'Among beings so nearly equal in power and capacity as men of the

---

Bee-Hive Newspaper: its Origin and Early Struggles', in *Essays in Labour History*, edited by A. Briggs and J. Saville (1960; rev. edn., 1967), pp. 174–204.

[1] Shelley is referring to the favourite Whig complaint that the 'influence of the Crown' had increased inordinately.

[2] Modern historians might consider that Shelley overstates the degree of control possessed by the Commons over ministers before 1832 (see B. Kemp, *King and Commons*, pp. 139–40). But even in the eighteenth century the Commons were able to make at least 'occasional claims to supremacy, not only . . . over King and Lords, but also . . . over the electorate and over the King's choice of ministers' (ibid., p. 143).

same community are it is impossible that a solitary tyrant should exist. Laws that are designed to operate unequally on society, must offer an exclusive interest to a considerable portion of its members, to ensure their execution on the rest.'[1] Shelley considered that even the aristocratic oppressors 'experience the reaction of their own shortsighted tyranny, in all those sufferings and deprivations which are not of a distinctly physical nature, in the loss of dignity, simplicity and energy and in the possession of all those qualities which distinguish a slave driver from a proprietor' (*Works*, vii. 30). Most of Shelley's political pronouncements are directed to his own class, and are intended to show them their own real interests.

The positive demands of the democratic revolution can be summed up in Shelley's dictum that 'no individual who is governed can be denied a direct share in the government of his country without supreme injustice'. This, he adds, was the position of the 'advocates of universal suffrage' (*Works*, vii. 40). He was referring to the radical Reformers who had by 1819 adopted the position that what constituted the difference between 'a *free man* and a *slave*' was 'simply this, that the free man, if he be in a state of civil society, *partakes in the making of the laws by which he is governed*; and, the slave is governed by the *will of another, or of others*'.[2] But not even the Radicals carried out the full programme of the democratic revolution as Shelley saw it, and he pointed out that the arguments used to justify universal suffrage would lead to republicanism and the redistribution of property.[3] He was well aware, as we shall see in Chapter V, that his own position was far more 'radical' than that of the Radicals; we shall also see why his proposals were so much more moderate than theirs. Shelley's point is demonstrated by the fact that the most consistent Radical theorist, Major Cartwright, did in fact become a republican in the end.[4] But few Radicals cared to take democratic theories to a republican conclusion. Such extremism was beyond the political pale, thanks to the general loss of nerve suffered by all progressive politicians after the débâcle of the democratic movement in the French Revo-

---

[1] *Advice to the Privileged Orders*, Part I (1792), in *The Works of Joel Barlow*, Facsimile reproductions, with an Introduction by William K. Bottorff and Arthur L. Ford (2 vols., Gainesville, 1970), i. 100–1.

[2] *Political Register*, 15 Nov. 1817, p. 1002.

[3] *Works*, vii. 41. See also vi. 68.

[4] Corinne Comstock Weston, *English Constitutional Theory and the House of Lords 1556–1832* (1965), pp. 221–30.

lution.[1] The only thing worse than being a republican was being an atheist, and Shelley was that too; indeed his atheism was intimately connected with his political revolt. In 1811 he wrote, 'It is this empire of terror which is established by Religion, Monarchy is it's prototype, Aristocracy may be regarded as symbolising with [sic] its very essence. They are mixed—one can now scarce be distinguished from the other.' (*Letters*, i. 126) In his open letter to the *Examiner* on the trial of Richard Carlile in 1819 his concern is with the political implications of religion (*Letters*, ii. 143–4). In 1816 he had nailed his colours to the mast-head in a Greek inscription in the visitors' book at Chamonix which may be translated: 'I am a philanthropist, an utter democrat, and an atheist.'[2]

Tracing the genesis of Shelley's political views is difficult because so much of what he learnt from other sources is overlaid by, absorbed into, or modified by Godwinian elements, as we saw in discussing Shelley's involvement with Whig ideology. It is however valuable to locate and follow the specifically Whig and Paineite strands in his political education since they in turn modified what he took from Godwin. In their ways Paine and Godwin were both followers of the democratic revolution, and some of Godwin's thinking follows clues provided by Paine. Where they diverged Shelley did not automatically follow Godwin and he retained a practical admiration for 'the celebrated Paine . . . that great & good man' as late as 1819.[3] In what follows we shall see references to Paine's ideas in Shelley's two Irish pamphlets, in his two Reform pamphlets, and in *A Philosophical View of Reform*. I shall concentrate on Paine's political ideas, though it should be noted that Shelley drew heavily on *Rights of Man* (1791–2) for his ideas concerning religion and toleration in the Irish pamphlets, and he probably had Paine's kind of Deism in mind in providing arguments for the Deist Theosophus in *A Refutation of Deism* (1814), in which he may be drawing on Paine's *Age of Reason* (1794). Shelley's allusions to Paine's works are too many for them all to be

---

[1] See M. Roberts, *The Whig Party*, pp. 176–7; Philip Anthony Brown, *The French Revolution in English History* (1918; 1965), Ch. IX.

[2] Gavin de Beer, 'An "Atheist" in the Alps', *K–SMB* ix (1958), 9. The translation is by the present author.

[3] *Letters*, ii. 143. There is what may well be an allusion to Paine's writings in Shelley's last work, *The Triumph of Life* (see G. M. Matthews, 'On Shelley's "The Triumph of Life" ', *Studia Neophilologica*, xxxiv (1962), 127n.).

discussed, but it should be possible to give a more complete account of the Paineite elements in Shelley's thought than has yet been given.[1]

For Shelley, Paine must have seemed the archetypal hero of the whole revolutionary movement. He inspired and fought for one revolution in America, participated in and wrote propaganda for another in France, and tried to instigate yet a third in England. While Godwin satisfied the young Shelley's thirst for justice, it was Paine who provided him with a satisfyingly comprehensive and vigorous denunciation of the actual injustices of existing society. He had some claim to be regarded as combining the philosopher and the man of action. With the example of Paine and America before him, it is easier to understand how Shelley might have thought he could achieve something similar in Ireland.[2] Indeed Shelley showed considerable interest in Paine just at the time he was planning his expedition to Ireland, and he quotes freely from him in his Irish pamphlets. He took comfort from the fact that Paine, whose 'writings were far more violently in opposition to government than mine perhaps ever will be', died in bed. He spoke of pasting his own voluminous pamphlets on the walls of Dublin 'as Paine's works were', and he set his sister-in-law to collecting 'the usefu[l] passages' from Paine for republication.[3] It is significant that Shelley never mentions his interest in Paine when writing to Godwin, which suggests that the divergence between them was quite apparent to him, and that his own loyalties were still divided.

Paine's political philosophy is by no means as coherent and plausible as his lucid and persuasive style would have us believe, and there is no question of Shelley having adopted his ideas in any systematic way. Indeed it is a style of politics as much as a philosophy that Shelley inherits from Paine. But Paine does expound certain preoccupations and concepts that are of great relevance to Shelley's thinking on politics. Rather than giving a catalogue of all the connections between Paine's thinking and

[1] Paine's importance for Shelley seems to me to be understated by Carl Woodring, *Politics in English Romantic Poetry* (Cambridge, Mass., 1970), p. 233. It is stressed by Gerald McNiece, *Shelley and the Revolutionary Idea* (Cambridge, Mass., 1969), pp. 14, 95–6, and some parallels are cited by K. N. Cameron, *The Young Shelley*, pp. 56–9, 319–20.
[2] See John P. Guinn, *Shelley's Political Thought* (The Hague, 1969), p. 12.
[3] *Letters*, i. 221, 239, 255.

Shelley's that could be made, I prefer to discuss in a little detail four main issues: the myth of America; the revolutionary view of history; Paine's analysis of the origin and justification of government; and the question of the 'rights of man'.

Paine's optimism concerning the possibility of a totally new order of politics was derived mainly from the experience of America. In his later years he came to have misgivings about the course of events in his adopted country, but he never doubted that a renovation had occurred there and that its effects could be made universal. The theme of the uniqueness of the American opportunity is present in his work as early as *Common Sense* (1776).

Every spot of the old world is overrun with oppression. Freedom hath been hunted round the globe. Asia and Africa have long expelled her. Europe regards her like a stranger, and England hath given her warning to depart. O! receive the fugitive, and prepare in time an asylum for mankind. (*Complete Writings*, i. 30–1)

If America was freedom's last refuge, Paine also came to see her as the base for a counter-attack on its enemies. The French Revolution provided the perfect opportunity. Why should not America make it her mission to bring the new political light to the benighted old world and thus become the '*Mother Church* of government' (ii. 1350)? Even before American independence had been achieved Paine was urging the English, 'Your present king and ministry will be the ruin of you; and you had better risk a revolution and call a Congress, than be thus led on from madness to despair, and from despair to ruin. America has set you the example, and you may follow it and be free.' (i. 155) Paine's life and talents were to be devoted to propagating the spirit and the principles of a revolution which 'has contributed more to enlighten the world, and diffuse a spirit of freedom and liberality among mankind, than any human event (if this may be called one) that ever preceded it' (i. 232).

It was Paine as much as anyone who popularized the image of America as the land of liberty for later reformers.[1] It was an important image for Shelley, in the second generation of Romanticism. The older Romantics saw France as the 'peuple législateur,[2] and

---

[1] See John W. Derry, *The Radical Tradition: Tom Paine to Lloyd George* (1967), p. 43.

[2] Constantin François Chasseboeuf, comte de Volney, *Les Ruines, ou Méditation sur les révolutions des empires* (Paris, 1791), p. 116.

consequently their political hopes were involved in its downfall. But even after 'the last hope of trampled France had failed', as Shelley puts it in the opening line of *Laon and Cythna* (1817), the flourishing American republic still served as an inspiration to those who held to the ideals of the democratic revolution. This is the role it plays in *Laon and Cythna*, where it is seen both as an asylum for oppressed liberty and the source of future renovation.

> There is a People mighty in its youth,
> A land beyond the Oceans of the West,
> Where, tho' with rudest rites, Freedom and Truth
> Are worshipped; from a glorious Mother's breast
> Who, since high Athens fell, among the rest
> Sate like the Queen of Nations, but in woe,
> By inbred monsters outraged and oppressed,
> Turns to her chainless child for succour now,
> It draws the milk of Power in Wisdom's fullest flow.
> (XI. xxii)

America draws its principles of liberty from England, its 'glorious Mother'—Paine's own English origins are surely relevant here—and now oppressed England must turn to America for help.[1] The reference to 'high Athens' points forward to the more detailed tracing of the tradition of freedom in the 'Ode to Liberty' (1820), and to *Hellas* (1822) and the unfinished 'Charles I' (1821–2), in which America is seen as 'the new Hellas in the West'.[2] Many other references could be given for Shelley's enthusiasm for the infant republic.[3]

Medwin records some rather more critical comments by Shelley on the American form of government.[4] It is possible that he has not totally misrepresented Shelley's views, for while Shelley admired the 'system of Government in the United States of

---

[1] This view had been expressed by Mary Wollstonecraft, *An Historical and Moral View of the Origin and Progress of the French Revolution; and the Effect it has produced in Europe*, Vol. i (1794; no more published), p. 234. Justice has not been done to Mary Wollstonecraft's strong presence in *Laon and Cythna*.

[2] Earl R. Wasserman, *Shelley: A Critical Reading* (Baltimore and London, 1971), p. 403. Wasserman has an interesting discussion of the way Shelley's political enthusiasms relate to his poetic symbolism (ibid., pp. 403–4, 407–10).

[3] See *Letters*, i. 193, 239, 272; 'To Liberty' (in *The Esdaile Notebook: A Volume of Early Poems by Percy Bysshe Shelley*, edited by K. N. Cameron (1964), p. 59); *Works*, iii. 50, 51, iv. 164; Edward John Trelawny, *Life*, ii. 201–2.

[4] Medwin, p. 345.

America' as 'the first practical illustration of the new philosophy' in morals and politics, he did express some reservations (*Works*, vii. 10). It should be pointed out, however, that Shelley had no doubts at all about the *relative* superiority of the American republican system, and he insisted that America presented 'an example compared with the old governments of Europe and Asia of a free, happy and strong people'.[1] If he qualified his praise by noting that the American system is still 'Sufficiently remote . . . from the accuracy of ideal excellence' this is a comment which must apply to any actual society for a believer in Perfectibility (*Works*, vii. 10).

The doctrine of Perfectibility seems to have betrayed Shelley into a misreading of Paine by which he attributes to the American constitution a virtue that it did not possess. 'It constitutionally acknowledges the progress of human improvement, and is framed under the limitation of the probability of more simple views of political science being rendered applicable to human life. There is a law by which the Constitution is reserved for revision every ten years.' (*Works*, vii. 11) It has already been pointed out that this is incorrect, though the suggestion is in harmony with the thought of some of the Founding Fathers, especially Jefferson.[2] For Godwin and Shelley it was crucially important that a system of government, however good in its own time, should also be open to change in the future. Paine was in fact acquainted with Condorcet, a leading perfectibilarian, and sometimes speaks like one himself; it would have been easy for Shelley to misread this.

The constitutions of America, and also that of France, have either fixed a period for their revision, or laid down the mode by which improvements shall be made.

It is perhaps impossible to establish any thing that combines principles with opinions and practise, which the progress of circumstances, through a length of years, will not in some manner derange, or render inconsistent; and therefore, to prevent inconsistencies accumulating, till they discourage reformations or provoke revolutions, it is best to regulate them as they occur. (*Complete Writings*, i. 396)

In fact Paine does not address himself to the possibility of positive progress (in which he has little real faith), and he is referring, not

---

[1] *Works*, vii. 12. Shelley went on to stress the advantages of *not* possessing the aristocratic institutions of England.

[2] D. L. Clark, *Shelley's Prose*, p. 234 n. 13.

to the federal constitution, but to the individual constitutions of the various states. This is also true of the passage quoted by Peck as a note to Shelley's passage.[1]

Paine's suggestion that the possibility of future change should be left open follows naturally from his insistence that the present should not be shackled to the past. 'Every generation is, and must be, competent to all the purposes which its occasions require. It is the living, and not the dead, that are to be accomodated.' (*Complete Writings*, i. 251) Paine however does not follow this reasoning through as Godwin and Shelley were to do. They insisted that the future must not be shackled by the present. Paine made no secret of his belief that a final and virtually perfect form of government would be arrived at within 'a few years' (i. 396). At that point further progress would become unnecessary, and the ideal government could be embodied in a definitive constitution. But as Godwin noted with disapproval, any settled constitution acts as a check on progress.[2] Shelley follows Paine rather than Godwin when he assigns a useful function to constitutional law, and, even more eclectically, he follows Burke in arguing that such law may consist in 'written institutions or traditions' (*Works*, vi. 289–90). His comments on the English constitution in the Irish pamphlets apparently reflect a more orthodox Paineite line. Shelley never echoes Paine's insistence that a valid constitution must be written, but he does argue that 'at no time did the individuals that compose them [England and Ireland] constitute a system for the general benefit' and thus they have no real constitution (*Works*, v. 260). This is essentially Paine's argument that the government of England 'arose out of a conquest, and not out of society, and consequently it arose over the people . . . the country has never regenerated itself, and is therefore without a constitution' (*Complete Writings*, i. 279). But where Paine clearly wants a valid constitution Shelley borrows his arguments for the negative purpose of showing that England does not have one, whatever Whig rhetoric may say.

Godwin's distrust of constitutional settlements rests on his willingness to appeal to the future against the inadequacies of the present. Paine appealed rather to the common sense of the present against the obscurantism of the past. This distinction between past

[1] *Complete Writings*, i. 395, quoted in *Works*, vii. 334 (as a note to vii. 11, line 35).
[2] See *Political Justice*, ii. 283–96.

and present is the only one relevant to Paine's revolutionary view of history, and it lends special resonance to his use of terms like the 'old' and the 'new' world. He assured the Americans, 'We have it in our power to begin the world over again', an early expression of that faith in the 'American Adam' which was to affect American culture so profoundly.[1] Paine's famous attack on the English constitution is founded explicitly on his rejection of 'the dead weight of the past'.[2] Provoked by Burke's praise for the Glorious Revolution of 1688 and the subsequent settlement, Paine made a clean sweep of all the historic achievements enshrined in Whig mythology.

There never did, there never will, and there never can exist a parliament, or any description of men, in any country, possessed of the right or the power of binding and controlling posterity to the "*end of time*", or of commanding forever how the world shall be governed, or who shall govern it. . . .

Every age and generation must be as free to act for itself, *in all cases*, as the ages and generations which preceded it. (*Complete Writings*, i. 251)

From a similar point of view, though in more Godwinian language, Shelley attacked the Revolution Settlement as an attempt to 'arrest the perfectibility of human nature' (*Letters*, i. 264).

Paine saw the defence of the present against the encroachments of the past as the point at issue between himself and Burke: 'I am contending for the rights of the *living* . . . and Mr. Burke is contending for the authority of the dead over the rights and freedom of the living.' (i. 252) Paine neglects the need to make provision for the freedom of the unborn from the authority of the living. He consequently fails to see the positive implications of Burke's traditionary vision of the state as 'a partnership not only between those who are living, but between those who are living, those who are dead, and those who are to be born'.[3] That Burke chooses to make his point in terms of a 'partnership' and elsewhere of a 'family settlement'[4] is unfortunate in that it serves to remind his

---

[1] *Complete Writings*, i. 45. See R. W. B. Lewis, *The American Adam: Innocence, Tragedy and Tradition in the Nineteenth Century* (Chicago, 1955), p. 5.

[2] 'Paine believed in casting off the dead weight of the past. In some moods he talked as if all the ills of the world were the result of a submissive regard for tradition and he was rarely sympathetic to appeals to custom and precedent' (J. W. Derry, *The Radical Tradition*, p. 11).

[3] Burke, *Works*, ii. 368.

[4] Ibid. ii. 306–7.

opponents of certain objectionable institutions in existing society that affect the transmission of property. But a change in terms would hardly have made Paine more sympathetic to his position, for Paine was fundamentally opposed to any appeal to tradition. Shelley, as a poet who deeply admired the European literary tradition, is in many ways nearer to Burke than to Paine.[1] Shelley's reference to 'that great poem, which all poets, like the co-operating thoughts of one great mind, have built up since the beginning of the world' recalls Burke's vision of human society as 'a partnership in all science; a partnership in all art; a partnership in every virtue, and in all perfection'.[2] He remarks that Keat's 'fate and fame' will inspire men 'till the Future dares/Forget the Past' (*Adonais*, line 7), implying that such a break in the continuity of human history would be ominous. From his original disgust at 'that record of crimes & miseries—History'[3] Shelley came to appreciate by 1817 that the past is a repository of inspiring examples as well as of disheartening failures (*Works*, vi. 252). *A Philosophical View of Reform* contains a sustained effort to find positive value in what has been, and acknowledges the need to preserve as well as to change.[4] Shelley would always lament political reaction as 'the slow victory of the spirit of the past over that of the present' (*Letters*, ii. 358), but he did not share Paine's belief that a single revolutionary act could wipe out the past and realize a perfect present. If the democratic dream were to become a reality it could only be by sustained and patient effort directed to the future. In their concern for the potential of the future Godwin and Shelley could appreciate the force of Burke's remark that 'A spirit of innovation is generally the result of a selfish temper, and confined views. People will not look forward to posterity, who never look backward to their ancestors.'[5]

One of Paine's most seminal distinctions is that between society and government. His intention is to stigmatize government as a negative institution and from there to press for its reduction, but at the same time his argument serves to present the essential justification for some measure of coercive government.

---

[1] See G. McNiece, *Shelley and the Revolutionary Idea*, pp. 13–14.
[2] *Works*, vii. 124; Burke, *Works*, ii. 368.
[3] *Letters*, i. 340.
[4] See William Royce Campbell, 'Shelley's Philosophy of History: A Reconsideration', *K–SJ* xxi–xxii (1972–3), 57; J. P. Guinn, *Shelley's Political Thought*, p. 66.
[5] Burke, *Works*, ii. 307.

Society is produced by our wants and government by our wickedness; the former promotes our happiness *positively* by uniting our affections, the latter *negatively* by restraining our vices. . . .

Society in every state is a blessing, but government, even in its best state, is but a necessary evil. . . . Government, like dress, is the badge of lost innocence; the palaces of kings are built upon the ruins of the bowers of paradise. For were the impulses of conscience clear, uniform and irresistibly obeyed, man would need no other lawgiver.[1]

This position can certainly be developed in an anarchist direction, as it is by Joel Barlow when he argues that if there were a nation in which 'those moral habits by which men are disposed to mutual justice and benevolence . . . should exist in a perfect degree, that nation would require no government at all'.[2] If Barlow takes this possibility seriously Paine does not. Man can no more do without government than he can do without clothes. The allusion to the Fall suggests that man's need for the restraints of government is an ineradicable part of his nature, and Paine himself supported the Constitution of 1787 which established a strong central government for America.[3]

Godwin and Shelley are happy to take Paine's point that government is an evil—as we shall see they had moral objections to government going beyond Paine's—but they questioned the necessity which he accepted. When Shelley borrows Paine's terms he is careful to drop the reference to the Fall, with its suggestions of a depravity which is innate. 'In proportion as mankind becomes wise, yes, in exact proportion to that wisdom should be the extinction of the unequal system under which they now subsist. Government is in fact the mere badge of their depravity.' (*Works*, vi. 249) Man's depravity, which justifies coercive government, is a matter of empirical fact, not an unalterable condition of his existence, and if his wisdom allows him to escape from it he need no longer wear the badge of servitude. Shelley makes a similar point elsewhere by adding a third term to Paine's pair: 'Society is produced by the wants, Government by the wickedness, and a state of just and happy equality by the improvement and reason of

---

[1] *Complete Writings*, i. 4–5. Part of this famous passage is quoted by Godwin (*Political Justice*, i. 124), but Shelley was probably acquainted with its original context in *Common Sense*.

[2] *Works of Joel Barlow*, i. 36–7.

[3] See Eric Foner, *Tom Paine and Revolutionary America* (New York, 1976), pp. 204–5.

man' (*Works*, v. 232). That such a fundamental improvement in man could be posited as a serious possibility would never have occurred to Paine, and this is part of his indifference to the future. The consequences of this radical extension of Paine's position will be discussed in Chapter III.

One further aspect of Paine's thought, or it might be better to say of his rhetoric, must be considered, for it influenced Shelley in a way that could not be reconciled to the ideas of Godwin. I refer to Paine's insistence on the notion of the *rights of man*, natural and civil. Political philosophers are not very happy with this concept, and they argue that talk of 'natural rights' is only a way of expressing personal preferences.[1] The situation would seem to be that political philosophers would like to talk about politics objectively, while politics as an activity is inseparably involved with questions of value. Paine is certainly unconvincing when he tries to explain how man got his inalienable rights (at the Creation), nor is it easy to see how one could derive a complete catalogue of these rights. But pronouncements concerning 'rights' are more than rhetorical value-judgements; they are ways of making political demands, something Godwin prefers not to do. Before considering Godwin's position on this question, however, we should make some attempt to decide what are the important rights for Paine or for any follower of the democratic revolution. The crucial assumption is that made by Shelley in a note which only survives in Mary Shelley's transcript. 'The institutions, opinions, feelings and habits by which human society is regulated, have no meaning or use, except as they tend to produce the advantage of the individuals of which it is composed.'[2] Moreover the individuals themselves are to be judges of what is for their own advantage: 'All government existing for the happiness of others is just only so far as it exists by their consent, and useful only so far as it operates to their well-being.'[3] From this follows the basic, tripartite political right whose enunciation by Richard Price provoked Burke to touch off the whole debate on the democratic revolution: 'The right to choose our own governors; to cashier them for misconduct; and to frame a government for ourselves.'[4]

[1] See Margaret MacDonald, 'Natural Rights', in *Philosophy, Politics and Society*, edited by Peter Laslett (Oxford, 1956), pp. 49–55.
[2] Bodl. MS Shelley adds. d. 6, p. 107.   [3] *Works*, v. 260. See also v. 271.
[4] *A Discourse on the Love of our Country* (1789), in *The Debate on the French Revolution 1789–1800*, edited by Alfred Cobban (1950; 2nd edn., 1960), p. 61.

Godwin, arguing from the point of view of the moral philosopher rather than of the politician, put the democratic case in terms of justice rather than of rights. This may seem to be a distinction without a difference, since Godwin's view of how society ought to be organized is not very different from Paine's but Godwin saw good reason to oppose the implications of Paine's rhetoric. For Godwin man was primarily a moral being, on whom the claims of duty were imperative: 'there is no situation in which I can be placed, where it is not incumbent on me to adopt a certain conduct in preference to all others' (*Political Justice*, ii. 496). To talk of 'rights' implied a discretionary element, a privilege of deciding whether or not to pursue a course of action. For Godwin man had only one right, the right to do his duty. Shelley certainly understood Godwin's position, and praised him for having evolved 'the first moral system explicitly founded upon the doctrine of the negativeness of rights and the positiveness of duties,—an obscure feeling of which has been the basis of all the political liberty and private virtue in the world' (*Works*, vi. 219). But Shelley was reluctant to renounce the aggressive and politically active stance inherent in the language of rights. Sometimes he ignores Godwin's objections, as in his *Declaration of Rights* (1812), with its provocative conclusion from Satan's exhortation to the fallen angels: 'Awake!—arise!—or be for ever fallen'.[1] Elsewhere he makes a sophisticated attempt to reconcile his mentors by arguing that a Godwinian duty includes a Painean right.

Man has a right to feel, to think, and to speak, nor can any acts of legislature destroy that right. He will feel, he must think, and he *ought* to give utterance to those thoughts and feelings with the readiest sincerity and the strictest candour. A man must have a right to do a thing before he can have a duty; the right must permit before his duty can enjoin him to any act.[2]

---

[1] *Works*, v. 271–5, quoting Milton, *Paradise Lost*, I. 330. Some of the rights that Shelley asserts have sources in Godwin (see A. H. Koszul, *La Jeunesse de Shelley* (Paris, 1910), p. 115). But the conception of the *Declaration* as a whole owes more to the 'Declaration of the Rights of Man and of Citizens by the National Assembly of France' (1789), in whose authorship Paine is believed to have had a hand (see Paine, *Complete Writings*, i. 313–15). The sources of Shelley's *Declaration* have been traced in detail by Walter Edwin Peck, *Shelley: His Life and Work* (2 vols., 1927), i. 236–48.

[2] *Works*, v. 262. See also v. 272, 275, vi. 65. Paine had argued, 'Speech is . . . one of the natural rights always retained; and with respect to the National Assembly, the use of it is a *duty*' (*Complete Writings*, i. 295).

The repetitiousness of this indicates that Shelley is rather bothered by his awareness that Godwin and Paine do not consort easily together. His ingenious argument, deriving the duty of sincerity from the right of free speech, only begs the question. Godwin asserts that the duty to perform a certain act at a certain time does not extend a licence to perform the same act under different circumstances, and without this licence the notion of a 'right' is an empty category. The most Godwin will concede is that certain rights are generally acknowledged because they allow certain duties to be fulfilled; thus the right to private property provides the necessary scope for the exercise of independent judgement.[1] But a man only has the right to do with his own property what is dictated by duty.

The significance of the difference between Paine and Godwin on the issue of rights is connected with their different attitudes to political action. Paine justifies man in actively resisting any attempt to infringe his rights, and in taking appropriate steps to guarantee or recover them. Godwin allows man a moral claim to the performance by others of their duty as it affects him, but pointedly leaves him no way of making this claim good. This is no accident, for we shall see that Godwin consistently evades the problems of political action. As John Clark tactfully puts it, for Godwin, 'The means by which society should be brought into conformity with justice is a question distinct from that of what is justly due to its members'.[2]

We are in a position now to sketch in broad terms the essential contrast between Paine's politics and Godwin and Shelley's. A good point to start is with the complex meanings of the term 'revolution', which underwent crucial shifts in the late eighteenth and early nineteenth centuries.[3] During the eighteenth century the accepted meaning of 'revolution' in its political sense was any important change in the form or personnel of a government, usually (though not always) effected by force, either from within the country affected or from without.[4] When Paine contrasts the

---

[1] *Political Justice*, ii. 433–4.

[2] John P. Clark, *The Philosophical Anarchism of William Godwin* (Princeton, 1977), p. 136.

[3] For a discussion of the various senses of the term see Aileen Ward, 'The forging of Orc: Blake and the idea of revolution', in *Literature in Revolution*, edited by G. A. White and C. Newman (New York, 1972), pp. 205–9. Contemporaries were well aware that it was an 'indefinite and equivocal term' (J. Mackintosh, *Vindiciae Gallicae*, p. viii; see also ibid., pp. 16–17).

[4] See R. R. Palmer, *The Age of the Democratic Revolution*, i. 21.

American and French revolutions with all previous events bearing that title he is giving 'revolution' a new and more modern meaning.

The revolutions that have taken place in other European countries, have been excited by personal hatred. The rage was against the man, and he became the victim. But, in the instance of France, we see a revolution generated in the rational contemplation of the rights of man, and distinguishing from the beginning between persons and principles.[1]

The new kind of revolution does not merely replace the personnel of government—as the Glorious Revolution did in England—but includes 'a revolution in the principles and practise of governments' (*Complete Writings*, i. 354). The change is radical, and the agents are the citizens of the country itself, the 'people'. For this kind of revolution to occur, the people must first undergo a 'mental revolution': 'The mind of the nation had changed beforehand, and the new order of things had naturally followed the new order of thoughts', as Paine commented on the French Revolution (i. 298). Paine was not the only one to grasp this point, and at this period we begin to hear quite frequently phrases like 'a revolution of *character*', 'revolution in opinion', '*revolution of sentiment*', 'revolutions in the *character* of nations'.[2] We shall see that the necessity for a mental and moral revolution in the people as a prelude to any political change is a central point for Godwin and Shelley. But, looking back at the experience of the French Revolution, they would be reluctant to follow Paine in believing that the 'new order of thoughts' had already arrived.

The French experience added yet another meaning to the word 'revolution' by associating it with mob-rule, revenge, tyranny, militarism, and the perversion of the best ideals to justify the worst crimes. The fate of the French Revolution, like the fate of Christ's teachings, provides the evidence for the gloating conclusion of the Fury that 'all best things are thus confused to ill'.[3] If Christ's name had become a curse, as Prometheus says, 'revolution' had become a bogy with which to frighten even the well-intentioned

[1] *Complete Writings*, i. 258. See also i. 354, 360–1, ii. 219.
[2] J. Mackintosh, *Vindiciae Gallicae*, p. 81; M. Wollstonecraft, *View of . . . the French Revolution*, p. 12; Henry Yorke, quoted in *The Debate on the French Revolution*, edited by A. Cobban, p. 133; Edward Lytton Bulwer, *England and the English* (1833), edited by Standish Meacham (Chicago and London, 1970), p. 19.
[3] *Prometheus Unbound*, i. 628.

into support of the existing order. Paine himself saw no necesssary connection between political revolution and violence. He insisted that 'The moral principle of revolutions is to instruct, not to destroy', and he argued that 'the greatest forces that can be brought into the field of revolutions, are reason and common interest'.[1] Hindsight is generally perfect, and it was clear to men of Shelley's generation that what had frustrated the good intentions of men like Paine was their impatience to put them into action. There is a revealing passage in the Dedication of Part Second of *Rights of Man*, to Lafayette.

The only point upon which I could ever discover that we differed was not as to principles of government, but as to time. For my own part, I think it equally as injurious to good principles to permit them to linger, as to push them on too fast. That which you suppose accomplishable in fourteen or fifteen years, I believe practicable in a much shorter period. (i. 347)

Elsewhere he declared, 'I do not believe that monarchy and aristocracy will continue seven years longer in any of the enlightened countries of Europe' (i. 352); the magical turn of the century clearly played a large part in the fixing of his revolutionary timetable. Paine's secular chiliasm predisposes him to believe that the preparatory mental revolution has already occurred, and hence to disregard his own warning: 'The danger to which the success of revolutions is most exposed, is that of attempting them before the principles on which they proceed, and the advantages to result from them, are sufficiently seen and understood.' (i. 356) Experience was to show that the warning had more foundation than his optimism.

Paradoxically Paine's impatience is a result of his moderation rather than his extremism. The fact that he only wanted to abolish monarchy and aristocracy, that his dream of a democratic society commanded a good deal of popular support, betrayed him into exaggerated expectations and undue haste.

The politician who aims at a limited object, and has shut up his views within that object, may be forgiven, if he manifest some impatience for its attainment. But this passion cannot be felt in an equal degree, by him who aims at improvement, not upon a definite, but an indefinite scale. . . . That progress, which may be carried on, through a longer time, and a

[1] *Complete Writings*, ii. 587, i. 446.

greater variety of articles, than his foresight can delineate, he may be expected to desire should take place in a mild and gradual, though incessant advance, not by violent leaps, not by concussions which may expose millions to risk, and sweep generations of men from the stage of existence. (*Political Justice*, i. 266–7)

Godwin was never in any danger of believing that the perfect political system was in immediate reach; the more extreme the demands he makes on the future, the more willing he is to rely on gradualist methods of achieving them. Godwin and Shelley desire a democratic republic, just as Paine does—Godwin could find no higher compliment to pay his young disciple than to call him 'a plain, philosophical republican' (*Life*, i. 352)—but, intending to go on even further when that is achieved, they do not see revolution as an appropriate way of achieving it. They are more cautious than Paine because they are playing for higher stakes—no less than the complete and final abolition of government, 'that brute engine, which has been the only perennial cause of the vices of mankind' (*Political Justice*, ii. 212).

We can bring out Shelley's adherence to Godwin's gradualism rather than Paine's impatience by a discussion of *Laon and Cythna* (1817), a poem which has caused commentators some difficulty. The main problem is how we reconcile Shelley's statement that he intended to describe 'the *beau ideal* of the French Revolution' (*Letters*, i. 564) with the patent fact that the revolution he describes is a failure. The poem will remain puzzling until we recognize that Shelley intended right from the start to describe a revolution that failed. His intention was not to redress the balance of history by showing how the French Revolution might have succeeded, but to snatch moral victory from actual defeat by showing how a revolution which cannot achieve its aims ought to be conducted. *Laon and Cythna* describes the '*beau ideal*' of a revolution which is doomed to failure, on the immediate historical plane at least. Shelley's own account of the poem suggests why this failure is inevitable.

It is in fact a tale illustrative of such a Revolution as might be supposed to take place in an European nation, acted upon by the opinions of what has been called (erroneously as I think) the modern philosophy, & contending with antient notions & the supposed advantages derived from them to those who support them. It is a Revolution of this kind, that is, the *beau ideal* as it were of the French Revolution, but produced by the influence of individual genius, & out of general knowledge. The authors of it are supposed to be my hero & heroine whose names appear in the title. (*Letters*, i. 563–4)

The crucial words here, though not perhaps as clear as we would like, are 'but produced by the influence of individual genius, & out of general knowledge'. It seems to me that Shelley intends a contrast here, though he expresses himself carelessly; 'out of' must be taken to mean something like 'without', or as a slip for 'not of'. If this interpretation is correct it is not difficult to see why the revolution must fail; it is only sustained by the individual genius of the hero and heroine, not by the assimilation of their principles into 'general knowledge', and thus the final reaction is inevitable.

Such an interpretation is certainly compatible with Shelley's view of the French Revolution. In the early *Proposals for an Association* he accepted, with some reservations, the myth that 'the Revolution of France was occasioned by the literary labours of the Encyclopædists', and attempted to demonstrate that its failures could be directly traced to the inadequacies of its sponsors (*Works*, v. 264–5). But he also argued that 'The murders during the period of the French Revolution, and the despotism which has since been established, prove that the doctrines of Philanthropy and Freedom, were but shallowly understood' (*Works*, v. 264). Paine's optimism about the occurrence of the 'mental revolution' is seen to have been unfounded, partly because Shelley will only allow the doctrines of the Enlightenment to have been fully understood if they become active factors in determining men's conduct; he demands a moral revolution, rather than the intellectual assent with which Paine was satisfied. As we shall see, good principles were generally adopted in the Golden City of *Laon and Cythna*, but not understood in Shelley's sense. The Preface to the poem argues that the necessary moral revolution cannot be an overnight affair.

Could they listen to the plea of reason who had groaned under the calamities of a social state, according to the provisions of which, one man riots in luxury whilst another famishes for want of bread. Can he who the day before was a trampled slave, suddenly become liberal-minded, forbearing, and independent? This is the consequence of the habits of a state of society to be produced by resolute perseverance and indefatigable hope, and long-suffering and long believing courage, and the systematic efforts of generations of men of intellect and virtue. Such is the lesson which experience teaches now.

Shelley was indeed fortunate in being able to take it all as a lesson of experience. He escaped the exaggerated hopes and consequent disillusion of the first generation of Romantics.

In the light of experience Shelley could see that the French Revolution was a premature attempt to gain what could only come by a programme of gradualism. An examination of the course of events in *Laon and Cythna* makes it clear that the same is true of the revolution in that poem. Even as a youth Laon aspires to the position of a revolutionary leader.

> It must be so—I will arise and waken
> The multitude, and like a sulphurous hill,
> Which on a sudden from its snows has shaken
> The swoon of ages, it shall burst, and fill
> The world with cleansing fire; it must, it will—
> It may not be restrained!—and who shall stand
> Amid the rocking earthquake stedfast still,
> But Laon? on high Freedom's desert land
> A tower whose marble walls the leagued storms withstand!
> (I. xiv)

In such a consistently high-pitched poem as *Laon and Cythna* it is difficult to be sure about such a point, but it seems to me that we are meant to detect a certain overweening excess of optimism in Laon's volcanic utterance, in which he is posited as the sole revolutionary agent, standing isolated in the 'desert' caused by his own eruption. Certainly his attempts to spread the revolutionary message meet with disillusion after apparent success.

> and another,
> And yet another, I did fondly deem,
> Felt that we all were sons of one great mother;
> And the cold truth such sad reverse did seem,
> As to awake in grief from some delightful dream.
> (I. xvii)

At this point Laon is a revolutionary poet, not an activist, and can expect to continue to encounter such mixed reactions. Gerald McNiece argues that the revolt 'had apparently been inspired by his own early hymns to hope or freedom'.[1] But this is only partly

---

[1] G. McNiece, *Shelley and the Revolutionary Idea*, p. 193.

true. The real beginning of the revolt is the visit of the tyrant's minions to recruit Cythna for his harem, and Laon's reaction; he slays three of them, and calls his countrymen 'to death or Liberty!' (III. x) This hasty resort to force is wrong, and Laon must expiate it by his agony on the tower and the years of subsequent madness or alienation from himself. Such a beginning for the revolution is inauspicious. Laon is nursed back to health by a hermit, in whom the *Quarterly Review* recognized William Godwin.[1] This Hermit is Godwinian enough to have only lent his aid to the revolt after it was already under way (IV. ix–x). He informs Laon that his illness lasted seven years, during which the revolt has gathered head; we might remember here Paine's rash prophecy that monarchy and aristocracy would not exist 'seven years longer in any of the enlightened countries of Europe'.[2] During this seven years the Hermit has been propagating revolutionary principles, in the name of Laon (IX. xi–xvii). But the Hermit is a philosopher, not a leader, and Laon has returned to himself in good time, for the revolutionary crisis has arrived. So far the revolt has been bloodless, and the Hermit is determined that it should stay so.

> If blood be shed, 'tis but a change and choice
> Of bonds,—from slavery to cowardice
> A wretched fall!
> (IV. xxviii)

But he does not seem very optimistic.

> Perchance blood need not flow, if thou at length
> Wouldst rise; perchance the very slaves would spare
> Their brethren and themselves; great is the strength
> Of words . . .
> (IV. xviii)

The power of words has recently been demonstrated by the activities of 'a maiden fair' (who turns out, of course, to be Cythna), who has managed to win over the tyrant's slaves, and stay the people from violence.

---

[1] *The Unextinguished Hearth: Shelley and His Contemporary Critics* (1938), edited by Newman Ivey White (New York, 1966), pp. 139–40. The *Quarterly* also identifies Cythna with Mary Shelley, but it seems more likely that Shelley modelled his heroine on Mary's mother, Mary Wollstonecraft.

[2] See above, p. 67.

> So in the populous City, a young maiden
> Has baffled havock of the prey which he
> Marks as his own, whene'er with chains o'erladen
> Men make them arms to hurl down tyranny,
> False arbiter between the bound and free; . . .
> (IV. xxiii)

Without her influence the revolution would presumably have descended to violence and anarchy. And even now the situation is ominous: 'Blood soon, although unwillingly to shed,/The free cannot forbear' (IV. xxiv). Only the presence of Laon himself can hope to stave off disaster. Clearly an enormous amount rests on the 'individual genius' of the hero and heroine.

Laon arrives in the Golden City just in time, and for a time manages to hold his followers back from revolutionary violence. When the tyrant's guards slaughter the people Laon stands between them and popular vengeance, and succeeds in reconciling them to the people (v. vi–xiii). Later he saves the tyrant himself from summary execution (v. xxxii–xxxv). Some critics see this as a great mistake; Paul Foot considers that the revolution fails precisely because the opportunity to liquidate the tyrant was not taken.[1] But Shelley has his eye on history. The execution of Louis XVI didn't save the French Revolution from defeat, in that its apparent victory was involved with the collapse of all the values it was supposed to establish. The revolutionaries in *Laon and Cythna* have in fact two choices open to them: to be defeated by the forces of the counter-revolution, or to be defeated by the corruption of their own ideals. In such a situation, where you're damned if you do and damned if you don't, it is better, Shelley suggests, to at least keep your hands clean, and pass on the revolutionary ideals uncompromised to the future.

The revolution is in fact destroyed by massive force provided by Othman's brother tyrants. At this moment of crisis the true weakness of the revolution itself is revealed. When the counter-revolutionary armies attack the people are struck with panic.[2] The 'rage and grief and scorn' that Laon feels are directed not at the enemy but at his own followers as he strives to stem 'Their miserable flight' (VI. ii–iii, v). Finally he manages to rally 'A band

[1] *Red Shelley* (1979), Ch. vi.
[2] G. McNiece (op. cit., p. 208) also notes this point.

of brothers', who stand firm, defending themselves with pikes (weapons of Swiss liberty) until all but Laon are cut down (VI. viii–xviii). At this point, about half-way through the poem, the revolution is definitively over. It was, as Cythna admits, 'a false dawn' (IX. v). What follows emphasizes this. The panic and superstition that follow famine and plague cause a swing of public opinion back to the tyrant. The 'maniac multitude' concur in the decision to sacrifice Laon and Cythna to divine wrath, and when he gives himself up the rejoicing is general (X. xlii, XII. i). In the second half of the poem the public realm is abandoned to its fate in the gruesome aftermath of unsuccessful revolution and the hero and heroine retire to consummate their personal union.

> Oblivion wrapt
> Our spirits, and the fearful overthrow
> Of public hope was from our being snapt,
> Tho' linked years had bound it there . . .
> (VI. xxx)

But this retirement is not necessarily retreat, more a continuation of the revolution by other means. If their society has turned away from revolutionary ideals, they are still preserved in Laon and Cythna themselves, who will ensure that their message is passed on by their voluntary martyrdom.

Laon and Cythna must be seen as the attempt of a poet who considers violent revolution to be counter-productive to come to terms with the fact of a violent revolution carried out in the name of ideals to which he is profoundly committed. The fate of the French Revolution will irrevocably compromise those ideals unless a version of it can be stage-managed to demonstrate the possibility of a moral revolution, which can then be distanced as an image of heroism that will serve to inspire more efficacious forms of political action. The intention and effect of *Laon and Cythna* is to preserve the revolution as a monument, which functions to inspire and to warn at the same time. The cumbersome framework of the poem is essential to achieving this purpose. For a revolutionary like Paine the only reality is action, but *Laon and Cythna* is only a vision of action, and a vision directed at a particular audience. Just as *Queen Mab* is addressed to the virtuous Ianthe, so *Laon and Cythna* is directed to the narrator of Canto I, and through him to all who are in his situation and need to be preserved from 'visions of despair' in the dark days after 'the last hope of trampled France had failed' (I. i). In the Chinese box of narratives that make up the poem we easily lose sight of the fact that all of the poem from the beginning of Canto II is addressed by Laon to the narrator, and it is told for the latter's sake. He is told,

> Thou must a listener be
> This day—two mighty spirits now return,
> Like birds of calm, from the world's raging sea,
> They pour fresh light from Hope's immortal urn;
> A tale of human power—despair not—list and learn!
> (I. lviii)

What he learns he will later teach; the voice emphasizes that he will only be a listener 'This day', and recognizes that he will later revert to his true role—that of poet, who will write the poem in which all this is recounted. The Temple of the Spirit is in fact a metaphor for the poem *Laon and Cythna*. In the Temple events on earth can be seen *sub specie aeternitatis*, just as the poem can extract a timeless message from the flux of 'the world's raging sea'. When history has thus become vision it can be viewed with hope rather than despair. This hope is to be found less in the events of the revolution—though the initial response to Cythna's campaign was encouraging—than in the characters of Laon and Cythna themselves, who appropriately take their seats in the immortal senate that sits in the Temple. When all men feel and act as they revolutions will not fail; or, rather, revolutions will not be necessary. They are the image of the new order, or rather its seeds, who must accept their own death if it is to come in the natural order of events.

> This is the Winter of the world;—and here
> We die, even as the winds of Autumn fade,
> Expiring in the frore and foggy air,—
> Behold! Spring comes, tho' we must pass, who made
> The promise of its birth . . .
> (IX. xxv)

The similarity of these lines, and of Cythna's whole magnificent ode to the future, to the 'Ode to the West Wind' has frequently been pointed out. They are also similar to a fragment jotted down by Shelley in a notebook, probably in 1821 or 1822: 'the Spring rebels not against Winter but it succeeds it—the dawn rebels not against night but it disperses it'.[1] The conclusions of Shelley's revolutionary epic are, in fact, profoundly anti-revolutionary. If Shelley sometimes seems to set his own heroes up, giving them the task of guiding a revolution which he has decided beforehand will fail, we must recognize that Shelley himself has been put on the spot by history. If the French Revolution had not occurred there would have been no need to write *Laon and Cythna*. Shelley's ideals are revolutionary, but they preserve themselves in spite of the historical experience of revolutionary practice. For the precise nature of these ideals, and the way in which Shelley hopes to make them prevail, we must turn from the democratic activist, Paine, to the philosophical theorist of anarchism, William Godwin.

[1] Bodl. MS Shelley adds. e. 18, inside front cover. See E. R. Wasserman, *Shelley*, p. 387.

CHAPTER III

Philosophical Anarchism

IT WOULD be impossible to give an exhaustive account of the presence of Godwinian ideas in Shelley's work, partly because these ideas are so pervasive, and partly because Shelley himself was, as Middleton Murry put it, '*anima naturaliter Godwiniana*'.[1] Shelley's response to Godwin's doctrines was so positive, so deep, and so enduring—surviving even the vexatious business of helping Godwin in his financial difficulties—because Godwin voiced aspirations that were already his own, and gave him the framework of a rational faith and a political vision that were in complete harmony with his own feelings and needs. In Shelley's mature work it is often difficult—and would be of doubtful value—to determine whether Shelley is borrowing from Godwin, or merely thinking in the same way. In either case a consideration of Godwin's thought will illuminate Shelley's thinking. In this chapter we shall consider first of all why Shelley found Godwin's system so attractive. Then we shall examine the three central concepts of Godwin's (and Shelley's) political thinking: Independence, Perfectibility, and Opinion. Finally I shall attempt to give a reading of *Prometheus Unbound* in which the relevance of Shelley's political philosophy to some of his greatest poetry will be brought out.

The evidence that Shelley became acquainted with *Political Justice* in 1809, while still at Eton, consists of Shelley's own statement to Godwin in January 1812: 'It is now a period of more than two years since first I saw your inestimable book on "Political Justice"' (*Letters*, i. 227). Hogg hazarded the reasonable assumption that the book had been 'borrowed from Dr. Lind', while making it clear that he considered that Shelley had been carried away by a sense of occasion in asserting that it had influenced him very strongly while at Eton (*Life*, i. 313–14). Hogg is probably correct; initially Shelley only claims that he 'saw' the work. When he goes on to assure Godwin that 'it opened to my mind fresh & more

[1] John Middleton Murry, *Heaven—and Earth* (1938), p. 311.

extensive views, it materially influenced my character, and I rose from its perusal a wiser and a better man', it seems likely that his words should be referred to a later period.[1] Embarrassingly aware of the fact that his juvenile works showed little trace of this supposedly decisive influence Shelley was forced to claim that his two Gothic novels had been 'written prior to my acquaintance with your writings', and hence to assert that they were written at least a year earlier than we know to be the case.[2] But the fact that he fibs about the dates of his own works suggests that he is telling the truth about the date of his first acquaintance with *Political Justice*. What he was unwilling to reveal to Godwin was that any real knowledge on his part of its principles and arguments dated from November 1810, when he requested Stockdale to send him a copy (*Letters*, i. 21). The negative evidence of his works and letters written previously can only lead us to conclude, with Paul Elsner, that any earlier reading of Godwin's work can only have been 'vorüber-gehend und flüchtig'.[3]

Godwin made his initial impact upon the young Shelley at precisely the period that we might have expected, during his first term at Oxford. We have seen that Shelley's family and the Duke of Norfolk were busy grooming him for a career in Parliament, and Oxford would have been the last stage before he entered the Commons. Shelley had serious misgivings about such a career, misgivings that centred around the morality of the politics in which he was to participate. The result was a strong negative reaction to politics as he saw it carried on, which Hogg chose to interpret as a rejection of all political activity (*Life*, i. 129–30). Hogg regularly misrepresents Shelley on this issue, but on this point he could have adduced considerable evidence under Shelley's own hand. In April 1811 Shelley wrote to Hogg, 'I will no longer mix politics and virtue they are incompatible.' In the next month he wrote, 'I now *most perfectly* agree with you that political affairs are quite distinct from morality, that they cannot be united.' And the month after that brought an even more explicit repudiation of

---

[1] *Letters*, i. 227. Shelley's praise is pointed, for Godwin wrote in his Preface that he had been 'desirous of producing a work from the perusal of which no man should rise, without being strengthened in habits of sincerity, fortitude and justice' (*Political Justice*, i. vii).

[2] *Letters*, i. 231, 266.

[3] *Percy Bysshe Shelleys Abhängigkeit von William Godwins Political Justice*, (Berlin, 1906), p. 66.

the family plans: 'Political or literary ambition IS VICE. Nothing but one thing is virtue.'[1] Shelley was experiencing the effect of an intolerable split between political ideals and political realities, between the devotion to liberty of Whig ideology and the party politics and boroughmongering of Whig practice. Like Blake he concluded that the latter was 'something Else besides Human Life'.[2]

> They have appropriated human life
> And human happiness, but these weigh nought
> In the nice balanced Politician's scale,
> Who finds that murder is expedient
> And that vile means can answer glorious ends.[3]

What Shelley objects to, and finds incompatible with morality, is the cynical appeal to expedience. From 1817 onwards he becomes rather more flexible himself, but his immediate reaction is to reject a field where expedience apparently is the supreme value.

It was as an antidote to this kind of scepticism about public affairs—the very violence of Shelley's reaction revealing that he has not been able to divest himself of concern—that *Political Justice* was most valuable to Shelley. Godwin, who began his political career as a Whig hack, came to have his own doubts concerning party politics, which he saw as 'a sort of dexterous game, the perfection of which is supposed to lie in falsehood and hypocrisy, and the making men believe our intentions to be other than they are'.[4] His reaction was to redefine politics in strict moral terms.

> just political regulations are nothing more than a certain select part of moral law.
>   ... the subject of our present enquiry is strictly speaking a department of the science of morals. Morality is the source from which its fundamental axioms must be drawn ... (*Political Justice*, 121, 125)

---

[1] *Letters*, i. 66, 82, 112.
[2] William Blake, *Complete Writings with variant readings*, edited by Geoffrey Keynes (1969), p. 600.
[3] 'The Voyage' (Aug. 1812), lines 267–71 (*The Esdaile Notebook*, p. 106). The lines quoted come from a part of the poem that may have been written earlier than the rest of the poem (see ibid., p. 231).
[4] *New Annual Register* (1789), 'British and Foreign History', p. 45. For Godwin's authorship see Jack W. Marken, 'William Godwin's Writing for the *New Annual Register*', *MLN* lxviii (1953), 477–9.

If politics as he had seen it conducted seemed incompatible with morality, Shelley found in Godwin the theory of another kind of politics which was explicitly founded on morality. He seized these new weapons eagerly, and we find him trying to convince Southey

that the most fatal error that ever happened in the world was the sepera- tion of political and ethical science, that the former ought to be entirely regulated by the latter, as whatever was a right criterion of action for an individual must be so for a society which was but an assemblage of individuals, 'that politics were morals more comprehensively enforced.' (*Letters*, i. 223)[1]

If we would understand the more obviously political thinking of Godwin and Shelley we must first appreciate that it is intimately connected with their moral values.

The very 'justice' of Godwin's title is a moral principle, which he is applying to the political sphere. 'By justice I understand that impartial treatment of every man in matters that relate to his happiness, which is measured solely by a consideration of the properties of the receiver, and the capacity of him that bestows' (*Political Justice*, i. 126). In practice Godwin's conception of justice depends more on abstract moral worth as one of the 'properties of the receiver' than does that of the more egalitarian Shelley. But both Godwin and Shelley see justice, linked to man's 'happiness', as intimately connected with the essential ends of morality.

Morality is that system of conduct which is determined by a consideration of the greatest general good: he is entitled to the highest moral appro- bation, whose conduct is . . . governed by views of benevolence, and made subservient to public utility. In like manner the only regulations which any political authority can be justly entitled to inforce, are such as are best adapted to public utility. (*Political Justice*, i. 121)[2]

This utilitarian morality is preserved from erecting expedience as its supreme value—exactly what repelled Shelley in the political practice of his day and in the moral philosophy of Paley—by the

---

[1] I have not found the concluding quotation in so many words in *Political Justice*, but Godwin does lament that politics has been 'violently separated from morality', and asserts that 'Society is nothing more than an aggregation of individuals' (*Political Justice*, i. 123, 136).

[2] In the first edition Godwin defined justice as 'the treating every man precisely as his usefulness and worth demand, the acting under every circumstance in the manner that shall procure the greatest quantity of general good' (*Political Justice*, iii. 266). He assumes that the two are equivalent, but never explains how.

emphasis on justice (however it may be understood), which is considered as an immutable and sacrosanct principle. 'Is it not the same, are not it's decrees invariable; and for the sake of his earth-formed schemes has the politician a right to infringe upon that which itself constitutes all right and wrong?—surely not.' (*Letters*, i. 127) Significantly this enthusiasm for justice is communicated to the sympathetic Miss Hitchener, while at the same time Shelley reiterates his disillusion with all politics to the cynical Hogg.

Godwin thus provided Shelley with a moral principle in terms of which the politics he knew could be judged and rejected, while it held out the possibility of a new kind of politics, which would allow moral values to become operative in the real world. Simultaneously Godwin furnished Shelley with a very welcome opportunity for self-devotion. The very austerity of Godwin's moral system, the stringent demands it made upon its adherent, were among its main attractions for Shelley, and must have seemed in refreshing contrast to the cynical appeals to self-interest made by the Duke of Norfolk.

Morality is nothing else but that system, which teaches us to contribute upon all occasions, to the extent of our power, to the well-being and happiness of every intellectual and sensitive existence. But there is no action of our lives, which does not in some way affect that happiness. Our property, our time, and our faculties, may all of them be made to contribute to this end. (*Political Justice*, i. 159)

To be 'anxiously alive to the inspirations of virtue' is to realize that 'every shilling of our property, and every faculty of our mind, have received their destination from the principles of unalterable justice' (i. 198). Godwin urged this point of view personally to Shelley, claiming that it lay 'at the basis' of *Political Justice* (*Life*, i. 352–3). To the young Shelley, deeply disturbed by the fear of being swayed by the '*howl* of self interest', the appeal to complete disinterestedness was a revelation and an inspiration.[1] As Middleton Murry has remarked, with Godwin and Shelley it is impossible to separate political from religious faith.[2] Shelley's language is rather too pointed for us to assume that this was unconcious on his part. 'The

---

[1] *Letters*, i. 101. Shelley's letters of 1811–12 supply abundant evidence of his fear of the self and of the strength of self-interest; see ibid. i. 29, 30, 34, 36, 44, 47, 48, 77–8, 95, 151, 171, 173, 178, 179–80, 188, 192, 207, 252, 257, 268.

[2] *Heaven—and Earth*, p. 314.

society of peace and love!' he enthused to Miss Hitchener. 'Oh! that I may be a successful apostle of this only true religion, the religion of philanthropy . . .'[1] Godwin provided Shelley with alternatives to both the politics and the religion that he had repudiated, and helped him to release his talents and energies without compromising his integrity. Shelley once asked Miss Hitchener respecting her father, 'Is he one who makes a distinction between the profession of certain principles and acting up to that profession?—If he is then he is a man unworthy of my highsouled friend.' (*Letters* i. 314) No doubt he had his own father in mind. He embraced the Godwinian gospel because it offered a positive alternative to a worldliness that effectively denied the claims of morality.

Godwin's apparent philosophical rigour is no more trustworthy a guide than is Paine's plausibility to the coherence of their respective systems. Godwin professes to argue as a consistent utilitarian, but his central concepts often seem to possess an independent validity quite apart from any utilitarian justification.[2] Similarly he ostensibly derives the most important doctrine of his (and Shelley's) philosophical anarchism from empiricist premises, while the reader may have a suspicion that the conclusion is more important than the premises and that he would sacrifice the latter if there was a possibility of conflict. In fact there is no conflict, and while Godwin's system would suffer from any rigorous philosophical analysis, his positions do manage to retain a certain coherence among themselves. Godwin likes to play the role of the impassive and exact philosopher—a role very different to that of the political agitator adopted by Paine—and his apparent objectivity and logical rigour had an enormous appeal to his original readers. In fact Godwin has a certain obtuseness which, while it prevents him from solving some of the problems he has consequently to beg, also gives him a useful flexibility in directing his arguments in the direction in which he wishes them to go. Godwin does have some things of interest to say, and they are

---

[1] *Letters*, i. 255. Shelley may have known about Paine's Deist sect of 'Theophilanthropy', of which his own 'religion of philanthropy' would be a fully secularized version.

[2] See F. E. L. Priestley, in *Political Justice*, iii. 15–16. The fullest and most useful account to date of Godwin's philosophy, John P. Clark's *The Philosophical Anarchism of William Godwin*, seems to me to suffer from Clark's insistence on reading Godwin as a consistent utilitarian.

connected. In considering his system we shall do well to focus on these aspects.

Godwin's epistemology is in the empiricist tradition of Locke, his immediate mentor being Helvétius. Godwin is in accord with this tradition when he insists that man's moral possibilities are not determined or limited by any innate factors. 'The actions and dispositions of men are not the offspring of any original bias that they bring into the world in favour of one sentiment or character, rather than another, but flow entirely from the operation of circumstances and events acting upon a faculty of receiving sensible impressions.' (*Political Justice*, i. 26–7) Godwin escapes the conclusion that moral growth is purely a matter of chance by adopting the loaded terminology of Helvétius, and arguing that 'the characters of men are determined in all their most essential circumstances by education'; 'education' is defined so as to include 'every incident that produces an idea in the mind, and can give birth to a train of reflections', but the term encourages us to believe that the process is amenable to rational control.[1] One leading merit of the empiricist account is that it furnishes arguments against the concepts of original sin and innate depravity and the pessimistic conclusions respecting man's ability to improve his condition to which they lead. 'Man', insists Godwin, 'is not originally vicious.' (ii. 210) Shelley makes explicit the attack on Christian dogma that Godwin prudently leaves implicit.

It will not appear surprising that some original taint of our nature has been adopted as an opinion by the unthinking when they perceive how very early depraved dispositions are exhibited; but when it is considered what exhaustless pains are taken by nurses and Parents to make wrong impressions on the infant mind, I cannot be surprised at the earliest traits of evil and mistake. (*Letters*, i. 237–8)[2]

The point is taken up in *Queen Mab*, where Shelley insists that the 'ruin, vice, and slavery' that afflict man are not to be put to the account of 'Nature'.

---

[1] *Political Justice*, i. 45. '. . . examinant ce que pouvaient sur nous la nature et l'éducation, je me suis aperçu que l'éducation nous faisait ce que nous sommes' (Claude Adrien Helvétius, *De l'esprit* (1758), Discours III, Ch. iii, edited by F. Châtelet (Verviers, 1973), p. 371). See also *Letters*, i. 199.

[2] Shelley was delighted to find that Southey was 'no believer in original sin' and that he considered that all vice could be traced to 'the prejudices of education and sinister influence of political institution[s]' (*Letters*, i. 216). F. L. Jones's editorial pluralization is redundant.

Let priest-led slaves cease to proclaim that man
Inherits vice and misery, when force
And falshood hang even o'er the cradled babe,
Stifling with rudest grasp all natural good.
(IV. 117–20)

The idiom of *Queen Mab* fails to provide Shelley with a very rich poetical medium, but he uses it with great competence for his rhetorical purposes. The movement of the verse brings the emphasis on to 'Inherits', which is exactly where he intends that it should fall; he is not denying that 'vice and misery' exist, but repudiating the notion that corruption is innate, a legacy from our first parents.

On the other hand Shelley does occasionally invoke the idea of 'natural good', assuring Miss Hitchener, 'I know how much of *good* there is in human nature, spite of the overwhelming torrent of depravity which education unlooses.' (*Letters*, i. 263) Godwin more consistently recognizes that the arguments against innate depravity (which are also good arguments against inequality) are equally valid against innate goodness. The empiricist account wipes the slate completely clean, and establishes man's original *innocence*; but 'Innocence', remarks Godwin, 'is a sort of neutral character, and stands in the mid way between good and harm'.[1] Shelley pays lip-service to this point of view when he declares that 'the character of virtue' is 'distinct from that of either innocence or vice' (*Works*, v. 263), but his early writings show that he is frequently tempted to see the state of innocence as Blake does, as one in which man's impulses, although untutored, are basically good. But it is very difficult to specify the environmental causes of benevolence, and Shelley would find it hard to point to any passages in *Frankenstein* that would justify his Godwinian assertion that the Monster's 'mind was such as its first impressions framed it, affectionate and full of moral sensibility' (*Works*, vi. 264). I shall argue in Chapter VI that Shelley is obliged to look beyond Godwin in order to arrive at a satisfactory account of the origin of benevolence.

Godwin makes a strict distinction between innocence and virtue

---

[1] *Political Justice*, iii. 151. 'Innocence is not virtue. Virtue demands the active employment of an ardent mind in the promotion of the general good' (ibid. i. 105). Godwin allows more scope to innate goodness in his later works (see Lois Whitney, *Primitivism and the Idea of Progress in English Popular Literature of the Eighteenth Century* (1934; New York, 1965), p. 209).

because the tendency of his philosophy is progressive, and directed to the improvement of man. Hence he wants no truck with primitivist accounts of human nature.[1] It is worth insisting in this context that Shelley, received opinion to the contrary notwithstanding, was not a primitivist. The so-called 'Essay on Christianity' (1817) makes it clear that he does not take seriously the nostalgic myth of the state of Nature, nor will he endorse any primitivistic attempt to return to it.

Nothing can well be more remote from truth . . . than that it were best for man that he should abandon all his acquirements in physical and intellectual science, and depend on the spontaneous productions of Nature for his subsistence. Nothing is more obviously false than that the remedy for the inequality among men consists in their return to the condition of savages and beasts. (*Works*, vi. 247)[2]

In this work Shelley draws considerably on Rousseau's first two Discourses, but he is astute enough to recognize that Rousseau's apparent primitivism is not a positive programme, but a critical device, a way of bringing out what is wrong with man's present state.

Rousseau certainly did not mean to persuade the immense population of his country[3] to abandon all the arts of life and destroy their habitations and their temples and become the inhabitants of the woods. He addressed the most enlightened of his compatriots, and endeavoured to persuade them to set the example of a pure and simple life, by placing in the strongest point of view his conceptions of the calamitous and diseased aspect which, overgrown as it is with the vices of sensuality and selfishness, is exhibited by civilized society. (*Works*, vi. 247–8)

Deciding what Rousseau 'really' means is a matter of some difficulty, but it seems to me that Shelley is more perceptive about the Discourses than most of his contemporaries. Shelley has his own bias, in that he wishes to build the future rather than yearn

[1] Unless one argues that Godwin's preference for simplicity in government is slightly primitivistic (see L. Whitney, op. cit., p. 219).

[2] For Shelley's view of the 'natural man', as child, savage, or illiterate, see *Works*, vii. 74–6. Edward Duffy has also noted that 'Shelley's dalliance with primitivism is critical in intent' and in no way contradicts 'progressive Godwinianism' ('The Image of Jean-Jacques Rousseau in the Work of Shelley and Other English Romantics', unpublished Ph.D. dissertation, Columbia University, 1971, p. 145).

[3] Shelley has clearly forgotten that Rousseau was Swiss, not French – except by what we might call cultural naturalization.

for the past, as is clear in his critique of the classical poets and their myth of the Golden Age.

They represented equality as the reign of Saturn, and taught that mankind had gradually degenerated from the virtue which enabled them to enjoy or maintain this happy state. Their doctrine was philosophically false. Later and more correct observations have instructed us that uncivilized man is the most pernicious and miserable of beings, and that the violence and injustice which are the genuine indications of real inequality obtain in the society of these beings without mixture and without palliation. (*Works*, vi. 250)

But their visions of a 'natural' state, in the sense of a state best fitted to the moral nature of man, were not merely trivial fictions. 'Their imaginations of a happier state of human society were referred indeed to the [wrong] period, they ministered indeed to thoughts of despondency and sorrow. But they were the children of airy hope, the prophets and the parents of mysterious futurity.' (*Works*, vi. 250)[1] Not as man once was but as he will be—taken thus the myth of the Golden Age inspires hope rather than nostalgic 'despondency and sorrow', and by inspiring hope these visions become the 'parents' of what they foretell.

In his vigorous attack on the sentimental versions of 'natural goodness' Shelley reveals his understanding of Godwin's position. By denying the existence of innate determining factors in man Godwin is insisting that he must take the responsibility for the creation of his own nature. As Shelley argues, 'Virtue is thus entirely a refinement of civilised life, a creation of the human mind or rather a combination which it has made according to elementary laws contained within itself, of the feelings suggested by the relations established between man and man.' (*Works*, vii. 76) To be able to suggest that man can create his own moral nature it is necessary to smuggle in some assumptions not included in the basic empiricist account. This account has been slanted towards Godwin's preferred conclusions by his decision to refer to environmental forces as 'education', in preference to more neutral terms like 'experience' or 'sensation'. For all his insistence on the impersonal operation of Necessity Godwin does believe that man

---

[1] 'wrong' is my own suggestion to supply a blank in the manuscript. The received reading, 'Saturnian', was supplied by Lady Jane Shelley (*Shelley Memorials* (1859; 3rd edn., 1875), p. 286).

can co-operate in a rational way in the development of his own nature. This aspect of Godwin's thought is acutely and sympathetically seized on in Wordsworth's account, in which he stresses

> The freedom of the individual mind,
> Which, to the blind restraint of general laws
> Superior, magisterially adopts
> One guide, the light of circumstances, flash'd
> Upon an independent intellect.[1]

Not unadvisedly does Wordsworth refer to 'the *light* of circumstance' and call it a 'guide'. Man is not the helpless product of his environment, for it is open to him to understand and to act in accord with what Godwin is fond of calling the 'nature of things'. For Godwin such understanding is only attainable by the 'independent intellect'. The emphasis on 'education' could easily be made to lead to an elitism, according to which men's natures are to be moulded by a class of enlightened educators, as Marx noted in his Third Thesis on Feuerbach.[2] Godwin does not entirely avoid this danger.[3] But Godwin's elitism is in contradiction to the real core of his thought, which is a fierce insistence on the necessity for complete intellectual independence. This is a moral imperative, for any action that is not derived from an 'independent intellect's' apprehension of 'the light of circumstances' is not a valid moral act.

Man is an intellectual being. There is no way to make him virtuous, but in calling forth his intellectual powers. There is no way to make him virtuous, but by making him independent. He must study the laws of nature, and the necessary consequences of actions, not the arbitrary caprice of his superior. . . . It can only be by the most deplorable

---

[1] William Wordsworth, *The Prelude* (1805 version), x. 826–30, edited by Ernest de Selincourt, revised by Helen Darbishire (Oxford, 1959), p. 414. Leslie F. Chard argues that Godwin's influence on Wordsworth was over long before he began *The Prelude*, and certainly he does not write as a disciple, though he writes of Godwin's position with a more sympathetic understanding than Chard's account would lead us to expect (*Dissenting Republican: Wordsworth's Early Life and Thought in their Political Context* (The Hague, 1972), pp. 188–204).

[2] See Karl Marx, *Early Writings*, introduced by Lucio Colletti, translated by Rodney Livingstone and Gregor Benton (Harmondsworth, 1975), p. 422.

[3] See Burton R. Pollin, *Education and Enlightenment in the Works of William Godwin* (New York, 1962). A certain elitism in Shelley's attitude has been stressed by James Rieger, *The Mutiny Within: The Heresies of Percy Bysshe Shelley* (New York, 1967).

perversion of reason, that we can be induced to believe any species of slavery, from the slavery of the school-boy to that of the most unfortunate negro in our West India plantations, favourable to virtue. (*Political Justice*, ii. 388–9)

The reference to 'the slavery of the school-boy' indicates the kind of extreme to which Godwin is willing to push his claim for independence (though his own pedagogical practice was less liberal than his philosophy would seem to demand).

From the moral claim for complete independence naturally flows Godwin's anarchist political philosophy. As George Woodcock has argued, 'In [the] insistence that freedom and moral self-realization are interdependent . . . lies the ultimate lesson of true anarchism.'[1] For Godwin freedom is not just one good among others, to be balanced against them until a satisfactory compromise is arrived at, as it is for Paine; it is an inescapable duty, not a right which can be partially given up to preserve other rights. Man's responsibility to truth and morality imposes on him the necessity of preserving his independence against all outside authorities that claim the right to determine his actions: 'the conviction of a man's individual understanding, is the only legitimate principle, imposing on him the duty of adopting any species of conduct'.[2] It is hardly surprising that Godwin totally rejects government, where Paine accepts it with qualifications. But Godwin's anarchism can be seen as taking to an extreme the ideas common to the democratic revolution. Where Paine only wanted to extend man's control over the government and hence over those activities controlled by government, Godwin wanted to restore to man all control over his own conduct. Joel Barlow, a democratic theorist more sympathetic to anarchism than Paine, would take Godwin's point that 'the exercise of *private judgment* is the foundation of *moral virtue*; and consequently, that all operations of government carry destruction to the latter, in proportion as they deprive us of the former'.[3] But if government is detrimental to the interests of

---

[1] George Woodcock, *Anarchism: A History of Libertarian Ideas and Movements* (1962; Harmondsworth, 1971), p. 451. See J. M. Murry, *Heaven—and Earth*, pp. 257–8.

[2] *Political Justice*, i. 181. Even Malthus, who considered Godwin's scheme as a whole 'little better than a dream', was impressed by his vindication of the 'unlimited exercise of private judgment' (*An Essay on the Principle of Population* (1798; 5th edn., 3 vols., 1817), ii. 244).

[3] *Works of Joel Barlow*, i. 245.

virtue, it may be asked, is it not essential to repress tendencies to evil and crime? Even Barlow is willing to allow for the use of 'compulsion and restraint' against the small number of possible 'refractory persons' in his ideal society.[1] This issue can best be treated in the course of a discussion of Shelley's treatment of the concept of independence.

Shelley's early enthusiasm for the doctrine of independence may well have been based on temperamental as much as rational grounds, as in his assurance to Miss Hitchener: 'I would take my own opinion, particularly when it springs from my own reasonings & feelings before that of any man.' (*Letters*, i. 291) He told Godwin that even before reading *Political Justice* his mind had been 'jealous of its independence' (*Letters*, i. 228). In the same letter he expounded his profound opposition to the supposed virtue of obedience, which he, like Godwin, regarded as the abdication of individuality and moral responsibility (i. 227). We have already seen how large 'independence' bulked in the rhetoric of Shelley's family circle, and it is clear that Godwin helped Shelley to see the full implications of a position he was already very willing to adopt. Shelley's concern with obedience suggests that it was a position chosen at least partly as a way of opposing his father. But Shelley also appreciated the moral dimensions of the case against obedience.

> The man
> Of virtuous soul commands not, nor obeys.
> Power, like a desolating pestilence,
> Pollutes whate'er it touches; and obedience,
> Bane of all genius, virtue, freedom, truth,
> Makes slaves of men, and, of the human frame,
> A mechanized automaton.
> (*Queen Mab*, III. 174–80)

The language of this is Godwinian, and Shelley quotes Godwin in denouncing the soldier, who is, thanks to his habits of obedience, 'of all descriptions of men the most completely a machine'.[2] When he considers the moral status of the soldier again some seven years

---

[1] Ibid. i. 246–7.

[2] Note to *Queen Mab*, IV. 178–9. Shelley quotes in this note from Godwin, *The Enquirer. Reflections on Education, Manners, and Literature* (1797), pp. 234–6. For further attacks on military obedience see *The Esdaile Notebook*, pp. 62, 64, and *Works*, vii. 41, and on obedience in general, *Letters*, i. 146, and Note to *Queen Mab*, VII. 135.

later, his aside sums up the Godwinian doctrine of independence. 'He is taught obedience; his will is no longer, which is the most sacred prerogative of man, guided by his own judgement.' (*Works*, vii. 41) The assumptions that lie behind this have become a second nature to Shelley. In what may well be his last prose work he reads these assumptions into the teachings of Christ.

The doctrines indeed, in my judgement, are excellent and strike at the root of moral evil. If acted upon, no political or religious institution could subsist a moment; every man would be his own magistrate and priest; the change so long desired would have attained its consummation, and man exempt from the internal evils of his own choice would be left free to struggle with the physical evils which exist in spite of him. . . . Doctrines of reform were never carried to so great a length as by Jesus Christ; the Republic of Plato and the Political Justice of Godwin are probable and practical systems in the comparison. (*Works*, vi. 255)[1]

As Donald Reiman remarks, 'The moral law that governed Shelley's mature thought and action insisted upon both the right and the duty of each individual to rule his own destiny.'[2] To aspire to a society in which 'every man would be his own magistrate and priest' is to take to their logical extreme the demands of the democratic revolution; such a position also turns out to have important implications for Shelley's poetic style.

There is nothing very surprising about the republican fervour with which Shelley prays,

> O, that the free would stamp the impious name
>   Of KING into the dust!
> ('Ode to Liberty' (1820), lines 211–12)

It might however give us pause to find that Shelley himself invokes the 'impious name', in a poem clearly intended as a central statement of political belief.

> Man who man would be,
> Must rule the empire of himself; in it
> Must be supreme, establishing his throne
> On vanquished will,—quelling the anarchy

---

[1] The received text is seriously inaccurate at this point. The manuscript, being written on paper identical to that used for portions of *Charles I*, the translation from *Faust*, and *The Triumph of Life*, probably dates from 1822.

[2] *Shelley's 'The Triumph of Life': A Critical Study Based on a Text Newly Edited from the Bodleian Manuscript* (Urbana, Illinois, 1965), p. 3.

Of hopes and fears,—being himself alone.—
('Sonnet: To the Republic of Benevento' (1821),
lines 10–14)

In an early draft for this poem Shelley described his ideal man as 'A King establishing his throne'. This draft also shows that he experimented with several titles to underline the basic paradox. The first attempt seems to have been 'The Republican', then altered to 'The Eng[lish?] Republican'. Shelley cancelled all this and tried 'Rex [Im?]'.[1] Finally he settled for a topical dedication to the tiny (and short-lived) republic of Benevento, which declared its independence from Papal domination in sympathy with the Neapolitan revolution.[2] Shelley is clearly quite deliberate in presenting his republican ideals in the language of monarchy, and, as we shall see, he does much the same in *Prometheus Unbound*. There would seem to be a problem here which has been largely ignored. Richard Cronin seems to be the only one of Shelley's critics who has faced squarely the implications of his language, and his attempt to unravel the knot deserves consideration.[3] After an illuminating discussion of some passages in which, as Mr Cronin puts it, 'Shelley takes prisoner the vocabulary of his enemies, and forces it to fight against its former comrades' (p. 212), he goes on to suggest that there is something essentially self-contradictory about this practice. 'In struggling against the emotive power of language, the poet can succeed only by diverting, not by destroying, that power. So, Shelley must celebrate republicanism in the language of monarchy, and use, in rejecting marriage, a nuptial vocabulary.' (p. 214) In other words, Shelley is trying to dress himself in borrowed robes; his language does not serve his ideals positively, but is, in Mr Cronin's phrase, a 'Language of Dissent'. It seems to me that this interpretation underestimates Shelley's radicalism. There is no reason why he 'must' use the language of his enemies if it does not suit him, for republicanism has its own rhetoric. But when we fully understand the implications of

[1] Bodl. MS Shelley adds. e. 8, p. 150. Shelley probably intended to write 'Rex Imperator', the title of the British monarch.

[2] The dedication appears in Shelley's fair copy of the sonnet; see *The Shelley Notebook in the Harvard College Library*, edited by G. E. Woodberry (Cambridge, Mass., 1929), p. 152 of the facsimile. For the history of Benevento see A. Coppi, *Annali d'Italia del 1750 al 1861* (17 vols., Rome, 1848–67), iii. 274, iv. 170, 203, vi. 208, vii. 120–1, 211.

[3] 'Shelley's Language of Dissent', *Essays in Criticism*, xxvii (1977), 203–15.

Shelley's politics we shall see that the language of monarchy suits him very well.

Over sixty years ago Helen Rossetti Angeli made the perceptive comment that Shelley's notion of 'intellectual independence' involved 'the supremacy of reason over passion from within' as well as over 'compulsion from without'.[1] The same point was made by Donald Reiman when he remarked that the Furies who torture Prometheus represent 'two threats to human moral autonomy—external power and the anarchy of internal passions'.[2] Shelley somewhat extends Godwin's position by his recognition that independence can only be preserved by a battle on two fronts. As a consequence 'rule' becomes a Janus-faced concept. Man must assert his moral independence by repudiating all exterior claims to rule over him, but at the same time he must himself rule 'the anarchy/Of hopes and fears' within. Thus the great ones in *The Triumph of Life* are simultaneously denounced for having been rulers and for not having been rulers.

> 'And who are those chained to the car?' 'The Wise,
>
> 'The great, the unforgotten: they who wore
>   Mitres and helms and crowns, or wreathes of light
> Signs of thought's empire over thought; their lore
>
>   'Taught them not this—to know themselves; their might
> Could not repress the mutiny within,
>   And for the morn of truth they feigned, deep night
>
> 'Caught them ere evening.'
> (lines 208–15)

Paradox is piled on paradox here, and not without reason. It was precisely because they chose to be rulers in the obvious sense that the great were unable to rule themselves: 'The man/Of virtuous soul', as Shelley says in *Queen Mab*, 'commands not, nor obeys.' (III. 174–5) These leaders, religious, military, civil, or intellectual, all enslaved their fellow-men, and paid the price by becoming slaves to their own worse selves. As Shelley comments with reference to imperial Rome, 'Freedom left those who upon the free/Had bound a yoke which soon they stooped to bear' (lines

---

[1] *Shelley and His Friends in Italy* (1911), p. 305.
[2] *Percy Bysshe Shelley* (1969; 1976), p. 82. See also his *Shelley's 'The Triumph of Life'*, pp. 19, 31.

115–16). The 'triumph' of the title alludes to the triumphal processions of ancient Rome, and the analogy is exact, for those chained to the Car of Life are conquered kings, like the captives chained to the chariots of the emperors.[1] Such triumphs are always ironic, for the conquerors have failed to achieve the true conquest of self, and thus have made themselves as much slaves as those they conquered.

> Conquerors have conquered their foes alone,
> Whose revenge, pride, and power they have overthrown:
> Ride ye, more victorious, over your own.
> ('An Ode written October 1819', lines 26–8)

By appropriating the language of rule (and with it the vocabulary of victory, conquest, triumph, and so on) Shelley is suggesting that there is a true rule which, properly understood, provides the best defence against the forms of false rule. This false rule comes about by an evasion of human responsibility, and a consequent perversion of the instinct to rule which is in itself quite proper. 'Too mean spirited and too feeble in resolve to attempt the conquest of their own evil passions, and of the difficulties of the material world, men sought dominion over their fellow men as an easy method to gain that apparent majesty and power which the instinct of their nature requires.' (*Works*, vi. 244) Shelley does not take the vocabulary of his enemies prisoner so much as liberate it from the false application they make of it.

Shelley's recognition that human independence was threatened by passion from within and oppression from without, and his distinction between true and false kinds of rule, come into clearer focus when we put them in the context of the liberal tradition of political debate. It was a commonplace of this tradition that 'The great use of government is as a restraint'.[2] Government is seen as a coercive agency, whose only real function is to preserve the peace by restraining the vices and passions of its subjects. We have already considered Paine's argument that government is the result of man's 'wickedness', that it is in itself evil, but 'a necessary evil', so long as conscience is inadequate to restraining this wickedness. In other words, to adopt Shelley's terms, oppression from without

---

[1] Lines 111–16. Shelley mentions the Roman triumphs elsewhere, with evident disapproval; see *Works*, vi. 303n., vii. 309.

[2] Burke, *Works*, v. 83.

is justified precisely by the existence of the unruly passions within. On this point Paine joins hands with his famous antagonist Burke.

Society cannot exist unless a controlling power upon will and appetite be placed somewhere, and the less of it there is within, the more there must be without. It is ordained in the eternal constitution of things, that men of intemperate minds cannot be free. Their passions forge their fetters.[1]

Burke's argument and his concluding metaphor were taken up by Coleridge in a poem for which Shelley is known to have felt great admiration.

> The Sensual and the Dark rebel in vain,
> Slaves by their own compulsion! In mad game
> They burst their manacles and wear the name
> Of Freedom, graven on a heavier chain!
> ('France: An Ode' (1798), lines 85–8)[2]

Shelley would also have known Coleridge's assertion that 'the universal necessary Laws, and pure IDEAS of Reason were given us . . . that by an energy of continued self-conquest, we might establish a free and yet absolute Government in our own Spirits'.[3] Coleridge would accept that if man could truly rule himself there would be no necessity for coercion from without. 'The necessity for external government to man is in inverse ratio to the vigour of his self-government. Where the last is most complete, the first is least wanted. Hence, the more virtue the more liberty.'[4] It is clear, however, that neither Paine, Burke, nor Coleridge seriously believed that man could ever subdue 'the anarchy of hopes and fears' within him so completely as to supersede the necessity for external government.

Shelley may not have believed so either, but he was committed

---

[1] Ibid. ii. 555.
[2] For Shelley's admiration see *Medwin's Conversations of Lord Byron*, edited by E. J. Lovell, Jr (Princeton, 1966), p. 114. Coleridge's lines find an echo in Demogorgon's 'All spirits are enslaved which serve things evil' (*Prometheus Unbound*, II. iv. 110).
[3] *The Friend*, edited by Barbara E. Rooke (2 vols., 1969), ii. 110–11. I cite the text as published in 1812, in which form it was probably known to Shelley; see Charles E. Robinson, 'The Shelley Circle and Coleridge's *The Friend*', *ELN* viii (1971), 269–74.
[4] *Specimens of the Table Talk of Samuel Taylor Coleridge*, edited by H. N. Coleridge (1835; 4th edn., 1851), p. 252 (15 June 1833).

to holding that it must happen. Unlike the theorists of the liberal tradition he could not balance one kind of government against another, internal against external, and be satisfied so long as the requisite quantum was preserved. In Godwin's moral philosophy to restrain man's vices by external coercion was to thwart the development of his moral independence, and thus make him even less capable of ruling himself—and thus even more in need of government. Godwin saw all government as an evil because it was 'an usurpation upon the private judgment and individual conscience of mankind' (*Political Justice*, ii. 2). And this is government at its best; at its worst it fosters as many vices as it restrains. Clearly no Godwinian can acquiesce in the usurpation by government of the role of the individual conscience, a role that government can fulfil only indifferently. Shelley defers to the theorists of the liberal tradition to the extent of agreeing that moral reform must precede the abolition of coercive restraints: 'where there is no virtue there will be crime, and where there is crime there must be government. Before the restraints of government are lessened, it is fit that we should lessen the necessity for them. Before government is done away with, we must reform ourselves.' (*Works*, v. 232) Here Shelley plays on the two senses of 'reform', moral and political. In his mature verse he puns with equal earnestness on the two senses of 'rule'. In doing this his intention is not to dress himself in stolen plumage but to reclaim what is due to man, and enlarge his readers' sense of what is possible. If the true rule is self-rule, and political government is no more than a perversion of and an inadequate substitute for it, and if men can be brought to realize this, then it may be possible to realize Godwin's hope that 'the principle of private judgment . . . in proportion as it impresses itself on the minds of men, may be expected perhaps to supersede the possibility of the action of society in a collective capacity' (*Political Justice*, ii. 291). That is rather a lot of 'ifs'; it is largely to allow scope for their fulfilment that the philosophical anarchists are so attached to the doctrine of Perfectibility.

An account of man which stresses his responsibility to create his own moral nature is naturally committed to seeing him as progressive. A comparison between what man has become (however much that still leaves to be desired) and what he once was establishes that some progress has been made. Why should not this tendency continue into the future?

Such was man in his original state, and such is man as we at present behold him. Is it possible for us to contemplate what he has already done, without being impressed with a strong presentiment of the improvements he has yet to accomplish? There is no science that is not capable of additions; there is no art that may not be carried to a still higher perfection. If this be true of all other sciences, why not of morals? If this be true of all other arts, why not of social institution? (*Political Justice*, i. 118–19)

Shelley uses the same kind of empirical evidence in rebuking the classical poets for only seeing the Golden Age in the past. 'Man was once as a wild beast, he has become a moralist, a metaphysician, [a] poet and an astronomer,—Lucretius or Virgil might have referred the comparison to themselves and as a proof of progress of the nature of man challenged a comparison with the cannibals of Scythia.' (*Works*, vi. 250) In these terms the case has some strength. Godwin's attempts to provide it with a theoretical underpinning are more dubious. It is axiomatic for Godwin that 'In whatever light we consider virtue . . . its degree must be intimately connected with the degree of knowledge' (*Political Justice*, i. 310). Although Shelley came to see the problem in rather different terms he always agreed with Godwin that 'wisdom and virtue may be said to be inseparables and criteria of each other'.[1] It is clear that in the individual the acquirement of knowledge is progressive[2] and it is not unreasonable to expect this to be connected with moral growth. In society too the acquirement of knowledge is progressive, as are the arts (the mechanical rather than the fine arts) and sciences. But is this kind of intellectual progress synonymous with or even conducive to moral progress? In the perspective of philosophical anarchism it is moral progress that is really at issue. Does the acquirement of factual and scientific knowledge, the improvement of technological resources—the whole Baconian enterprise—really serve to make society juster or more moral? Shelley certainly saw good reason to doubt whether it did, and even to suspect that it had the opposite effect.[3] If Godwin's doctrine of Perfectibility is taken as an account of the laws of individual and social progress, and a proof of the necessary connection between intellectual

---

[1] *Works*, vii. 75–6. This question is considered in more detail in Chapter VI (see below, pp. 229–37).
[2] See *Political Justice*, i. 94–5.
[3] See *Works*, vii. 134.

progress and moral improvement, it is quite inadequate and leaves far too many facts out of the account. But it would be a mistake to see the issue in these terms. 'Perfectibility' is less a theory than it is an attitude of mind, and an attitude that it is indispensible to anyone holding to an anarchist political philosophy. It is an attitude that is registered in Shelley's thinking, but even more intimately in his poetic style.

'Perfectibility' is Godwin's preferred term for the thesis that there is a tendency on the part of the individual and of society to improve constantly.[1] The term is ill-chosen because it is bound to mislead readers into assuming that it implied that man was capable of achieving final perfection. This was pretty much the direct opposite of what Godwin wanted to say.

By perfectible, it is not meant that he [Man] is capable of being brought to perfection. But the word seems sufficiently adapted to express the faculty of being continually made better and receiving perpetual improvement; and in this sense it is here to be understood. The term perfectible, thus explained, not only does not imply the capacity of being brought to perfection, but stands in express opposition to it. If we could arrive at perfection, there would be an end to our improvement. (*Political Justice*, i. 93)

As Godwin later acknowledged, his meaning would have been clearer if he had been content to speak of 'the progressive nature of man, in knowledge, in virtuous propensities, and in social institutions'.[2] The progress in question is not to be limited by any goals, its final scope is infinite; and if we bear this in mind Godwin's pet term 'perfectibility' will serve our purposes. If we demand a more appropriate term we could do no better than adopt a word which has become current in Shelley criticism—'potentiality'. As some excellent studies have shown, the concept of potentiality is intimately connected with the distinctive qualities of Shelley's

[1] The doctrine of perfectibility is lucidly summarized by J. P. Clark, *The Philosophical Anarchism of William Godwin*, pp. 76–80. Clark follows Godwin in blurring the distinction between individual and social perfectibility, a distinction that Godwin chooses to ignore, though he recognizes its existence, as when he records a conversation on 'perfectibility individual & general' (Journal entry for 22 Sept. 1792; on microfilm in the University Library, Cambridge).

[2] 'Thoughts occasioned by . . . Dr. Parr's Spital Sermon' (1801), in *Uncollected Writings (1785–1822)*, edited by J. W. Marken and B. R. Pollin (Gainesville, Florida, 1968), p. 337.

poetry.[1] The fact that potentiality in Shelley has not hitherto been connected with Godwin's perfectibility has served to obscure the political implications of Shelley's style.

Godwin uses the doctrine of perfectibility to underwrite his own reluctance to engage in or countenance any form of political action. Since men and society had an inherent tendency to improve Godwin considered that it was safest to leave this natural process to work itself out in its own good time. Sceptical about man's ability to help it he was only too aware that the best intended efforts could hinder it. We have already seen his opposition to Paine's demand for a settled constitution, and to violent revolution as counteracting society's slow but certain improvement. His distrust of government itself rests on similar grounds, for 'positive institution' is the most effective brake on progress of all.

By its very nature positive institution has a tendency to suspend the elasticity and progress of mind. Every scheme for embodying imperfection must be injurious. That which is to-day a considerable melioration, will at some future period, if preserved unaltered, appear a defect and disease in the body politic. (*Political Justice*, i. 246)

Godwin would like to believe that man's tendency to improve would bring him to a state where the coercive restraints of government would no longer be necessary. The catch is that, on Godwin's own account, government operates rather successfully to hold back man's moral improvement. There is a vicious circle here which Godwin lacks the courage to break; as we shall see in Chapter IV Shelley argues more boldly and more consistently from Godwin's own premises, devising an endless dialectic of political reform and moral improvement by which man can break into the circle and take the responsibility for his own social destiny. Godwin's error lies in relying on perfectibility as if it expressed an invariable law, providing the grounds for predictions whose fulfilment was quite independent of human action. This reliance on Necessity is to be found in *Queen Mab* but not in Shelley's mature work. There Necessity is not an inevitable force which relieves man of

[1] D. J. Hughes, 'Potentiality in *Prometheus Unbound*' (1963), in *Shelley: Modern Judgements*, edited by R. B. Woodings, pp. 142–61; Timothy Webb, 'Shelley's Negatives', to be published as part of the proceedings of the Shelley Conference held at Gregynog in September 1978, edited by Kelvin Everest (forthcoming from the Harvester Press, Hassocks, Sussex).

the need actively to create his destiny but a reminder that actions are not to be divorced from their consequences.

> one comes behind,
> Who aye the future to the past will bind—
> Necessity, whose sightless strength forever
> Evil with evil, good with good, must wind
> In bands of union, which no power may sever:
> They must bring forth their kind, and be divided never!
> (*Laon and Cythna*, IX. xxvii)

History is only on the side of those who use good means to produce good ends. Used in this way 'Necessity' has none of the quietist overtones present in Godwin's reliance on it. Shelley holds up Necessity as a warning to those who are committed to political action.

Perfectibility is a vivifying element in Shelley's thinking because he recognized that what force and truth the idea possessed lay in the effect it had on human actions, by inspiring human actors with faith and moral strength. He does not make a fetish out of perfectibility, and retains a certain scepticism about its dogmatic claims, which is well expressed by another Godwinian poet, Joel Barlow.

I cannot expect that every reader, nor even every republican reader, will join me in opinion with respect to the future progress of society and the civilization of states; but there are two sentiments in which I think all men will agree: that the event is desirable, and that to believe it practicable is one step towards rendering it so. This being the case they ought to pardon a writer, if not applaud him, for endeavouring to inculcate this belief. (Preface to *The Columbiad* (1807))[1]

Barlow suggests that perfectibility is a fiction, which the belief of human actors might turn into a truth. The attitude he expresses is extremely common in Shelley, and it has been the cause of a good deal of impatience among readers who have failed to recognize the scepticism involved in it and have insisted on taking Shelley's own speculations literally. Shelley's own warnings against this are clear enough. He comments on a passage in *Hellas*, which embodies the Christian concept of an afterlife, in terms that are strongly reminiscent of those used by Barlow.

---

[1] *Works of Joel Barlow*, ii. 383. See also ii. 852.

The concluding verses indicate a progressive state of more or less exalted existence, according to the degree of perfection which every distinct intelligence may have attained. Let it not be supposed that I mean to dogmatize upon a subject concerning which all men are equally ignorant, or that I think the Gordian knot of the origin of evil can be disentangled by that or any similar assertions. . . . That there is a true solution of the riddle, and that in our present state the solution is unattainable by us, are propositions which may be regarded as equally certain; meanwhile, as it is the province of the poet to attach himself to those ideas which exalt and ennoble humanity, let him be permitted to have conjectured the condition of that futurity towards which we are all impelled by an inextinguishable thirst for immortality. (Note to *Hellas*, lines 197–238)

This is more than a defence of poetic fictions, for Shelley uses similar arguments to justify the appeal to fictions in the practical activity of politics. Thus he says of complete material equality that it cannot be part of any immediate practical programme, while insisting that it is 'one of the conditions of that system of society, towards which with whatever hope of ultimate success it is our duty to tend' (*Works*, vii. 43) The fact that it is beyond our present grasp, may never in fact be attainable, does not prevent if from being valuable as an ideal by which to regulate political action.

Towards whatsoever we regard as perfect, undoubtedly it is no less our duty than it is our nature to press forward; this is the generous enthusiasm, which accomplishes not indeed the consummation after which it aspires, but one which approaches it in a degree far nearer, than if the whole powers had not been developed by a ⟨delusion⟩.— (*Works*, vi. 46)

This kind of idealism is pervasive in Shelley's poetry, and has drawn frequent charges of naïvety from his hostile critics. For my own part I am astounded by the tough-mindedness with which Shelley manages to be totally committed to ideals which he fully recognizes to be fictions. His choice of the word 'delusion', his cancellation of it, and his inability to find a replacement say it all.

The difference between the Shelleyan and the Godwinian senses of perfectibility can be illuminated by reference to a distinction made by Kant, who will also serve to bring out the radicalism of Shelley's use of the concept. In adducing Kant here I prefer to ignore the question of how familiar Shelley was with Kant's writings. I think René Wellek was justified in concluding that 'there is no evidence for any real acquaintance of Shelley with

Kant's philosophy'.[1] We do not need to establish any direct influence in order to see the relevance of certain parallels between Kant's thought and Shelley's. Kant makes a distinction between 'constitutive' and 'regulative' ideas that can be usefully applied to the idea of perfectibility.[2] For Godwin perfectibility is a 'constitutive' idea, one giving valid information about the nature of reality, on which conclusions and predictions about the real world can confidently be based. For Shelley it is a 'regulative' idea, which gives no reliable information about reality but serves to guide men's practical activity, and which is therefore to be accepted 'as if' it were true. I have used these terms rather loosely here, but in a way that Kant would recognize, to judge by his comments on Plato's *Republic*.

This perfect state may never, indeed, come into being; none the less this does not affect the rightfulness of the idea, which, in order to bring the legal organisation of mankind ever nearer to its greatest possible perfection, advances this maximum as an archetype. For what the highest degree may be at which mankind may have to come to a stand, and how great a gulf may still have to be left between the idea and its realisation, are questions which no one can, or ought to, answer. For the issue depends on freedom; and it is in the power of freedom to pass beyond any and every specified limit.[3]

This ability to 'pass beyond any and every specified limit' is at the heart of the doctrine of perfectibility. Kant also enables us to make another distinction here, between what I would call 'open' and 'closed' forms of perfectibility.[4] Kant posits a 'closed' system: the society described by Plato is probably unattainable, but for Kant it is a 'maximum', and if it were attained there would be no question of progressing beyond it. Godwin and Shelley would argue that human freedom can go beyond 'any and every specified limit', including the limit that Kant specifies by setting up a supposed 'maximum'. In their 'open' system whatever goals man may have set himself will be passed as soon as achieved, for the

---

[1] *Immanuel Kant in England 1793–1838* (Princeton, 1931), p. 182.
[2] This distinction is lucidly explained in G. N. G. Orsini, *Coleridge and German Idealism* (London and Amsterdam, 1969), pp. 130–1.
[3] *Immanuel Kant's Critique of Pure Reason* (1781; 2nd edn., 1787), translated by Norman Kemp Smith (1929; 1970), p. 312.
[4] A similar distinction between progress seen as a 'closed system' and as 'indefinite' is made by J. B. Bury, *The Idea of Progress: An Inquiry into its Origin and Growth* (1920), p. 236.

very achievement of these goals will put him in a position to conceive of fresh goals that were previously inconceivable.[1]

Shelley's adherence to perfectibility as an 'open' system means that in his mature work he was not a Utopian writer, though this label has often been applied to him. A Utopian, like Plato, or Kant in his comments on Plato, presents us with a state conceived of as being perfect, with the clear implication that if it were attained further progress would be out of the question and any change could only be detrimental. But the doctrine of perfectibility explicitly excludes any question of achieving a final perfection. In only one of Shelley's works can he be called a Utopian, and that is *Queen Mab*, which has been described as Godwin in verse, quite wrongly for it is really the least Godwinian of all Shelley's major works.[2] In *Queen Mab* Shelley does indeed suggest that perfection can be achieved, and he hails the regenerated world as 'happy Earth! reality of Heaven!' (IX. 1, 11) In Canto IX, as Robert Pack observes, Shelley has created 'a world perfected'. 'He takes history to its end, implying that history will cease once the millennium comes.'[3] This is a more traditional conception and an easier one to comprehend than the infinite potentiality that is invoked in Shelley's mature poems. Meyer Abrams finds it all too easy to misread the end of Act III of *Prometheus Unbound* as though nothing more were involved than a reprise of Canto IX of *Queen Mab*. According to Professor Abrams's account, 'man, having become what he might always have been, "made earth like heaven" and, "equal, unclassed, tribeless, and nationless", takes up residence in his achieved paradise'. Abrams goes on to pay Shelley an undeserved compliment by suggesting that his idealism is ballasted with wholesome realism: 'Shelley's is a paradise of this earth, in which man remains inescapably conditioned by passion and by "chance, and death, and mutability"; otherwise he would not be earthly man but a disembodied idea in a Platonic heaven . . .'[4] Shelley, however,

---

[1] The clearest exposition of this way of thinking is worked out by Anthony Beavis in Aldous Huxley's novel *Eyeless in Gaza* (1936), Ch. 54.

[2] See H. N. Brailsford, *Shelley, Godwin and Their Circle* (1913; 1949), p. 218; Crane Brinton, *The Political Ideas of the English Romanticists* (1926; Ann Arbor, Michigan, 1966), p. 164.

[3] 'Shelley and History: The Poet as Historian' (unpublished Ph. D. dissertation, University of Pittsburgh, 1970), pp. 39–40.

[4] *Natural Supernaturalism: Tradition and Revolution in Romantic Literature* (1971), p. 306.

does not say that man is 'inescapably conditioned' by the conditions of mortal existence, he says that he is '[not] *yet* exempt' from them (III. iv. 200, emphasis added). This important passage will be discussed at more length in the course of my reading of the whole drama, when we will see that for Shelley no limits are to be accepted as inescapable.

There are in Shelley's works passages that we might be tempted to label as 'Utopian', but we would be using the term loosely and somewhat misleadingly. These are the passages in which Shelley envisages an ideal world into which to retreat from the repellent and alienating aspects of the world at large, most notably 'Lines written among the Euganean Hills', lines 335–73; *Prometheus Unbound*, III. iii. 10–63; and *Epipsychidion*, lines 422–587. These dream worlds are not unrelated to Shelley's political ideals, as the ironic Advertisement to *Epipsychidion* suggests.

The Writer of the following Lines died at Florence, as he was preparing for a voyage to one of the wildest of the Sporades, which he had bought, and where he had fitted up the ruins of an old building, and where it was his hope to have realised a scheme of life, suited perhaps to that happier and better world of which he is now an inhabitant, but hardly practicable in this.

In his more aggressive moments Shelley would not let the apparent impracticability of a scheme deter him from urging its adoption. In *Epipsychidion* he is consciously in retreat from the public world, and the 'scheme of life' he describes in it is not a plan of social life which is rendered 'hardly practicable' by the world's resistance to reform, but a personal scheme of life which is frustrated by the corrupting influence of the world on individuals. In his moments of disillusion Shelley was often tempted to the conclusion that only retreat could preserve the virtuous from corruption and allow them any kind of truly human life, and he wrote to his wife:

My greatest content would be utterly to desert all human society. I would retire with you & our child to a solitary island in the sea, would build a boat, & shut upon my retreat the floodgates of the world.— . . . If I dared trust my imagination it would tell me that there were two or three chosen companions beside yourself whom I should desire.—But to this I would not listen.—Where two or three are gathered together the devil is among them, and good far more than evil impulses—love far more than hatred—has been to me, except as you have been it's object, the source of all sort[s] of mischief. So on this plan I would be *alone* & would devote either to oblivion or to future generations the overflowings of a mind which, timely withdrawn from the contagion, should be kept fit for no baser object—But this it does not appear that we shall do.— (*Letters*, ii. 339)

Such a plan is not really Utopian, for a Utopia is a complete blue-print for a regenerated society, and what Shelley is concerned with here is the tactics of self-preservation in an obstinately unregenerated society. If society were amenable to improvement there would no longer be any call for retreat. It may be objected that Prometheus plans to retire from a regenerated world, but the point there is that Prometheus and Asia have no business in such a world, for they are immortals. Prometheus' job is done, the world is a fit place for humanity, and humanity will live in it without needing a retreat. When a man seeks retreat it either implies a repudiation of public hope, or signifies a temporary retirement which will allow him to renew the struggle later or to contribute to it by spreading the influence of good. 'If', says Shelley, 'there must be no response to my cry', then he and Mary will watch over man from their retirement.

> thou and I,
> Sweet Friend! can look from our tranquillity
> Like lamps into the world's tempestuous night,—
> Two tranquil stars, while clouds are passing by
> Which wrap them from the foundering seaman's sight,
> That burn from year to year with unextinguished light.
> (Dedication to *Laon and Cythna*, xiv)

The retreat envisaged in 'Lines written among the Euganean Hills' may serve as a kind of moral nursing home where those corrupted by the world can convalesce.

> We may live so happy there,
> That the Spirits of the Air,
> Envying us, may even entice
> To our healing Paradise
> The polluting multitude;
> But their rage would be subdued
> By that clime divine and calm . . .
> They, not it, would change . . .
> (lines 352–8, 370)

This retreat is not so much a miniature of a perfected world as a working model of the spirit which makes moral and social improvement come to pass.

The doctrines of Independence and Perfectibility are at the very heart of the moral vision that Shelley elaborated upon a Godwinian basis, and have demanded consideration at some length. With the issue of Opinion we come to the link between morality and politics in the scheme of philosophical anarchism, a question of some importance but which may be treated rather more briefly. 'Opinion' is Godwin's own term and, as usual, it may confuse rather than illuminate his reader. In his usage the term covers moral disposition as well as rational conviction, the two being connected in his moral philosophy. The term is congenial, firstly because it hints at the political power of 'public opinion', a concept coming into currency at the time and often invoked by Shelley;[1] and secondly because it suggests that our convictions and our habits are relative, since, like everything else about man, they are perpetually progressing.[2] Godwin is concerned both with the political limitations imposed by the present state of opinion, and with the future possibilities that progress in opinion will bring. The importance that Godwin attaches to opinion is connected with his rationalism, with his belief that man is capable of moral action according to his own judgement, not determined by innate factors or environment. 'Man is not a vegetable to be governed by sensations of heat and cold, dryness and moisture. He is a reasonable creature, capable of perceiving what is eligible and right, of fixing indelibly certain principles upon his mind, and adhering inflexibly to the resolutions he has made.' (*Political Justice*, i. 79) Man's judgement is not infallible, but it is the crucial determining factor in his actions, and hence, as Godwin proclaims in the title of Book I, Chapter v of *Political Justice*, 'The Voluntary Actions of Men originate in their Opinions'.

The concept is extended from Godwin's moral philosophy into his political thought by his conviction that social institutions, no less than individual actions, originate in 'opinion'—a conviction that is possibly connected with his belief that 'Society is nothing more than an aggregation of individuals' (i. 136). In the final analysis no government can be imposed on men without their

---

[1] See *Works*, v. 241, vi. 270, vii. 44–5, 51.
[2] See *Political Justice*, i. 151, 199.

own beliefs co-operating to rivet the shackles. 'All government is founded in opinion. Men at present live under any particular form, because they conceive it their interest to do so.' (i. 145) Either they actively approve of it, or they think submission wiser than resistance, or they lack the imagination to conceive of any alternative. Godwin's rationalistic view of moral action allows him to argue that those who accept a particular system are morally unfit for anything better. '. . . no persons are ripe for the participation of a benefit, the advantage of which they do not understand. No people are competent to enjoy a state of freedom, who are not already imbued with a love of freedom.' (i. 257) When men are morally prepared for better government the support of their rational conviction is withdrawn from the old system, and it cannot stand: 'In reality the chains fall off of themselves, when the magic of opinion is dissolved.' (i. 99) This conclusion is clearly intended to preclude the necessity of revolutionary action. If political institutions are the products and reflections of the state of opinion in society as a whole, then it must follow that it is worse than useless to effect changes in social institutions before the opinions on which they are founded have been changed. These institutions may be palpably pernicious but the fault lies primarily with the very men who suffer under them. 'Opinion' both creates the future and ties man to his present condition.

Opinion as a negative force will be more familiar to readers of Shelley under the appellation of 'Custom'.[1] It is the adherence to 'Custom' that enslaves man to the past. Even in *Queen Mab* it is not true that Shelley makes 'Kings, priests, and statesmen' solely responsible for all the ills of the world. Evil comes through them, but it is their slaves who confer upon them the power to do evil. Behind the denunciatory rhetoric Shelley is already aware that if man is enslaved it is because

> on his own high will, a willing slave,
> He has enthroned the oppression and the oppressor.
> ('Ode to Liberty', lines 244–5)

The gods and tyrants of whom he goes in awe are in reality projections of his own fears and doubts, the internal 'anarchy' that

---

[1] See *The Esdaile Notebook*, pp. 86, 158; *Queen Mab*, I. 127, III. 98, IX. 201; *Laon and Cythna*, IV. ix, xxiv, VIII. xxvii; *Prometheus Unbound*, I. 621; 'Fragments probably intended for *Otho*', line 2 (*Works*, iii. 165); *The Witch of Atlas*, line 493.

he is unable to rule. The failure on man's part to rule himself provides the justification for external rule, as we have already seen; it also leads him to a state of self-doubt in which he is willing to let himself be ruled. In these terms moral disposition and political 'opinion' are indeed connected, as Godwin suspected, but failed to demonstrate. A society in which man is ruled by other men is one in which man is ruled by his own worst self, and in such a society man is both slave and tyrant—the two are inseparable sides of the same coin.[1] Shelley conveys his vision of a society ruled by its own anarchic impulses through the imagery of shadows, seen as projections from man himself. The Christian God is just such a shadow.

> What is God? Some moon-struck sophist stood
> Watching the shade from his own soul upthrown
> Fill Heaven and darken Earth, and in such mood
> The Form he saw and worshipped was his own,
> His likeness in the world's vast mirror shewn . . .
> (*Laon and Cythna*, VIII. vi)[2]

This imagery is a powerful structural motif in *The Triumph of Life*, where some 'mournfully within the gloom/Of their own shadow walked, and called it death . . .' (lines 58–9). When man thus stands in his own light he can put others in the shade, as did the great divines of the Christian Church

> Who rose like shadows between Man and god
>   Till that eclipse, still hanging under Heaven,
> Was worshipped by the world o'er which they strode
>
>   For the true Sun it quenched.—
> (lines 289–92)

The climax of the poem is Rousseau's Dantean vision of all the political and moral ills that plague mankind, in the shape of flitting 'shadows'. At first they seem to be external to men, a plague of tormenting demons, but the simile of 'A flock of vampire-bats' with which they are introduced turns out to be horrifyingly apt.

---

[1] This is a point on which Shelley frequently insists. See *Letters*, ii. 325; 'An Ode written October 1819', line 9; *Hellas*, line 557.

[2] Leigh Hunt borrowed this imagery for a sonnet addressed to Shelley (in *The Unextinguished Hearth*, p. 341).

They live by draining the vitality of their victims, who are moreover the ultimate source of their existence.

> each one
> Of that great crowd sent forth incessantly
> These shadows, numerous as the dead leaves blown

> In Autumn evening from a popular tree—
> (lines 481, 484, 526–9)

Like the leaves these shadows are a part of that whence they come,
though they are not likely to 'quicken a new birth' like the leaves
in the 'Ode to the West Wind' (line 64). The oppressive forms of
government and religion are mere 'shadows' without substance
outside the minds of men. Nevertheless they rule them as surely
as anything physical or exterior. This consideration helps to
explain the curious strategy by which Shelley in *Queen Mab*
simultaneously denies the existence of the Christian God and
arraigns and defies him as if he did exist. In one sense a mere word
by which men express their ignorance, he is in another sense the
'prototype of human misrule' (VI. 105) whose example is used to
justify earthly tyrannies, and thus he has a potent existence in
the sphere of 'opinion'.

It seems likely that it was the Godwinian doctrine of Opinion
that predisposed Shelley to adopt the idealist philosophy of
Berkeley—or as much of that philosophy as is contained in Shelley's
formulation: 'All things exist as they are perceived: at least in
relation to the percipient. "The mind is its own place, and of
itself can make a heaven of hell, a hell of heaven." ' (*Works*, vii.
137)[1] Shelley does in fact take no more from Berkeley than is
contained within his own explicit statements, and it would be
wrong to assume that Shelley shares Berkeley's concerns. Shelley
is not interested in questions of ontology. He does not say that all
things exist by being perceived, or that they only exist in so far as
they are perceived. One should rather gloss his words as meaning
that the manner in which all things exist is conditioned by the
manner in which they are perceived. He does not commit himself
on the vexed issue of whether objects have any existence apart
from their being perceived, this being a matter of great indifference

---

[1] Bishop Berkeley would have been surprised to see his philosophy illustrated
from Satan's speech of defiance (*Paradise Lost*, I. 254–5).

for him. Shelley was really less interested in abstruse metaphysical questions than in their moral implications[1] and the significance of his allusions to Berkeley is indicated by a passage in the draft of *A Defence of Poetry*: 'our existence becomes greater in proportion to our [creed?] the nobility of intellectual philosophy'.[2] As Jerome McGann has remarked, '*Esse est percipi* came to mean, in Romantic thought, that man's mind creates its own existential condition.'[3]

Since opinion is so powerful a determinant of man's social existence it follows that all political reform must begin with a reform of opinion. In the words of one of Godwin's disciples, 'To counteract a bad moral influence . . . you must create a good moral influence. Reformed opinion precedes reformed legislation.'[4] Godwin has a serene confidence in the inevitable progress of opinion, from which political progress will follow with equal inevitability. 'In reality the chains fall off of themselves, when the magic of opinion is dissolved. When a great majority of any society are persuaded to secure any benefit to themselves, there is no need of tumult or violence to effect it. The effort would be to resist reason, not to obey it.' (*Political Justice*, i. 99) Godwin is afraid of the consequences of premature political reform: 'The only method according to which social improvements can be carried on, with sufficient prospect of an auspicious event, is, when the improvement of our institutions advances, in a just proportion to the illumination of the public understanding.' (i. 273) His hostility to revolution is understandable, especially in view of the fact that revolution, by substituting force for reason, violates the intellectual independence of the individual as much as government itself (i. 257). But Godwin often takes his caution to extreme lengths and virtually declares a moratorium on all political action. After the abortive attempt at direct reform in Ireland Shelley was more inclined to accept Godwin's advice, and to direct his activities into literary channels, reforming society by reforming its opinions.[5] But Shelley never abandoned political activity entirely, and, as we shall see, he was justified in this by the principles of *Political*

---

[1] See *Works*, vii. 71.
[2] *Shelley's Prose in the Bodleian Manuscripts*, edited by A. H. Koszul (1910). p. 112n.
[3] *Don Juan in Context* (1976), p. 148.
[4] Edward Lytton Bulwer, *England and the English*, p. 381.
[5] See Mary Shelley's 'Note on the Early Poems' (*Works*, iii. 120).

Justice. Shelley also differed from Godwin in his understanding of 'opinion'. Godwin often talks as if opinion can be reformed merely by the intellectual enlightenment of the members of society—a mistake that Paine made. Since the crucial issue is the moral condition of a society one has to share Godwin's rationalism to find this an adequate conception of the problem. Shelley came to consider that the opinions and moral condition of a person depend ultimately on his total experiential vision of the world—and thus on imagination rather than reason.

Most of the [*illegible word*] of philosophy have erred from considering the human being in a point of view too detailed and circumscribed. He is not a moral and intellectual,—but also, and preeminently, an imaginative being. His own mind is his law; his own mind is all things to him. If we would arrive at any knowledge which should be serviceable from the practical conclusions to which it leads, we ought to consider the mind of man and the universe as the great whole on which to exercise our speculations.— (*Works*, vii. 65)

The point of the last sentence is to emphasize that the transformation of existing reality depends directly or indirectly on a transformation of man's consciousness of the world which he both creates and experiences. The world must be transformed in imagination before it can be changed politically, and it is here that the poet can exert an influence over 'opinion'. This imaginative re-creation of existence is both the subject and the intended effect of *Prometheus Unbound*.

James Rieger has hazarded the illuminating assertion that 'Obscurantism enters the main tradition of English verse with Shelley'.[1] Rieger has in mind particularly *Prometheus Unbound*, and his remark does point to some disturbing aspects of the poem. After the failure of *Laon and Cythna* (or *The Revolt of Islam*, to give it the title by which it was to become known to the public) Shelley resigned himself perforce to seeing the poems he himself cared most about rejected by the contemporary public. He commented, 'if I may judge by its merits, the "Prometheus" cannot sell beyond twenty copies' (*Letters*, ii. 174). Shelley is always a difficult poet, but there is some evidence to support Rieger's suspicion that the difficulties of *Prometheus Unbound* are at least partly wilful. There is a certain smugness about Shelley's remark to Hunt that *Prome-*

---

[1] *The Mutiny Within*, p. 15.

theus 'will not sell—it is written only for the elect. I confess I am vain enough to like it.' (ii. 200) If the public were determined not to understand, Shelley would puzzle them with a vengeance. It is true that in his drama Shelley 'loaded every rift with arcane learning', and Rieger has some grounds for his accusation that he was 'showing off' (pp. 16–17). But the real problem does not lie there, though it suits Rieger to think it does, since he intends to display some arcane learning himself and to demonstrate that 'Demogorgon is the product of Platonic and Gnostic syncretism and by virtue of that ancestry an exact emblem of the Shelleyan Imagination' (p. 17). Such an attempt to crack Shelley's code would be valid if the only problem was that Shelley had deliberately encoded his meaning in esoteric terms, since he could at least be expected to keep to the rules. But *Prometheus Unbound* does not in fact puzzle us primarily by the reconditeness of its allusions. Most of the allusions are to the classical and biblical sources which were notionally available to an educated audience of Shelley's day. What is problematic about the work seems rather to arise from uncertainties in Shelley's own mind about what he was doing. Several promising interpretations of the main course of the drama are available, but none of them is capable of explaining everything in it. This may not seem entirely surprising in view of the fact that Shelley is known to have altered his mind concerning some points in the actual course of composition. Shelley initially considered that the drama was 'finished' with the completion of the first three acts in April 1819 (*Letters*, ii. 94), and the fourth act does not seem to have been begun until after John Gisborne had left for England on 12 September with the first three acts.[1] At least one other change of intention seems to have left its mark on the play as it stands. Abrams has argued that 'since, by the conditions of Shelley's inherited story, Prometheus must remain fixed to his precipice, the function of the self-educative journey is given over to his alter ego, Asia'.[2] In terms of the drama as we have it this is correct, but it seems likely that Shelley originally planned to solve the problem rather differently. When Prometheus desires the 'recall' of his Curse the Earth prepares the way with a long and complex piece of mythology.

[1] See *Journal*, p. 124.
[2] *Natural Supernaturalism*, p. 304.

> Ere Babylon was dust,
> The Magus Zoroaster, my dead child,
> Met his own image walking in the garden.
> That apparition, sole of men, he saw.
> For know, there are two worlds of life and death:
> One that which thou beholdest, but the other
> Is underneath the grave, where do inhabit
> The shadows of all forms that think and live
> Till death unite them, and they part no more;
> Dreams and the light imaginings of men
> And all that faith creates, or love desires,
> Terrible, strange, sublime and beauteous shapes.
> There thou art, and dost hang, a writhing shade
> 'Mid whirlwind-peopled mountains; all the Gods
> Are there, and all the Powers of nameless worlds,
> Vast, sceptred phantoms; heroes, men, and beasts;
> And Demogorgon, a tremendous Gloom;
> And he, the Supreme Tyrant, on his throne
> Of burning Gold.
>
> (I. 191–209)

The opening allusion is so recondite that no scholar has yet tracked it down, and I am inclined to believe that Shelley invented it himself. But the real problem is structural. It seems strange that this elaborate and powerful conception of the double worlds should be completely absent from the drama after the invocation of the Phantasm of Jupiter. But since Demogorgon is specifically mentioned as inhabiting the world of shadows it would seem likely that in Shelley's original conception it was Prometheus, not Asia, who was to confront Demogorgon by invoking his Phantasm—a device that would get round Prometheus' necessary immobility. It is certainly better for Asia to question Demogorgon, and for this to be the culmination of a 'self-educative journey', but in adopting this superior solution Shelley left himself saddled with a piece of machinery with which he could not dispense (because of the recalling of the Curse) but for which he no longer had any more use.

With respect to other aspects of the play we may be tempted to believe that Shelley did not so much change his mind as fail to make it up. This issue is most urgent in so far as it affects the conception of Prometheus. The question can be simplified in the following terms. Rieger admits that the drama is 'on one level a maddeningly recondite allegory of the operations of the human mind'.[1] In terms of this allegory does Prometheus represent the human mind itself in its totality, or one of its faculties or powers? In other words, is Prometheus to be seen as the subject—in the philosophical sense—of the drama, as the only truly active character of whom the others are aspects or projections, with the exception of Demogorgon? Or is Man the true subject, never appearing as a character, while his mental operations are figured in the activities of the characters? Each of these alternative interpretations can be carried to illuminating lengths, without it being possible finally to choose either or to reconcile them in a third.

The first interpretation is the most immediately attractive, and is what might be called the orthodox reading now current. Wasserman adopts it by seeing Prometheus as a figure of the 'One Mind' of which individual human minds are portions; this reading does not exactly interpret him as representing the human mind, but it clearly sees him as more than an aspect of it.[2] Abrams also takes Prometheus to be the central subject: 'Various clues in the text, moreover, invite us to regard all the *dramatis personae*, except one, as externalized correlatives of the powers, aspects, and activities of Prometheus' own divided and conflicting self, and to regard even the altering natural setting as projections of Prometheus' mental states.'[3] An interpretation along such lines is strongly hinted at by Shelley himself when he describes Prometheus as 'the type of the highest perfection of moral and intellectual nature, impelled by the purest and the truest motives to the best and noblest ends' (Preface). Shelley's words serve to remind us that he is concerned with the moral rather than the metaphysical operations of the mind. Prometheus is presented as exemplary, a symbol of the true humanity to which each man should aspire. Along these lines we can construct an allegorical structure which fits the first three acts, by which Prometheus is enslaved not by exterior force but by his own 'opinion', and freed by his determination to rule himself and hence to refuse allegiance to any external power—a course followed by man at the close of Act III.

---

[1] *The Mutiny Within*, p. 16.
[2] *Shelley: A Critical Reading*, p. 257.
[3] *Natural Supernaturalism*, p. 302.

The words of the Curse make it clear that Jupiter's power was originally vested in him by Prometheus.

> Aye, do thy worst. Thou art Omnipotent.
>   O'er all things but thyself I gave thee power,
> And my own will.
> (I. 272–4)

Later Prometheus tells Mercury,

>   I gave all
> He has, and in return he chains me here
> Years, ages, night and day . . .
> (I. 381–3)

The same basic account is given by Asia.

>   Then Prometheus
> Gave wisdom, which is strength, to Jupiter
> And with this law alone: 'Let man be free,'
> Clothed him with the dominion of wide Heaven.
> (II. iv. 43–6)

It is never made clear why Prometheus handed over this power to Jupiter, but I am inclined to suspect that Shelley is implying an allegory of the liberal account of the origin of government, by which man submits to government in order to gain protection from his own unruly passions and impulses; he chooses to be ruled because he is incapable of self-rule. We are told that under Saturn's reign men were denied 'Self-empire and the majesty of love' (II. iv. 42), and their submission to the rule of Jupiter follows naturally from this. The condition made by Prometheus alludes to the liberal assumption that government can only be understood as an arrangement for the benefit of the governed, and hence the ruler is only entrusted with power as part of a tacit contract by which he is obliged to exercise it as a trust. But, as Hobbes saw, such a contract is self-defeating, since its terms endow the ruler with a power that enables him to evade his part of the bargain. To be a ruler, as Asia observes, is 'To know nor faith nor love nor law' (II. iv. 47–8). That Jupiter represents civil rule is undeniable; he is referred to as 'cruel King' (I. 50), 'Heaven's fell King' (I. 140), 'our almighty Tyrant' (I. 161), 'the Supreme Tyrant' (I. 208), 'the great King' (I. 457). He is also God, the 'prototype of human misrule'. The divine ruler is, as we have seen, a fiction created by man himself out of his ignorance and fear, but so is the human ruler; both ultimately derive their power from the acquiescence of their subjects. Hence Prometheus continues to uphold the power of Jupiter by continuing to believe in it—his alienation of power was not a single act once and for all, but is continued by his own acceptance of the reality of Jupiter's power, which cannot subsist without such acquiescence.[1] Even while he ostensibly denies Jupiter's power over him he sees his own situation as a parody of what he takes to be the reality of Jupiter's rule.

> me, who am they foe, eyeless in hate,
> Hast thou made reign and triumph, to thy scorn,
> O'er mine own misery and thy vain revenge.—
> Three thousand years of sleep-unsheltered hours
> And moments—aye divided by keen pangs
> Till they seemed years, torture and solitude,
> Scorn and despair,—these are mine empire:—
> More glorious far than that which thou surveyest
> From thine unenvied throne, O Mighty God!
> (I. 9–17)

Prometheus does not yet fully appreciate the truth he expresses here in all its bearings. A little more of what is here hinted at is revealed in the words of the Curse, where Prometheus erroneously calls Jupiter 'Omnipotent', even while stating that Jupiter does not have power over himself or over Prometheus' will. When he uttered the Curse Prometheus assumed that the latter was the vital exception, and the Curse itself represents the resistance of Prometheus' self-will to Jupiter's tyranny. As we have already seen, this negative attitude confirms Jupiter's power rather than destroying it. Jupiter's real weakness lies in his inability to rule himself, which Prometheus is able to do, if only by controlling his 'own misery' and refusing to bow to Jupiter's 'vain revenge'. The implicit suggestion that there are two kinds of rule, the true and the false, is made explicit by Prometheus in a flash of insight that arises from his awareness that he can endure the tortures of the Furies.

---

[1] See Stuart Curran, *Shelley's Annus Mirabilis: The Maturing of an Epic Vision* (San Marino, Calif., 1975), p. 196.

> Yet am I king over myself, and rule
> The torturing and conflicting throngs within
> As Jove rules you when Hell grows mutinous.
> (I. 492–4)

Again Prometheus sees a parallel between Jupiter's rule and his own, but a contrast between them is also implied: Prometheus rules himself, while Jupiter only rules the exterior creatures of his will. Simultaneously the terms of the simile tend to collapse into one another. The Furies *are* 'The torturing and conflicting throngs within'; it is only when man fails to repress the 'mutiny within' that they are projected out of himself and seen as external entities controlled by some superior power. An illustration of this occurs in *The Triumph of Life*, in the description of the shadows thrown off by men.

> Each, like himself and like each other were,
> At first, but soon distorted, seemed to be
>
> Obscure clouds moulded by the casual air;
> And of this stuff the car's creative ray
> Wrought all the busy phantoms that were there
>
> As the sun shapes the clouds—
> (lines 530–5)

This description is given by Rousseau, and it is clear that he is in error. Man has abdicated his control over these shapes—his own thoughts, words, and deeds—but there is no other 'creative' force that controls them. The shapes they take are bestowed by the human imagination, which similarly sees shapes in the clouds or in flames.[1] When Prometheus asserts control over the anarchy within he makes Jupiter's rule redundant, and simultaneously withdraws from him the materials from which his Hell was constructed. When Jupiter in his extremity calls on 'Hell' to wreak revenge on his behalf he discovers that the universe no longer acknowledges his rule: 'The elements obey me not . . .' (III. i. 80) The torturing of Prometheus by the Furies is paralleled by the consolation he receives from the Spirits. But the Spirits do not merely replace the

---

[1] On several occasions Shelley ascribes the perception of shapes in clouds or in the fire to the activity of the imagination (see *Works*, vii. 107, 228). See also 'Ode to Liberty', lines 61–4.

Furies—they *are* the Furies in another form. When Prometheus has resisted and mastered the tendency of his thoughts to lead him to despair, the same thoughts can minister to hope. The Spirits draw a lesson of love from the same incidents—war, shipwreck, dream, reverie—that the Furies invoked to tempt Prometheus to despair.[1] No doubt Shelley is making a distant allusion to Aeschylus' play *The Eumenides*, in which the Erinyes (Furies) are transformed into the Eumenides (Kindly Ones).

The hints in Act I concerning the ambivalent nature of 'rule' and the ultimate source of tyranny are developed in Act II when Asia interrogates Demogorgon. Paul Foot has offered an intriguing reading of this scene, seeing Asia as a revolutionary agitator whose questions are not seeking information, but are quite rhetorical, directed to the unawakened masses (Demogorgon) in order to stir them to action.[2] This interpretation cannot be pushed very far, but it does describe accurately enough the situation as Asia initially conceives it. Her opening questions concerning the creation of the world and what is good in the world are certainly designed to elicit the answers she receives—answers that are less helpful than she imagines, since they are implicit in the terms of her questions: 'I spoke but as ye speak' (II. iv. 112), Demogorgon laconically comments, when she later presses him to give some content to the term 'God'. But when Asia goes on to demand who created moral evil ('terror, madness, crime, remorse . . . Abandoned hope, and love that turns to hate;/And self-contempt' II. iv. 19, 24–5) she does not get the answer she was expecting. Demogorgon merely replies 'He reigns' (II. iv. 28). Asia wanted a *name*, and she wanted it for a very specific purpose.

> Utter his name—a world pining in pain
> Asks but his name; curses shall drag him down.
> (II. iv. 29–30)

Asia's intention now becomes only too clear: to extract from Demogorgon the name of the culprit, and to curse him. We have already seen what comes of curses. Demogorgon is not being as obstructive as Asia might think, for he is helping her to avoid Prometheus' error. By ascribing moral evil to 'He reigns' he both

---

[1] Compare the Chorus of the Furies (I. 495–520) with the speeches of the Spirits (I. 694–751).

[2] *Red Shelley*, Ch. vi (page refs. not available).

hints that the real problem is not located in the identity of the ruler (Asia clearly expected Jupiter to be named) but in the very existence of rule as the domination of one man by another, and also prompts her to question herself as to who really reigns, who is in ultimate control. Her reflections lead her to the surprising conclusion that this certainly cannot be Jupiter.

> Not Jove: while yet his frown shook Heaven, aye when
> His adversary from adamantine chains
> Cursed him, he trembled like a slave. Declare
> Who is his master? Is he too a slave?
> (II. iv. 106–9)

Asia is coming close to the central paradox of rule, as Demogorgon acknowledges by his confirmation of her guess.

> All spirits are enslaved who serve things evil:
> Thou knowest if Jupiter be such or no.
> (II. iv. 110–11)

Only a slave can be a tyrant—only a man devoid of the liberty that is self-rule can enslave others. Since Demogorgon can only tell Asia what she knows already, his highly uninformative, even evasive reply to her question 'Who is the master of the slave?' indicates either that she would not understand the answer if he gave it, or that she is asking about freedom which is a mystery about which nothing can be said. However Asia's own speech on human history has provided pointers as to where to look for ultimate power. She herself states that Prometheus 'Clothed [Jupiter] with the dominion of wide Heaven' (II. iv. 46), while her description of Prometheus' activity as patron of man draws on metaphors of power and rule: Prometheus 'tamed fire', he 'tortured to his will/Iron and gold', and 'taught to rule . . . The tempest-winged chariots of the Ocean' (II. iv. 66, 68–9, 92–3). The source of rule is in Prometheus himself, and moral evil is the result of his alienation of his own powers, by which Jupiter is allowed to establish the perverted rule of man over man. When Prometheus ceases to resist his self-caused evils by the sterile opposition of will, Love (Asia) can appeal to the eternal law by which causes are born from their effects (Demogorgon) for an abrogation of Jupiter's false and ultimately illusory rule. As he falls Jupiter himself recognizes that Prometheus has the ultimate power in the moral world.

> Gentle and just and dreadless, is he not
> The monarch of the world?
> (III. i. 68–9)

Prometheus could not save Jupiter, for all his repudiation of revenge, for true rule abolishes the false rule by a necessity which is unalterable.

Prometheus' repudiation of the false tyranny he had imposed on himself and his ascent to the autonomy of true rule is clearly presented as an example for man to follow. The closing lines of Act III celebrate a humanity that follows the Promethean model. The implications of these lines will lead us far.

> The painted veil, by those who were, called life,
> Which mimicked, as with colours idly spread,
> All men believed and hoped, is torn aside—
> The loathsome mask has fallen, the man remains
> Sceptreless, free, uncircumscribed—but man:
> Equal, unclassed, tribeless and nationless,
> Exempt from awe, worship, degree,—the King
> Over himself; just, gentle, wise—but man:
> Passionless? no—yet free from guilt or pain
> Which were, for his will made, or suffered them,
> Nor yet exempt, though ruling them like slaves,
> From chance and death and mutability,
> The clogs of that which else might oversoar
> The loftiest star of unascended Heaven
> Pinnacled dim in the intense inane.
> (III. iv. 190–204)

All the forms of Jupiter's reign are dismissed as a 'loathsome mask', a falsity that concealed man's true nature, which now emerges in its perfection.[1] This process includes a rejection of all that claims to rule or control man's activity; a repudiation of false rule that means an acceptance of the responsibilities of self-rule. Richard Cronin has pointed to the ambiguity by which 'the King' seems at first to belong with 'awe, worship, degree' as yet another negative condition to be rejected, and is then suddenly revealed as the positive description of the man who is free from external

---

[1] The simplistic conception of moral evil as a 'mask' which conceals man but is no part of him is implicitly criticized by Shelley's imagery elsewhere; see Chapter VII.

rule: 'King/Over himself'.[1] The phrase clearly recalls Prometheus' 'king over myself' (1. 492), and anticipates the sonnet to Benevento. The sonnet makes it clear that for Shelley to be 'the King over himself' is synonymous with being truly human: 'man who man would be', as he there puts it. To say that the true man is king over himself is to offer an analytic statement, rather than a synthetic one, in that it adds nothing to the first term but merely expounds its implications. It is worthy of note that the closing lines of Act III of *Prometheus Unbound* have virtually nothing to tell us about the regenerated man in positive terms. He is defined entirely by negatives. The preference for negative epithets is pervasive in Shelley's work, many of them being coinages of his own—*Prometheus Unbound* alone furnishes us with the following distinctively Shelleyan negatives: sleepless, eyeless, sleep-unsheltered, unenvied, unmeasured, shapeless, wingless, undefended, moveless, unresting, tongueless, inorganic, ineradicable, inarticulate, nameless, unaccustomed, undeclining, fruitless, boundless, unvanquished, endless, unimagined, unending, shelterless, unreprieved, unrepentant, lidless, unkindled, unchanted, untasted, slumberless, disenchanted, unwholesome, tearless, unremembered, cloudless, windless, unpent, headless, unupbraiding, woundless, printless, wordless, measureless, unspoken, undrawn, unenvying, ungazed upon, unbewailing, unheeded, friendless, fadeless, disunited, imageless, kingless, lampless, unrisen, unveiled, unextinguished, unsandalled, unrepressed, unbeheld, unbodied, dreadless, shoreless, bottomless, undazzling, unstain'd, sightless, unpastured, unexhausted, sunless, unwithering, uncommunicating, unwet, unwearied, undelaying, unerasing, untransmitted, untold, unmeant, unregarded, unreclaiming, sceptreless, uncircumscribed, unclassed, tribeless, nationless, passionless, unascended, unsealed, unpavilioned, unfathomed, lifeless, unremoved, unquiet, senseless, half unfrozen. That is a selective list, giving only those of Shelley's negatives which are out of the run of everyday speech. The extent to which Shelley's negatives are a distinctive part of his poetic

[1] 'Shelley's Language of Dissent', p. 211. The text as printed in 1820 reads 'awe, worship, degree, the king'. Reiman and Powers may have edited out a functional ambiguity by adopting the reading of Shelley's own final extant copy, 'awe, worship, degree,—the King' (see Lawrence John Zillman, *Shelley's Prometheus Unbound: A Variorum Edition* (Seattle, 1959), p. 259). Since Mary Shelley did not alter the reading of 1820 for her edition of 1839, it would seem that Shelley did not see fit to correct it in his list of *errata* to the 1820 edition.

style will be obvious to the reader who casts his eye over the above list and notes how often the individual words irresistibly recall their contexts to his mind. Many readers have registered this aspect of Shelley's style, even if not consciously, for it is one of the main factors behind the accusation of 'vagueness' so often and so vaguely brought against Shelley. Shelley has good reason to be 'vague', as Francis Berry recognizes in commenting that 'an understanding of Shelley's nature, as one which involved a detachment from the Present, in favour of the Future of his vision, explains the remoteness of his language from human actuality'.[1] Shelley exercises considerable ingenuity and inventiveness to keep his language remote from actuality, and this should cause us no surprise. It would seem rather obvious that a poet who is profoundly opposed to existing social conditions, and committed to what is no more than possible, will not always find the language of concrete realities the most suited to his purposes. Some of that language can be redeemed—as Shelley does with the language of rule—but much of it can only be negated. To refer to the regenerated man as 'passionate' would be to invite misunderstanding by readers who took for granted the hostility between passion and reason, a hostility that Shelley insists is peculiar to man's present condition; so Shelley can only indicate that he will be *not* 'passionless'. Since most of the forms of actuality are really negations of man's true being—a 'loathsome mask' in terms of which it can find no expression—Shelley's preference for negatives is really a negation of the negation, the nearest to a positive that is possible while this actuality continues to prevail.

The language of negation is the natural language of Perfectibility. In the final analysis Perfectibility does not offer any final goals, for it insists on continual change, and distrusts fixed goals as attempts to limit progress. It demands 'aspiration with no definable goal, or with a goal that can be defined only in terms of infinity'.[2] The poet who is a perfectibilarian—and Shelley has rightly been called 'the poet of perfectibility'[3]—will naturally adopt a language that negates all existing limits, while refraining from setting up new limits of its own. The best study to date of Shelley's fondness for negatives—the subject has been strangely neglected—recog-

[1] *Poets' Grammar: Person, Time and Mood in Poetry* (1958), p. 153.
[2] Wasserman, *Shelley: A Critical Reading*, p. 26.
[3] J. B. Bury, *The Idea of Progress*, p. 233.

nizes that it is intimately connected with his celebration of potentiality.[1] Kant, as we have seen, insisted that 'it is in the power of freedom to pass beyond any and every specified limit'. The transcendence of limit is hinted at in the very title of Shelley's drama, with its reference to Prometheus 'unbound'—this is moreover a calculated negation of the title of Aeschylus' *Prometheus Bound*. In Act IV 'unbound' becomes 'unbounded'. Shelley's critics have not scrupled to descend to personalities and to ascribe his opposition to limits to a narcissistic desire on his own part to be unconstrained and boundless. Such an argument is merely reductive, for Shelley acknowledges this desire too explicitly for it to be safe to assume that he has any need to pander to it covertly.

> I love all waste
> And solitary places; where we taste
> The pleasure of believing what we see
> Is boundless, as we wish our souls to be.
> (*Julian and Maddalo*, lines 14–17)

The deliberate overturning of all limitation in *Prometheus Unbound* has a political rather than a personal relevance. Shelley twice refers to the regenerated man as 'but man' (III. iv. 194, 197). The implication is partly '. . . and not some other, false thing', but it is also '*only* man, nothing superhuman'. But Shelley is not, despite the orthodox reading of these lines, concerned to deliver comfortable platitudes about human limitations—on the contrary. The repetition of 'but man' does not halt the movement of the verse, but checks it only to launch it on a fresh surge. To be man-and-nothing-but is not to be limited by human nature or the human condition, but to be in a state of boundless potentiality, a state only to be defined in negatives, for to ascribe positive attributes would be to limit it. Those things that appear to set limits should be regarded as obstacles—'clogs'—to be conquered and transcended. When man has negated the limits set by the moral evils he imposed on himself—'Which were, for his will made, or suffered them'—there remain other limits which may appear to be

---

[1] Timothy Webb, 'Shelley's Negatives.' Shelley's use of negative epithets has also been discussed, in Platonic rather than political terms, by John Buxton, *The Grecian Taste: Literature in the Age of Neo-Classicism 1710–1820* (London and Basingstoke, 1978), pp. 159–60.

inherent in the nature of man or the nature of things. Even regenerated man is not 'passionless'

> Nor yet exempt . . .
> From chance and death and mutability.

'*Nor yet*': the finality of such limits is only apparent. As a free agent man cannot accept any limits as final, because to do so is to make them final—to impose them on himself by his very acceptance. Jupiter's reign was eternal so long as his subjects thought it was; Paine, Burke, and Coleridge would make government eternal by their acknowledgement of its eternal necessity. Shelley is not indulging in any facile optimism about the possibility of conquering death, and those 'natural' evils he refers to as 'chance' and 'mutability'. He is insisting that man is not to acquiesce in them as limits; belief in his own eventual omnipotence must be his regulative principle, and he must always act 'as if', in Kantian phrase, his power can always be made equal to his desire. Not to do so would be to shirk his responsibility to become the master of his own fate, once he has become the master of his own soul. This responsibility is a moral imperative, and can therefore have no limit. There is no point to which man can come and then think he has done enough, for each conquest only brings him within sight of fresh realms to conquer. Shelley's concluding gesture towards 'the intense inane' is disturbing because it reveals the infinte perspectives in terms of which his thought operates. That 'star pinnacled dim in the intense inane' is the furthest goal man can set himself, so distant it seems unreachable. But when it is reached —and we must say *when* rather than *if*—more goals will be visible from it. Shelley was well aware that progress depends on setting up the reachable goal as the guide to immediate action, as we shall see in considering his political activities. But in *Prometheus Unbound*, where his concern is with the last word rather than with the next one, he would insist that no goal is to be ruled out *a priori* as unattainable.

Many readers seem to have been puzzled by Shelley's reference to regenerated man as

> Nor yet exempt, *though ruling them like slaves*,
> From chance and death and mutability.

Milton Wilson writes, 'it is difficult to decide exactly what is meant by "ruling them like slaves", unless it simply means the application of scientific discoveries which control disease, and thereby prolong life, but do not finally destroy mutability'.[1] I am no more satisfied with this explanation than Mr Wilson seems to be. A problem that resists so able a critic of Shelley deserves close attention. To understand what Shelley means we must consider his theory of evil. Melvin Rader has claimed that in *Prometheus Unbound* Shelley 'distinguishes . . . between two types of evil: one sort is ineradicable and objectively grounded; the other sort is subjective but deeply based'.[2] This is the distinction between 'physical' evil—death, disease, earthquakes, famine, and so on—and 'moral' evil—hatred, fear, self-contempt, slavery, tyranny, and so on—which I have already invoked implicitly. It is a most important distinction in Shelley's prose, though he deliberately blurs it in his poetry. We have already considered Shelley's remark that if Christ's doctrines were put into practice 'man exempt from the internal evils of his own choice would be left free to struggle with the physical evils which exist in spite of him'. He originally wrote 'which are his portion'.[3] It is easy to see why he corrected this; moral evil differs from physical evil in being within man's immediate control as the creation of 'his own choice' ('Which were, for his will made, or suffered them'), but that does not mean that he is to acquiesce in the existence of physical evil as an unalterable 'portion' (*pace* Rader). As Shelley elsewhere insists, man is committed to conquering both; men are 'to attempt the conquest of their own evil passions, and of the difficulties of the material world'.[4] The conquest of moral evil naturally comes first, and its achievement not only leaves man's energies free to ameliorate his physical condition but also makes physical evil itself less pernicious. Physical evil is bad in itself but is made far worse by man's inability to control his own passions, for this lack of self-rule leaves him helpless and morally vulnerable. Milton Wilson has well remarked that 'For Shelley the terrible thing about slavery and physical hardship is that the will may allow itself to be corrupted by them'.[5] Moral weakness lays man open to the onslaughts

---

[1] *Shelley's Later Poetry: A Study of his Prophetic Imagination* (New York, 1959), p. 174.
[2] 'Shelley's Theory of Evil' (1930), in *Shelley: A Collection of Critical Essays*, edited by G. M. Ridenour (Englewood Cliffs, N. J., 1965), p. 105
[3] *Works*, vi. 370 (note to vi. 255, line 15). See above, p. 89.
[4] See above, p. 92.   [5] *Shelley's Later Poetry*, p. 23.

of physical evil, and they breed moral evil within him. The man who can control 'the anarchy of hopes and fears' within is not exempt from physical suffering, but he is not corrupted by it. Carl Woodring puts the point wittily when he observes that, in Shelley's Paradise, 'thorns remain, but the virtuous man knows no pain from their pricking'.[1] This is an exaggeration; he feels the pricking, but he does not react with fear, anger, or resentment. What Shelley means in detail can be illustrated from the example of death, the one physical evil which *may* be 'ineradicable'. Even the virtuous man must die, but death and, even more, the fear of death need not poison his life. In *Prometheus Unbound* the Earth promises that

> death shall be the last embrace of her
> Who takes the life she gave, even as a mother
> Folding her child, says, 'Leave me not again.'
> (III. iii. 105–7)

It will be like this, because this is how man will approach death. In the achieved Paradise of *Queen Mab* Death remains, but is accepted as a 'slow necessity', with hope rather than with dread (IX. 57–61, 161–3). If man cannot escape death he can escape that fear of death which, as Shelley says, has been a 'contemplation of inexhaustible melancholy whose shadow eclipses the brightness of the world' (*Works* vi. 206). Shelley's intention in writing his own unfinished essay on 'A Future State' (1818–19) is made clear in a cancelled passage. 'The fear of death rather than the love of life then renders the grave terrible. If the world were not disquieted by this fear and the hope of transvital existence natural old age would sink down calmly upon its couch of rest'.[2] The bleak rationalism with which Shelley marshals the evidence against a future life has encouraged his editors to consider 'A Future State' an early work. It is in fact contemporary with the writing of *Prometheus Unbound* (probably composed between Act I and Act II), and Shelley's intention is to enable man to control the hopes and fears that plague him concerning death by showing him what certain knowledge he can have on the subject. To be sure that death is final may be valuable if it frees him from doubt.[3]

---

[1] *Politics in English Romantic Poetry*, p. 297.

[2] Bodl. MS Shelley adds. e. 11, pp. 128ᵛ–129ᵛ.

[3] Shelley evidently intended to consider the positive case for a future life, though all he wrote was the first sentence: 'But there is another point of view

Because the conquest of moral evil is the immediate task and the necessary prelude to the successful conquest of physical evil,[1] Shelley emphasizes the distinction between them in his prose speculations. In his poetry, however, he seems concerned to blur the distinction. Only a moral regeneration is within man's power in the immediate prospect, but in both *Queen Mab* and *Prometheus Unbound* Shelley suggests that this moral regeneration immediately produces, or rather is synonymous with, the abolition of major physical evils. In *Queen Mab* Shelley seems to be deliberately superimposing the results of regenerated man's activity upon his regeneration, telescoping the time involved to suggest that the world will be transformed at a stroke. In *Prometheus Unbound* he suggests that carnivorous birds will become vegetarians and poisonous berries will then be wholesome food for them (III. iv. 78–83). The implication that a total restructuring of the world's ecology will be a direct result of man's moral reform is clearly not to be taken literally. Such passages function as potent images of desire, and serve as reminders that to establish a rigid distinction between moral and physical evil may lead to acquiescence in the latter as constituting an unpassable limit to what man can achieve. The only inescapable limits and ineradicable evils are those that are accepted as such; and Shelley's purpose in *Prometheus Unbound* is to enlarge our imaginative apprehension of the world to such a point that we can see that such acceptance is neither necessary nor desirable.

When man enters on the path of infinite perfectibility he is fulfilling the demands of his own nature, but he cannot be said to be following the example of Prometheus. Progress into the infinite has no meaning for Prometheus, who is immortal, and therefore not subject to chance, death, or mutability. But without such obstacles there can be no progress, for progress is the successive conquest of obstacles. The only obstacles for Prometheus were

---

from which the Universe may be considered, totally different' (Bodl. MS Shelley adds. e. 11, p. 112ᵛ). Shelley clearly recognized that a positive view of the subject demanded an imaginative transformation of the way in which it was viewed.

[1] 'The cultivation of those sciences which have enlarged the limits of the empire of man over the external world, has, for want of the poetical faculty, proportionally circumscribed those of the internal world; and man, having enslaved the elements, remains himself a slave' (*Works*, vii. 134).

imposed on him by himself, and he must free himself from these at
a stroke; having done so, he has come to the end, where man has
found his beginning. Prometheus bound suffered under the same
self-imposed evils as man, and the process of liberation into self-
rule is the same for both. But the liberated Prometheus cannot
be the model for liberated man. While the latter extends his
dominion over the universe, Prometheus retires with Asia. Act IV,
the celebration of human potentiality, takes place without
Prometheus, and without Asia or Jupiter for that matter; the three
immortals have disappeared from the scene. I am indebted to a
pregnant observation made by Richard Cronin in conversation, to
the effect that all three disappear to the same place. When Jupiter
falls he is dragged down to 'the abyss', 'to the dark void' (III. ii. 10)
which is the realm of Demogorgon. The last we hear of Prometheus
and Asia is their retreat to a Cavern, once the source of poisonous
vapours which are now harmless and even beneficial (III. iii. 124–
47). The same cavern was earlier described as

> the mighty portal,
> Like a volcano's meteor-breathing chasm,
> Whence the oracular vapour is hurled up . . .
> (II. iii. 2–4)

But this 'portal' is the entrance to 'the realm/Of Demogorgon'
(II. iii. 1–2). The natural conclusion would seem to be that Jupiter,
Prometheus, and Asia have all been reabsorbed into this realm,
the ultimate source of all potentiality. This is death, as far as
death is possible for immortals. Prometheus accepts with perfect
equanimity the prospect of retiring to his Cave

> Where we will sit and talk of time and change
> As the world ebbs and flows, ourselves unchanged—
> What can hide man from Mutability?—
> (III. iii. 23–5)

That this is essentially a farewell is made clear by the echoes of
Lear's speech to Cordelia.

> so we'll live
> And pray, and sing, and tell old tales, and laugh
> At gilded butterflies, and hear poor rogues
> Talk of court news; and we'll talk with them too—
> Who loses and who wins; who's in, who's out—

And take upon's the mystery of things
As if we were God's spies; and we'll wear out
In a wall'd prison packs and sects of great ones
That ebb and flow by th'moon.
(*King Lear*, v. iii. 11–19)

The pathos of Lear's speech lies in the fact that the only retreat from the world that he and Cordelia will know will come through their death. Prometheus and Asia too are fated to extinction as separate existences, though, their work completed, this is a fate they can face with tranquillity, unlike Jupiter, who resists the fall into non-entity desperately and vainly. If we follow the implications through we shall conclude that Prometheus, Asia, and Jupiter are all aspects or faculties of the human mind, who disappear as separate entities when the mind heals its own divisions. If we previously argued that Jupiter's existence depended on Prometheus, it would seem from this perspective that Prometheus, depends on Jupiter. Prometheus can only exist in a mind already divided against itself, so that he and Jupiter, antidote and poison, are brought about by the same act of the mind; hence the symbiotic relationship between them in the drama. The outlines of a fairly coherent moral allegory begin to emerge, in which Prometheus stands for Will, Asia represents Love, and Jupiter is (to hazard a borrowing from Blake) the principle of Selfhood, or perhaps a perversion of the Will that cannot be reconciled with Love. In fact Jupiter stands for too much for a single allegorical reading to be adequate. At one level he represents the original selfish instincts of human nature as Shelley describes them.

The immediate emotions of his nature especially in its most inartificial state prompt him to inflict pain and to arrogate dominion. He desires to heap·superfluities to his own store letting others perish with famine. He is propelled to guard against the smallest invasion of his own liberty, though he reduces others to a condition of the most pitiless servitude. He is revengeful, proud and selfish. (*Works*, vii. 73)

Jupiter is also the fear that leads to the creation of false gods, the self-mistrust and self-contempt that prompts despair, and so on. When this 'anarchy of hopes and fears' is, by some inexplicable original error, released, then the only hope lies in resolute fortitude, a negative resistance by the Will. Shelley's hopes for man's self-rule unavoidably give an important function to the will, by which the internal anarchy is to be repressed and controlled. The will is frequently invoked by Prometheus, who reproaches the Earth,

> Mother, thy sons and thou
> Scorn him, without whose all-enduring will
> Beneath the fierce omnipotence of Jove
> Both they and thou had vanished like thin mist
> Unrolled on the morning wind!
> (I. 113–17)

In the Curse he explicitly excepts his 'own will' from the power of Jupiter (I. 274). As we have seen, this negative resistance of the Will perpetuates what it is opposed to. The Curse, the very embodiment of counter-productive opposition, must be withdrawn and Will join with Love, before the reign of Jupiter will end. Thus Mary Shelley missed Shelley's meaning when she claimed that he believed 'that mankind had only to *will* that there should be no evil, and there would be none'.[1] Even if Mary Shelley only means moral evil, she is wrong to see will as a positive force. John Flagg has marshalled considerable evidence in support of his view that for Shelley the concept of will is essentially negative.[2] The will can certainly impose evil on man—

> it is our will
> That thus enchains us to permitted ill—
> (*Julian and Maddalo*, lines 170–1)

but it does not follow that the will alone can release us from this self-imposed prison. Julian is right to draw the conclusion that 'We might be otherwise' (line 172), but being 'otherwise' depends on the exercise of the Imagination, or, to use terms that are interchangeable for Shelley, on Love.

The proper relation between Will and Love is defined in the Earth's lyric in Act IV of *Prometheus Unbound*, which draws together most of the strands we have been considering in our discussion of the drama.

> It [Love] interpenetrates my granite mass,
> Through tangled roots and trodden clay doth pass

---

[1] 'Note on *Prometheus Unbound*' (emphasis added).
[2] Prometheus Unbound *and* Hellas: *An Approach to Shelley's Lyrical Dramas* (Salzburg, 1972), pp. 58–84.

Into the utmost leaves and delicatest flowers;
  Upon the winds, among the clouds 'tis spread,
  It wakes a life in the forgotten dead,
They breathe a spirit up from their obscurest bowers

  And like a storm, bursting its cloudly prison
  With thunder and with whirlwind, has arisen
Out of the lampless caves of unimagined being,
  With earthquake shock and swiftness making shiver
  Thought's stagnant chaos, unremoved forever,
Till Hate and Fear and Pain, light-vanquished shadows,
    fleeing,

  Leave Man, who was a many-sided mirror
  Which could distort to many a shape of error
This true fair world of things—a Sea reflecting Love;
  Which over all his kind, as the Sun's Heaven
  Gliding o'er Ocean, smooth, serene and even,
Darting from starry depths radiance and light, doth move,

  Leave Man, even as a leprous child is left
  Who follows a sick beast to some warm cleft
Of rocks, through which the might of healing springs
    is poured;
  Then when it wanders home with rosy smile
  Unconscious, and its mother fears awhile
It is a Spirit—then weeps on her child restored.

  Man, oh, not men! a chain of linked thought,
  Of love and might to be divided not,
Compelling the elements with adamantine stress—
  As the Sun rules, even with a tyrant's gaze,
  The unquiet Republic of the maze
Of Planets, struggling fierce towards Heaven's free
    wilderness.

  Man, one harmonious Soul of many a soul
  Whose nature is its own divine controul
Where all things flow to all, as rivers to the sea;
  Familiar acts are beautiful through love;
  Labour and Pain and Grief in life's green grove
Sport like tame beasts—none knew how gentle they could be!

His Will, with all mean passions, bad delights,
And selfish cares, its trembling satellites,
A spirit ill to guide, but mighty to obey,
Is as a tempest-winged ship, whose helm
Love rules, through waves which dare not overwhelm,
Forcing life's wildest shores to own its sovereign sway.

All things confess his strength.—Through the cold mass
Of marble and of colour his dreams pass;
Bright threads, whence mothers weave the robes their
children wear;
Language is a perpetual Orphic song,
Which rules with Dædal harmony a throng
Of thoughts and forms, which else senseless and
shapeless were.

The Lightning is his slave; Heaven's utmost deep
Gives up her stars, and like a flock of sheep
They pass before his eye, are numbered, and roll on!
The Tempest is his steed,—he strides the air;
And the abyss shouts from her depth laid bare,
'Heaven, has thou secrets? Man unveils me, I have none.'
(IV. 370–423)

A full commentary on this important lyric would occupy more
space than we have available here. It is an unequivocal celebration
of Man as ruler. The movement of the first four stanzas refuses to
be contained by the limits of the poetic form, as the sense runs
across line endings, and even leaps the gaps between stanzas. The
effect is of an exuberance that verges on the chaotic. The challenge
is met in the last five stanzas, where the poet is successsful in
reducing his material to order by a creative imposition of his control.
The lioes thus enact what is their subject, man's rule over
himself and over the external world. Since man and his world are
interdependent the distinctions between physical and mental,
internal and external are deliberately broken down. The concepts
of physical forces (gravitation), morality (self-rule), and social
activity (domestication of animals, exploration and colonization,
the arts and sciences) illustrate each other to the point that tenor
and vehicle become difficult to distinguish. It is not just that Shelley
is moving from image to image because no single image is adequate,

as he often does, but that all the images here are relevant and serve to qualify each other. We are being asked to envisage a control exercised by man over himself which is absolute, yet at the same time in harmony with the processes of the outside world. By ruling himself man is not doing violence to his nature, for ideally reason and passion, law and impulse should be identical. At this point one can glimpse a private fear that Shelley generally suppresses. The tenets of philosophical anarchism naturally lead to extreme individualism; but a world of unconnected individuals would be no ideal world for Shelley. It is significant that Godwin concluded in *Political Justice* that 'We ought to be able to do without one another', and then went on to make the anguish of moral isolation the subject of virtually all his fiction.[1] Shelley feels compelled to repudiate an atomistic individualism ('Man, oh, not men!') and to invoke Love as the force that will make 'one harmonious Soul of many a soul'. 'Love' can mean many things of course, and to appreciate what Shelley means we must look at his definition of it in terms of the Imagination. 'The great secret of morals is love; or a going out of our own nature, and an identification of ourselves with the beautiful which exists in thought, action, or person, not our own. . . . The great instrument of moral good is the imagination . . .' (*Works*, vii. 118).[2] The Will is executive only, and is easily perverted to the assertion of the self; this is Jupiter's condition. Love or Imagination gives access to what is outside the self, and it must give guidance to the Will. Hence the regeneration of man is not moral in a limited sense but is an imaginative transformation of his condition. The whole of Act IV celebrates man's birth into a universe that is alive because it is apprehended imaginatively. A hint is dropped at the end of Act III when the Spirit of the Earth asks,

> wouldst thou think that toads and snakes and efts
> Could e'er be beautiful?—yet so they were
> And that with little change of shape or hue . . .
> (III. iv. 74–6)

The world has changed less in reality than in the Spirit's vision of

---

[1] *Political Justice*, ii. 505. See D. H. Monro, *Godwin's Moral Philosophy: An Interpretation of William Godwin* (1953), pp. 7, 67.

[2] The development and nature of Shelley's ideas on the Imagination are treated in detail in Chapter VI.

it. As George Wilson Knight recognized there is an echo here of
Coleridge's *Ancient Mariner*, where the Mariner suddenly finds
himself blessing the water-snakes which he had previously found
loathsome.[1] In both cases 'a changed expression in the self precedes
and generates the changed recognition of what is without'.[2]

On this interpretation the true subject—again in a philosophical
sense—of the drama is man. The three immortals, Prometheus,
Jupiter, and Asia, are potentialities contained within man, immortal
because they are present in all men at all times as potentialities.
As Demogorgon reminds us at the end of Act IV, Jupiter may have
fallen, but his return is an ever imminent possibility; if it should
happen Prometheus and Asia must also return to play their
respective roles. It follows that Prometheus is not an absolute but
a relative ideal; and in Act I he is treated with an irony that would
be hard to reconcile with his apparent role as a complete model
of man. Prometheus may revoke the Curse, but he never seems to
realize why it was wrong, nor does he come to full awareness of
the extent to which he and Jupiter are interdependent. It would
also seem that Jupiter is relatively rather than absolutely evil. In
the complete man Jupiter too has a role to play, if a strictly
subordinate one. The imagery of Act IV makes it clear that regenerated man will have scope for the absolute domination
previously associated with Jupiter. Even Prometheus sees a parallel
between his kind of rule and Jupiter's.

> Yet am I king over myself, and rule
> The torturing and conflicting throngs within
> As Jove rules you when Hell grows mutinous.
> (I. 492–4)

Demogorgon's gloss on Jupiter's fall—'Conquest is dragged
Captive through the Deep' (IV. 556)—serves as a paradoxical
reminder that, if conquest is to be repudiated, the desire for
conquest must itself be conquered.

> Conquerors have conquered their foes alone,
> Whose revenge, pride, and power they have overthrown:
> Ride ye, more victorious, over your own.
> ('An Ode written October 1819', lines 26–8)

---

[1] *The Starlit Dome: Studies in the Poetry of Vision* (1941; 1971), p. 217.
[2] Michael Cooke, *The Romantic Will* (New Haven and London, 1976), p. 35.

Prometheus Unbound is an astonishing work, but by no means an unflawed one. We may christen it a 'psychodrama', but we cannot deny that the dramatic reality of the characters sometimes conflicts with their roles as psychological entities. Some confusion concerning the basic conceptual scheme seems to exist in Shelley's own mind. Prometheus is presented both as an ideal and a model for man—this is how he is described in the Preface, presumably written when the drama was complete—and also as one of several faculties in the human mind. The active role assigned to Asia (itself probably a departure from Shelley's original plan), and the absence of Prometheus and the other immortals during the lyrical celebration of Act IV, both suggest the latter interpretation, without it being possible for us to discard the former. Part of the fascination of the work lies in the fact that we not only see Shelley's mature political ideas embodied in it, but in its very uncertainties we are able to detect them in the process of crystallizing out.

CHAPTER IV

Shelley in Ireland

IN CHAPTER I we considered some ideological aspects of the background to Shelley's political mission to Ireland in February and March of 1812. We need now to look briefly at some preceding events in the sister island. In 1809 a new period of Catholic organization had begun under the newly formed Catholic Committee.[1] The moving force behind the Catholic agitation was now the young lawyer Daniel O'Connell, a radical who opposed the preponderance of aristocratic influence in Catholic counsels and was determined to break with the 'Ryan faction' of moderates who had compromised the Catholic claims in order to co-operate with the Whigs.[2] O'Connell, like Shelley, considered that the Irish cause was not to be promoted by the Catholic aristocrats and their Foxite allies, and he looked instead to an appeal to popular feeling and the establishment of a country-wide organization in communication with the central Committee—a project that was in danger of running foul of the Convention Act of 1793 which forbade the setting up of representative bodies.[3] The appointment of a committee of delegates in 1811 to draw up various addresses and petitions so alarmed the Irish Secretary that he ordered the arrest of those concerned in the elections under the provisions of this Act.[4] The Catholic proposal to hold elections for a new committee in July was met by a government Proclamation forbidding it—John Philpot Curran, whom Shelley met through Godwin's introduction, was one of the privy councillors who refused to sign this proclamation. The Catholic Committee decided to persevere and to bring the issue of the right to petition to a head. When Dr Sheridan was brought to trial for his part in the elections the

[1] See Thomas Wyse, *Historical Sketch of the late Catholic Association of Ireland* (2 vols., 1829), i. 9–10; and *State of the Catholic Cause, from the Issuing of Mr. Pole's Circular Letter, to the Present Day* [edited by W. H. Hamilton] (Dublin, 1812), pp. 5–6.
[2] Wyse, op. cit. i. 138–40.
[3] Ibid. i. 144, 173–4.
[4] Ibid i. 175–6.
[5] Hamilton, op. cit., pp. 30–56.

result was acquittal.[1] A leading Dublin opposition newspaper (itself Protestant) hailed this event in significant terms.

the union of Protestant, Catholic, and Presbyterian . . . this IMMORTAL VERDICT, has CEMENTED, we trust, for ever. A Jury composed of PROTESTANTS and PRESBYTERIANS has found a Verdict in favour of the aggrieved Catholic—in favour of Public Right—in favour of Ireland—in favour of the Empire.[2]

Whatever the attitude of the government, public opinion favoured the Catholics. When in the following month a meeting of the Catholic Committee was dispersed and Lords Fingal and Netterville taken into custody the Catholics decided to submit temporarily. They still had faith in the good intentions of the Regent, whom they toasted as 'the early and enlightened Friend of Ireland, and her proudest Hope'; and an Aggregate Meeting held on 26 November showed, to the satisfaction of the Whig *Morning Chronicle*, 'their confidence in the PRINCE'.[3] The meeting agreed to wait until the restrictions on the Regent expired in February 1812, in the expectation that their claims would then be satisfied, and voted to present an Address to the Regent and adjourn until 28 February, when they would reassemble in the Fishamble Street Theatre.[4]

When they did reassemble their hopes in the Regent had been shattered. The same issue of the *Dublin Weekly Messenger* that greeted the philanthropic efforts of 'Pierce Byshe Shelly, Esq' had as its leader a long and ironically italicized article on the perfidy of the Regent.[5] However, the dismayed Catholics could find no response to this treachery beyond yet another Address, though Sir Thomas Wyse lamented the Prince's desertion of the principles of Fox and his adherence to 'a shameful coalition'.[6] However the possibility that their disappointment might drive them into a more radical position must have occurred to Shelley, and he took good care to be present at the long-awaited meeting

---

[1] For a full account of the trial see ibid., pp. 266–323.
[2] *Dublin Evening Post*, 23 Nov. 1811 (quoted from the *Morning Chronicle*, 27 Nov. 1811).
[3] *Morning Chronicle*, 25, 31 Dec. 1811.
[4] *Morning Chronicle*, 31 Dec. 1811.
[5] *Dublin Weekly Messenger*, 7 Mar. 1812.
[6] Home Office report of the meeting, quoted in MacCarthy, *Shelley's Early Life*, p. 238.

on 28 February.[1] It is not clear whether he had intended to do so when he first decided to go to Ireland. He placed more reliance on the written word, and in defending the project to Godwin he asserted with vigour the value of written discussion and early practice in composition (*Letters*, i. 231, 242–3). Determined to spread the teachings of Godwin (rather against the master's will), Shelley had written most of his first pamphlet, *An Address, to the Irish People*, before he left England.[2] Before we condemn him for making up his mind before having examined the situation at first hand we should remember that English politicians were quite prepared to legislate for Ireland from a similar position of ignorance, that Ireland was treated as an aspect of domestic politics, and that the problems of the sister island were notorious. As Cobbett put it, 'To know the state of Ireland we need not go thither. . .'.[3] I hope to show that Shelley's views were by no means ill-informed, however clumsy his expression of them may have been on occasions.

Shelley's *Address* was a deliberate attempt to popularize his own advanced ideas; 'it consists of the benevolent and tolerant deductions of Philosophy reduced into the simplest language,' he assured Godwin, 'and such as those who by their uneducated poverty are the most susceptible of evil impressions from Catholicism may clearly comprehend.' (*Letters*, i. 243) Popularizing is more difficult than Shelley seems to have realized—he was always more at ease when addressing a cultured audience of his own class—and the pamphlet suffers from what may appear to be a rather condescending tone, and from an over-emphatic iteration of the main points; Shelley was only too acurate in referring to 'The pains which I have taken even to tautology to insist on pacific measures' (*Letters*, i. 268). Shelley might well have taken a hint from the work of a more experienced propagandist, here given in its entirety—brevity being one of its great merits.

Roman Catholics of Ireland.
For Christ's sake, and for the tender mercy of God, do not take up arms in your defence or any one else's on any account whatsoever; in that respect act exactly like the Quakers (bear and forbear) suffer wrongs

---

[1] There is no evidence to support Richard Holmes's assertion that Shelley was 'invited' to speak by the Catholic Committee (*Shelley: the Pursuit* (1974), p. 120).
[2] *Letters*, i. 233–4, 238–9, 243.
[3] *Political Register*, 15 May 1813, p. 723.

patiently for Christ's sake, and the Lord in time will relieve you; do not be foolishly led away by any show or false promise, to leave your poor parents, wife, or families breaking their hearts after you; forfeiting your religion, or duty to God, the Church, and your neighbour.

Remember. 'He that lives by the sword, must die by the sword.'—Therefore, for the Lord's sake, enter not into combination or private meetings of any sort that may give the least offence to Government. Be thoroughly resigned to the will of the Lord, and God will bless you and your's.[1]

The *Morning Chronicle* noted with disdain that this broadsheet was 'said to be distributed, as will be seen by the style it could be intended for none other, among the very lowest of the Catholics of Dublin'—precisely the audience that Shelley wished to reach. It was evidently circulated by the Catholic Committee, who hoped to gain their ends peacefully and were concerned to prevent popular disturbances which could only harm the cause.[2] The anonymous writer (clearly an educated man) and Shelley were concerned to recommend the same pacific course of action to their common audience, but it is clear that the former had a better chance of gaining a hearing, since he refrained from making excessive demands on its attention, and was able to draw on the language of Catholic devotion. We have no information as to how Shelley's pamphlet was received, apart from his own statement that it had 'excited a sensation of wonder in Dublin' (*Letters*, i. 263). Since it was addressed to the uneducated and inarticulate masses the lack of recorded response is hardly surprising. But a pamphlet representing the viewpoint of a single individual (and that an extreme one) could have attracted only passing attention in an age of eccentric pamphleteering. The Irish were more inclined to place their trust in their own leaders and in the Regent than in the schemes of an individual enthusiast.

Closer acquaintance with conditions in Ireland—or rather in Dublin—seems to have confirmed Shelley in his existing opinions. First-hand experience only gave a sharper edge to the knowledge that all well-informed Englishmen had concerning the distress and

---

[1] *Morning Chronicle*, 10 Jan. 1812.

[2] In January 1812 the Catholic leaders themselves took the lead in exposing the plot of the schoolmaster Keegan, who boasted when in his cups that he was 'secretary to the new association established for the purpose of separating Ireland from England by force of arms'; John O'Connell considered that the affair was a government plot intended to discredit the Catholics (see *The Life and Speeches of Daniel O'Connell, M.P.*, edited by John O'Connell (2 vols., Dublin, 1846), i. 131–4).

misery that existed in Ireland. Even so, to be brought face to face with the reality caused Shelley a shock which is registered in his report to Godwin.

I had no conception of the depth of human misery until now.—The poor of Dublin are assuredly the meanest & most miserable of all.—In their narrow streets thousands seem huddled together—one mass of animated filth! With what eagerness do such scenes inspire me, how selfconfident too, do I feel in my asumption to teach the lessons of virtue to those who grind their fellow beings into worse than annihilation. These were the persons to whom in my fancy I had addressed myself; how quickly were my views on this subject changed! yet how deeply has this very change rooted the conviction on which I came hither. (*Letters*, i. 268)

What is surprising here is the air of optimism with which Shelley announces his disillusion. An interesting contrast is afforded by a letter written by Keats over six years later. Keats may well have had Shelley's Irish adventure in mind, which he would have seen as a good example of what he elsewhere called, not without irony, Shelley's 'magnanimity'.[1] Having seen the misery and d egradation of the Irish poor, Keats commented, 'What a tremendous diffi-culty is the improvement of the condition of such people—I cannot conceive how a mind "with child" of Philanthropy could gra[s]p at possibility—with me it is absolute despair.'[2] 'Philan-thropy' was a favourite word with Shelley, especially in his Irish pamphlets. He was able to 'grasp at possibility' at least partly thanks to his quick instinct for practical charity, and he devoted considerable exertions to alleviating the misery with which he came in contact. We have seen his attempts to help the Irish expatriate Redfern, and he made similar attempts to help victims of oppression in Dublin, on occasion remonstrating with the agents of the law (*Letters*, i. 270–1). The inevitable realization of how little such isolated exertions could effect brought Shelley close to disgust if not despair. 'I am sick of this city,' he wrote to Miss Hitchener, '& long to be with you and peace' (i. 271). His experiences only strengthened his conviction that political changes were necessary to bring improvement on the necessary scale; an issue on which, as we shall see, he came into conflict with Godwin.

The letter to Godwin just quoted makes it clear that his views

---

[1] See *The Letters of John Keats 1814–1821*, edited by Hyder E. Rollins (2 vols., Cambridge, 1958), ii. 323.
[2] Ibid. i. 321.

as to the nature of the necessary political changes did not alter. He gives the impression that his plan of an association, expounded in his second pamphlet, was a response to his own experience of Irish conditions (*Works*, v. 246), but, as we shall see, it had been germinating in his mind for at least a year. He was willing to adapt his plans somewhat to Irish conditions and opinion but fundamentally they did not change. His exposition of these plans, *Proposals for an Association*, was conceived by 14 February, in the press by 24 February, and printed before 8 March.[1] This rapidity suggests that Shelley was merely applying ideas on political action which had been formed previously. Before this pamphlet was published Shelley took the opportunity to air his views at the Aggregate Meeting on 28 February. Despite their disgust at the Regent's treachery this meeting had little recourse but to approve, 'unanimously', an Address to the Regent and a Petition to Parliament as prepared by the Committee. These documents (substantially identical) stressed the Catholics' determination to act only within the framework of the constitution and by legal means.[2] It was therefore hardly likely that they would endorse Shelley's proposed association whose legality was dubious. The Address, with its 'respectful, but firm and explicit, language', is but one indication of the 'state of moderation' in which the hope of relief kept the Catholics until the rejection of their appeals by Parliament—by which time Shelley was back in England.[3] The good order and discipline of the Catholics prevented their 'indignation' at the Regent's conduct spilling over into 'blind insurrections' as Shelley had feared (*Letters*, i. 258). But this moderation also defused the crisis on which he had relied to provide support for his plans.

We do not know all the contents of Shelley's speech at the Aggregate Meeting since the newspaper reports omitted passages that the audience disapproved of (*Letters*, i. 275). All the reports agree that he attacked the Union with England and that he repeated his opinion that Repeal was of more moment than Emancipation.[4] Since the declared business of the meeting was to

[1] *Letters*, i. 255, 258–9, 268. Publication had been scheduled for 2 March (ibid. i. 263).
[2] *Morning Chronicle*, 3 Mar. 1812.
[3] *Annual Register* (1812), 'General History', p. 134. For the text of the Address see 'State Papers', pp. 342–6.
[4] The newspaper reports are reprinted in *Works*, vii. 317–18.

petition for Emancipation Shelley was clearly attempting to radicalize its position and extend its frame of reference (he also directed its attention to 'the state of the representation'). But to attack the Union was quite in accord with the avowed policies of the more aggressive and popular Catholic leaders. O'Connell himself went so far as to say: 'I abandon all wish for emancipation if it delays that Repeal.'[1] Repeal was a national rather than a purely Catholic cause and Shelley was following the example of the Irish leaders in seeking to sink sectarian differences in issues of universal concern. Apart from the newspaper reports, whose bias is admitted by Shelley, we do not really know how this speech was received. One member of the audience recorded his impression of Shelley's manner but said nothing of his matter.[2] O'Connell's son praised his speech, but he had not been present and must have gathered Shelley's views from his writings.[3] O'Connell himself, who spoke at the meeting, might have had something of interest to say; but when questioned by MacCarthy he had no recollection of Shelley.[4]

We also lack detailed information concerning Shelley's last month in Dublin. His last letter from there is dated 20 March, about three weeks before his departure. We may conjecture that, having published the *Proposals*, he was waiting for some response to his suggestions. He would soon have found that, while he was treated with respect and even esteem by the Irish, there was no sign that they intended to adopt his scheme. They were glad of support from a Protestant, an Englishman, and a man of rank—but it was to their own leaders that they looked for guidance. When Shelley confessed to Godwin that his scheme of an association was 'ill-timed' it is probable that his failure to enlist support for it weighed more with him than the exaggerated fears of Godwin (*Letters*, i. 276). He had already admitted to Miss Hitchener, 'As to an Association, my hopes daily grow fainter on the subject, as my perceptions of its necessity gain strength.'[5] Perhaps he was already beginning to realize that the reformer must work with existing movements and organizations rather than hoping to create

---

[1] *Life and Speeches of Daniel O'Connell*, i. 54.

[2] Chief Baron Woulfe, quoted in [John Anster], 'Life and Writings of Percy Bysshe Shelley', *North British Review*, viii (1847), 236.

[3] *Life and Speeches of Daniel O'Connell*, i. 135–8. John O'Connell quotes from Shelley's *Proposals*.

[4] MacCarthy, *Shelley's Early Life*, pp. xiii–xiv.

[5] *Letters*, i. 275. See also i. 271.

them to order. The projects that came to occupy his attention as the association scheme waned were more literary and more individual. Isolated cases of misery and oppression occupied more of his time.[1] He toyed with the idea of taking a share in a newspaper, which he hoped, rather vaguely, to make into 'a powerful engine of melioration'.[2] He intended to achieve this with the aid of John Lawless, a Catholic publicist and later one of the leaders of the Catholic Association. Lawless was an O'Connellite radical and it is significant that this group supplied virtually the only Irish politician to show any serious interest in Shelley's schemes. Shelley reported that 'tho he regards my ultimate hopes as visionary, [he] is willing to acquiesce in my means' (*Letters*, i. 275). Shelley had anticipated that few would consider his aims attainable and he stressed the fact that he only expected agreement and co-operation in the means of progress that he proposed.[3] Cynical commentators have assumed that Lawless was mainly interested in Shelley's pecuniary 'means',[4] and it is true that Shelley tried to raise £250 to print a 'voluminous History of Ireland', probably Lawless's *Compendium of the History of Ireland* (Dublin, 1814).

By now Shelley had already decided upon a date for his departure, and was meditating a similar campaign for his association in Sussex, a campaign that was never launched.[5] He left Ireland around 10 April, and summed up the results of his expedition with some realism. 'We left Dublin because I had done all that I could do, if its effects were beneficial they were not greatly so, I am dissatisfied with my success, but not with the attempt . . .' (*Letters*, i. 282). His first sally into the real world of human affairs is not to be evaluated solely in terms of what he managed to achieve. It served as a necessary stage in his political education, giving him an opportunity to bring his abstract doctrines to the test of practice, and to discover the difficulties involved in trying to make them operative. We must look now in some detail at the issues that preoccupied Shelley at this time.

---

[1] *Letters*, i. 270–1.   [2] *Letters*, i. 272, 275.
[3] *Works*, v. 244, 257, 267.
[4] See especially John Cordy Jeaffreson, *The Real Shelley: New Views of the Poet's Life* (2 vols., 1885), ii. 85–8.
[5] *Letters*, i. 271. Elizabeth Hitchener sent an extract from Shelley's *Address* to the *Sussex Weekly Advertiser*, which complimented her on her 'patriotic sentiments', and assured her that it was 'under consideration' (6 April 1812). Nothing more was heard of it.

Shelley's decision to go to Ireland and engage in overt political agitation was the occasion of a debate between him and Godwin which would have been bound to occur eventually, and which defines for us the differing conceptions they held of the best way to actually implement a programme on which, in substance, they were in accord. The debate concerned means rather than ends but is no less important for that. Godwin had fought this battle before, when he opposed the direct methods of the radical societies in the 1790s.[1] When Godwin objected to Shelley's scheme of an association he argued that the 'pervading principle' of *Political Justice* was 'that association is a most ill-chosen and ill-qualified mode of endeavouring to promote the political happiness of mankind'.[2] Shelley replied that his scheme was 'not . . . contradictory but strictly compatible with the principles of "Political Justice" ' (*Letters*, i. 267). In fact both Godwin and Shelley are right, and the dispute between them arises from the fact that Shelley has drawn his own conclusions from the 'principles' of philosophical anarchism—conclusions that are not necessarily less valid than Godwin's. Godwin did indeed oppose the idea of political associations,[3] but the real point at issue between him and Shelley concerns the status and necessity of direct political action. Shelley's stand on this issue does indeed reveal that 'his social and political views are more practical and institutional than Godwin's'.[4]

In reply to Godwin's criticisms Shelley puts his view of the matter very clearly.

Political Justice was first published in 1793; nearly twenty years have elapsed since the general diffusion of its doctrines. What has followed? . . . I think of the last twenty years with impatient scepticism as to the progress which the human mind has made during this period.—I will own that I am eager that something should be done. (*Letters*, i. 267)

---

[1] See Isaac Kramnick, 'On Anarchism and the Real World: William Godwin and Radical England', *American Political Science Review*, lxvi (1972), 114–28. See also John P. Clark, 'On Anarchism In An Unreal World: Kramnick's View of Godwin and the Anarchists', Kramnick's 'Comment' on Clark's article, and Clark's 'Rejoinder' to Kramnick's 'Comment', in ibid. lxix (1975), 162–7, 168, 169–70.

[2] *Life*, i. 321. Hogg printed Godwin's letters to Shelley from Godwin's own drafts or copies (now in Bodleian Dep. c. 524); Hogg's versions have been checked against his originals.

[3] See *Political Justice*, i. 285–99.

[4] McNiece, *Shelley and the Revolutionary Idea*, p. 95.

This frank avowal of 'impatient scepticism' did not fail to draw down a predictable rebuke from Godwin.

You say, 'What has been done within the last twenty years?' Oh, that I could place you on the pinnacle of ages, from which those twenty years would shrink to an invisible point! It is not after this fashion that moral causes work in the eye of him who looks profoundly through the vast and, allow me to add, venerable machine of human society. . . . He that would benefit mankind on a comprehensive scale, by changing the principles and elements of society, must learn the hard lesson—to put off self, and to contribute by a quiet, but incessant activity, like a rill of water, to irrigate and fertilize the intellectual soil. (*Life*, i. 329)

Godwin's reply is dignified and not without cogency, but we should not be too hasty to take his part against Shelley. Godwin's ability to take a long view and his reliance on 'moral causes' represent a strength in his thinking, but at the same time a weakness that led him to reject all possibility of constructive political action. One need not be a hothead to believe that a certain amount of creative intervention in the course of events is possible and at times essential.

For Godwin the proper levers of progress are 'Discussion, reading, inquiry, perpetual communication' (*Life*, i. 321). This is one of the doctrines of *Political Justice* which Shelley expounded to his Irish audience. 'Be calm, mild, deliberate, patient; recollect that you can in no measure more effectually forward the cause of reform than by employing your leisure time in reasoning, or the cultivation of your minds. Think and talk, and discuss.' (*Works*, v. 224) Shelley repeatedly insisted that the only means of resistance he would countenance were 'intellectual resistance', 'intellectual opposition', 'intellectual force'.[1] But even this is more radical than Godwin would like, for Shelley is suggesting that the progress of 'opinion' can become an effective political pressure, as intellectual weapons are brought to bear on a reactionary government. Godwin prefers to trust to the inevitable progress of 'opinion' to reform the political order. This process is seen as an impersonal one, not dependent on human action. 'This thing has its time. "In the hour that ye think not, the Son of Man cometh" '.[2] The danger is not that the opportunity will pass but that precipitate attempts at change will destroy what progress has been made. Godwin pre-

---

[1] *Works*, v. 244, 245, 246.
[2] *Life*, i. 333. Godwin is paraphrasing Luke 12: 40.

ferred, as he told Shelley, 'to keep up the intellectual, and in some sense the solitary, fermentation, and to procrastinate the contact and subsequent action' (*Life*, i. 333). The duty of the reformer was not to take the lead in effecting reform but to work on society behind the scenes by transforming 'opinion'. 'Every change of sentiment, from moral delusion to truth, every addition we make, to the clearness of our apprehension on this subject, and the recollectedness and independence of our mind, is itself, abstracted from the absolute change of our institutions, an unquestionable acquisition.'[1] Godwin deprecated the idea of a public association even for the purposes of discussion, for his trust in man's reason did not extend to man in a crowd. It is possible that his own experiences as a teacher helped to form his conviction that truth is best spread in intimate, face-to-face discussion. By 'unreserved communication' under such conditions enlightened individuals could strengthen and extend their own grasp on truth, and even, in a loose and limited association, a kind of study-group, provide a focus for its spread, while avoiding the 'brute and unintelligent sympathy' prompted by large public meetings. This domestic intercourse between reformers Godwin saw as promising 'consequences of inestimable value' (*Political Justice*, i. 294–7). Godwin actually drew up a prospectus for a '*Select Club*' of this sort, to consist of doctors, law students, artists, mathematicians, 'philosophic *minds*, in search of *truth*' (political truth, since Godwin cites Holcroft, Priestley, Fox, Sheridan, and Mackintosh), and foreign guests and correspondents. There were to be '*No Rules*' except that 'truth, knowledge[,] *mind* being the chief object, no subject is to be excluded'.[2] This proposed study-group is the nearest that Godwin ever comes to institutionalizing 'opinion'.

Godwin's reliance on the power of opinion to reform society and his consequent refusal to consider direct political action is based on the neglect of one of his own perceptions—that society also influences opinion. A main source of the individual's 'education', on which all else depends, is provided by the 'political institution' under which he lives (*Political Justice*, i. 48–51). The political state of society inevitably and often imperceptibly conditions its members.

---

[1] *Political Justice*, i. 277–8. See also *Letters*, i. 162.
[2] The manuscript of these proposals is now in the Bodleian, Dep. c. 532 (4).

It is beyond all controversy, that men who live in a state of equality, or that approaches equality, will be frank, ingenuous and intrepid in their carriage; while those who inhabit where a great disparity of ranks has prevailed will be distinguished by coldness, irresoluteness, timidity and caution. . . . As long as parents and teachers in general shall fall under the established rule, it is clear that politics and modes of governments will educate and infect us all. They poison our minds, before we can resist, or so much as suspect their malignity. (*Political Justice*, i. 49)

Since 'government by its very nature counteracts the improvement of individual intellect' (i. viii), it would seem vain to hope that intellectual and moral progress alone could ever reform government. It must follow from Godwin's own position that, just as moral and political corruption produce each other, so progress must come about through the reciprocal action of moral and political reform.

To begin to reform the Government, is immediately necessary, however good or bad individuals may be; it is the more necessary if they are eminently the latter, in some degree to palliate or do away the cause; as political institution has ever the greatest influence on the human character, and is that alone which differences the Turk from the Irishman. (*Works*, v. 237)[1]

Shelley is here more faithful to the principles of philosophical anarchism than is Godwin. Shelley is aware that at every point moral progress must be translated into political progress in order to preserve what has already been gained and to prepare for further advances. In the next chapter we shall see how Shelley's Reform programme embodies this dialectic of moral and political progress.[2]

Godwin's distrust of political action often comes close to throwing him into the camp of the reactionaries. His insistence on the priority of individual moral reform is very similar to a favourite argument of the defenders of things as they were.

Tom I'm a friend of the people. I want reform.
Jack Then the shortest way is to mend thyself.

[1] 'ever' is corrected from 'even' in the original.
[2] A passage in the first edition of *Political Justice* (iii. 288–9) suggests that at one time Godwin would have taken Shelley's point: 'When therefore some considerable advantage is sufficiently understood by the community to induce them to desire its establishment, that establishment will afterwards react to the enlightening of intellect and the generating of virtue. It is natural for us to take our stand upon some leading truth and from thence explore the regions we have still to traverse.'

Tom   But I want a *general* reform.
Jack   Then let every one mend one.[1]

Major Cartwright's retort to Hannah More and all those who were 'laborious in preaching up individual or private reform, in exclusion of parliamentary or public reform' will do for Godwin as well. 'No rational advocate of public reform ever thought otherwise, than that private virtue is the surest foundation for public order and happiness; but what sort of morality is that, which discommends all direct attempts at public reformation, until private reform shall be so complete, as that public reform shall be unnecessary?'[2] For Shelley it was essential that the reformer should be ready and willing to seize the favourable moment at which the moral forces working in society could be consolidated in the form of political melioration. His view of history was hence a 'crisis' view.

Robert Pack has already pointed to Shelley's fondness for 'a "crisis" theory of history'.[3] A theory of this kind sees 'the course of history as a series of climactic events which, when dealt with properly, affect the future course of events'. Such a theory, based on the assumption that man can intervene effectively and even decisively in history, is in contradiction to the Godwinian doctrine of Necessity, as Pack observes. Actually the notion of a 'crisis' is often treated in Shelley's poetry in a way that implicitly invokes Necessity. In an early poem actually entitled 'The Crisis' the miseries and oppressions of Shelley's society are presented as the cause of their own destruction; when they are apparent,

> Then may we hope the consummating hour
> Dreadfully, sweetly, swiftly is arriving.
> (lines 13-14)

Nothing is said about how this desirable consummation is to come about; it seems to be in the natural course of events, without recourse to deliberate human activity. Similarly in 'The Devil's Walk' (1812) the end of Satan's rule is heralded by an 'earthquake's

---

[1] Hannah More, *Village Politics* (1793), quoted from *Politics and Literature in the Eighteenth Century*, edited by H. T. Dickinson (1974), p. 210. See also William Hamilton Reid, *The Rise and Dissolution of the Infidel Societies in this Metropolis* (1800), p. 3.
[2] *An Appeal, Civil and Military, on the Subject of the English Constitution* (1799), p. 92.
[3] R. F. Pack, 'Shelley and History', pp. 51-3.

crash' (line 128), a crisis whose nature Shelley does not specify. In the first poem of *Posthumous Fragments of Margaret Nicholson* (1810) 'enthusiast ears' hear sounds that promise 'the last eventful day' when 'heaven' will somehow bring an end to monarchy and war. In all these poems the implication seems to be that the very extent and severity of the evil brings about the renovating 'crisis' which begins an upward trend; when things are so bad they can't get any worse they must get better. I suspect however that Shelley is presenting this as a necessary process largely in order to evade his own suspicion that this kind of crisis will take the form of violent insurrection. His prophetic vision clouds just before the crucial moment of the crisis he anticipates, because his hatred of warmongering kings has to struggle against his commitment to peaceful methods of reform.

> Woe be the tyrants' and murderers' meed,
> But Nature's wound alone should make their Conscience bleed,

as he says in 'On leaving London for Wales' (November 1812). The philanthropist, with his 'soul to indignation wrought', still has an obligation as 'the friend of the unfriended poor' not to 'madly stain their righteous cause in gore'.[1] This pacifist commitment naturally inhibits Shelley from anticipating with any relish the inevitable crisis, and he prefers to present it as independent of human agency. A similar nervousness is apparent in *Prometheus Unbound*, where the 'consummating hour' is personified as 'A spirit with a dreadful countenance' who announces himself as 'the shadow of a destiny/More dread than is my aspect'.[2] If Cameron is correct in his very reasonable speculation that this is 'the Hour of the revolutionary overthrow of the old order'[3] then it must be acknowledged that Shelley only alludes in a covert way to the revolutionary crisis which he feared was imminent but could hardly bring himself to welcome. If it is necessary Shelley would prefer to see it as inevitable.

When Shelley spoke of a crisis in the Ireland of 1812, however, he was not thinking of it as a potentially revolutionary situation but as a critical conjuncture of affairs which presented a real

---

[1] Lines 53–4, 57, 62–3 (*The Esdaile Notebook*, pp. 54–5).
[2] II. iv. 142, 146–7.
[3] K. N. Cameron, 'The Political Symbolism of *Prometheus Unbound*' (1943), in *Shelley: Modern Judgements*, ed. R. B. Woodings, p. 119.

opportunity for creative intervention on the part of a reformer who rejected violence. The situation in Ireland was above all 'part of a great crisis in opinions' (*Letters*, i. 234). It thus offered 'an opportunity which if I thus disengaged permit to pass unoccupied I am unworthy of the character which I have assumed' (i. 243). As Godwin may have observed with some unease, Shelley did not seem to have noted the passage in *Political Justice* which urged, 'Let us not over-anxiously watch for occasions and events: of particular events the ascendancy of truth is independent' (ii. 546). Shelley made some efforts to explain to Godwin his conception of the nature of the Irish crisis. 'I conceive that the benevolent passions of their breasts are in some degree excited, and individual interest in some degree generalized by catholic disqualifications and the oppressive influence of the Union act; that some degree of indignation has arisen, at the conduct of the prince which might lead to blind insurrection.' (*Letters*, i. 258) The crisis constituted a threat, but also a great opportunity for the reformer—an opportunity 'for fixing the fluctuation of public feeling' (*Works*, v. 245). To the educated and liberal audience to which he addressed his *Proposals* Shelley is very frank about his own enlightened opportunism: 'Men cannot make occasions, but he may seize those that offer.'[1] The opportunity that Shelley hoped to seize lay in the kind of public feeling that events in Ireland had generated. It was no longer a blind response to immediate and personal grievances, for the Irish had begun to assign their miseries to general causes and to experience a fellow-feeling with all who suffered from them. '. . . I perceive that individual interest has, in a certain degree, quitted individual concern to generalize itself with universal feeling.' (*Works*, v. 254) Shelley has in mind the attempt on the part of the radical Catholic leaders to make the opposition to government policies a national rather than a merely Catholic cause. O'Connell put Repeal before Emancipation for the Union with England affected all Irishmen. Shelley did not share O'Connell's nationalism but he welcomed any sign of the spread of disinterested feeling. It was only in so far as it sprang from such feeling that the cause of the Irish could serve 'the great ends of virtue and happiness', for, as Shelley insisted, 'an action, or a motive to

---

[1] *Works*, v. 253. Shelley is echoing Paine: 'Man cannot, properly speaking, make circumstances for his purpose, but he always has it in his power to improve them when they occur . . .' (*Complete Writings*, i. 301).

action, is only virtuous so far as it is disinterested'. Realizing perhaps that he was making excessive demands on his audience he qualified this by adding 'or partakes (I adopt this mode of expression to suit the taste of some) of the nature of generalized self-love'.[1] In fact this distinction is more than a matter of 'taste'. For Shelley or an Irish Protestant to work for Emancipation would be 'disinterested'; for a Catholic to do so, or for any Irishman to work for Repeal, would only partake 'of the nature of generalized self-love', for they would expect to have a share in benefits which would also be extended to their fellows. But even 'generalized self-love' is a move away from complete enslavement to purely individual interests. The possibility of altruism, even in a limited form, is of great importance for Shelley since he wishes men to work for the future in which they can have no personal interest. He notes that occasions which 'generalize and expand private into public feelings' also make the individual feel 'for posterity' (*Works*, v. 253). It is ironic that the collapse of his Irish schemes left him with the same cold comfort he had been offering the Irish. '. . . I will look to events in which it will be impossible that I can share, and make myself the cause of an effect which will take place ages after *I* shall have mouldered into dust. I need not observe that this resolve requires Stoicism.' (*Letters*, i. 277) It would clearly require rather exceptional circumstances for a whole nation of individuals to make the sacrifice of personal interests in order to work for a general cause. For a short while it seemed that the moral situation of Ireland had reached this point, and Shelley paid the Irish the high compliment of believing that they were ready to practise what he preached in his two pamphlets.

It may be argued that Shelley misread the state of Irish opinion, mistaking the nationalist ardour that O'Connell was busily fanning for his own brand of moral fervour. But Shelley was not the only observer to detect a 'crisis in opinions' by which particular interests were being merged into a national interest.

The present important crisis in the affairs of Ireland, occupies, as it ought to do, the attention of all ranks and religions of the people. The great Cause which now agitates the Country is not of a partial, but of a general nature—as such we have ever viewed it, and as such alone, do we wish it to undergo the grave and unprejudiced consideration of not

---

[1] *Letters*, i. 243; *Works*, v. 263.

only the Irish, but the English Subjects of his Majesty. If this great Cause ever carried with it an individual, a party, or an isolated character, such features have been long since obliterated; they have been broken down and blended in the generality of its interest, and universality of its importance. It is no longer the particular Cause of the individuals composing the Catholic Body of Ireland; it embraces the whole of our population; it connects itself with the stability of the Throne, and safety of the Empire, for satisfied are we, that in Catholic Emancipation will be found the best security of Protestant freedom.[1]

This testimony carries the more weight in that it comes from a *Protestant* source.[2] National unity in Ireland depended above all on the ability to rise above sectarian differences. Shelley had personal reasons for being concerned with the issues of religion and tolerance, but it would have been impossible to discuss the Irish situation without dealing with them, and they naturally bulk large in his Irish pamphlets. His statements on religion were not all well received by his audience. But he was less the victim of Catholic bigotry (as Hogg thought) than of his own clumsiness and misinformation. It is certainly not true to say that his religious pronouncements reveal him as being naïve or ignorant about the state of opinion in Ireland. On the contrary, his advocacy of mutual toleration between Protestants and Catholics was fully in accord with the policy adopted by the Irish leaders.

We have already seen that Shelley's 'philanthropy' was as much a religion as a moral code.[3] Like other religions it could lead to a rather militant attitude to other creeds, and it cannot be denied that Shelley's pronouncements betray hostility to Catholicism. What is only implied in the first pamphlet is stated far more openly in the second. 'I hear the teeth of the palsied beldame Superstition chatter, and I see her descending to the grave! Reason points to the open gates of the Temple of Religious Freedom, Philanthropy kneels at the altar of the common God!' (*Works*, v. 255) An opponent of Shelley's views, signing himself 'A Dissenter' (whether from those views or the established Church is not clear), hastened to point out that this passage was an attack on Catholicism from a Deist standpoint, no doubt in order to dis-

---

[1] *Dublin Evening Post*, 31 Aug. 1811 (quoted in Hamilton, *State of the Catholic Cause*, pp. 104–5).

[2] See Hamilton, op. cit., p. 84.

[3] The religious aspect of Shelley's Irish expedition has been, perhaps, overemphasized by F. A. Lea, *Shelley and the Romantic Revolution* (1945), p. 26.

credit Shelley with his mainly Catholic audience.[1] The accusation was not without point. In recommending a rational, natural religion to his readers Shelley was only following up what he had done in the *Address*, which had been, he said, '*secretly* intended also as a preliminary to other pamphlets to shake Catholicism at its basis, and to induce Quakerish and Socinian principle[s] of politics' (*Letters*, i. 239). As T. W. Rolleston noted, Shelley 'desired the emancipation of Catholics from their legal disabilities, but he avowedly desired still more their emancipation from Catholicism . . .'[2]. Of course Shelley was as much opposed to Protestant Calvinism as he was to Catholicism (even his Deism may have been assumed as a concession to his audience). A large part of the *Address* was devoted to attacking the past crimes and excesses of both denominations, thus endorsing their mutual accusations in order tacitly to recommend a third position (a technique he was to use again with rather more poise in *A Refutation of Deism*).[3] As Shelley's friend Lawless was later to warn the Irish, 'the Deist and the Atheist rejoice' at the quarrels of Christians.[4] It is unfortunate that Catholicism appeared to bear the brunt of Shelley's attack; and even more unfortunate that his remarks seemed to stem from typical Protestant prejudices. He cautioned the Irish Catholics about virtually all the distinctive features of their religion: confession, the influence of the clergy, 'ceremonies', 'burials', 'processions', and 'wonders' (*Works*, v. 219). At the root of this attack was a Godwinian concern for the independent judgement of the individual, but the Irish could hardly be expected to appreciate this. He sadly admitted, 'Prejudices are so violent in contradiction to my principles that more hate me as a freethinker, than love me as a votary of Freedom. . . . The spirit of Bigotry is high.' (*Letters*, i. 271–2) Commenting on his speech to the Aggregate Meeting he referred to 'the hisses with which they greeted me when I spoke of *religion*, tho' in terms of respect' (i. 275).

[1] 'A Dissenter' to the Editor, *Dublin Journal*, 21 Mar. 1812 (quoted from *Works*, vii. 324). K. N. Cameron has suggested that 'this letter, ostensibly attacking Shelley, may have been written by Shelley himself in order to arouse a controversy' (*The Young Shelley*, p. 356 n.80).

[2] Introduction to *An Address, to the Irish People*, edited by T. J. Wise (1890), p. 21.

[3] *Works*, v. 216–20.

[4] *The Belfast Politics, enlarged; being a Compendium of the Political History of Ireland, for the last Forty Years* (Belfast, 1818), pp. 4, 7n.

In view of his published comments on Catholicism the displeasure of his audience is not hard to understand. Even sixty years later they provoked one author (himself a Catholic) to denounce Shelley's 'atrocious calumnies on the religion of the people of Ireland'.[1] We shall consider shortly the reasons for Shelley's tactlessness in his references to Catholicism, but first it must be stressed that Shelley's audience did not object to his appeals for toleration and co-operation between Catholics and Protestants. The myth that they did so can be traced back to Hogg's account.

On one occasion, he told me that at a meeting—probably at the meeting of Philanthropists—so much ill-will was shown towards the Protestants, that thereupon he was provoked to remark that the Protestants were fellow Christians, fellow subjects, and as such were entitled to equal rights, to equal charity, toleration, and the rest. He was forthwith interrupted by savage yells; a tremendous uproar arose, and he was compelled to be silent. At the same meeting, and afterwards, he was even threatened with personal violence. This unreasonable display of popish and party bigotry went far to disgust him with his rash enterprise, to open his eyes, and to convince him that Irish grievances consisted not in a denial of equal rights, these the Philanthropic Association did not seek, but the power and opportunity to tyrannize over and to oppress their Protestant brethren. (*Life*, i. 337)

Hogg's account is palpably false. There never was a meeting of Shelley's proposed 'Philanthropic Association', nor indeed anything worthy of being called an Association. The only public meeting at which Shelley spoke was the Catholic Aggregate Meeting in the Fishamble Street Theatre. At this meeting, far from 'ill-will' being shown to Protestants, Shelley rose to address the audience in response to a resolution of thanks to the 'DISTINGUISHED PROTESTANTS' like himself who were lending their countenance to the Catholic meeting. The seconder of this resolution, Sir Thomas Wyse, invoked the 'Spirit of UNDISTINGUISHED BROTHERHOOD AND UNIVERSAL EMANCIPATION'.[2] Shelley himself had preached 'Universal emancipation' in his *Address*, having found the phrase in Curran's great speech on behalf of Hamilton Rowan in 1794.[3] Similar phrases were widely current, and we find

[1] MacCarthy, *Shelley's Early Life*, p. xiv.

[2] Ibid., pp. 247–8.

[3] *Works*, v. 237; see *Speeches of the Right Honourable John Philpot Curran* (3rd edn., Dublin, 1811), pp. 137–8, 169–70.

Lawless urging 'the application of the *omnipotent* principle of *universal toleration* to all sects'.[1]

To recommend toleration in the Ireland of early 1812 was not to be contentious but quite the contrary. Such sentiments were the expected thing and were greeted with dutiful applause. The leaders of the Irish opposition were only too well aware that religious disunity was the greatest and most immediate threat to any campaign to win reform in Ireland. As Cobbett remarked, 'If I were to choose a people to hold in a state of complete subjection, it should be a people divided into several religious sects, each condemning the other to perdition.'[2] Curran attributed the Union with England to the 'reciprocal animosity' of religious sects, and O'Connell urged the Irish to abandon the 'religious discord' which had enabled England to enslave Ireland.[3] O'Connell was reported to have said, 'I am, I confess, first and chiefly anxious for Emancipation, that the attention of the Irish people being taken off from this *family quarrel*, we may have leisure to look to our country.'[4] Co-operation between the members of the different denominations was also a tactical necessity. Until O'Connell's successful exploitation of the numerical strength of the Catholics in the 1820s they could only get a hearing for their case with the help of friendly Protestants in Parliament. The Protestants, on the other hand, could not hope to get the Union repealed without the support of the Catholic masses.[5] Consequently the trend of Irish public opinion was not just towards toleration but towards an exaggerated display of toleration. The reports of the county meetings held to elect Catholic delegates in 1811 are full of scrupulous acknowledgements of Protestant aid and support.[6] At the end of the year the 'Friends of Religious Liberty' held a dinner which was attended

[1] *The Belfast Politics, enlarged*, p. 3. Coleridge mocked '*Universal Toleration*' as a popular catch-phrase in the *Courier* for 1 Apr. 1812 (*Essays on His Times*, ii. 342).

[2] *Political Register*, 6 Feb. 1813, p. 176.

[3] *A New and Enlarged Collection of Speeches, by the Right Honourable John Philpot Curran* (London, 1819), p. 274; *Life and Speeches of Daniel O'Connell*, i. 54.

[4] Quoted by Coleridge in the *Courier* for 5 Aug. 1811 (*Essays on His Times*, ii. 243).

[5] Catholics were prevented from sitting in Parliament by the terms of the oath exacted; but they still possessed considerable political strength since many of them were able to vote (a point which is not appreciated by Gillian Carey, *Shelley* (1975), p. 20).

[6] Hamilton, *State of Catholic Cause*, pp. 63–254 *passim*.

by the Catholic leaders Lord Fingal and O'Connell, the Protestant politicians Curran, Henry Grattan, and Archibald Hamilton Rowan, and the Quaker educationalist Joseph Lancaster.[1] Grattan extended the olive branch on behalf of the Protestants by urging the acknowledgement that Emancipation was 'not a Catholic, but a National and an Irish question'. He went on to hope that it would be not 'the victory of one party over the other—but the victory of both over a wretched code of nonsensical incapacities'. O'Connell for the Catholics was quick to acknowledge Protestant support, adding that 'the principle upon which the Catholics sought for freedom was not narrow or selfish—it was not confined to themselves, but embraced the rights, the undoubted rights of the Dissenters in England—of the Protestants among our Allies in Spain and Portugal'.[2]

It is clear that Shelley's audience would not have disapproved of platitudes concerning toleiation. As he realized himself, it was his explicit hostility to Catholicism that they objected to. It is clear that this was a tactical error, but no satisfactory explanation has yet been given of why Shelley made it. I believe that he misinterpreted the state of opinion in Ireland, and assumed that the willingness to ignore doctrinal differences expressed by both Catholics and Protestants implied that they were ready to abandon the tenets of Christianity and embrace a more 'natural' religion. As A. M. D. Hughes shrewdly pointed out, Shelley seems to have approached the Irish situation in 1812 with assumptions that would have been more appropriate to the eighteenth century.[3] He failed to realize that the nascent nationalism of the Irish was intimately bound up with those very peculiarities of their religion that he found most irrational and objectionable. When Shelley accused the Catholics of bigotry, he did not mean anti-Protestant prejudice but sincere attachment to their own faith. If he was misinformed as to the strength of this attachment part of the blame may rest with one of the works on which he drew for an understanding of the Irish situation.

About four months after the Shelleys had left Dubl'n Harriet

---

[1] *Morning Chronicle*, 25 Dec. 1811.

[2] See also the Catholic Address to the Regent: 'We would cheerfully concede the enjoyment of civil and religious liberty to all mankind; we ask no more for ourselves' (*Annual Register* (1812), 'State Papers', p. 344); and O'Connell's speech, quoted in Hamilton, op. cit., p. 179.

[3] *The Nascent Mind of Shelley* (1947; Oxford, 1971), p. 132.

wrote to an Irish friend, 'Percy intends to print some proposals for printing Pieces of Irish History saying that everyone whether Irish or English ought to read them' (*Letters*, i. 321). It is accepted that Shelley was referring to the same work when he wrote to Hookham:

I send you a copy of a work which I have procured from America, & which I am exceedingly anxious should be published. It developes as you will perceive by the most superficial reading, the actual state of republicanized Ireland, & appears to me above all things calculated to remove the prejudices which have too long been cherished of that oppressed country, to strike the oppressors with dismay. (*Letters*, i. 324)

The work to which Shel ey was referring was a compilation of various documents, published by two Irish republicans who sought refuge in America after the failure of the Rebellion in 1798, William James MacNeven (a Catholic) and Thomas Addis Emmet (a Protestant, and the brother of Shelley's hero Robert Emmet). The full title reads: *Pieces of Irish History, illustrative of the Condition of the Catholics of Ireland, of the Origin and Progress of the Political System of the United Irishmen; and of their Transactions with the Anglo-Irish Government* (Bernard Dornin, New York, 1807). MacNeven and Emmet had been members of the Executive Directory of the United Irishmen, and their book evidently provided Shelley with most of his knowledge concerning this society, whose attitudes and policies were very attractive to him. But he was mistaken if he thought that their 'System' could be revived in the Ireland of 1812. *Pieces of Irish History* was already out of date when it was published, for the collapse of Robert Emmet's revolt in 1803 spelt the end of the United Irishmen as an effective political force. By 1812 'republicanized Ireland' was in exile in America along with its authors.

The United Irishmen shared the concern of the Irish leaders already quoted to sink religious differences in a general cause. As Wolfe Tone put it, they w shed 'to substitute the common name of Irishman in place of the denominations of Protestant, Catholic, and Dissenter'.[1] The society was formed as a result of a decision by the Protestant and Dissenting radicals of Belfast and the

[1] Quoted from Frank MacDermot, *Theobald Wolfe Tone: A Biographical Study* (1939), p. 200.

Catholic leaders of Dublin to found 'societies . . . for uniting together the great objects of Parliamentary Reform and Catholic Emancipation'.[1] The Protestant radicals took up the cause of Emancipation largely for tactical reasons, and Wolfe Tone published his *An Argument on Behalf of the Catholics of Ireland* (1791) in order 'to shew to the protestant friends of reform that they could never hope for success, unless by embodying with their measure a repeal of the popery laws, and thus giving to the mass of population an interest in its favour'.[2] The Belfast radicals, many of them Dissenters, were genuinely opposed to civil disqualifications for religious opinions,[3] but their real political objective was Reform and they only included Emancipation in their programme in order to win support; like Shelley they 'had not the slightest sympathy for catholicism as a creed'.[4] Many of them were probably Deists, again like Shelley—the society was originally based on the organization of the Freemasons.[5] Their attitude to Catholicism was thus condescending at best.[6] They liked to argue that Emancipation was a symbolic issue even for the Catholics; they resented the measure of Emancipation granted in 1793, seeing it as an attempt to deprive them of Catholic support; and they were frankly contemptuous of wholly Catholic societies like the 'Defenders'.[7]

In the 1790s it was these Protestant radicals who took the lead and the Catholics had to accept their political aid on whatever terms were available. By 1810 the situation had changed greatly. The Protestants were still tempted by the numerical strength of the Catholics and still willing to support Emancipation, and the Catholics still valued that support. But the Catholics had gained both strength and self-confidence and were in a position to demand far more respect from their political allies. They were no longer in a mood to tolerate sneers or condescension towards their faith. John Mitchel roundly condemned the Duke of Richmond for having 'the sanctimonious audacity to express his wonder that religion, being only occupied with a great object of eternal concern, men should be excited to rancorous enmity because they sought

---

[1] *Pieces of Irish History*, p. 15.
[2] Ibid., p. 16.
[3] Ibid., pp. 12, 172–3, 229.
[4] R. B. McDowell, *Irish Public Opinion 1750–1800* (1944), p. 181.
[5] See Lawless, *The Belfast Politics, enlarged*, p. 440.
[6] R. B. McDowell, *Irish Public Opinion 1750–1800*, pp. 193–4.
[7] *Pieces of Irish History*, pp. 92–3, 206; 40, 42, 45; 118–19.

the same great end by paths somewhat different'.[1] Live and let live was all very well, but the Catholics were not prepared to be told that their religion wasn't important. It is hardly surprising, in view of this sensitivity, that Shelley's audience did not take kindly to his suggestion that religious differences should be not merely shelved but virtually abolished, and the Catholic and the Protestant absorbed into the Deist. O'Connell was careful to appear an orthodox and even fervent Catholic in public, though he had been a Deist and an admirer of Paine's *Age of Reason*, and at least one biographer doubts the sincerity of his Catholicism.[2] Shelley certainly failed to exercise the tact demanded by his Catholic audience; but what they hissed in 1812 they would probably have received in silence in 1792.

We can best conclude our consideration of Shelley's Irish expedition by a discussion of his scheme for an Association in relation to the various models that he had in mind. Shelley was hardly novel in his plan—the idea of organizing public opinion and giving it expression through a body either associated or representative had been in the air for over forty years.[3] The Whigs were the first to find it necessary to combine in a regular way in order to support certain general policies; as an opposition party they found it greatly to their advantage to organize public opinion against government policies, as they did in the county associations of the 1780s. To counter the accusation of factiousness they were wont to invoke Burke's famous dictum: 'When bad men combine, the good must associate.'[4] By Shelley's day the idea of political associations was far less novel and problematic than it had been in Burke's, but Shelley remained in the Whig tradition to the extent of justifying association as a defensive response to the combination of the supporters of oppression. In 1819 the spectacle of the *Quarterly Review*'s systematic campaign against the 'cause of improvement' led him to exclaim, 'If a band of staunch reformers, resolute yet skilful infidels were united in so close & constant a

---

[1] *The History of Ireland, from the Treaty of Limerick to the Present Time* (1868; 2 vols., Burns, Oates & Washbourne, London, no date), ii. 137.

[2] Seán O'Faolain, *King of the Beggars: A Life of Daniel O'Connell, the Irish Liberator, in a Study of the Rise of the Modern Irish Democracy 1775–1847* (1938; Dublin, 1970), p. 74.

[3] See E. C. Black, *The Association: British Extraparliamentary Political Organization 1769–1793* (Cambridge, Mass., 1963).

[4] Burke, *Works*, i. 372.

league as that in which interest & fanaticism have joined the members of that literary coalition!'[1] His first association project was explicitly defensive. It was addressed to Leigh Hunt, editor of the *Examiner*, a leading Reform journal; however there is no evidence to warrant Professor Cameron's assertion that Shelley was proposing a Reform association, on the lines of the later Hampden Club.[2] Shelley's letter was prompted by the emergence of Hunt and his brother, acquitted but financially damaged, from their third prosecution for seditious libel in as many years. What Shelley proposed was an association to safeguard Hunt and other 'fearless enlighteners of the public mind' from the effects of such prosecutions, 'a methodical society which should be organized so as to resist the coalition of the enemies of liberty which at present renders any expression of opinion on matters of policy dangerous to individuals'. It would seem that the 'scheme of mutual safety and mutual indemnification for men of public spirit and principle' (described by Shelley in an 'address' which has not survived) was intended to be a kind of insurance scheme for journalists, by which the costs of standing trial and paying fines would be defrayed from a fund raised by regular contributions.[3] Such a scheme would almost have been within the framework of *Political Justice*, for Godwin, generally opposed to all political associations, makes an explicit exception for 'the remedy of some pressing and momentary evil', such as the relief of an individual 'unjustly attacked by the whole force of the party in power'.[4] However Shelley evidently had in mind something more permanent than Godwin would have been willing to countenance.

In the letter to Hunt Shelley cites '*Illuminism*' as a model for the organization of his own association. His knowledge of Adam Weishaupt's notorious secret society was gained from the perusal of the Abbé Barruel's *Mémoires pour servir à l'histoire du jacobinisme* (1797–8). Barruel saw the Jacobins of the French Revolution as merely the heirs of the Illuminati (the 'Sophisters of Impiety and

---

[1] *Letters*, ii. 81. See also *Independent Whig*, 19 Jan. 1817, p. 20; and *The Complete Works of William Hazlitt*, edited by P. P. Howe (21 vols., 1930–4), vii. 257.

[2] *The Young Shelley*, p. 53.

[3] *Letters*, i. 54–5. There is some evidence to suggest that Shelley sent similar proposals to other journalists (see MacCarthy, *Shelley's Early Life*, pp. 63–5, 71–2).

[4] *Political Justice*, i. 229. No doubt Godwin anticipated that he might himself need to take advantage of such a loophole.

Anarchy'), who had carried on the vast conspiracy against Christian civilization initiated by the Philosophes ('Sophisters of Impiety') and the Freemasons ('Sophisters of Rebellion').[1] As John Roberts has shown, the historical importance of 'Spartacus' Weishaupt's Illuminati lay less in what they actually did than in the frenzied reactions of conservative writers like Barruel to what they saw as 'the most general, most astonishing, and most dreadful Conspiracy that ever existed'.[2] Hogg, who himself laid Barruel under contribution for the 'Eleutherarchs' episode of his *Memoirs of Prince Alexy Haimatoff* (1813), recorded that the Abbé's work was 'a favourite book' with Shelley at Oxford, and added that he swallowed 'with eager credulity the fictions and exaggerations of that readily believing, or readily inventing author' (*Life*, i. 376). Professor Roberts has pointed out that Shelley's 'credulity' 'does not apply to Barruel's conclusions but only his evidence'.[3] He was well aware that the book was 'half filled with the vilest and most unsupported falsehoods', but considered it 'worth reading' for anyone who knew how to 'distinguish truth' (*Letters*, i. 264). It was no doubt convenient to be able to reject any unpalatable facts about the Illuminati as hostile fabrications. However Barruel presents enough hard evidence to show Shelley the points of difference between his own ideas and those of Weishaupt. These are worth discussing, for the Illuminist influence on Shelley's scheme of an association has been greatly exaggerated.[4]

Shelley explicitly disavowed 'the visionary schemes of a completely-equalized community' that were part of the Illuminati's programme (*Letters*, i. 54). This may have been more than an attempt to appear respectable in Hunt's eyes, for the Illuminist Utopia was a vulgarization of Rousseauistic primitivism, with which Shelley may well have had little sympathy.[5] Shelley, as a philosophical anarchist, would have been more impressed by Weishaupt's reiterated emphasis on the concept of self-rule as an

---

[1] Augustin de Barruel, *Memoirs, illustrating the History of Jacobinism*, translated by Robert Clifford (4 vols., 1797–8), i. xxi–xxiii. Shelley possessed this translation, and his copy of Volume I is in the Berg Collection of the New York Public Library. The only annotations in this volume are Shelley's autograph with the date 1810 (letter from the Berg Collection to the author, 9 Mar. 1976).

[2] Barruel, *Memoirs*, iii. 109–10. See John Roberts, *The Mythology of the Secret Societies* (1972), pp. 134–45.

[3] Roberts, op. cit., pp. 201–2n.

[4] See J. O. Fuller, *Shelley: A Biography*, p. 116.

[5] See Barruel, *Memoirs*, iii. 23–4.

ideal. 'Why should human nature be bereft of its most perfect attribute, that of governing itself? Why are those persons to be always led who are capable of conducting themselves? Is it then impossible for mankind or at least the greater part, to come to their majority?' the candidate for Epopt (Priest) in the Order was asked (*Memoirs*, iii. 188). He was then informed that 'true morality' was 'the art of teaching men to shake off their wardship, to attain the age of manhood, and thus to need neither princes nor governments' (iii. 199). The consummation of the Order's work was the '*Man-King, sole king, sole sovereign* of his actions as of his thoughts' (iii. 408), and it looked forward to a time when 'each man shall recognize no other law but that of his reason' (iii. 265–6). Clearly Shelley would have been very sympathetic towards the Order's political ends. However he is careful to disavow the means recommended by Weishaupt. The Order was very definitely a secret society: 'Silence *and secresy are the very soul of the order.*' (iii. 63) It was not only secret to the world at large, but some of its hierarchy and philosophy were to be concealed from the lower grades of initiates (iii. 401). This was clearly in violation of Godwinian Sincerity (and secret associations were still illegal under the Corresponding Societies Act of 1799). Shelley was careful to point out that no such concealment would operate in his association. 'I propose not an Association of Secrecy. . . . I disclaim all connexion with insincerity and concealment. . . . It is a very latitudinarian system of morality that permits its professor to employ bad means for any end whatever.' (*Works*, v. 259) The rejection of expedience in this context makes it clear that he has the Illuminati in his sights, for 'Weishaupt's grand principle' was 'that EVERY THING WHICH IS USEFUL IS AN ACT OF VIRTUE' (*Memoirs*, iii. 95). When Shelley declared, 'Weapons which vice *can* use are unfit for the hands of virtue' (*Works*, v. 259), he was explicitly repudiating the injunction of Weishaupt to 'employ the same means for a good purpose which impostors employ for evil' (*Memoirs*, iii. 115). These means included the use of violence or, as Weishaupt coyly put it, 'means drawn from the greatest degree of force of which human nature is capable' (iii. 108). At the same time the writings of the Order disclaimed violence in terms that Godwin and Shelley would have heartily endorsed. 'Every violent reform is to be blamed, because it will not ameliorate things *as long as men remain as they are, a prey to their passions; and because*

wisdom needeth not the arm of violence.' (iii. 133) The insistence
that 'Morality shall alone produce this great Revolution' (iii. 187)
may have been sincere or it may have been intended for public
consumption; in any case there is ample evidence to support the
widespread suspicion that the Illuminati favoured the selective
liquidation of the perpetrators of 'public crimes which every wise
and honest man would wish to suppress' (iii. 107). Shelley found
this notion tempting enough to develop it in his description of the
sect of tyrannicidal philanthropists in his romance 'The Assassins',
which he started in August 1814 following a rereading of Barruel.[1]
It is hardly surprising that Shelley never completed the romance,
for tyrannicide can only commend itself to a thinker who believes
that tyrants are the source of evil; it has already been made clear
that the mature Shelley sees tyranny as being a symptom as much
as a cause. Finally, although the Illuminati aimed at freeing man
to be his own ruler, the Order itself was strictly regimented and
disciplined. Weishaupt had been educated by the Jesuits, and he
adopted from them a pyramidal hierarchy designed to keep the
Order subservient to his personal control.[2] Here was the 'fictitious
unanimity' (*Letters*, i. 277) that Shelley disavowed with a
vengeance! Shelley considered that the members of his association
would agree on the means of achieving progress but would differ
concerning final ends, and he was careful to make full provision
for the secession of dissentients.[3] Weishaupt's control was confirmed by the exaction of an oath of unconditional obedience
which (unlike the Jesuit oath) left no scope at all for the exercise
of conscience.[4] Shelley's respect for the moral autonomy of the
individual would never have allowed him to take or demand such
an oath. It was the oath of obedience that proved too much for
Hogg's hero, who abandoned the order of the 'Eleutheri' when it
was demanded, though he had passed through all the other stages
of initiation.[5]

According to Barruel's 'conspiracy' theory the Jacobins and
other political societies of the French Revolution had been
spawned by the Illuminati. It seems probable that these societies

[1] *Journal*, pp. 11–12.
[2] Barruel, *Memoirs*, iii. 13–14, 409–11.
[3] See *Works*, v. 267, and *Letters*, i. 267.
[4] Barruel, *Memoirs*, iii. 75–8.
[5] Thomas Jefferson Hogg, *Memoirs of Prince Alexy Haimatoff* (1813), edited
by Sidney Scott (1952), pp. 127–9.

were in Shelley's mind when he planned his own association.[1] He would have approved of the openness of their operation and the way they served to develop public opinion by acting as public forums for debate on the course and aims of the Revolution. Moreover they nourished the spirit of the Revolution by fostering feelings of solidarity and brotherhood.[2] In the England of his day Shelley would have seen the moral rather than the directly political influence of such societies as being most valuable. One of the French societies, the 'Cercle Social des Amis de la Vérité', which was founded by Nicholas Bonneville, a friend of Paine's, hoped 'to establish a network of branches or lodges throughout France, and gradually to extend these beyond the frontiers. These cells would propagate the true principles of political philosophy; they would form the centres from which the regenerating power would operate; ultimately they would form the nucleus of a universal federation of peoples.'[3] Shelley similarly hoped that, having founded branches of his association in Ireland and Wales, he would be able to 'extend them all over England, and *quietly* revolutionize the country' (*Letters*, i. 264). McNiece has suggested that they would achieve this end not so much by direct intervention in political affairs as by functioning as 'embryo utopias' which 'might realize microcosmically now the ideal future society which would ultimately result from continuing progress'.[4] To borrow Paine's terms, they would be miniature 'societies' working inside the frame of 'government' to subvert it by rendering it redundant.[5]

Shelley certainly hoped that his association could be brought to bear on 'whatever moral or political evil it may be within the compass of human power to assuage or eradicate', but he also assigned it a more narrowly political role and saw its first task as the achievement of Emancipation and Repeal (*Works*, v. 253). His decision to found his association in Ireland initially was certainly based on his knowledge of the activities of the society of United Irishmen as chronicled in *Pieces of Irish History*. The United Irishmen, one of many British societies inspired by the French

---

[1] See McNiece, *Shelley and the Revolutionary Idea*, Ch. V.

[2] See Robespierre's defence of the Jacobin clubs, quoted in *French Revolution Documents*, Vol. i, edited by J. M. Roberts (Oxford, 1966), p. 373.

[3] Joan McDonald, *Rousseau and the French Revolution 1762–1791* (1965), p. 76.

[4] McNiece, op. cit., p. 103.

[5] Ibid., p. 96.

Revolution, had begun as a political pressure group in the Whig tradition, modelled on the earlier Irish Volunteer movement, and devoted to Reform and Emancipation.[1] The 'conspiracy' theorists saw it as yet another front for the Illuminati, arguing that its avowed aims were mere 'pretexts' to cover its 'real objects', which were 'Liberty, Equality, Secrecy, Union, and the Rights of man'.[2] These accusations are largely founded on the confounding of the original society and the later 'system of secret associations' which was founded in 1794 and also called the United Irishmen. This later society 'looked towards a republican government, founded on the broadest principles of religious liberty and equal rights', and it changed the former pledge to work for radical Reform into an oath to fight for republicanism, also making its own structure far more democratic.[3] What had happened was that the Irish opposition, exasperated by the government's counter-attacks on the democratic revolution, had gone underground, finally organizing 'a provisional representative government' and soliciting French aid.[4] This revolutionary movement was crushed in the Rebellion of 1798 and Emmet's revolt of 1803. Shelley would no doubt have felt great sympathy for the aims of this society, while disapproving of its methods, and he obviously saw the former United Irishmen as ideal recruits for his own association. He was initially eager to meet Curran, who had defended members of the society during the Rebellion (*Letters*, i. 259). He sent copies of his *Address* to Hamilton Rowan, who had been found guilty of treason and pardoned (i. 262); it is not known whether Rowan returned any reply, but it seems likely that it would have been a case of once bitten twice shy. Shelley was pleased to get Lawless's support at least partly because he had been a former United Irishman.[5] As he wrote to Miss Hitchener, 'The remnant of United Irishmen whose wrongs make them hate England I have more hopes of.—I have met with no determined Republicans, but I have found some who are DEMOCRATIFIABLE.' (*Letters*, i. 264–5) But his attempts to

---

[1] See *Pieces of Irish History*, p. 15.

[2] [Robert Clifford], *Application of Barruel's Memoirs of Jacobinism, to the Secret Societies of Ireland and Great Britain* (1798), p. 4.

[3] *Pieces of Irish History*, pp. 76–8.

[4] Ibid., p. 3. There is of course a close connection between their representative structure and their democratic aims (see R. R. Madden, *The United Irishmen, their Lives and Times* (2 vols., 1842), i. 146).

[5] R. R. Madden, op. cit. ii. 342.

revive the spirit of the 1790s were doomed to disappointment. *Pieces of Irish History* was no reliable guide to Irish public opinion in 1812. The driving force behind the United Irishmen had been the Dissenting radicals of Belfast; by 1810 the shock of the Rebellion had driven them into actual support of the Union, and it was clear that the wind of change would not blow again from that quarter.[1] Henceforward the Irish cause would be led by the Catholic radicals under O'Connell, and the O'Connellites had learnt the lesson of history too well to want anything to do with the republican aims and the violent methods of the United Irishmen.[2] Even Lawless, a former United Irishman, still, as Shelley found, a 'republican', only chronicled the first phase of the society, when their methods were still 'legal and constitutional'.[3]

Nevertheless, Shelley's scheme of an association was not irrelevant to Irish conditions, though he underestimated the extent to which Catholicism (rather than his own humanitarian Deism) would have to be the unifying force of any such organization in Ireland. When Catholic Emancipation was finally achieved it was won by the efforts of a national society using tactics similar to those recommended by Shelley.[4] On the eve of victory Thomas Wyse surveyed the history of the Catholic Association in order to show 'by what sure though tardy progress, the omnipotence of public opinion is ultimately, though gradually, brought to bear upon the most unmanageable questions of public policy, and in its good time to work those mighty moral changes in the national mind, which to the unphilosophic observer appear little less than miraculous'.[5] Shelley, and even Godwin, would have endorsed Wyse's conception of peaceful progress in harmony with general opinion. O'Connell's success was based on two factors: his realization that support for the Irish cause must come from the Catholic masses and that the opposition programme must be radicalized to secure this support;[6] and his recognition that the rea power of a mass movement lay in its moral rather than its

---

[1] See Gearóid Ó Tuathaigh, *Ireland before the Famine 1789–1848* (Dublin, 1972), pp. 38–9.

[2] See Hamilton, *State of the Catholic Cause*, pp. 10–11; Wyse, *Historical Sketch*, i. 131.

[3] *The Belfast Politics, enlarged*, p. 483.

[4] See Charles S. Middleton, *Shelley and his Writings* (2 vols., 1858), i. 217.

[5] Wyse, *Historical Sketch*, i. 6.

[6] Ibid. i. 205.

physical resources. He preferred to restrict himself to legal and constitutional methods, though he also knew how to hint at a resort to force when necessary.[1] His strongest weapon was the feeling of unity that he had instilled into the Catholics by the 1820s. The Catholic Rent, for example, was an inspired device, for it not only provided the Association with a fighting fund, but also served as 'a new means of binding the people in an open and visible fraternity, which extended from one end of Ireland to the other'.[2] The Association's great achievement was to produce that spirit which Shelley had glimpsed in 1812.

the Catholics . . . had, above all, the elevating enthusiasm of men, who fight not with selfish or factious motives, for private or partial ends, but with a really noble spirit, for a really glorious object—the rights of many millions of men, the extension of the blessings of a free constitution to generations yet unborn, the equalization of society throughout all its branches, and the security of an empire, which has continued for centuries one unbroken scene of discord and of danger.[3]

These are perhaps not precisely the objects that Shelley sought to gain, and he might have felt uneasy at the stress laid by the leaders of the Association on party discipline and 'Organization'.[4] They ran the movement like an army, deliberately creating and guiding opinion rather than merely responding to it; in this they revealed their commitment to the necessities of politics. Nevertheless Shelley would certainly have been gratified to see the way in which a great and necessary reform was achieved by the powers of public opinion, non-violent resistance, and popular association.

[1] See John Mitchel, *The History of Ireland*, ii. 140.
[2] Wyse, op. cit. i. 208.
[3] Ibid. i. 351–2.
[4] Ibid. ii. 82–3.

CHAPTER V

Liberty and Free Election[1]

AT NO period in his life was Shelley completely indifferent to political issues and events. Nevertheless his interest was certainly more lively and active at some times than at others. The period between his return from Ireland in 1812 and his return from the Continent in 1816 was, as Gerald McNiece has noted, the most apolitical in his life.[2] A partial explanation may be found in his private life: the break-up of his first marriage, the development of the relationship that led to his second, two trips abroad, struggles to secure a regular income, harrowing games of hide-and-seek with his creditors—all this was a heavy drain even on Shelley's immense energies. But Shelley always lived at this hectic pace, and it did not prevent him from taking an active interest in public events in 1811–12 or after his move to Italy. Perhaps more inhibiting was the emotional crisis he suffered in 1813–14, leading to the crippling sense of moral isolation recorded in *Alastor*—to which public despair may have contributed as much as personal emotional difficulties. If we consider Shelley's life in the context of his times changes in the political climate may offer more useful clues to the rhythm of his political engagement than any merely personal factors. It is a fact of some significance that the periods in which Shelley was most actively involved with political issues (1810–12, 1816–17, 1819–20) were also the periods when the movement for Parliamentary Reform was most active.[3] His willingness to engage in political debate from the end of 1816 registers his belief that there had come into existence a kind of politics that promised to forward his own views. When the Irish situation had failed to live up to his expectations there had been no other issue that could

---

[1] The legend on a patch-box formerly in Shelley's possession and bearing his name inside, now on display in the Bodleian Library, Oxford.

[2] *Shelley and the Revolutionary Idea*, p. 52.

[3] This point has been made by Gerald McNiece, 'Shelley's Practical Politics and Philosophical Opinions related to his Vision of Society' (unpublished B. Litt. thesis, University of Oxford, 1951), p. 263, and by Paul Foot, *Red Shelley*, Ch. vi (page refs. not available).

tempt him into the political arena at that time. It had been only too clear that there would be no possibility of achieving any productive reforms while the war against Napoleon continued; too few people were willing to take the risks involved in trying to repair the national house while the hurricane was raging. In the issue of the war itself Shelley, who had no more love for Napoleon than for any other tyrant, could have no interest. At the end of 1812 he commented, with reference to the events that led to the débâcle at Moscow, 'With respect to these victories in the North, if they tend towards Peace they are good—if otherwise they are bad.' (*Letters*, i. 346) Only peace held out any hopes of real political change.

When peace came it brought prospects of change with a vengeance, which aroused fear as much as hope, even for someone as convinced of the need for change as Shelley was. As always peace brought more problems than it solved, and the first rejoicings were soon overshadowed. When the ministerial *Courier* complacently announced, 'The play is over: let us go to supper', Cobbett retorted by putting his finger on the problems that the war had left behind it: '*The play* may be over; but, oh! no! we cannot "*go to supper*". We have something to do. We have *forty-five millions a year for ever to pay for the play*. This is no pleasant thing.'[1] The war had meant an enormous increase in the National Debt, and Shelley adopted Cobbett's figure for the annual interest.[2] Moreover the government's fulfilment of its pledge to abolish the Property Tax meant that the burden of taxation was thrown on to the labouring classes by direct taxes on necessities.[3] In addition the return to the conditions of peace led to over-production and hence to underemployment (also contributed to by demobilization), creating the classic conditions for post-war distress, as the economist David Booth explained to Fanny Imlay, who passed his account on to the Shelleys.[4] The inevitable consequences were misery and unrest among the working classes. Twenty-six thousand found themselves out of work in Staffordshire and

[1] *Political Register*, 29 July 1815, pp. 98–9.
[2] *Works*, vi. 79. See K. N. Cameron, 'Shelley, Cobbett and the National Debt'.
[3] See above, pp. 49–50.
[4] See Fanny Imlay to Mary Shelley, 29 July 1816, in Mrs Julian Marshall, *The Life and Letters of Mary Wollstonecraft Shelley* (2 vols., 1889), i. 148.

Shropshire alone; colliers on their way to put their case to the Regent (anticipating the March of the Blanketeers of 1817) dragged their coals as far as Oxford and St. Albans before being turned back by the authorities; there was widespread unemployment in Glasgow, and 'Bread or Blood' riots in the inland agricultural counties.[1] Such cases, all of which came within the observation of a single member of Shelley's circle, could be multiplied indefinitely from the newspaper reports of 1816, as the unusually cold and wet summer threatened the final calamity, a bad harvest.

The resulting unrest could not be dismissed, as the Luddite riots of 1811–12 had been, as merely a temporary and blind response to misery, the result of 'hunger' without political dimensions.[2] Writers like Cobbett and speakers like Henry ('Orator') Hunt had begun to direct the attention of working men to 'the true cause of their sufferings—misgovernment; and to its proper corrective—parliamentary reform'.[3] The radical Reformers had made little headway during the war, but now they found a ready audience for their analysis of the political causes of social suffering. Cobbett had no hesitation in pleading guilty to the charge 'that we *took advantage of the distressed state of the people*', adding, 'had we not a *right* so to do . . . Was it not our duty to call upon the people to demand a Reform, when they were tasting of all the evils of a want of Reform . . . ?'[4] To the charges that they were stirring up discontent and inciting the people to violence the Reformers could, however, plead innocence with a clear conscience. 'Their concern was to prevent economic distress from venting itself in such forms of direct action as machine-breaking, strikes and demonstrations of violence, and to turn the energies of the sufferers to political association for the immediate political purpose of reforming the House of Commons.'[5] But of course the new association of distress and political awareness was more dangerous to the aristocratic system than any amount of sporadic violence.

---

[1] Ibid. i. 148–9.

[2] *Letters*, i. 297. Shelley's reaction was typical of educated public opinion; see Frank O. Darvall, *Popular Disturbances and Public Order in Regency England* (1934; Oxford, 1969), p. 319.

[3] Samuel Bamford, *Passages in the Life of a Radical* (1839–41; 3rd edn., 2 vols., London, Edinburgh, and Manchester, 1844), i. 7.

[4] *Political Register*, 2 Aug. 1817, p. 546.

[5] Reginald J. White, *Waterloo to Peterloo* (1957; Harmondsworth, Middlesex, 1968), p. 111.

'The time never existed', warned Robert Owen in 1818, 'when knowledge and misery were so closely and extensively united.'[1]

There is clearly a parallel between the Reformers' attempts to turn popular discontent into political channels and Shelley's concern that the Irish crisis should not degenerate into 'blind insurrection' but should provide the driving force for a political association. Shelley's Irish expedition can be seen as a displaced response to the Luddite disturbances. Shelley did not take them seriously as political manifestations, but he was clearly alarmed by these outbreaks of popular violence, which he saw as signs that the English were 'willfully rushing to a Revolution, the natural death of all great commercial Empires, which must plunge them in the barbarism from which they are slowly arising'.[2] It is clear that Shelley does not relish the prospect, and his attitude in 1812 is the same as his attitude will be in 1819.

I desire to establish on a lasting basis the happiness of human-kind. Popular insurrections and revolutions I look upon with discountenance; if *such things must be* I will take the side of the People, but my reasonings shall endeavour to ward it from the hearts of the Rulers of the Earth, deeply as I detest them. (*Letters*, i. 221)

Shelley was not the only observer to be alarmed by the phenomenon of Luddism. John Cartwright, already by 1812 a veteran of the Reform movement, also appreciated the dangers of destructive violence inherent in the unrepresented and uneducated masses, and he had the foresight to see that if they could be converted to the cause of Reform it would be possible both to forestall a revolution and to forward the work to which he had devoted his life. While the government responded to Luddism with military force—the army stationed in the Midlands in 1811–12 was larger than the forces in the Spanish Peninsula—'social cranks' like Shelley and Cartwright were experimenting with more thoughtful solutions, designed to canalize discontent into political forms. Shelley's attempt to '*quietly* revolutionize the country' by the establishment of a network of philanthropical associations failed at the outset. Cartwright, with long experience in the organization of political societies, was far more successful, but it should be noted that what he was doing was not at all dissimilar to Shelley's project.

---

[1] *A New View of Society and Other Writings*, edited by John Butt (1972), p. 134.
[2] *Letters*, i. 110. See also i. 213.

Cartwright was as dissatisfied as was Shelley with '*the time-servingness of temporizing reform*' (*Works*, v. 246), and it is now known that his intention in 1812 was to outflank the moderate and Whig Reformers of the metropolis and to build a popular Reform movement on the feeling in the country at large.[1] He built well, for his tours as a self-appointed 'political missionary' from 1812 onwards sowed the seeds among the industrial workers of the North and Midlands that were to bear fruit in the Hampden Club movement of late 1816.[2] He had created the kind of association that Shelley had wished for.

Shelley's failure saved him from the embarrassments that the establishment of a political association of the politically excluded would inevitably have caused him. The Hampden Club movement was just such an association, and his attitude to it is interestingly ambivalent. It is usual to discuss the political situation of post-war England in terms of a split between 'radical' and 'moderate' Reformers.[3] These terms have some point, and I make use of them myself, but it can usefully be argued that the basic distinction is really between the *metropolitan* Reformers like Burdett, Francis Place, Leigh Hunt, and the more radical Whigs, and the *provincial*, working-class Reformers, who had their own local leaders, and followed the political line of the more extreme national figures like Cartwright, Cobbett, and Henry Hunt, who had recognized the potential of this large popular movement.[4] There was inevitably tension and even friction between the two groups. To a Manchester man like Samuel Bamford, for example, London was 'the great Babylon'. He found the genteel Burdett unsympathetic, and looked for guidance to Cartwright, 'our venerable political Father'.[5] Shelley had a surprisingly clear awareness of what had happened, though this alone could not free him from the limitations of his own situation. He knew that since the end of the seventeenth

---

[1] See Naomi Churgin Miller, 'Major John Cartwright and the Founding of the Hampden Club', *English Historical Journal*, xvii (1974), 615–19.

[2] See Edward P. Thompson, *The Making of the English Working Class* (1963; Harmondsworth, Middlesex, 1968), pp. 665–8. See also N. C. Miller, 'John Cartwright and radical parliamentary reform, 1808–1819', *English Historical Review*, lxxxiii (1968), 705–28.

[3] See for example K. N. Cameron, 'Shelley and the Reformers', *ELH* xii (1945), 63–4, and *Shelley: The Golden Years* (Cambridge, Mass., 1974), pp. 122–5.

[4] See R. J. White, *Waterloo to Peterloo*, pp. 155–6.

[5] *Passages in the Life of a Radical*, i. 29, 32.

century there had appeared in England what he called a 'fourth class', 'the unrepresented multitude' who 'had no constitutional presence in the state', for it was no longer possible to claim that their interests were 'virtually' represented by the existing political classes (*Works*, vii. 23). Shelley had a vivid sympathy for them as victims of social injustice, but he also feared and mistrusted them. His own political experience and connections always lay within the circle of metropolitan radicalism—what could he have known of the political consciousness developing among the unrepresented masses? To him they were 'the helots of luxury', 'the untutored multitude' (*Works*, vi. 79–80). Their condition, their hopes, fears, and aspirations were opaque to him. The utmost that his imaginative sympathy could achieve was to envisage that this shapeless and potentially destructive force could, like Demogorgon, also be a force for beneficial change.[1]

Shelley appreciated that, while popular distress and discontent presented a fearsome danger, it also provided an unequalled opportunity. That the mass of the population should have come to see that their grievances originated in an unjust system of government and should demand its reform was, however alarming, a great and significant movement in 'opinion'. Such a movement of opinion portended and made inevitable great social changes. 'The cloud of mind is discharging its collected lightning, and the equilibrium between institutions and opinions is now restoring, or is about to be restored.' (Preface to *Prometheus Unbound*) Shelley has in mind a poetical discharge here, but the imbalance between institutions and opinions is to be restored politically too. From 1817 on Shelley's writings abound in images of thunderstorms, earthquakes, volcanoes, avalanches, and the like, all registering his conviction that beneath the surface of his society were mighty forces struggling to attain a new state of equilibrium—forces beyond human control which might only attain equilibrium by violent and destructive outbreaks. Occasionally the allegorical

---

[1] The possibility of reading 'Demogorgon' as *demos* (the people) and *gorgon* (terrible) has already been noted by G. M. Matthews, 'A Volcano's Voice in Shelley', p. 187. See also Paul Foot, *Red Shelley*, Ch. vi (page refs. not available). Scholars tracing the background of Shelley's use of the name have failed to note that it had a contemporary political sense, no doubt with a pun on 'demagogue'; see G. E. Bentley, Jr., *Blake Records* (Oxford, 1969), pp. 46, 70, and *The Complete Works of Walter Savage Landor*, edited by T. Earle Welby and Stephen Wheeler (1927–36; 16 vols., New York and London, 1969), v. 2 n. 3.

conceit proves too much for the poetry, as when Shelley pains-
takingly images the growth of 'opinion' as an avalanche

> whose mass,
> Thrice sifted by the storm, had gathered there
> Flake after flake, in Heaven-defying minds
> As thought by thought is piled, till some great truth
> Is loosened, and the nations echo round
> Shaken to their roots: as do the mountains now.
> (*Prometheus Unbound*, II. iii. 37–42)[1]

These lines seem to echo Prometheus' earlier vision of the French
Revolution.

> The nations thronged around, and cried aloud
> As with one voice, "Truth, liberty and love!"
> (I. 650–1)

Certainly it was the French Revolution which provided the
immediate example of the dangers attending any political movement that involved the masses. Its shadow lies over all of Shelley's
pronouncements on the political situation of England. If the
'equilibrium between institutions and opinions' were not restored,
there would be an upheaval like that in France which had been
produced by 'a defect of correspondence between the knowledge
existing in society and the improvement or gradual abolition of
political institutions'.[2] When Shelley warned of the dangers of
placing power 'in the hands of men who have been rendered brutal
and torpid and ferocious by ages of slavery' (*Works*, vi. 68) he had
in mind the atrocities committed in France by men 'rendered
brutal, ignorant, servile, and bloody, by long slavery' (vii. 13).
Their crimes were to be put to the account of tyranny itself, but
that did not make revolutionary excesses seem any more desirable.
It is not until 1819 that Shelley can muster the moral courage to
prefer even revolution to continuing despotism.

We must look briefly at the development of the post-war Reform
crisis in order to understand Shelley's Reform activities. During
the winter of 1816–17 the new-found strength of the Reform

---

[1] Carl Woodring, who reads this passage as an image of movements in thought
and poetry, also quotes W. J. Linton's application of it to describe a popular
political movement (*Politics in English Romantic Poetry*, pp. 287, 353). See also
G. McNiece, *Shelley and the Revolutionary Idea*, p. 221.

[2] Preface to *Laon and Cythna*.

movement led its leaders to hope for a speedy victory when Parliament reassembled in January. Cobbett wrote:

The country, instead of being disturbed, as the truly *seditious* writers on the side of Corruption would fain make us believe; instead of being *"irritated"* by the agitation of Reform, is kept, by the hope, which Reform holds out to it, in a state of tranquillity, wholly unparalleled in the history of the world, under a similar pressure of suffering.[1]

Cobbett's account is confirmed by so unlikely a witness as Coleridge, who observed with some shrewdness that 'The mere looking forward to the meeting of Parliament keeps up the spirits of the nation, and inspires a feeling of hope not the less effective from its expectations being indefinite'.[2] Shelley saw the ominous undercurrents, but felt able to report to Byron that 'the people appear calm, and steady even under situations of great excitement; and reform may come without revolution'. What worried Shelley was the new power of 'the popular party', and in particular the growing influence of 'illiterate demagogues'.[3] His fears proved to be justified, for Henry Hunt responded to the initiative of the extreme Spencean Philanthropists by addressing two mass meetings in support of Reform in Spa-fields, the second of which was the occasion of an abortive putsch by the Spenceans. Shelley was later to warn Reformers against such 'partial assemblies of the multitude' (*Works*, vi. 64), and his objection does not stem from genteel fastidiousness; the Spa-fields fiasco served to frighten moderate Reformers away from the popular movement, and gave the government an excuse to look for plots and introduce legislation against the Reformers in general.[4] The sailor Cashman was executed for his part in the riots; he was hanged opposite Godwin's shop in Skinner Street, and this case may have been in Shelley's mind when he later discussed the effect on the public of capital punishment for political crimes.[5]

---

[1] *Political Register*, 21 Dec. 1816, p. 800.

[2] *Essays on His Times*, ii. 462.

[3] *Letters*, i. 513. Shelley's distaste for Henry Hunt (shared by all moderate Reformers) led him to neglect Hunt's achievement in creating a 'mass platform', a logical development of Cartwright's proselytization of the movement (see J. C. Belchem, 'Henry Hunt and the evolution of the mass platform', *Eng. Hist. Rev.* xciii (1978), 739–73).

[4] E. P. Thompson, *The Making of the English Working Class*, pp. 691–7.

[5] *Works*, vi. 187–8. See Ford K. Brown, 'Notes on 41 Skinner Street', *MLN* liv (1939), 329.

Moderate fears would hardly have been allayed by the convention of delegates from the northern Hampden Clubs which met in January 1817. Such conventions tended to have the appearance of being intended as alternative parliaments; they reminded the cautious of the French National Convention, and they were technically illegal.[1] Godwin's most successful pamphlet was written to defend the leaders of the London Corresponding Society and the Society for Constitutional Information when in 1794 they were indicted for treason for organizing just such a convention.[2] In 1817 the convention was dominated by the radicals who, championed by Henry Hunt, forced through resolutions in favour of the popular programme of Universal Suffrage, Annual Parliaments, and the secret ballot, rejecting the more moderate proposals that would have been acceptable to Burdett and the Whigs. Significantly it was the arguments of one of the provincial Reformers, Samuel Bamford, that won over Cobbett, formerly a Burdettite; Cobbett was beginning to appreciate that a mass movement needed a radical and popular programme.[3] The convention met at the Crown and Anchor, and it is perhaps no coincidence that Shelley proposed the same venue for a meeting in his first Reform pamphlet, published at the end of February or beginning of March.[4] His *Proposals* have all the marks of being intended as a reply to the radical convention, for in it he criticizes those who split the Reform movement by debating the contentious details of Reform (*Works*, vi. 67–8). His tendency to take his stand with the moderate Reformers of the metropolis is evident in the list of people to whom he wished copies of the pamphlet to be sent; the only radicals on the list were Cobbett and Cartwright (Henry Hunt being significantly absent), and no copies were ordered to be sent to the really radical journals.[5]

It should be stressed that Shelley's support for a moderate Reform programme was the result of a tactical decision on his part—he thought that moderate Reform was attainable with

[1] E. P. Thompson, *The Making of the English Working Class*, p. 675.

[2] See *The Life of Thomas Holcroft. Written by himself, continued . . . by William Hazlitt* (1816), edited by Elbridge Colby (2 vols., 1925), ii. 26–69.

[3] E. P. Thompson, op. cit., pp. 697–9.

[4] *Works*, vi. 64. Copies of the pamphlet seem to have been available by 2 March (*Examiner*, 2 Mar. 1817, p. 139).

[5] The list is printed in *Letters*, i. 533–4. See K. N. Cameron, *Shelley: The Golden Years*, pp. 123–4.

support from the respectable political classes, and he considered that a more extreme Reform would be dangerous *at that time*. We cannot understand Shelley's pronouncements on Reform unless we realize that theoretically he is in complete agreement with the democratic aspirations of the radicals. He explicitly grants the abstract soundness of their arguments in favour of Universal Suffrage, and adds that from their premises they should arrive (as he had already done) at the republican conclusions of Paine. He makes it clear that he recommends a more restricted suffrage purely on the grounds of temporary expedience (*Works*, vi. 68). As an alternative to the radical tactics of mass meetings and conventions of delegates Shelley proposed a nation-wide canvass of opinion to determine 'whether the majority of the adult individuals of the United Kingdom of Great Britain and Ireland desire or no a complete representation in the Legislative Assembly' (vi. 64). This, as Crane Brinton saw, is to take for granted 'the concession of just that principle of popular sovereignty the opponents of Reform were denying'.[1] Behind Shelley's proposal is Paine's suggestion that there should be 'a method of occasionally ascertaining the state of public opinion with respect to government'.[2] The contradictions present in the pamphlet are not the result of ignorance or illogical thinking on Shelley's part but stem from his attempt to effect a working compromise between democratic theory and gradualist practice.

The events of 1817 were hardly encouraging to anyone who hoped to solve England's problems by an appeal to compromise. What seemed to be developing was a rising spiral of violence on the part of the radicals and repression on the part of the government. The abortive Spencean rising and the famous 'air-gun' attack on the Regent in January led to the appointment of parliamentary Committees of Secrecy, whose reports (which read like a supplement to Barruel) were used to justify legislation suspending Habeas Corpus and directed against radical organizations and publications.[3] In March 1817 the weavers of Manchester attempted to bring their grievances directly to the attention of the govern-

---

[1] *The Political Ideas of the English Romanticists*, p. 170.

[2] Paine, *Complete Writings*, i. 446. Paine also supplied Shelley with the ideas that the Government could rebel against the people, and that a nation was entitled to prefer bad government to reform (see *Works*, vi. 64, 63–4, and Paine, *Complete Writings*, i. 446, 447).

[3] E. P. Thompson, op. cit., pp. 699–700.

ment with the 'March of the Blanketeers', quickly suppressed by the government who detected an ominous reminiscence of the march from Marseilles to Paris of 1792.[1] The authorities soon began to use their new powers to round up suspected radicals under the suspension of Habeas Corpus, especially in the Manchester area.[2] The climax of these disturbing events drew from Shelley his most eloquent contribution to the Reform cause. On Monday, 7 November, Jeremiah Brandreth, William Turner, and Isaac Ludlam were executed for high treason at Derby as the ringleaders of an abortive rising in Derbyshire the previous June.[3] The day before, the heir presumptive Princess Charlotte had died in childbirth, an event that attracted far more public attention than the fate of the rebels.[4] There was a dangerous lack of proportion here that Shelley rebuked by his apposite quotation of Paine's riposte to Burke: 'We Pity the Plumage, but Forget the Dying Bird'.[5] This was prefixed to his second Reform pamphlet, *An Address to the People on the Death of the Princess Charlotte*,[6] in which he argued that the death of the Princess, however regrettable, was in the common course of nature, while the fate of Brandreth, Ludlam, and Turner resulted from a train of events originating in the wills of men and over which men might recover control if they were able to see how significant such events were for the moral and political state of the country.

Shelley's account of these events is founded on a widespread myth of the time, according to which unrest was deliberately fomented by government *agents provocateurs* in order to produce a general alarm and thus justify repression. He saw the Derbyshire rebels as 'innocent and unsuspecting rustics', 'A few hungry and ignorant manufacturers'—modern historians might consider them

---

[1] R. J. White, *Waterloo to Peterloo*, pp. 163–4.

[2] Samuel Bamford, *Passages in the Life of a Radical*, i. 42–5, 60, 64.

[3] See E. P. Thompson, *The Making of the English Working Class*, Ch. 15, section 4, and R. J. White, *Waterloo to Peterloo*, Ch. 14.

[4] The Princess had been the white hope of the Whigs, 'an Heir Apparent avowedly brought up in the principles of the late Mr. Fox' (*Examiner*, 24 Jan. 1813, p. 49). The national mourning is described in *The Times* (7, 8 Nov. 1817), which put its own columns into mourning for the Princess.

[5] *Works*, vi. 71. See Paine, *Complete Writings*, i. 260.

[6] This was composed on 11 and 12 November (*Journal*, p. 86). The only extant copies are of an edition produced by Thomas Rodd in the 1840s, but there is some evidence to support Rodd's own account, according to which Shelley had a limited private edition printed, presumably in November or December 1817 (see *SC* v. 125 n. 7).

rather more serious revolutionaries than that would suggest.[1] Elsewhere Shelley shows himself quite well aware that a popular revolution might well occur even unsponsored by government agents, though the known involvement of the informer known as 'Oliver' in the revolt tempted many Reformers to claim that without the existence of a government plot there would have been no insurrection. Shelley in fact does not go so far as to claim that 'the higher members of the government' were so cynical as to be directly 'involved in the guilt of their infernal agents'. His accusation was that they exploited the alarm generated by popular violence to justify the 'extraordinary powers' that they had assumed to repress the call for Reform (*Works*, vi. 80). As a Whig spokesman put it, while the government did not make the rebellion, 'they made the most of it'.[2] Shelley in fact has no more sympathy for the rebels than he has for the government, but he expresses far more bitterness against the latter because when the country called for Reform the government deliberately relinquished the opportunity of guiding change into peaceful channels. Their intransigence goaded the people to courses of violence to which they could offer no reply but repression. England was being forced to choose between government despotism and popular revolution, an impossible choice which could only be evaded by embracing the third alternative—reform (*Works*, vi. 80).

By late 1817 Shelley had good reason to fear that the third option was no longer available. The peroration of the *Address* attempts to redirect the national mourning, which may be only too well founded.

A beautiful Princess is dead:—she who should have been the Queen of her beloved Nation, and whose posterity should have ruled it for ever. . . . LIBERTY is dead. Slave! I charge thee disturb not the depth and solemnity of our grief by any meaner sorrow. . . . Let us follow the corpse of British Liberty slowly and reverentially to its tomb: and if some glorious Phantom should appear, and make its throne of broken swords and sceptres and royal crowns trampled in the dust, let us say that the Spirit of Liberty has arisen from its grave and left all that was gross and mortal there, and kneel down and worship it as our Queen. (*Works*, vi. 82)

The anagnorisis that Shelley manages here is a brilliant stroke

---

[1] *Works*, vi. 80. See E. P. Thompson, op. cit., Ch. 15, section 4.
[2] Quoted from A. Mitchell, *The Whigs in Opposition 1815–1830*, p. 112.

consider the *Address* only as a political pamphlet—it is
ough typical, irony that this was the only one of his
phlets that he was unable to distribute at the time,
ight well have been the most effective of all. It anticipates by nearly two years his deployment of the rhetoric of rule,
redirecting as it does the language of external majesty to the realm
of the principles that rule man's moral life—we might compare
this passage directly with his revision of the National Anthem,
where he hails the Queen, Liberty, whose throne is to be 'in our
hearts alone'. The possibility of this Queen receiving due allegiance
in the England of 1817 or 1819 was as remote as that of a resurrec-
tion from the grave, an image that is repeated at the end of his
'Sonnet: England in 1819'. The Gothic imagery of the charnel-
house, so prevalent in his early verse, now functions to convey his
sense of what was happening to the moral life of a nation which
had rejected the opportunity for peaceful progress.[1]

Shelley's clock stopped in 1817, politically speaking. His move
to Italy in 1818 cut him off from many sources of information,
and from all possibility of an intimate knowledge of the state of
opinion in England. The events of 1819, culminating in the famous
'Peterloo Massacre' served to convince almost all sectors of
English opinion that the great 'crisis' had arrived. Richard
Carlile's *Republican* carried a series of leading articles under the
heading 'The Crisis', and in December 1819 he wrote, 'It might
be said without presumption, or without the fear of false predictions, or of contradiction, that the CRISIS has arrived.'[2] But if it
took Peterloo to convince a radical Whig like Henry White that
the government's policies would end in '*Anarchy and revolution!*
Brothers will arm against brothers in unholy warfare . . .' and that
the choice was 'REFORM or REVOLUTION',[3] Shelley had foreseen as
much two years previously. Peterloo certainly served to precipitate
out feelings and convictions that Shelley had been developing

---

[1] See 'Lines written during the Castlereagh administration'; 'Song to the Men
of England', lines 29–32; 'To Sidmouth and Castlereagh'; 'A New National
Anthem', lines 2–3; *The Triumph of Life*, lines 503–5. Less specifically political
examples are 'Ode to the West Wind', lines 5–8, 23–5, and *Adonais*, lines 348–51.
On Shelley's political use of Gothic imagery see Anne Thompson, 'Shelley and
"Satire's scourge" ', in *Literature of the Romantic Period 1750–1850*, edited by
R. T. Davies and B. G. Beatty (Liverpool, 1976), pp. 146–9.

[2] *Republican*, 3 Dec. 1819, p. 225.

[3] *Independent Whig*, 5 Dec. 1819, p. 1519.

since November 1817 at least. It was the occasion of two of his greatest political works, *The Mask of Anarchy* and *A Philosophical View of Reform*, but not their cause. The events at Manchester tended to mislead Shelley if anything, for he assumed that they would be the first of a series of similar incidents, and he set himself to writing the scenario for an ideal Peterloo, as he had done for the French Revolution in *Laon and Cythna*.[1] Like all political thinkers Shelley was at times liable to see 'the Past in the To-come',[2] to let his reactions to what had already happened obscure his perception of what was happening and falsify his predictions of what was going to happen.

We must now look in some detail at the content of Shelley's activities on behalf of Reform. I shall not have anything to say about *Swellfoot the Tyrant* (1820), Shelley's contribution to the flood of ephemera spawned by George IV's attempts to divorce his wife, since this work has already received adequate critical attention.[3] It is ironic that this was the only one of Shelley's specifically Reformist works to attract any attention at the time. Horace Smith, who saw the work through the press for Shelley, received a visit from a 'burly alderman' (probably Sheriff Richard Rothwell) who demanded the name of the author 'in order that he might be prosecuted for a seditious and disloyal libel'. To save the publisher from prosecution Smith gave up the remainder of the edition (all but seven copies in one account) to be burnt.[4] Smith said that Rothwell came on the part of 'The Society for the Suppression of Vice', but I think this may be an error. This Society (founded 1802) concerned itself with the suppression of 'blasphemous or obscene publications';[5] Shelley's work was considered objectionable for political reasons, and seditious publications were the concern of Dr Stoddart's Constitutional Association

[1] See *The Mask of Anarchy*, lines 262–363, and *Works*, vii. 48–9. Some Reformers thought that further mass meetings would detract from the moral victory gained at Peterloo, and preferred to press their advantage in the lawcourts (J. C. Belchem, loc. cit. 760).

[2] Prologue to *Hellas*, line 161.

[3] See Newman Ivey White, 'Shelley's *Swell-foot the Tyrant* in Relation to Contemporary Political Satire', *PMLA* xxxvi (1921), 332–46, and Carlos Baker, *Shelley's Major Poetry: The Fabric of a Vision* (Princeton, 1948), pp. 173–81.

[4] Arthur H. Beavan, *James and Horace Smith* (1899), p. 176; K. N. Cameron, *Shelley: The Golden Years*, p. 628 n.38.

[5] Élie Halévy, *England in 1815* (1913), translated by E. I. Watkin and D. A. Barker (1924; 1961), p. 452.

(founded 1820).[1] Smith recorded that *Swellfoot* was burnt at 'the Inquisition Office, in Bridge Street, Blackfriars', and the Constitutional Association was known as 'the Bridge Street Gang' because its headquarters were there.

We have seen how Shelley was forced to abandon his early attempts to form an association of the enlightened to work for political reform. It is to be doubted that he ever completely renounced his faith in the potential of a union of the benevolent to influence opinion and promote change. As late as 1819 he felt that there was a need for an association of the good to counter the combination of the bad.[2] What he had specifically in mind was a literary alliance, and his hopes in this direction were finally to bear fruit in the short-lived magazine *The Liberal*.[3] In the more active field of politics he still believed in the value of 'such open confederations among men of principle and spirit as may tend to make their intentions and their efforts converge to a common centre' (*Works*, vii. 48). But he no longer believed that such an association could be willed into existence by individual efforts. It had to arise spontaneously as the representative of a general movement of opinion. The Reform movement, which united thousands all over the country in the agitation for a common object (whatever their differences as to details), provided the foundation for just such an association. This movement could not be amenable to the whims of an individual, and if Shelley wished to influence it he would have to find some compromise between its aims and his own beliefs. It is important to remember that, while Shelley believed in the necessity of Reform, he was well aware that he possessed ulterior objectives which other Reformers did not share. As an opponent of all forms of government Shelley could not accept a mere reform of the existing system as a final goal. It was a means of peaceful progress towards his own political goals, but it possessed a relative rather than an absolute importance. As Shelley was aware, it would be out of place for a Reformer to express such scepticism.

---

[1] See A. Aspinall, *Politics and the Press*, p. 64; *The Letters of William and Dorothy Wordsworth: The Middle Years*, edited by E. de Selincourt, revised by M. Moorman and A. G. Hill (2 vols., Oxford, 1969–70), ii. 657.

[2] See above, pp. 157–8.

[3] See William H. Marshall, *Byron, Shelley, Hunt, and* The Liberal (Philadelphia, 1960).

the advocate of a new system of diet is held bound to be invulnerable to disease, in the same manner as the sectaries of a new system of religion are held to be more moral than other people, or as a reformed parliament must at least be assumed as the remedy of all political evils. No one will change the diet, adopt the religion, or reform parliament else. (*Letters*, i. 543)

Shelley had more moderate expectations. In promoting Reform he did not hope (as other Reformers clearly did) to find a remedy to 'the universal evils of all constituted society' but only to 'the peculiar system of misrule under which those evils have been exasperated now' (*Letters*, ii. 22). That would be a great benefit in itself, and would clear the ground for further progress thereafter. In order to achieve this it was worth sinking political differences so that all those who supported Reform (for whatever reason) could co-operate to achieve it.

To do this it would be necessary to temper Godwinian Sincerity with a certain measure of expedience, a moral crux that Shelley debated with himself in the so-called 'Essay on Christianity', written towards the end of 1817.

it is of no small moment to the success even of a true cause that the judges who are to determine on its merits should be free from the national and religious predilections which render the multitude both deaf and blind. Let not this practice be considered as an unworthy artifice. It were best for the cause of reason that mankind should acknowledge no other authority but its own, but it is useful to a certain extent, that they should not consider those institutions which they have been habituated to reverence as opposing an obstacle to its admission. All reformers have been compelled to practice this misrepresentation of their own true feelings and opinions. . . . The interests . . . of truth require that an orator should so far as possible produce in his hearers that state of mind in which alone his exhortations could fairly be contemplated and examined. (*Works*, vi. 242–3)

These remarks are addressed as much to Shelley's situation as to Christ's. By 1817 Shelley was far more willing to listen to the voice of prudence than he had been in his youth.[1] If he had thought like this in 1812 he might have avoided giving offence to the susceptibilities of his Catholic audience. It was common for

---

[1] See G. McNiece, *Shelley and the Revolutionary Idea*, p. 80.

Reformers to claim Christ as one of themselves.[1] Shelley seems to have been the only one who took this trope seriously enough to model his own tactics on what he took to be Christ's practice.

> He said—However new or strange my doctrines may appear to you they are, in fact, only the restoration and reestablishment of those original institutions, and ancient customs of your own law and religion. The constitution of your faith and policy, altho' perfect in their origin, have become corrupt and altered, and have fallen into decay. I propose to restore them to their pristine authority and splendour . . .
>
>   Having produced this favourable disposition of mind Jesus Christ proceeds to qualify and finally to abrogate the system of the Jewish law. (*Works*, vi. 242)

Whether or not Christ made such claims the Reformers of Shelley's day notoriously did so, presenting their 'Re-form' as a return to the former perfection of the Constitution.[2] I doubt whether they had the ulterior views that Shelley attributes to Christ, but Shelley himself certainly did, as we must realize when considering his adoption of Reformist rhetoric. He had no desire to turn the clock back to the days of the Saxon commonwealth. He refers approvingly to 'Saxon Alfred' in the 'Ode to Liberty', but his survey of European history in *A Philosophical View of Reform* is quite free of the Reformist myth of the Gothic Constitution, Saxon liberties, and so on. But he appreciated the emotional force of an appeal to traditional liberties, and felt free to make it in his poems intended for a popular audience.

> Let the Laws of your own land,
> Good or ill, between ye stand . . .
>
> The old laws of England—they
> Whose reverend heads with age are grey,
> Children of a wiser day . . .
> (*The Mask of Anarchy*, lines 327–8, 331–3)[3]

---

[1] See Paine, *Complete Writings*, i. 469; John Horne Tooke, *The Diversions of Purley*, Part II (1805), p. 490; *Memoirs of Henry Hunt, Esq. Written by Himself* (3 vols., 1820–2), ii. 67; John Cartwright, *The English Constitution Produced and Illustrated* (1823), p. 249.

[2] See E. P. Thompson, *The Making of the English Working Class*, pp. 91–6.

[3] Crane Brinton takes Shelley rather too literally in finding his devotion to the old laws 'touching' (*The Political Ideas of the English Romanticists*, p. 175). Shelley wrote quite bluntly: 'The English nation does not, as has been imagined, inherit freedom from its ancestors' (*Works*, vi. 270).

The Reformers liked to make much of 'the laws which once were the security of the person and property of this country' (Habeas Corpus, the Bill of Rights, and so on), laws which they claimed had been 'SUBVERTED'.[1] Shelley chose to defer to such feelings without necessarily sharing them.[2] His real opinions can be read between the lines; he refers to the old laws as 'good or ill' and at line 337 he calls them 'sacred heralds', forerunners of the future society, rather than the survivals of a vanished perfection.

Shelley's intention to follow Christ's example and 'to qualify and finally to abrogate' certain features of English law, regardless of their venerable antiquity, is also clear. The plan of *A Philosophical View* seems to have included a discussion of capital punishment; on an otherwise blank leaf of the notebook is written 'On the punishment of death'.[3] Shelley probably intended to insert at this point an untitled fragment which Mary Shelley printed under this title.[4] In his opposition to the death penalty Shelley was willing to risk offending his audience, for he can hardly have been unaware that the 'numerous class of little tradesmen . . . richer and more powerful than those who are employed by them' who supported capital punishment were also the backbone of the Reform movement in the metropolis.[5] More congenial to Reformers would have been the attack on the landed aristocracy in 'On the Game Laws' (1817).[6] Shelley blamed the Game Laws for 'corrupting the tastes and morals' of the country, and it is clear that he conceived the duty of the enlightened Reformer to guide the opinion of his associates as committing him to animadversions on moral as well as legal topics. Thus he attempted to 'startle the reader from the trance of ordinary life' and 'to break through the crust of those outworn opinions on which established institutions

---

[1] *Republican*, 27 Aug. 1819, p. 4. John Scott confessed to 'an almost superstitious devotion' to 'the ancient laws' (*Champion*, 23 Mar. 1817, p. 92). See E. P. Thompson, op. cit., pp. 85–91.

[2] Carl Woodring has plausibly suggested that Shelley intended to parody claims for a 'Gothic' or 'Saxon' ancestry for English Liberties in *Swellfoot* (*Politics in English Romantic Poetry*, p. 272). Such claims were, *pace* Woodring, Reformist rather than Whiggish by Shelley's day.

[3] *SC* vi. 1066.

[4] See *Works*, vi. 185–90.

[5] *Works*, vi. 188. This class set the tone politically even in the 'Jacobin' constituency of Westminster (see E. P. Thompson, *The Making of the English Working Class*, p. 509).

[6] See above, pp. 49–50.

depend' by a sympathetic portrayal of incest in *Laon and Cythna*.[1]
Less bizarre were the attacks on revenge and remorse in the same
work (VIII. xxii). In 1817 the Shelleys had been alarmed by the
vindictive tone of Cobbett's attacks on the boroughmongers, and
Mary complained, 'He encourages in the multitude the worst
possible human passion *revenge*.'[2] Shelley was opposed to revenge
and to punishment conceived as retaliation because they were
impotent to reform the person against whom they were directed,
and only served to enslave the future to the evil done in the past.
He condemned revenge at length in the 'Essay on Christianity'
(*Works*, vi. 236–40), and *A Philosophical View* as it stands ends
with a passage urging Reformers to repudiate such negative
emotions (vii. 55).

Shelley's own willingness to compromise and sink points of
ideological difference in order to work within and influence a great
popular movement lies behind his appeals to other Reformers to
make similar sacrifices for the sake of unity. His own Reform
proposals were extremely moderate because he wished to construct a programme which should attract widespread support as a
kind of highest common factor of all available programmes. He
suspected, with good reason, that it would be wiser to postpone
discussion of the details of Reform until agreement had been
reached on the necessity of *some* kind of Reform.

the most eloquent, and the most virtuous, and the most venerable
among the Friends of Liberty,[3] should employ their authority and
intellect to persuade men to lay aside all animosity and even discussion
respecting the topics on which they are disunited, and by the love which
they bear to their suffering country conjure them to contribute all their
energies to set this great question at rest—whether the nation desires a
Reform in Parliament or no? . . . It is trivial to discuss what species of
Reform shall have place, when it yet remains a question whether there
will be any Reform or no. (*Works*, vi. 65, 67)

---

[1] Preface to *Laon and Cythna*. Shelley himself realized that to advertise his
adherence to such extreme views only tended to alienate his readers (*Letters*,
i. 582).

[2] *The Letters of Mary W. Shelley*, edited by Frederick L. Jones (2 vols.,
Norman, Oklahoma, 1944), i. 37. Mary's letter was quoted by Leigh Hunt in
the *Examiner* (5 Oct. 1817, p. 626). For Shelley's similar criticism of Cobbett
see *Peter Bell the Third* (1819), III. 91–3, and note to VI. 95.

[3] I think Shelley intends a specific reference to Burdett, Leigh Hunt, and
Cartwright.

Shelley is here speaking the language of the moderate and Whig Reformers.[1] He suspected, with some reason, that it was the Radicals who were likely to be most intransigent, as a cancelled passage in the draft of his *Proposal* makes clear: 'The advocates of annual Parliaments & Universal Suffrage It requires some sacrifise of the selfish the envious'.[2] But the whole Reform movement was by nature fissiparous, for reasons both ideological and personal.

On the face of it Reform should have provided the rallying point for a wide spectrum of opinion opposed to the policies of the government. All those between the more radical Whigs at one extreme and republicans like Carlile at the other should have felt able to co-operate in achieving a Reform which would make Parliament more accountable to those it governed. In practice no two groups, and hardly any two individuals, could agree on what they wanted and how to get it. As Southey observed, the question 'what is meant by Parliamentary Reform?' acted like 'the apple of discord' among the Reformers themselves.[3] Self-interest exacerbated these disputes. The Whigs, considering themselves the traditional leaders of 'the people', distrusted even Burdett's brand of Reform.[4] The Burdettites in return scorned the timidity and time-servingness of the Whigs. However it was complained that there was 'too little co-operation' between Burdett and the other parliamentary leader of the Reformers, Lord Cochrane.[5] As the call for Reform grew, Burdett found his own popularity being threatened by the more extreme Reformers from the provincial Hampden Clubs and their leaders, and early in 1817 he refused to present their petition, commenting, 'I am determined not to be made a cat's paw of . . .'[6] By 1818 he had formed an alliance with

[1] See the speeches delivered by Burdett and Thomas Brand at a meeting of 'The Friends of Public Order, Retrenchment, and Reform' held on 22 February 1817 (*Examiner*, 2 Mar. 1817, pp. 141–2), and the Declaration proposed to the same meeting by William Peter (*The Times*, 24 Feb. 1817). All three were on the list of those who were to be sent copies of Shelley's *Proposals*.

[2] *A Proposal for putting Reform to the Vote throughout the Kingdom . . . Facsimile of the Holograph Manuscript with an Introduction by H. Buxton Forman* (1887), p. 14.

[3] *Essays, Moral and Political* (1832; 2 vols., Shannon, 1971), i. 376.

[4] See H. W. Carless Davis, *The Age of Grey and Peel* (1929; Oxford, 1964), pp. 207–8.

[5] *Reformists' Register*, 8 Feb. 1817, p. 33.

[6] Quoted from M. W. Patterson, *Sir Francis Burdett*, ii. 415.

Jeremy Bentham, and was defending the latter's ultra-democratic scheme (including Universal Suffrage and the secret ballot) to the Commons; Burdett and Bentham shared a healthy contempt for 'the *Cobbett* with his penmanship' and 'the *Henry Hunt* with his oratory'.[1] The radical Reformers were even less tractable. They poured contempt on the Whigs as 'enemies of Reform';[2] denounced 'what are called *moderate* Reforms' with gibes about 'moderate' honesty;[3] attacked Burdett on the score of his vanity and his ambition;[4] quarrelled with the radical 'City Whigs' such as Robert Waithman;[5] sneered at the propertied Reformers of the London Hampden Club;[6] ridiculed Bentham's *Plan*;[7] and attacked Leigh Hunt and his *Examiner*.[8] At the same time they denounced anyone who was more extreme than they were, such as the Spenceans or the advocates of pure republicanism.[9] Nor were they safe from each other. In 1808 Cobbett had denounced Henry Hunt as a man of 'bad character', and even when they were colleagues his praise for Hunt was (not without reason) qualified.[10] Hunt deplored the 'shyness' that developed between them, but did not hesitate to attack Cobbett for fleeing to America in 1817.[11] That all this in-fighting often had its source in personal vanity and rivalry is clear from some revealing remarks made by Cobbett's daughter in 1820.

Papa never did a better thing than cutting the old Major (Cartwright), Hunt, and the whole tribe calling themselves Reformers. He has never until now been able to do anything or go anywhere without having to drag some of them along with him, and they always kept him back; but

---

[1] Ibid. ii. 462–4; Jeremy Bentham, *Plan of Parliamentary Reform* (1817), p. cxiii.

[2] *Political Register*, 28 Apr. 1810, p. 644; *Memoirs of Henry Hunt*, i. 508–10.

[3] *Political Register*, 6 Sept. 1817, p. 735.

[4] Ibid., 13 Sept. 1817, pp. 762–3; *Memoirs of Henry Hunt*, ii. 57, 59; [William Hone], *Full Report of the Third Spa-Fields Meeting* ([1817]), pp. 6–7.

[5] *Political Register*, 25 Jan. 1817, pp. 120–8; *Memoirs of Henry Hunt*, ii. 78, iii. 163.

[6] *Political Register*, 18 Jan. 1817, p. 72.

[7] Ibid., 12 Dec. 1818, pp. 359–61.

[8] Ibid., 2 Mar. 1816, p. 273; *Memoirs of Henry Hunt*, ii. 415–16, iii. 18–19.

[9] *Political Register*, 27 Mar. 1819, pp. 828–9, and 13 Nov. 1819, p. 384.

[10] 'Lewis Melville', *The Life and Letters of William Cobbett* (2 vols., 1913), ii. 13–14; *Political Register*, 18 Oct. 1817, pp. 884–5.

[11] *Memoirs of Henry Hunt*, ii. 259–60, iii. 22–4, 472–5. By the late 1820s there was a full 'feud' between the former colleagues (*Life and Struggles of William Lovett* (1876; 1967), p. 44).

now that he is rid of the whole swarm he is able to do more for himself, for the cause, and is of much more consequence in himself.[1]

This desirable freedom of action might be purchased at too heavy a price if it made it impossible for Reformers to co-operate even to achieve what they held in common.

As William Hazlitt pointed out, with his customary shrewdness, a man who was amenable to appeals for compromise and unity was not the kind of man who was likely to become a Reformer in the first place.

A Reformer is not a gregarious animal. . . . To procure unanimity, to get men to act in *corps*, we must appeal for the most part to gross and obvious motives, to authority and passion, to their vices, not their virtues . . . A man to be a Reformer must be more influenced by imagination and reason than by received opinions or sensible impressions. With him ideas bear sway over things; the possible is of more value than the real; that which is not, is better than that which is. He is by the supposition a speculative (and somewhat fanatical) character; but there is no end of possible speculations, of imaginary questions, and nice distinctions; or if there were, he would not willingly come to it; he would still prefer living in the world of his own ideas . . .[2]

This passage is of particular interest because Hazlitt in his attack on Shelley a year later clearly saw him as a case in point, a 'philosophic fanatic' who dealt in wild speculations and fruitless paradoxes, and thus frustrated the efforts of practical men like Hazlitt himself.[3] Leigh Hunt reported Hazlitt's justification to Shelley. 'He says that Shelley provokes him by his going to a *pernicious* extreme on the liberal side, and so hurting it. I asked him what good he would do the said side by publicly abusing the supporters of it, and caricaturing them? To *this* he answers nothing.'[4] A pertinent question; but Hazlitt had the vices he denounced and would not sacrifice his own opinion even to heal the disunity he lamented. His attack was the more unjust in that Shelley fully took his point and (I suspect) paid him the compliment of borrowing his arguments in attempting to enforce the necessity of compromise. '. . . no thing is more idle than to reject

[1] 'Lewis Melville', *Life and Letters of William Cobbett*, ii. 186–7.
[2] *The Complete Works of William Hazlitt*, vii. 13–15.
[3] Ibid. viii. 148–50.
[4] *The Correspondence of Leigh Hunt*, edited by Thornton Hunt (2 vols., 1862), i. 166.

a limited benefit because we cannot without great sacrifices obtain an unlimited one. We might thus reject a Representative Republic, if it were attainable, on the plea that the imagination of man can conceive of something more absolutely perfect.' (*Works*, vii. 46) This restates in a more positive form the content of Hazlitt's gibe that the typical Reformer 'would rather have slavery than liberty, unless it is a liberty precisely after his own fashion; he would sooner have the Bourbons than Buonaparte; for he truly is for a Republic, and if he cannot have that, is indifferent about the rest'.[1] Shelley, like Hazlitt, 'truly is' for a Republic, if not something even more unattainable in the present; but he fully accepts the need to face 'the difficult and unbending realities of actual life' (*Works*, vii. 43), to compromise in practice, and to accept a moderate gain where no better was to be had. As he told Leigh Hunt: 'You know my principles incite me to take all the good I can in politics, for ever aspiring to something more. I am one of those whom nothing will fully satisfy, but who am ready to be partially satisfied by all that is practicable.' (*Letters*, ii. 153) Shelley would only have been 'partially satisfied' by the achievement of all his Reformist aims. In working for them he never lost sight of his larger objectives, and his activities as a Reformer can only be understood if they are related to those objectives.

As a believer in unending progress Shelley was more concerned with the process of continual amelioration than with the achievement of particular goals.[2] Since there was nothing final about whatever degree of Reform could be achieved in the immediate future Shelley could make his initial demands very moderate.

If Reform shall be begun by the existing Government, let us be contented with a limited, with any whatsoever opening ... it is no matter how slow, gradual and cautious be the change; we shall demand more and more with firmness and moderation, never anticipating but never deferring the moment of successful opposition ... (*Works*, vii. 46)

Most moderate Reformers saw a moderate Reform as an end—for Shelley it was only the beginning. When the Whigs superintended the passing of the first Reform Act they hoped that this purification of the old order would make it resistant to further calls for

---

[1] *Complete Works of William Hazlitt*, vii. 15. Shelley cited Hazlitt as a leading writer on the Reform side elsewhere in *A Philosophical View* (see below, p. 195).
[2] See *Political Justice*, i. 266–7, quoted above, pp. 67–8.

change; Shelley was more prescient in realizing that once the door had been opened it could never be shut again. Shelley chooses moderation because it is the most effective form of radicalism. His views are conditioned by his rejection of revolution as a means of political progress, not only for humanitarian reasons, but because he considered it was always counter-productive. The evidence for this opinion is marshalled in the opening chapter of *A Philosophical View*, in which Shelley surveys the course of European history from the fall of Rome to his own day, and expounds the theory of political change that underlies his Reform programme. In his survey Shelley is concerned to demonstrate the perfectibilarian thesis of continual social progress, but he focuses his attention on the moments of crisis at which progress emerges from conflict— this is hardly surprising, since he felt himself to be living through just such a crisis. The historical crises to which he pays most attention are the Reformation, the 'Glorious Revolution', and the French Revolution. From the study of these events a pattern emerges. In each case, according to Shelley's analysis, the cause of liberty made positive gains, but those gains were strictly limited. What the French Revolution and the Revolution of 1688 have in common is the relative nature of their achievements. 'The Authors of both revolutions proposed a greater and more glorious object than the degraded passions of their countrymen permitted them to attain. But in both cases abuses were abolished which never since have dared to shew their face.' (*Works*, vii. 15) Such crises necessarily lead to such compromises, for 'opinion' (in the moral sense—'degraded passions') sets strict limits to institutional progress. The lesson of France is that it is futile to attempt to outstrip opinion by abolishing more of the old forms than the nation at large is really in a position to do without. '. . . as it only partially extinguished those passions which are the spirit of these forms a reaction took place, which has restored in a certain limited degree the old system.' (*Works*, vii. 14) The good that was achieved could have been had without a revolution, since anything the revolution achieved beyond that was automatically undone by an inevitable reaction. Clearly such forms could not be abolished in England either before 'the public mind, through many gradations of improvement, shall have arrived at the maturity which can disregard these symbols of its childhood' (*Works*, vi. 68). This condition is not to be reached by premature revolutionary action but by the spreading of enlightenment among the people. 'It is better that they should be instructed in the whole truth, that they should see the clear grounds of their rights, the objects to which they ought to tend; and be impressed with the just persuasions, that patience and reason and endurance, [produce][1] a calm yet irresistible progress.' (*Works*, vii. 41)

These considerations helped to shape Shelley's actual Reform programme. In theory he fully agreed with the radical Reformers who demanded Universal Suffrage as a right.[2] But he considered that to grant it would be, 'in the present unprepared state of public knowledge, a measure fraught with peril' (*Works*, vi. 68). It is the 'vulgar eagerness' of the radical Reformers that he objects to[3] rather than their policies in themselves, and he suggests that they have not followed out the logic of their own premisses. Universal Suffrage would lead, in Shelley's view, to the abolition of the monarchy and the House of Lords, to an 'agrarian distribution' on the model of the Spenceans' plan,[4] and the institution of a republic. Personally Shelley would like nothing better than a republic, but one which arose in this fashion could only be 'as rapid in its decline as in its growth'.[5] Rather than such an 'immature attempt' at the grand object it would be better to 'temporize', so that when such advances 'shall be accomplished they may be rendered permanent' (*Works*, vii. 43–4). Shelley himself was willing to 'temporize' so far as to endorse as a starting-point the extremely moderate measure of Reform proposed by Lord John Russell in the Commons in December 1819. 'Let the rotten boroughs be disfranchised, and their rights transferred to the unrepresented cities and districts of the Nation.'[6] He naturally approved of the more vigorous programme of the moderate and Whig Reformers, who called for a suffrage based on the payment of direct taxes or the possession of a certain amount of property.[7]

---

[1] Not in the manuscript.   [2] *Works*, vi. 68, vii. 40.
[3] *SC* vi. 1040.
[4] K. N. Cameron also considers that Shelley has the Spencean plan in mind here (*Shelley: The Golden Years*, p. 146). For the Spenceans and Shelley's reactions to them see ibid., pp. 116–17.
[5] *Works*, vii. 41. Godwin had similar views; see C. Kegan Paul, *William Godwin: His Friends and Contemporaries* (2 vols., 1876), ii. 265.
[6] *Works*, vii. 46. For Russell's proposal to disenfranchise Grampound and transfer its seats see John Cannon, *Parliamentary Reform 1640–1832* (Cambridge, 1973), pp. 176–80. Russell announced his plan in July 1819.
[7] *Works* vi. 68, and vii. 46. See J. Cannon, op. cit., pp. 174–5.

This would widen the franchise without throwing power into the hands of the masses. In a cancelled passage Shelley speculated on the merits of a scheme of 'virtual' representation. 'It would perhaps be adviseable to begin by establishing a suffrage which should be universal in ⟨point⟩ of extension, and of rights rather than in point of numbers.'[1] Shelley would seem to be suggesting here that the whole population could be represented as classes rather than as individuals. The working classes would be represented 'virtually' if some of their members had the vote, without possessing a dangerous preponderance.[2] While most moderate Reformers were most concerned with excluding the uneducated classes Shelley felt that it was of great importance that they should be able to participate in some way in the political process.

As part of a moderate programme that could gain support from influential sections of the ruling class Shelley was willing to settle for 'triennial parliaments' (*Works*, vii. 46), that is, a reduction of the maximum life of a parliament from seven years to three. The Radicals insisted on annual parliaments, and in 1817 Shelley had agreed with them, for reasons that deserve our attention.

It appears to me that Annual Parliaments ought to be adopted as an immediate measure, as one which strongly tends to preserve the liberty and happiness of the nation; it would enable men to cultivate those energies on which the performance of the political duties belonging to the citizen of a free state as the rightful guardian of its prosperity, essentially depends; it would familiarize men with liberty by disciplining them to an habitual acquaintance with its forms. (*Works*, vi. 67)

Shelley's argument is that those who are at present unfit to be entrusted with power can be educated politically by frequent participation, even if only as spectators, in the political process.[3] We must remember that he is concerned both to restore the

---

[1] *SC* vi. 1046.

[2] A similar suggestion was voiced by Sir James Mackintosh (*Edinburgh Review*, xxxi (1818), 182–4). For the theory of 'virtual' representation and representation of interests see J. F. Lively, 'Ideas of Parliamentary Representation in England 1815–1832' (unpublished M. Litt. thesis, University of Cambridge, 1959), Ch. II.

[3] Godwin noted that frequent elections revived in the actual voters 'the practical and healthful feeling, that they are freemen' (*Uncollected Writings*, p. 447). Mackintosh argued that the exercise of the franchise by 'the humbler classes' tended to make them 'conscious of the moral dignity of their nature' (*Edinburgh Review*, xxxi. 179–80). Shelley saw beneficial effects in frequent elections even for those who could not actually vote.

equilibrium between institutions and opinion, and also to provide institutions that could help opinion to develop itself progressively in the future. His main criticism of the American system was that, while it did represent 'the will of the People as it is', it fulfilled only 'imperfectly and indirectly the last and most important condition of perfect government', namely 'To provide that that will should *be as wise and just as possible*' (*Works*, vii. 335). Many Reformers recognized the need for education for Reform, and the possibility of gaining Reform by education;[1] Shelley was almost alone in seeing that the right kind of Reform would itself provide the necessary political education for further Reform.[2] Thus the attainment of Reform would be a continuing process in which 'the people may become habituated [to] exercising the functions of sovereignty, in proportion as they acquire the possession of it' (*Works*, vii. 46). This conception evades Godwin's dilemma by seeing moral and political reform as the mutually supporting elements of an unending dialectic. Timely and intelligent reform in institutions educates those subject to them and enables them to make further institutional reforms, and so on.

If Reform is to fulfil the educative function that Shelley envisages it must make politics an activity open at least to the inspection, if not the active participation, of all. It is largely for this reason that Shelley rejects the secret ballot, which the radicals saw as essential to prevent the bribery or intimidation of voters.[3] Many politicians had moral misgivings about the secret ballot— what was the worth of a vote which the voter dared not acknowledge?[4] Some Reformers shared these misgivings, and Shelley commented that a voter's motives 'if concealed cannot but be dishonourable'.[5] But it is of more interest to note that Shelley's objections really rest on the fact that the casting of a vote in secrecy

---

[1] See Samuel Bamford, *Passages in the Life of a Radical*, i. 12, and *Life and Struggles of William Lovett*, passim.

[2] Cartwright seems to have glimpsed a similar possibility, and he stressed the importance of Annual Parliaments (*An Appeal . . . on the Subject of the English Constitution*, pp. 2–3).

[3] See Cartwright, *Take your choice!* (1776), p. 70; Bentham, *Plan of Parliamentary Reform*, pp. lxi–lxv, clxxi–clxxxii; [George Grote], *Statement of the Question of Parliamentary Reform* (1821), pp. 98–9.

[4] A good summary of the arguments against the secret ballot is given by Norman Gash, *Politics in the Age of Peel*, pp. 19–23.

[5] *Works*, vii. 44. See also Cobbett, quoted *Examiner*, 26 Jan. 1817, p. 58; and Capel Lofft, letter to the Editor, *Reformists' Register*, 29 Mar. 1817, p. 320.

denatures the whole moral act upon which he relies to provide an education in political responsibility. It is regrettable that he did not fully work out his ideas on this point, but he said enough to indicate his line of thought.

The elector and the elected ought to meet one another face to face, and interchange the meanings by actual presence and share some common impulses, and in a degree understand each other. There ought to be the common sympathy of their [sic] excitements of a popular assembly, among the electors themselves. The imagination would thus be strongly excited, and a mass of generous and enlarged and popular sentiments be awakened, which would give the vitality of [. . .][1]

Imponderables like opinion and public spirit are of central importance in the political morality of Godwin and Shelley, and we must not be surprised to find them invoked in the discussion of the practical details of Reform. Godwin also rejects the secret ballot, one of his objections being that any system of secrecy leads men to act with 'frigidity'.[2]

Public opinion enters both into the substance of Shelley's Reform and into his tactical considerations on how it is to be attained. He considered that Reform was important enough to justify the last resort of the oppressed, 'resistance' and finally 'insurrection'.[3] Anything would be preferable to allowing the public mind to sink into Oriental apathy (*Works*, vii. 50). But Shelley (unlike Byron) did not relish the prospect of civil war, not because he was squeamish about bloodshed, but because he knew that violence was always counter-productive; what was the lesson of the French Revolution if not that 'There is secret sympathy between Destruction and Power, between Monarchy and War'?[4]

---

[1] *Works*, vii. 44. Compare Mackintosh: 'In elections, political principles cease to be mere abstractions. They are embodied in individuals; and the cold conviction of a truth, or the languid approbation of a measure, is animated by attachment for leaders, and hostility to adversaries' (*Edinburgh Review*, xxxi. 197). Both Shelley and Mackintosh use language reminiscent of Burke, where utilitarian advocates of the ballot like Bentham and Grote favour an appeal to rationality and self-interest.

[2] *Political Justice*, ii. 319–20. See also *Thoughts on Man, his Nature, Productions, and Discoveries* (1831), pp. 319, 342.

[3] *Works*, vii. 52–3. Art Young has shown how the justification of resistance is consistent with Shelley's belief in non-violence (*Shelley and Nonviolence* (The Hague, 1975), pp. 152–4).

[4] *Works*, vii. 53. For a good summary of the rationale of Shelley's opposition to violence see Art Young, op. cit., p. 8.

Armed revolt is playing the game of the oppressors, and can only be justified in self-defence, when the government has resorted to military force first (*Works*, vii. 53). The best response even then is passive resistance, as Shelley insists in *The Mask of Anarchy* and *A Philosophical View*; as the Reformers frequently argued, the soldiers were also citizens and would make common cause with a people who offered no active resistance.[1] Virtually all critics have seen a contradiction between Shelley's pacifism and his repeated reminder to the people, 'Ye are many—they are few'.[2] To see a contradiction is to miss the point, for this is no call to arms—on the contrary, Shelley is saying that a united people is so strong that conflict would be out of the question. The many would not need to resort to violence, and the few would not dare. What Shelley desires is 'such an unanimity as would preclude any thing amounting to a serious dispute'.[3] Violent conflict is an ominous sign that the nation is too divided for such conflict to issue in a beneficial reform.

Thus, although he faced the possibility that oppression might necessitate armed resistance, Shelley found the tactics of 'intellectual resistance' both preferable and more promising. He realized that the government's real strength was in public opinion, and it was here that it was also most vulnerable. 'The public opinion ⟨in⟩ England ought first to [be] excited to action, and the durability of those forms within which the oppressors intrench themselves brought perpetually to the test of its operation. No law or institution can last if this opinion be disti[nctly] pronounced against it.' (*Works*, vii. 51) Shelley was advocating a campaign of civil disobedience, involving the commission of the supposed 'crimes' of seditious libel and non-payment of taxes, so that the political issues involved would have to be canvassed before the juries, the organs of public opinion.[4] As he noted, some of the Reform leaders (Leigh Hunt, Burdett, Cobbett, William Hone, and possibly Richard Carlile) had been doing this with respect to

---

[1] *The Mask of Anarchy*, lines 340–59; *Works*, vii. 48–9. See Burdett, *Parliamentary Debates*, xl. 1461–2; *Political Register*, 17 Jan 1818, pp. 90–1; Cartwright, *A Bill of Rights and Liberties* (1817; [1821]), p. 6 (paragraph V).

[2] *The Mask of Anarchy*, lines 155 and 372.

[3] *Works*, vii. 50. Shelley's point has been taken by Carlos Baker, *Shelley's Major Poetry*, p. 163, and Richard Hendrix, 'The Necessity of Response: How Shelley's Radical Poetry Works', *K-SJ* xxvii (1978), 49.

[4] *Works*, vii. 51. See above, pp. 28–31.

seditious libel. Non-payment of taxes was more con'
the very name of the Hampden Club alluded to it, a'
Reformers who hinted at recourse to this weapon.[1] I'
and Peacock had themselves concocted a scheme to to...
example of Hampden.[2] The appeal to public opinion by the
defiance of unpopular legislation was indeed one of the most
effective weapons in the Reformers' armoury, and it was by acts
similar to those advocated by Shelley that sufficient pressure was
brought to bear on the government to force the passage of the first
Reform Act, over a decade later.[3]

Shelley also recommended an attack on the other main organ
of public opinion, Parliament, both by mass petitions and by
'memorials' from leading Reformist writers such as Godwin,
Hazlitt, Bentham, and Leigh Hunt.[4] It is not surprising that
Shelley should have been concerned to provide the Reform movement with an intellectual leadership, for he always insisted that the
agitation for Reform should be under the guidance of responsible
leaders. While the radicals exhorted the people to rely on their
own exertions and to distrust attempts at direction by members
of the ruling class, Shelley like many moderate Reformers distrusted and feared a movement controlled by the masses and their
self-appointed leaders; he warned that the people 'may be panic-
stricken and disunited by their oppressors and the demagogues'
(*Works*, vii. 48). His plans for the attainment of Reform assign an
important role to the 'true patriot' who 'will endeavour to enlighten
and to unite the nation and animate it with enthusiasm and confidence', a sort of Reformist Laon (vii. 48). This seems to be the
role that Shelley himself hoped to fulfil, by writing *A Philosophical
View*, intended as 'a kind of standard book for the philosophical
reformers politically considered' (*Letters*, ii. 201), and by preparing
his 'little volume of *popular songs* wholly political, & destined to
awaken & direct the imagination of the reformers' (ii. 191). His
reaction to Peterloo was to appeal to his own class, 'those whose

---

[1] See *Examiner*, 5 Jan. 1817, p. 12; Burdett, *Parliamentary Debates*, xl. 1461;
Donald Read, *Peterloo: The 'Massacre' and its Background* (Manchester, 1958)
p. 112; Southey, *Essays, Moral and Political*, i. 318.

[2] *Letters of Mary W. Shelley*, i. 18-19.

[3] See Michael Brock, *The Great Reform Act* (1973), pp. 297-9. See also Leigh
Hunt's Preface to *The Mask of Anarchy*, in *Works*, iii. 227.

[4] *Works*, vii. 51-2. Shelley originally included Byron and then cancelled his
name (*Works*, vii. 340).

hereditary duty it is to lead' the English people; similar appeals were made by Burdett and the radical Whig Henry White.[1] Like them Shelley believed (and with some reason) that only the co-operation of a sizeable element of the existing ruling class could ensure peaceful progress. As he assured Peacock, 'the change should commence among the higher orders or anarchy will only be the last flash before despotism'.[2] This conviction goes a long way towards explaining why Shelley thought it advisable to press only for the most moderate Reform in the first instance. The 'higher orders' could hardly be expected to sympathize with the radical aspirations of the working-class reformers; and to alienate the ruling classes would both weaken the Reform cause and bring nearer the prospect of a destructive conflict. It was in fact only with the co-operation of these classes that the first Reform Act was passed, which, as Shelley foresaw, was the first instalment in a series of measures that by 1921 had granted the Reformers all they fought for.[3] Shelley's moderation was tactical, and did not imply that he had given up any of his theoretical extremism. To oppose the Shelley of *Prometheus Unbound* to the Shelley of *A Philosophical View* is to misunderstand both works.[4]

So far we have considered Shelley's own Reform activities and his theoretical writings directed to the crisis of 1816–20. We must turn now to the literary implications of his political involvement, and consider the ways in which it shaped the poetry he wrote. Shelley's response to the Reform crisis issued in two forms. Of these the most obvious is the 'little volume of *popular songs* wholly political'. One can assume that it was for such a volume that the following poems and fragments were written: *The Mask of Anarchy*, 'Lines written during the Castlereagh administration', 'Fragment: To the People of England', 'A New National Anthem', 'Sonnet: England in 1819', 'A Ballad' (formerly known as 'Young Parson Richard'); closely associated with these poems is *Peter Bell*

---

[1] *Letters*, ii. 136. See also Burdett's letter to his constituents (*Examiner*, 29 Aug. 1819, p. 551) and the reaction of Henry White (*Independent Whig*, 22 Aug. 1819, p. 1395).

[2] *Letters*, ii. 115. This was written before Shelley heard of Peterloo.

[3] Major Cartwright wanted universal suffrage at eighteen which did not come until 1969.

[4] Shelley's moderation was interpreted as an ideological volte-face by Edward Dowden (*Transcripts and Studies* (1888), p. 102), and by A. Sen (*Studies in Shelley* (Calcutta, 1936), pp. 228–36).

the Third. This volume was never published, nor was *A Philosophical View*, the Reformers' handbook that Shelley seems to have intended as a companion work. But in 1820 Shelley did publish a volume of political verse, *Prometheus Unbound. A Lyrical Drama in four acts with Other Poems*, which contained, besides the title-poem, 'The Sensitive Plant', 'A Vision of the Sea', 'Ode to Heaven', 'An Exhortation', 'Ode to the West Wind', 'An Ode written October 1819', 'The Cloud', 'To a Skylark', and 'Ode to Liberty'; had they been ready in time one would have expected it also to contain 'Ode to Naples' and 'Liberty'. Unlike the projected volume of songs, the *Prometheus Unbound* volume is hardly 'wholly political'; the other poems in it are used to restate and explore the various facets of the drama, of which the political dimension is only one. But Shelley is not at any pains to conceal that an explicit political dimension is involved, though he is concerned to link it to his other imaginative and philosophical concerns. Where the abortive political volume would have constituted an address to the masses the *Prometheus Unbound* volume was addressed to 'the highly refined imagination of the more select classes of poetical readers'.[1] This cultured audience proved far from responsive, but at least in addressing himself to them Shelley did not feel any unease as to the possible consequences. To direct fairly inflammatory poems to the multitude in a potentially revolutionary situation was a very different matter. In fact Shelley did make efforts to get *Peter Bell the Third*, *The Mask of Anarchy*, and (probably) 'Sonnet: England in 1819' published,[2] efforts which were frustrated by the caution of his friends in England. The fact that Shelley did not press more strenuously for their publication, however, is evidence that he had some doubts himself. In the end events overtook his original intention. The prompt action of the government in incarcerating the Reform leaders, an improvement in economic conditions, and the absorption of the English public in the Punch and Judy show (as Shelley aptly termed it) of the royal divorce all worked to defuse the crisis which had seemed so menacing. Even by the end of 1819 Shelley could see that 'the passion of party will postpone the great struggle till another year', and as a consequence he contemplated dropping *A Philosophical View* (*Letters*, ii. 164). He still had hopes of

[1] Preface to *Prometheus Unbound*.
[2] See *Letters*, ii. 134–5, 152, 167.

publishing both it and the volume of popular songs as late as May 1820, but it seems likely that he finally decided that, if the final crisis of civil war was no longer imminent, it might be safer to let sleeping dogs lie.

A volume of poems centred on *The Mask of Anarchy* would have been both a more urgent and a more ephemeral production than the *Prometheus Unbound* volume. Directed as they are to the specifics of an actual political situation Shelley's popular poems contain a good deal of topical satire. Satire, as the fragment known as 'A Satire on Satire' shows, was something about which Shelley had misgivings. Mary Shelley dated this fragment to 1820, but the fact that it is drafted in a notebook that also contains drafts for *Adonais* and a partial copy of *A Defence of Poetry* makes 1821 a more likely date.[1] It may have been written after Shelley's visit to Byron in August 1821; it is evident that 'A Satire on Satire' records Shelley's dissent from Byron's kind of satire.[2] When Shelley had seen the Dedication of *Don Juan* to Southey in 1818 he had been appalled at what was 'more like a mixture of wormwood & verdigrease than satire' (*Letters*, ii. 42), and he did not regret its omission from the published version (ii. 198). Satirists are wont to justify their vituperation by reference to their reforming mission, thus making personal animus a public duty. Shelley feels obliged to scrutinize this moral argument, and finally to reject it; it is not the 'stagnant truisms of trite Satire' that can reform its victim.

> This cannot be, it ought not, evil still—
> Suffering makes suffering, ill must follow ill.
> Rough words beget sad thoughts,   and, beside,
> Men take a sullen and a stupid pride
> In being all they hate in others' shame,
> By a perverse antipathy of fame.
> 'Tis not worth while to prove, as I could, how
> From the sweet fountains of our Nature flow
> These bitter waters . . .
> ('Fragment of a Satire on Satire', lines 35–43)

---

[1] Bodl. MS Shelley adds. e. 20, fo. 44.

[2] See Charles E. Robinson, *Shelley and Byron: The Snake and Eagle Wreathed in Fight* (Baltimore and London, 1976), pp. 142–3.

This is far more thoughtful and humane than anything we could expect from Byron on this subject; but these admirable qualities would seem to disqualify Shelley from wielding Satire's scourge to any effect. But there is more than one kind of satire. Personal satire was Byron's forte, and it was that that Shelley mistrusted. There is also an impersonal kind of satire whose target is a whole society and which rests on an indignation stemming from public rather than merely personal wrongs. This is an important distinction for any adequate reading of *Peter Bell the Third*, an unjustly neglected work, which is too often dismissed as a sub-Byronic personal satire on Wordsworth. There certainly is personal satire in the work, but Wordsworth is made a target because his situation is a symptom of a general social condition. Shelley's critical comments on Wordsworth as a poet are perceptive, and generous even when he states his reservations (IV. 293–312). His satire is a serious moral act, and, rather than falling with glee on his victim's foibles, he prefers to appeal from Alexander drunk to Alexander sober, as when he quotes Wordsworth's own injunction

> Never to blend our pleasure or our pride
> With sorrow of the meanest thing that feels.

as a comment on his 'description of the beautiful colours produced during the agonising death of a number of trout' in *The Excursion*.[1] Wordsworth had betrayed his own better self; but in this he was not unique, for the subject of *Peter Bell the Third* is a whole society which has become alienated from itself.

The key to this alienation is in Shelley's view the acceptance of religious fictions. The orthodoxy of *The Excursion* prompted the Shelleys to dismiss Wordsworth as 'a slave',[2] and *Peter Bell the Third* identifies the slavish acceptance of a corrupt religion with devotion to a tyrannical social order. Wordsworth had himself associated religion with politics, and the famous passage in his 'Ode: 1815' was both offensive to radicals and fair game for their attack.

> But Thy most dreaded instrument,
> In working out a pure intent,

[1] Note to VI. 588, quoting Wordsworth's 'Hart-Leap Well' (1800), lines 179–80, and referring to *The Excursion* (1814), VIII. 556–71.

[2] *Journal*, p. 15.

> Is Man—arrayed for mutual slaughter,
> —Yea, Carnage is thy daughter.[1]

When Shelley parodied this in *Peter Bell the Third* he not only changed the reference from Waterloo to Peterloo, but also had his hero address the lines to what he took to be the true object of Wordsworth's devotion—the Devil.[2] Wordsworth seemed to provide exemplary documentation for Shelley's belief that the Christian God was a projection of man's own base passions and fears, the 'prototype of human misrule'. His incautious zeal in the defence of the ways of Providence left him open to the satiric inversion by which Shelley exposes the devotee of the God of Battles as a superstitious devil-worshipper. This is more than the scoring of points. Borrowing the scheme of *Peter Bell*, which chronicles the process of its hero's redemption, in order to parody it by tracing the course of Wordsworth's fall to the 'Double Damnation' of dullness (with a pun on 'damnation' in the sense of unfavourable critical reception), Shelley secularizes Wordsworth's conceptual scheme without trying to explain it away. God, the Devil, and Damnation may be absurd fictions, but men's belief in them has also made them palpable and sinister realities. The joke of describing Hell in terms of the concrete details supplied by London has a grim point to it, for the only Hell there is is that created by man on earth.

> Hell is a city much like London—
> A populous and a smoky city;
> There are all sorts of people undone,
> And there is little or no fun done;
> Small justice shown, and still less pity.
>
> (III. 147–51)

This shows Shelley's kind of impersonal satire at its best. The apparent doggerel of the form (itself a parody of Wordsworth's form) is controlled by an artistic intelligence that is concerned to

---

[1] This is the version of the text published in 1816; see *The Poetical Works of William Wordsworth*, edited by Ernest de Selincourt and Helen Darbishire (1940–9; revised edition, 5 vols., 1952–9), iii. 155.

[2] *Peter Bell the Third*, vi. 634–52. Shelley also satirized Wordsworth's lines in his attempt at a burlesque epithalamium for the marriage of God's daughter Carnage to the Prince of Hell; see *Note Books of Percy Bysshe Shelley*, ii. 172–5, 184–5.

walk the line between burlesque and earnestness. 'A populous and a smoky city' refers the pre-industrial smog of the metropolis to the traditional meteorology of Hell, and its phenomenal increase in numbers to the insistence of Calvinist theologians that the great majority of the human race would be damned; while the rhyme on 'undone' shows that Shelley could learn a trick from Byron when he chose. But the jesting is grim jesting at the best, and only adds force to the devastating literalness of the last line. In this man-made Hell damnation is a real enough condition.

> And this is Hell—and in this smother
>   All are damnable and damned;
> Each one damning, damns the other;
> They are damned by one another,
>   By none other are they damned.
> (III. 217–21)

As Shelley comments, ' 'Tis a lie to say "God damns!" ', both because the vindictive God of the Old Testament does not exist and because men impose their damnation on themselves.

> Statesmen damn themselves to be
>   Cursed; and lawyers damn their souls
> To the auction of a fee;
> Churchmen damn themselves to see
>   God's sweet love in burning coals.
>
> The rich are damned beyond all cure
>   To taunt, and starve, and trample on
> The weak and wretched: and the poor
> Damn their broken hearts to endure
>   Stripe on stripe, with groan on groan.
>
> Sometimes the poor are damned indeed
>   To take,—not means for being blessed,—
> But Cobbett's snuff, revenge; that weed
> From which the worms that it doth feed
>   Squeeze less than they before possessed.
>
> And some few, like we know who,
>   Damned—but God alone knows why—
> To believe their minds are given

> To make this ugly Hell a Heaven;
>   In which faith they live and die.
>   (III. 227-46)

Men 'damn themselves' by their acts, but they 'are damned' to the condition of imaginative poverty from which these acts proceed; damnation is both the activity by which man abdicates responsibility for his condition, and the condition to which he submits because he thinks it is unalterable.

Wordsworth's hypostatization of moral evil in the form of a divine diabolism is a good example of man's ability to conceal the realities of his situation from himself.[1] As Shelley commented, in the modern world 'Self-deceit is the veiled Image of unknown evil, before which luxury and satiety lie prostrate' (*Works*, vii. 117)—'unknown' because unacknowledged for what it is. Shelley's intention is to burlesque and demystify the fictions by which men conceal and justify their real condition, as is particularly clear in his account of the Devil, who is revealed to be 'what we are':

> sometimes
> The Devil is a gentleman;
> At others a bard bartering rhymes
> For sack; a statesman spinning crimes,
>   A swindler, living as he can;
>
> A thief, who cometh in the night,
>   With whole boots and net pantaloons,
> Like some one whom it were not right
> To mention;—or the luckless wight
>   From whom he steals nine silver spoons.
>   (II. 81-90)

Shelley's Devil is not the great Deceiver, but the great Self-deceiver, the paradigm of man's alienation from his own condition.

> The Devil knew not, his name and lot;
>   Peter knew not that he was Bell:
> Each had an upper stream of thought,

---

[1] Shortly after writing *Peter Bell the Third* Shelley produced his Voltairean essay 'On the Devil, and Devils', in which he made the quite serious suggestion that the Manichaean dualism is 'simply a personification of the struggle which we experience within ourselves, and which we perceive in the operations of external things as they affect us, between good and evil' (*Works*, vii. 87), and noted that this kind of psychological reductionism works to erode literal belief (vii. 92).

> Which made all seem as it was not;
>   Fitting itself to all things well.
> (II. 106–10)

A double alienation is involved. Man is alienated from his true self and hence from a truly human society; but he is at the same time wilfully alienated from the recognition of the false society and condition to which he condemns himself. He fears the Hell beyond the grave because he refuses to see that he has already created it on earth. When he realizes that he is not what he ought to be, and that what ought not to be is what is, he will be able to overcome both forms of his self-alienation and heal the divisions with which the Furies taunt Prometheus.

> Hypocrisy and custom make their minds
> The fanes of many a worship, now outworn.
> They dare not devise good for man's estate
> And yet they know not that they do not dare.
> The good want power, but to weep barren tears.
> The powerful goodness want: worse need for them.
> The wise want love, and those who love want wisdom;
> And all best things are thus confused to ill.
> Many are strong and rich,—and would be just,—
> But live among their suffering fellow men
> As if none felt: they know not what they do.
> (*Prometheus Unbound*, I. 621–31)

The farce of *Peter Bell the Third* restates the tragedy presented in *Prometheus Unbound*. Both works see man's present condition as a 'loathsome mask' that must be stripped away from his true nature. One of Shelley's favourite rhetorical strategies in his writings of 1819 is the revelation of the truth that lies behind the accepted appearances. Thus he glosses the National Debt as

> a scheme of Paper money,
> And means—being interpreted—
> "Bees, keep your wax—give us the honey
> And we will plant while skies are sunny
>   Flowers, which in winter serve instead."
> (*Peter Bell the Third*, III. 167–71)

A Philosophical View of Reform is full of such asides, in which the mask of custom is stripped from the true meaning of institutions and events. The Roman Empire is glossed as 'that vast and successful scheme for the enslaving the most civilized portion of mankind', while the Catholic Church with its secular allies 'means, being interpreted, a plan according to which the cunning and selfish few have employed the fears and hopes of the ignorant many to the establishment of their own power and the destruction of the real interest of all' (*Works*, vii. 5). Charles I is revealed as 'one of those chiefs of a conspiracy of privileged murders and robbers', while the Glorious Revolution is taken from its pedestal and shown to be a 'compromise between the unextinguishable spirit of Liberty, and the ever watchful spirit of fraud and tyranny' (vii. 7). The Holy Alliance is revealed in its true colours by being described as 'that hypocritical knot of conspiring tyrants' (vii. 16). Tyranny always tries to conceal its true nature by an abuse of language and the Reformer must become adept at stripping it of its disguises.

> 'Wilder her enemies
> In their own dark disguise,—
>   God save our Queen!
> All earthly things that dare
> Her sacred name to bear,
> Strip them, as kings are, bare;
>   God save the Queen!
> ('A New National Anthem', lines 22–8)

We have already seen how Shelley treats the rhetoric of rule and majesty as stolen finery, unjustly appropriated by the tyrants, and which the assertors of liberty are fully entitled to reclaim. The reassumption of true humanity is simultaneously the exposure of the real face of tyranny.

Stuart Curran has already shown how Shelley exploits traditions of popular chiliasm in *The Mask of Anarchy*.[1] The poem does indeed present an apocalypse, though what is revealed is not a divine order, but the true nature of social reality; in laying claim to vision Shelley specifies that he means 'the visions of Poesy' (line 4). The revelation involved is an unmasking, though Shelley's syntax suggests that the concept of 'mask' is rather more complex than we might expect.

[1] *Shelley's Annus Mirabilis*, pp. 182–6.

> I met Murder on the way—
> He had a mask like Castlereagh—
> (lines 5–6)

The literal meaning of these lines is that Murder wears a mask just as Castlereagh wears one. We must certainly read the descriptions of Eldon and Sidmouth in this way.

> Next came Fraud, and he had on,
> Like Eldon, an ermined gown;

> Clothed with the Bible, as with light,
> And the shadows of the night,
> Like Sidmouth, next, Hypocrisy
> On a crocodile rode by.
> (lines 14–15, 22–5)

Shelley may have hoped to avoid prosecution for libel by his use of similes; he does not in fact identify Murder and Castlereagh, Fraud and Eldon, Hypocrisy and Sidmouth. But the apparently loose phrasing of the comparison between Murder and Castlereagh is calculated to direct us to the real meaning of their similarity. The two terms in each comparison are disguised as each other: Castlereagh is the mask that Murder wears. There is a sceptic's irony here, for Murder, Fraud, and Anarchy only come into existence in the actions of men; like the Devil, they have no reality in themselves. They are

> foul masks with which ill thoughts
> Hide that fair being we spirits call man
> (*Prometheus Unbound*, III. iv. 44–5)

as the Spirit of the Earth puts it. Even Castlereagh, Eldon, and Sidmouth are men, but they have so subdued their humanity to the anti-human roles of Murder, Fraud, and Hypocrisy that it comes to seem as if the roles are playing the men. Murder and its companions are like the 'old anatomies' in *The Triumph of Life* which, according to Rousseau,

> laughed from their dead eyes
> To reassume the delegated power
> Arrayed in which these worms did monarchize

> Who make this earth their charnel.—
> (lines 502–5)

Kings are only masks for the devils who 'reassume' a power which
is said to be 'delegated' both as ironic allusion to the Lockean
doctrine that power is 'delegated' to the rulers by the ruled, and
as a reminder that both rulers and ruled have abdicated the
responsibilities of self-rule. Power itself is no more than a mask,
in which kings merely play the role of monarchs, or 'monarchize'.[1]
No wonder this earth is a 'charnel', when the dead forms and the
living men thus take on each other's roles. In this world 'Anarchy'
wears the mask of social order: 'I AM GOD, AND KING, AND LAW!'
The skeletal Anarchy (like the 'anatomies' of *The Triumph of Life*)

> Bowed and grinned to every one,
> As well as if his education
> Had cost ten millions to the Nation.
> (lines 75–7)

Shelley, prudently, does no more than hint at an identification
here; but the implication is that the lean and famine-ridden form
of Anarchy has disguised itself in the ample form of the Prince
Regent. The irony is only on the surface, for hunger and luxury,
poverty and prosperity, are undesirable extremes that mutually
depend on each other. The end of this masquerade, in which
nothing wears its true face, is signalled by the appearance of Hope,
herself disguised as Despair (lines 86–9). As so often with Shelley's
depictions of crisis, the details of the climax are not clear, though
it would seem that Anarchy is destroyed by its own forces.

> And Anarchy, the ghastly birth,
> Lay dead earth upon the earth
> The Horse of Death tameless as wind
> Fled, and with his hoofs did grind
> To dust, the murderers thronged behind.
> (lines 130–4)

[1] Shelley alludes here to the famous speech of Richard II beginning 'For God's
sake let us sit upon the ground/And tell sad stories of the death of kings'
(*Richard II*, III. ii. 155–77). This speech was a favourite with Shelley (see *Life*,
ii. 24, and *The Autobiography of Leigh Hunt*, pp. 270–1). In *The Triumph of Life*
he draws on Richard's histrionic vision of kingly state as a mask for Death for
his own republican purposes.

If we translate the vision into prophetic allegory, the Horse of Death is probably the army, described in 'Sonnet: England in 1819' as 'a two-edged sword to all who wield'.

At first sight it would appear that the rest of the poem takes place after the fall of Anarchy, but in fact the long speech of which it consists is directed to a state of oppression. We should read the 'masque' of Anarchy as a visionary prologue to the main substance of the poem, which is Shelley's own address to his readers. Shelley is claiming to speak for more than just himself: 'As if their Own indignant Earth . . . As if her heart had cried aloud' (lines 139, 146). Shelley disguises his voice as the voice of the Earth, or the voice of the Earth is making itself heard by borrowing the voice of the poet. The first section of the poem was a revelation of the true nature of England's condition, culminating in a vision of its possible redemption. The second half addresses itself responsibly, and with a realism that does not shun the banal, to directing the efforts of those who seek to redeem it. It is as if Shelley has recognized that it is too easy to solve the problem by an appeal to 'the visions of Poesy'; they can direct action but not inform it in detail. Having shown his audience that Anarchy is to be overthrown by the self-sacrifice of Hope invoking the Spirit of Liberty, he descends from this height of abstraction to tell them what this amounts to in real terms and how it may be supposed to work. It means standing in front of armed soldiers and daring them to kill you. Shelley has often been sneered at for inviting the Reformers to face cannon, bayonets, and sabres with folded arms and calm looks, but I am not sure that Shelley didn't have a better grasp of the situation. The army that beat Napoleon at Waterloo would have made short work of any *armed* resistance on the part of the Reformers. A completely peaceful resistance was more difficult to put down because no one was quite sure how the army would react if called on to kill unarmed civilians. It was known that at Peterloo the bloodshed was caused not by the army but by the Yeomanry, a badly trained amateur body who were inept at crowd control and eager to settle personal scores with the local Reformers; the army only intervened when the Yeomanry had provoked a riot, and a good deal of their attention was devoted to attempting to restrain the Yeomanry's lust for blood.[1] Shelley had good reason

---

[1] See E. P. Thompson, *The Making of the English Working Class*, p. 753.

to suspect that the regular soldiers would be 'ashamed of such base company' (line 359). Shelley knows that it is the weakness of Anarchy that it must wear a mask, that it must disguise itself as order and even as liberty. Those who serve Anarchy must be able to feel that they are acting by a valid code, and the slaughter of unarmed men can hardly be reconciled with such a code.

> They will hardly dare to greet
> Their acquaintance in the street.
> (lines 354–5)

The flatness of the expression here registers Shelley's scepticism about the ultimate values of the code of gentlemanly honour.[1] If the oppressors could live by a more enlightened code they would not be oppressors; in the meantime the moral imperatives of a shame culture are chinks in Anarchy's armour.

Shelley's awareness that he is addressing an audience of his social and cultural inferiors occasionally leads him to appear condescending, as does the reserve he maintains with respect to his real political principles. But it is a strength of his popular political verse that he has obliged himself to speak his mind explicitly and in detail. To do so he must demystify even the language of Reform, as he does in the justly praised definition of Liberty.

> What art thou Freedom? O! could slaves
> Answer from their living graves
> This demand—tyrants would flee
> Like a dream's dim imagery:
>
> Thou art not, as impostors say,
> A shadow soon to pass away,
> A superstition, and a name
> Echoing from the cave of Fame.
>
> For the labourer thou art bread,
> And a comely table spread
> From his daily labour come
> In a neat and happy home.

---

[1] I think Thomas Edwards is in error in thinking that Shelley himself shares 'the gentleman's code' he expounds, though he is right to suggest that the passive resistance Shelley advocates depends on this code (*Imagination and Power: A Study of Poetry on Public Themes* (1971), p. 166).

> Thou art clothes, and fire, and food
> For the trampled multitude—
> (lines 209–22)

The unreality of tyranny becomes completely apparent when access has been gained to the concrete details of what liberty means in human terms. This impressive concreteness of reference is rare in the political poems contained in the *Prometheus Unbound* volume, and it would indeed be unreasonable to expect it. This volume is not concerned with a particular political situation so much as the moral laws that are operative in the political realm. It moves at a higher level of abstraction than *The Mask of Anarchy*. That this is a process which entails losses as well as gains can be shown by a brief examination of the 'Ode to Liberty'.

The 'Ode to Liberty', like *The Mask of Anarchy*, is concerned with a critique of illusion and a rectification of those abuses of language which support tyranny and priestcraft.

> O, that the words which make the thoughts obscure
>   From which they spring, as clouds of glimmering dew
> From a white lake blot heaven's blue portraiture,
>   Were stript of their thin masks and various hue
> And frowns and smiles and splendours not their own,
>   Till in the nakedness of false and true
>   They stand before their Lord, each to receive its due!
> (lines 234–40)

'God' must be redefined as man's 'own aweless soul' or 'the power unknown' before it is to be worshipped, and 'King' must be understood as man himself, 'the King of Life', before receiving obedience (stanzas xvi–xvii). Judith Chernaik has shown how Shelley's imagery wrests the lightning from Jove and returns it to the people.[1] But Shelley is not always successful in his wrestling with language. The high style of the ode is unable to deal with political issues except in terms of empty abstractions, and this is what Liberty, the very subject of the poem, remains. Shelley does indeed try to give Liberty significant content by connecting it with 'Blind Love, and equal Justice, and the Fame/Of what has been, the Hope of what will be':

[1] *The Lyrics of Shelley* (Cleveland and London, 1972), p. 100.

> O, Liberty! if such could be thy name
>   Wert thou disjoined from these, or they from thee:
> (lines 264–7)

But this is all a matter of 'name'; Liberty is never more than an abstraction defined in terms of other abstractions. When in *The Mask of Anarchy* Freedom was defined in terms of Justice, Wisdom, Peace, and Love, each term received a commentary in concrete terms (lines 230–54). In the confines of the 'Ode to Liberty' this would be impossible, for Shelley is restricted within a Whiggish rhetoric that is deliberately designed to deal in abstractions. Judith Chernaik is right to distinguish between the patriotic odes to Liberty of Thomson and Collins, and the revolutionary ode of Shelley; but it is not clear that the 'difference in motive' will express itself in 'an altogether different character', as she goes on to argue. A 'Romantic sublime' that attempts to use the 'convention and vocabulary' of the earlier odes may well find that the political vision it is able to express is radically curtailed.[1] These conventions will work to separate the poet from his subject. The structuring image of the ode is, significantly, flight, a flight on 'the rapid plumes of song' (line 6) that gives him an overview of his subject in time and in space but only at the cost of separation from the ground of his concern. In his flight the poet becomes the mouthpiece of a prophetic voice, but it is not the voice of 'their Own indignant Earth', as in *The Mask of Anarchy*, but 'A voice out of the deep' (line 15). This is a psychological depth, of course, to be identified with 'the inmost cave/Of man's deep spirit' where Liberty abides (lines 256–7). Nevertheless, there is a disconcerting sense that we are being invited to spring from the depths to the heights in a movement that evades engagement with the living realities of the level Earth. The very form of the ode, an invocation to Liberty, makes Liberty seem like a transcendent principle outside man, though it is clear from what is said in the poem that this is far from Shelley's meaning.

[1] See ibid., pp. 97–8.

CHAPTER VI

The Unacknowledged Legislators

SHELLEY'S INABILITY to have any effect on events in England must have been as obvious to him as it is to us. After his burst of activity during the crisis of 1819–20 he seems to have accepted his immediate helplessness and to have realized that events would take their course, though he remained a concerned observer of and commentator on the English political scene. He was shrewd enough to realize that the bloodbath he had feared in the months after Peterloo was no longer inevitable. 'I neither believe that', he wrote to his wife in July 1820, 'nor do I fear that the consequences will be so immediately destructive to the existing forms of social order. . . . Let us hope we shall have a Reform.' (*Letters*, ii. 223) The fall from the high drama of imminent civil war to what Yeats might have called 'the casual comedy' of partisan polemic and the royal divorce was, all things considered, a blessing. The temporary defusing of the Reform crisis certainly allowed Shelley himself a breathing-space in which to reflect on his own roles of reformer and poet. If he was to accept his ineffectuality as a politician it was important that he should be able to reassure himself of his potency as a writer. He was well aware that he would never achieve the popularity gained by Byron, who had 'touched a chord to which a million hearts responded' (*Letters*, ii. 436). If he coveted such popularity it was for the sake of spreading his moral and political principles. Not having it he had to find a way of believing in the power of the poet to produce good even without the obvious advantage of a large and responsive audience. To adduce these personal factors is not necessarily to discredit Shelley's attempt to resolve the problem, which is in any case common to all intellectuals who find themselves committed to responsibility without power. Shelley's answer to it is addressed specifically to the situation of the poet, but only after he has defined 'poetry' in a far from exclusive way. In his defence of poetry in the narrower and more usual sense Shelley is concerned to trace the connection between artistic creation and social progress without resorting to the crude didacticism that he distrusted without always being able to avoid it.

The adoption of a didactic attitude is based on the assumption that there is at least a potential disjunction between art and morality. In *A Defence of Poetry* Shelley is concerned to demonstrate that there can be no such disjunction, but he had not always believed this. If a choice did have to be made the virtuous man would have to choose morality rather than art, as he assured his Irish audience: 'the man would be very dead to all generous feelings who would rather see pretty pictures and statues than a million free and happy men' *(Works,* v. 234). Consequently art can only be justified if it can be shown to contribute to moral and social improvement, and Shelley insisted to Miss Hitchener 'that all poetical beauty ought to be subordinate to the inculcated moral—that metaphorical language ought to be a pleasing vehicle for useful & momentous instruction' *(Letters,* i. 98). Art which is not thus 'subordinate' will be useless, or even mischievous, and many moralists and reformers have been suspicious of art which evades proper control and supervision. Plato is the most famous example, but the same attitude is to be found in a political reformer of Shelley's day. 'The fine arts are a family of much frailty; and unless we can give them a virtuous education and a right direction, they will be full as likely to produce moral and political evil as good. By wise legislation, they may, as I conceive, be made powerful instruments of moral and political improvement.'[1] Cartwright sees the arts as 'instruments', serving ends which are chosen without reference to the arts themselves or to the imaginative activity that produces them. What is not generally realized is that until 1819 Shelley's attitude is rather close to Cartwright's. Even in his youth Shelley frequently disavowed didacticism, but we must recognize that he did not use 'didactic' in quite the same way as we do. The modern sense of 'didactic' is covered by the third meaning given by the *Oxford English Dictionary,* 'having the giving of instruction as its aim or object'; Shelley understands the word in its more original sense, 'Having the character or manner of a teacher or instructor'. By 'didactic' poetry Shelley and his contemporaries would have understood poetry about beekeeping, the spleen, the wool trade, and other practical matters, which could serve the purposes of a textbook on the subject, rather than

[1] *Life and Correspondence of Major Cartwright,* i. 339–40.

poetry which has a moral design on its readers. Thus Shelley could claim that *Queen Mab* was not a didactic poem. 'The notes to Q.M. will be long & philosophical. I shall take that opportunity which I judge to be a safe one of propagating my principles, which I decline to do syllogistically in a poem. A poem very didactic is I think very stupid.' (*Letters*, i. 350) Didacticism for Shelley is a matter of presentation. His 'principles' are far from absent from *Queen Mab* as a poem, but the presentation of them in a reasoned and argued way is reserved for the prose notes.

In the Preface to *Laon and Cythna* Shelley insists that the poem is 'narrative, not didactic', and records the important insight that poetry has its moral effect by arousing the sympathies of its readers, rather than by explicit presentation.

I have sought to enlist the harmony of metrical language, the etherial combinations of the fancy, the rapid and subtle transitions of human passion . . . in the cause of a liberal and comprehensive morality; and in the view of kindling within the bosoms of my readers, a virtuous enthusiasm for those doctrines of liberty and justice, that faith and hope in something good, which neither violence, nor misrepresentation, nor prejudice, can ever totally extinguish among mankind.

Shelley claims to appeal not to the reason (tricking out the moral with the 'poetical beauty' and 'metaphorical language' of the letter quoted above), but to 'the common sympathies of every human breast'. It can be disputed whether Shelley fulfils such claims in the poem, a good deal of which is didactic even in his sense. But even setting this issue aside it is clear that *Laon and Cythna*, as Shelley conceived it, is didactic in the modern sense. He announces his intention to 'enlist' poetry in the service of a previously settled system of morality and to persuade his readers to adopt the 'doctrines' which constitute his own 'moral and political creed'. This is to make poetry a means to some exterior end, which is what we now understand by didacticism.

In the Preface to *Prometheus Unbound* Shelley essentially repeats what he had said in the Preface to *Laon and Cythna*.

it is a mistake to suppose that I dedicate my poetical compositions solely to the direct enforcement of reform, or that I consider them in any degree as containing a reasoned system on the theory of human life. Didactic poetry is my abhorrence; nothing can be equally well expressed in prose that is not tedious and supererogatory in verse. My purpose has hitherto been simply to familiarise the highly refined imagination of the more select classes of poetical readers with beautiful idealisms of moral excellence; aware that until the mind can love, and admire, and trust, and hope, and endure, reasoned principles of moral conduct are seeds cast upon the highway of life which the unconscious passenger tramples into dust, although they would bear the harvest of his happiness.

Shelley has recognized that a cultivation of the soil is necessary before 'reasoned principles of moral conduct' can bear fruit (an allusion to the Parable of the Sower is evidently intended). He will pray the West Wind to

> Drive my dead thoughts over the universe
> Like withered leaves to quicken a new birth!

—'withered leaves', rather than seeds. But elsewhere in the Preface to *Prometheus Unbound* Shelley betrays a nervousness concerning the precise moral effect of any fiction that he might present which reveals the inhibitions that constrain the didactic poet. It is as if he has been listening to Major Cartwright on the subject of the 'frailty' of the fine arts and the need to give them 'a virtuous education and a right direction'.

The only imaginary being resembling in any degree Prometheus, is Satan; and Prometheus is, in my judgement, a more poetical character than Satan because, in addition to courage and majesty and firm and patient opposition to omnipotent force, he is susceptible of being described as exempt from the taints of ambition, envy, revenge, and a desire for personal aggrandisement, which in the Hero of *Paradise Lost*, interfere with the interest. The character of Satan engenders in the mind a pernicious casuistry which leads us to weigh his faults with his wrongs and to excuse the former because the latter exceed all measure. . . . But Prometheus is, as it were, the type of the highest perfection of moral and intellectual nature, impelled by the purest and the truest motives to the best and noblest ends.

Shelley's unease here is expressed in otiose qualifications like 'resembling in any degree', 'in my judgement', 'susceptible of being described', 'as it were'. There is also an evasive confusion of moral and literary values. What can it mean to call one character more 'poetical' than another? Is this a way of describing human character (as it would be in *A Defence of Poetry*), or an attempt to confine poetry to the presentation of certain moral qualities only? And why should Satan's moral defects interfere with 'the interest' of Milton's poem? The consensus of readers is surely that they *increase* the interest. What worries Shelley is the possibility of the wrong kind of interest being established; the readers may admire Satan's good qualities so much that they imitate his bad ones as well. A character like Prometheus is much safer, since he has no bad qualities at all. Shelley can feel safe in presenting him to his readers and telling them to do likewise. Actually Prometheus in the poem is a more complex and more ambivalent entity than a mere model of moral excellence, and I have already tried to show that such an interpretation is inadequate. Shelley himself imposes this inadequate interpretation on his own drama in his Preface in order to reassure himself that he has ultimate control over the reactions of his audience. This is a didactic attitude, for it casts him in the role of the teacher, and his audience in that of passive learners. He has not quite reconciled himself to trusting the autonomous imagination of his readers, though such trust is demanded by the moral scheme of philosophical anarchism. He comes closer to realizing its necessity in the Preface to *The Cenci*, where he revokes his rejection of 'casuistry' as 'pernicious'. Beatrice is like Satan in being a character who meets her wrongs by doing evil, but this is no longer seen as debarring her from poetical treatment—on the contrary.

The highest moral purpose aimed at in the highest species of the drama, is the teaching the human heart, through its sympathies and antipathies, the knowledge of itself; in proportion to the possession of which know-ledge, every human being is wise, just, sincere, tolerant and kind. If dogmas can do more, it is well: but a drama is no fit place for the en-forcement of them. . . . It is in the restless and anatomizing casuistry with which men seek the justification of Beatrice, yet feel that she has done what needs justification; it is in the superstitious horror with which they contemplate alike her wrongs and their revenge; that the dramatic character of what she did and suffered, consists.

Theoretically this is a distinct advance on the Preface to *Prometheus Unbound*, and *The Cenci* itself, while a lesser work than the lyrical drama, is rather successful in avoiding didacticism. It is not difficult to discover what Shelley thought of Beatrice's story and what are the moral lessons that he thought it enforced; but there is room for interesting dispute as to whether the drama does really bear him out. As Asia learns,

> of such truths
> Each to itself must be the oracle.—
> (*Prometheus Unbound*, ii. iv. 122–3)

The Cenci poses the story of Beatrice as a problem, and impels the audience to an examination of their own reactions in order to work out its solution, rather than imposing authorial dogma. The process is anticipated and dramatized in *Julian and Maddalo*, where the abstract dispute between Julian and Maddalo is circumvented by the presentation of the agony of the Maniac. Both disputants think that he is an example which will support their side of the argument. The Maniac, says Maddalo, used to talk just like Julian, and now 'his wild talk will show/How vain are such aspiring theories'. Julian accepts the challenge, and retorts, 'I hope to prove the induction otherwise . . .' (lines 200–2). But the attempt to use the Maniac's story to point a moral is rightly rebuked by the powerful effect of his soliloquy, which removes the poem from the level of abstract debate to that of living human reality. Both Julian and Maddalo are refuted, so far as the argument goes, Julian because there seems no solution available to the 'problem' posed by the Maniac, Maddalo because his immediate reaction to the Maniac is to help him, which hardly squares with his aristocratic pessimism. At the same time both, by being thrown back on their own reactions, can hope to learn something about themselves that they could never have learnt by mere argument. As Shelley comments in his preface, anticipating the Preface to *The Cenci*, 'the unconnected exclamations of his [the Maniac's] agony will perhaps be found a sufficient comment for the text of every heart.'

By 1819 Shelley was beginning to see more clearly how poetry could have a beneficial moral effect, and to realize that the audience as well as the poet had to play an active role in the process. But he is still limited by his inability to transcend the assumption that morality and poetry are separate, an assumption that opens up the possibility of an embarrassing choice. In January 1819 he wrote to Peacock: 'I consider Poetry very subordinate to moral & political science, & if I were well, certainly I should aspire to the latter; for I can conceive a great work, embodying the discoveries of all ages, & harmonizing the contending creeds by which mankind have been ruled.' (*Letters*, ii. 71) This project, of an almost

Coleridgean ambitiousness, was probably in his mind when in the Preface to *Prometheus Unbound* he threatened his readers with his proposed 'systematical history of what appear to me to be the genuine elements of human society'. We can see *A Philosophical View of Reform* as being an attempt to carry out this project, though by the time he came to write it his general views had been localized and sharpened by the need to respond to a particular political crisis. But the work which best corresponds to the specifications of 1819 is in fact *A Defence of Poetry*, written in February 1821 as a topical response to Peacock's attack on poetry. It is ironic that in that work Shelley was countering views expressed by Peacock that are rather similar to those implied by Shelley himself in his letter to Peacock. Peacock claimed that when there occurs a contradiction between the useful and the ornamental, it is the useful that is to be preferred, and he could have adduced the pronouncements by Shelley cited above to support his position. It is difficult to see how Shelley would have been able to refute his friend's arguments in 1819. As it happened, Peacock's provocative account of the alternatives open to the early nineteenth-century intellectual reached Shelley at just the right moment, when many of the concerns touched on by Peacock were already in his mind, and it served to precipitate out conclusions which had been latent for several years. The text of *A Defence* incorporates many elements from Shelley's earlier prose speculations. The account of the moral effect of poetry draws on ideas developed in the 'Speculations on Morals' (1817), which, as we shall see, Shelley was reworking immediately before the arrival of Peacock's article. The comments on the religious elements in Dante and Milton are drawn from 'On the Devil, and Devils' (1820). The notion that poetry strips the veil of familiarity from the world, and restores a primal immediacy of vision, has sources in Wordsworth and Coleridge but it also echoes the argument of 'On Life' (1819). The distinction between Reason and Imagination and the theory of poetic inspiration were elaborated by Shelley in a review he wrote in Italian of the *improvvisatore* Tommaso Sgricci's performance of *La Morte d'Ettore* in January 1821.[1]

The longest and most explicit of Shelley's self-borrowings in the *Defence* is, of course, from *A Philosophical View of Reform*. The

---

[1] Bodl. MS Shelley adds. e. 17, pp. 11–21. See E. R. Wasserman, *Shelley: A Critical Reading*, p. 379 n. 12. See below, pp. 247–8.

peroration of the *Defence* is taken almost verbatim from the peroration of the first chapter of the earlier work.[1] Not quite verbatim, for the original phrase 'Poets and Philosophers are the unacknowledged legislators of the world' (*Works*, vii. 20) has become 'Poets are the unacknowledged legislators of the World' (vii. 140). The change is of some significance. Godwin could have written the sentence as it originally stood, for he declared himself 'persuaded that the cause of political reform, and the cause of intellectual and literary refinement, are inseparably connected'.[2] It was probably Godwin who provided Shelley with his famous slogan by his description of the poet as 'the legislator of generations and the moral instructor of the world'.[3] But it is evident that Godwin would see philosophers as the source of beneficial currents of opinion, though he recognized that poets could do incalculable good by spreading them in their works; in *A Defence of Poetry* Shelley argues that it is exactly the other way round. The location of the source of value is a problem that will be considered presently; we shall see that Shelley is forced to go beyond the assumptions of Godwin in order to solve this problem. But in what they have to say about the social role of the poet Godwin and Shelley are in substantial agreement. Godwin argued that a writer's influence on society extended far beyond the circle of those consciously affected by his works.

The poorest peasant in the remotest corner of England, is probably a different man from what he would have been but for these authors. Every man who is changed from what he was by the perusal of their works, communicates a portion of the inspiration all around him. It passes from man to man, till it influences the whole mass. I cannot tell that the wisest mandarin now living in China, is not indebted for part of his energy and sagacity to the writings of Milton and Shakespeare, even though it should happen that he never heard of their names.[4]

Godwin is rather vague about the details of the transmission of cultural influences, talking in terms that suggest a contagious disease as much as anything. He seems to think of the process as

---

[1] Compare *Works*, vii. 19–20 and vii. 140.
[2] *The Enquirer*, p. x.
[3] *Life of Geoffrey Chaucer* (2nd edn., 4 vols., 1804), ii. 71. I find this a more likely source than *Rasselas*, proposed by K. N. Cameron, 'A New Source for Shelley's *A Defence of Poetry*', *Studies in Philology*, xxxviii (1941), 635.
[4] *The Enquirer*, p. 140.

something along the lines of pass the parcel: the Chinese mandarin's debt to Shakespeare or Milton will be incurred through a long line of intermediaries which conceals from him the original source of his knowledge—say, through an article written by a journalist, who had read the work of a philosopher, who had met a western traveller, who was acquainted with the work of a German poet, who had been directly influenced by *Macbeth* or *Paradise Lost*. Thus Shelley uses Chaucer's debt to the Italian poets in order to argue that 'we owe, among other causes, the exact condition belonging to our own intellectual existence, to the generous disdain of submission which burned in the bosoms of men who filled a distant generation and inhabited another land' (*Works*, vii. 6). Where Godwin and Shelley part company is the issue of what is communicated in this process. For Godwin the content of a literary work is of primary interest. But he ignores the extent to which the message of a work will be distorted or trivialized by its passage through so many hands, a factor that Lionel Trilling recalls to our attention. 'The religious leader, the political thinker, the teacher, the artist everlastingly communicate their vision— their high intensity of understanding—and they win assent, but always at a lower level and consequently, therefore, to a different thing than they had intended.'[1] The more often the vision is communicated the weaker it must become; and this vision, this original creative energy, is of more importance than any paraphrasable content.

To describe the process of cultural transmission Shelley borrowed an image from Plato's *Ion*. Shelley chose to interpret the irony of this work as a humorous perplexity akin to his own.[2] He argued that poetry unifies and draws together human society in space and time by a process that can be imaged in terms of a chain constituted by the force of magnetism—a chain 'which descending through the minds of many men is attached to those great minds, whence as from a magnet the invisible effluence is sent forth which at once connects, animates and sustains the life of all'.[3] Godwin's account

---

[1] *Matthew Arnold* (1939; 1974), p. 267.
[2] There was of course a neo-Platonic tradition which discounted the hostile irony of the *Ion* and read it as a defence of inspiration (see Joseph E. Baker, *Shelley's Platonic Answer to a Platonic Attack on Poetry* (Iowa City, 1965), p. 51).
[3] *Works*, vii. 124. Shelley translated the relevant passage from the *Ion* (533d) in the notebook in which he drafted the *Defence* (Bodl. MS Shelley d.1, fo. 91ᵛ). The version of the passage given in *Works*, vii. 238 is actually by Mary Shelley.

is essentially mechanical, for it could be given in terms of the 'chain' alone; the best image might be the passing of buckets of water along a human chain. Shelley puts it very differently by seeing the chain as constituted by the power of magnetism, one of those concepts from the margin of the science of his day that interested him considerably. He considered that magnetism was analogous to electricity, and perhaps to life itself; all three being phenomena that were comprehensible only in their effects.[1] In the magnetic chain each mind energizes the next in line, turning it into a magnet itself. That is to say that poetry is not merely handed on from one man to another, for it works by making men poets themselves. The image suggests that there is no absolute distinction between the poet and his audience; both the magnet and that which it attracts must be iron, of the same substance, and the magnet passes on some of its essential power to whatever it attracts. Some of this power is lost in the process, of course; each new magnet in the series is weaker than the one before it. This is regrettable, but not to be avoided, for it is only in the struggle with matter that the power is to be communicated at all.

The essential community between poets and the rest of humanity is also implied by Shelley's use of the concept of 'legislator' as a metaphor for the poet. We must realize that Shelley is not using this term in the sense of 'lawgiver', a sense current among the *philosophes* of the Enlightenment. Condorcet argued that in ancient Greece the philosophers had great influence on 'mœurs', 'lois', and 'gouvernements', an influence which was only increased by the fact that they had no 'existence politique'—they were 'unacknowledged', in fact. They drew up codes of laws which were then presented to the people at large for ratification.[2] Diderot considered that philosophers influenced society by educating political leaders.[3] Kant thought that they ought to be consulted on certain important public decisions, adding, not without irony, that this should be done in secret to spare the rulers embarrassment.[4]

---

[1] See *Works*, vi. 48, 50, 207–8. Coleridge was also interested in magnetism, which he saw as the symbol of 'the power of an organized pattern to reproduce itself, or to repeat its structure, without actual contact' (Stephen Prickett, *Coleridge and Wordsworth: The Poetry of Growth* (Cambridge, 1970), p. 184).

[2] *Esquisse d'un tableau historique des progrés de l'esprit humain* (1793), edited by M. and F. Hincker (Paris, 1971), pp. 123–5.

[3] See Peter Gay, *The Enlightenment: An Interpretation* (1966–9; 2 vols., 1967–70), i. 128–9.

[4] *On History*, translated by Lewis White Beck (Indianapolis, 1963), pp. 115–16.

For all these thinkers the philosophers appeared as the agents of change, the rest of society as passive recipients of their decisions. The same pattern is evident in Rousseau's classic formulation of the *législateur* as Lawgiver. According to Rousseau's account, which alludes to Plato's *Statesman*, and draws on the examples of classical Lawgivers like Lycurgus and Moses, the *législateur* must formulate out of his own, virtually superhuman, wisdom a complete code of laws, which the rest of society has only to accept and obey. He is 'le mécanicien qui invente la machine', and the part of the actual ruler is merely to start it up and keep it running. In order to impose his code on the individuals he is trying to form into a society he must 'changer pour ainsi dire la nature humaine' and he is entitled to commit the *pia fraus* of claiming a divine mission, thus making religion an instrument of policy.[1] Shelley would hardly have been sympathetic to such conclusions. In *The Triumph of Life* he explicitly condemns those who tyrannize over opinion by pretending to a divine sanction, like the Christian theologians

> Who rose like shadows between Man and god
> Till that eclipse, still hanging under Heaven,
> Was worshipped by the world o'er which they strode
>
> For the true Sun it quenched.—
> (lines 289-92)

In the same work he also condemns both the *philosophes* and the rulers whose policies they hoped to influence, mentioning by name Voltaire and Kant, Frederick the Great of Prussia, Catherine of Russia, and Leopold of Austria (lines 235–6). Shelley has recognized the anti-democratic tendency of the *philosophes*, who wished to legislate for humanity by persuading the despots to impose their reforms on their subjects. This kind of reform could hardly forward Shelley's main political objective; it could not make men fit for freedom and able to do without external rule.

In the English political tradition a 'legislator' is thought of as being a representative, or even a delegate of the governed, rather than a ruler or the aide of a ruler. Even Burke thought that MPs

---

[1] *Du contrat social* (1762), edited by Ronald Grimsley (Oxford, 1972), pp. 138–41. A good exposition of the classical theory of the lawgiver is given by Joel Barlow in his 'Dissertation on the Genius and Institutions of Manco Capac' (*Works of Joel Barlow*, ii. 177–91 and 800–12).

should represent the interests of their constituents, if not their opinions.[1] Since 1817 Shelley had been actively involved in a movement which aimed to make the legislators of England even more directly responsible to the people as a whole. It would seem reasonable to associate his definition of poets as 'unacknowledged legislators' with the democratic constitutional theories of the Reformers, rather than with the classical notion of the Lawgiver on which the *philosophes* drew.[2] Poets do not influence society by imposing their ideas on it; the influence they possess is based on the fact that their creations are the representatives of the hopes and desires, which may also be unacknowledged, of all men. Poets do not possess the superhuman wisdom posited by Rousseau for his Lawgiver, but they are more sensitive than most people to the movements of thought and feeling that affect society as a whole. They are able to reinforce and define some of these movements by giving them expression, but it is not in their power to create them by their personal fiat; like democratic legislators, they guide the general will by expressing it. Shelley repeatedly insists upon the reciprocal action of poets and society upon each other: 'they cannot escape from subjection to a common influence which arises out of an infinite combination of circumstances belonging to the times in which they live, though each is in a degree the author of the very influence by which his being is thus pervaded.' 'Poets . . . are in one sense the creators and in another the creations of their age.'[3] When Shelley calls poetry 'The most unfailing herald, companion and follower of the awakening of a great people'[4] he is advisedly careful not to commit himself on the question of whether poetry produces social change or social change produces poetry. Both are equally cause and effect of each other. The unacknowledged legislators do not represent their age by passively reflecting it but by participating in what is dynamic and progressive in it—in what Shelley's contemporaries liked to call 'the spirit of the age'. They look beyond opinion in its fixed and dead form of 'Custom' and attach themselves to the new currents of feeling that are moving towards beneficial change. It is in this way that the

[1] Burke, *Works*, i. 446–7.
[2] Clearly I would disagree with Stuart Curran's argument that Shelley saw his 'legislator' on the model of the classical 'law giver' (*Shelley's Annus Mirabilis*, p. 199).
[3] Preface to *Laon and Cythna*, Preface to *Prometheus Unbound*.
[4] *Works*, vii. 140; see also vii. 19.

poet 'beholds the future in the present, and his thoughts are the germ of the flower and the fruit of latest time' (*Works*, vii. 112)—that he can prophesy, and by prophesying help to bring the future to pass.

Both the 'magnet' image and the metaphor of legislation involve what Stephen Prickett has called the 'fundamentally egalitarian' doctrine of the Romantic poets by which the poet 'differs not in kind, but merely in degree from that which makes us all human'.[1] Prickett ascribes this doctrine to Wordsworth and Coleridge primarily, but it is also present in Shelley, for one thing in the form of explicit allusions to Wordsworth's Preface to *Lyrical Ballads*.[2] All three would admit that the poet is different from other men, but they would strongly deny that his nature is distinct from theirs. For Shelley poetry is 'connate with the origin of man' and existed before there were poets by profession. The principles of all poetry are exemplified in the spontaneous behaviour of the child and of the savage, that is, of 'natural' man. Even befoı e recorded traditions ('in the infancy of society' or 'In the youth of the world') men created 'Poetry' by following 'a certain order in their words and actions', though such poetry was necessarily ephemeral (*Works*, vii. 109–11). If in the modern world poetry has become a specialized activity it is because in most men their native poetic impulse has been overlaid by dead 'Custom', and it is to be reawakened by the productions of those who have retained it in full force and who are termed 'poets'; their poetry 'purges from our inward sight the film of familiarity which obscures from us the wonder of our being. . . . It creates anew the universe after it has been annihilated in our minds by the recurrence of impressions blunted by re-iteration' (*Works*, vii. 137). When Shelley speaks of the poet as an exceptional and anomalous individual it is for the limited purpose of defending poets rather than of defining poetry. Even here he is evidently concerned to vindicate the honour of the poetical faculty itself, and he insists that poets should be better, wiser, and happier than other men, precisely because they possess more of what alone can make any man good, wise, or happy (*Works*, vii. 138–9). But the social role he assigns

---

[1] *Coleridge and Wordsworth*, p. 203.
[2] See Bruce R. McElderry, Jr., 'Common Elements in Wordsworth's "Preface" and Shelley's *Defence of Poetry*', *MLQ* v (1944), 176, and K. N. Cameron, *Shelley: The Golden Years*, p. 194.

the poet depends on the fact that he is of essentially the same nature as other men; what is at work in all works more strongly and more explicitly in him. In order to appreciate this we must investigate Shelley's concept of the Imagination, which he considers, not as the special prerogative of the Romantic artist, but as vitally involved in *all* purposeful and creative human activity.

Shelley's belief that all human activity has its source in the imagination lies behind his use of the term 'Poetry', a use that has caused his critics some trouble. Raymond Williams has praised Shelley for trying to present 'a wider and more substantial account of human motive and energy than was contained in the philosophy of industrialism', but he goes on to object that in doing so he limited 'this more substantial energy to the act of poetry, or of art in general'.[1] What is virtually the same objection has been made from the opposite direction by René Wellek who complains that the 'cosmic extension of the meaning of poetry' results in a situation where 'Poetry loses its identity completely in a loose synthesis of philosophy, morality, and art'.[2] Patrick Parrinder calls the Romantic extension of the term 'poetry' 'a species of linguistic imperialism', meaning, I take it, an attempt to inflate the importance of poetry by annexing to it provinces to which it has no right.[3] Such objections rather underestimate the problems encountered by Shelley in attempting to devise an appropriate technical vocabulary, and slight the responsibility with which he did so. The synthesis of philosophy, morality, art, and other human positives is far from being a loose one, since in his eyes they really are intimately connected as manifestations of man's creative potential, differing specifically to be sure, but not generically. All the 'inventive arts' are connected, for they are all 'no more than various expressions of one internal power, modified by different circumstances, either of an individual, or society' (*Works* vii. 223). This internal power Shelley calls the imagination. The confusion arises when he tries to find a single term for the generic product of the imagination, and settles on 'Poetry': 'Poetry, in a general sense,

[1] *Culture and Society 1780–1950* (1958), p. 43.
[2] *A History of Modern Criticism 1750–1950* (4 vols., 1955–66), ii. 18, 125. M. H. Abrams also considers that Shelley ignores or obscures important distinctions (*The Mirror and the Lamp: Romantic Theory and the Critical Tradition* (New York, 1953), pp. 127–8).
[3] *Authors and Authority: A Study of English Literary Criticism and its Relation to Culture 1750–1900* (London, Henley and Boston, 1977), p. 86.

may be defined to be "the expression of the imagination" . . .'
(*Works*, vii. 109). But, as Shelley was well aware, 'poetry' in
common usage refers to one of the specific products of the
imagination, and it can be argued that Shelley does not really
make a clear enough distinction between the two uses by reserving
the capital P for the generic sense. Coleridge, with his usual
fondness for 'desynomizing words originally equivalent', found a
more viable solution to the problem in wishing 'to use the word
"poesy" as the generic or common term, and to distinguish that
species of poesy which is not *muta poesis* by its usual name
"poetry" '.[1] Coleridge would certainly agree with Shelley in seeing
a close connection between at least all the fine arts. It is perhaps
not surprising that poets should take the art they themselves
practise as a synecdoche of all the ways in which the imagination
can express itself. For Shelley poetry was a particularly illuminating example, in that language, the material of poetry, is 'more
plastic and obedient to the controul of that faculty of which it is
the creation' (*Works*, vii. 113). Not everyone would be prepared
to grant the literary arts the privileged position that Shelley claims
for them, and his choice of 'Poetry' as a generic term serves to
alert us to the pressure exerted on the development of his argument
by his own particular preoccupations. But if he tends to overlook
the specific circumstances of the non-literary arts, he is very
concerned to demonstrate the connection between the art of poetry
and human activities whose imaginative dimensions are usually
ignored.

Shelley's account of the imagination was originally developed as
part of his moral philosophy, rather than of his aesthetics. Shelley's
moral philosophy, like Godwin's, is basically utilitarian. A utilitarian moral philosophy tends to be an unstable structure, that
can only work by incorporating a number of moral principles that
cannot really be justified in utilitarian terms.[2] Utilitarianism works

---

[1] *Biographia Literaria* (1817), edited by John T. Shawcross (2 vols., 1973),
ii. 255.

[2] F. E. L. Priestley has pointed out that Godwin's utilitarianism is part of the
intellectual climate, that it is compromised by his rationalism, and that it is
qualified by adherence to goals beside pleasure, such as moral autonomy and
sincerity (*Political Justice*, iii. 14–17). John P. Clark insists on seeing Godwin
as a utilitarian above all else, arguing that utility overrides moral autonomy, and
interpreting Godwin's elevation of sincerity as an example of rule-utilitarianism,
or dismissing such passages as 'lapses from consistency' (*The Philosophical
Anarchism of William Godwin*, pp. 93, 108–12).

best as a principle of legislation, which is basically how it was understood by Bentham. When he made the famous comparison between poetry and push-pin his point was that the legislator has no business to favour or disfavour activities which affect only those engaged in them, whatever his private opinion concerning their respective merits. Those who like Godwin and Shelley wish to make utilitarianism into a moral philosophy cannot be so indifferent to judgements of value, and utilitarian moralists have generally argued that some pleasures are better or more worthy than others. Shelley distinguishes between 'durable, universal, and permanent' and 'transitory and particular' pleasures. 'Utility' is the promotion of either kind of pleasure, but the higher utility is the promotion of the higher pleasure by 'whatever strengthens and purifies the affections, enlarges the imagination, and adds spirit to sense' (*Works*, vii. 132). As John Clark has pointed out with respect to Godwin, these arguments can be given a utilitarian twist; the higher pleasures are better in themselves and also more useful in being fertile of more secondary pleasures.[1] Poetry is better than push-pin because poetry has a lasting moral effect apart from the immediate pleasure it can give in common with push-pin. The kind of enlightened utilitarianism to which Shelley adheres is also more aware of the essential utilitarian ends than the crass version that Peacock exploited. For Peacock, as Shelley pointed out, utility consists in 'banishing the importunity of the wants of our animal nature, the surrounding men with security of life, the dispersing the grosser delusions of superstition, and the conciliating such a degree of mutual forbearance among men as may consist with the motives of personal advantage'.[2] Shelley has no objection to this in itself, but he would be entitled to point out that it really goes a very short way towards fulfilling the essential aim of utilitarianism, the promotion of pleasure. Utilitarians are prone to value means above ends. As Bentham commented, when he wished to replace 'Utility' by 'Greatest happiness principle', 'there may be a utility which stops short of the only materials of happiness, viz. pleasures and exemptions from pains, in such sort as to have no reference to it'.[3]

[1] Op. cit., pp. 95–7.
[2] *Works*, vii. 132. Ellsworth Barnard thinks this passage is directed against Godwin (*Shelley's Religion* (Minneapolis, 1937), p. 252).
[3] Quoted in Mary P. Mack, *Jeremy Bentham: An Odyssey of Ideas 1748–1792* (1962), p. 225.

A distinguishing mark of utilitarian moral systems is their replacement of the terms 'good' and 'evil' by 'pleasure' and 'pain', with a consequent redefinition of the aims of morality in terms of the promotion of pleasure and the avoidance of pain. Shelley's earlier defences of pleasure are directed against an ascetic (and Christian) morality. Such a morality only does violence to human nature.

Pleasure, in an open and innocent garb, by some strange process of reasoning, is called vice; yet man (so closely is he linked to the chains of necessity—so irresistibly is he impelled to fulfil the end of his being,) must seek her at whatever price: he becomes a hypocrite, and braves damnation with all its pains. (*Works*, vi. 214)

To divorce 'good' and 'evil', 'virtue' and 'vice', from human pleasures and pains is to create a whole class of 'crimes of convention', as Shelley puts it in the Preface to *Laon and Cythna*, adding, 'It is because there is so great a multitude of artificial vices, that there are so few real virtues.' Such artificial crimes would include for Shelley blasphemous and seditious libel, and most sexual crimes, such as incest. The Benthamites also disapproved of attempts to regulate the sexual instincts, seeing them as based on ascetic prejudices, and Shelley's defence of contraception anticipated the campaign of Francis Place.[1] Shelley's phenomenalist 'intellectual philosophy' would also have led him to mistrust any moral system that referred to states or actions being good or evil in themselves without any reference to a possible subject of experience. In *A Refutation of Deism* he argued that 'good and evil are words employed to designate that peculiar state of our own perceptions, resulting from the encounter of any object calculated to produce pleasure or pain. Exclude the idea of relation, and the words good and evil are deprived of import.' (*Works*, vi. 52–3) This position is implied in Shelley's claim in the *Defence* that 'All things exist as they are perceived: at least in relation to the percipient' (*Works*, vii. 137).

By concentrating on the actual pleasures and pains of human percipients Shelley is able to evade the claims of any moral theory whose demands are phrased in terms of an abstract 'duty', imposed by the will either of God or of human legislators. But utilitarian moral theories are prone to run into another danger

---

[1] Ibid., pp. 212–13. See above, p. 49.

which Shelley is equally concerned to avoid, that of reducing all moral questions to self-interest. Virtually all eighteenth-century philosophers operate from a position of psychological egoism which leads logically to the position described by de Sade.

est-il charitable de faire du mal aux autres pour se délecter soi-même? Les coquins vous répondent à cela qu'accoutumés, dans l'acte du plaisir, à se compter pour tout et les autres pour rien, ils sont persuadés qu'il est tout simple, d'après les impulsions de la nature, de préférer ce qu'ils sentent à ce qu'ils ne sentent point. . . . Avons-nous jamais éprouvé une seule impulsion de la nature qui nous conseille de préférer les autres à nous, et chacun n'est-il pas pour soi dans le monde? . . . Ah! croyons-le, croyons-le, Eugénie, la nature, notre mère à tous, ne nous parle jamais que de nous; rien n'est égoïste comme sa voix, et ce que nous y reconnaissons de plus clair est l'immuable et saint conseil qu'elle nous donne de nous délecter, n'importe aux dépens de qui.[1]

Sade presents this as an attack on Christian morality, but it strikes at cherished beliefs of those Enlightenment thinkers who thought they had rejected the absurdities of superstition in favour of Reason and Nature; his sophisms reveal that rationalism and naturalism tend to generate the conclusions that were originally fed in as prejudices. The chief aim of a utilitarian system is to promote the general good, or the greatest happiness of the greatest number. This aim depends on people acting at least occasionally in the interest of others, but from a legislative point of view this is compatible with a moral theory that accounts for everything in terms of self-interest. The legislator has simply to harness self-interest in favour of his own system by attaching penalties to actions that harm the general interest, and rewards to those that promote it; hence it becomes self-interest to work for the general interest. Such a solution would not satisfy a philosophical anarchist, for at this point utilitarian considerations come into conflict with the overriding claims of moral independence. People must act rightly as the result of their own moral choice, not by the coercion of legislative constraints. If they are to act in the general interest it must be possible to act either benevolently (for the sake of others rather than of themselves) or disinterestedly (for the sake of the general interest rather than of their own). There is a real distinction here whose force possibly escapes Shelley, who transforms

[1] *La Philosophie dans le boudoir; ou, Les Instituteurs immoraux* (1795), edited by Yvon Belaval (Paris, 1976), pp. 128–9.

Godwin's demand for disinterestedness into the imperative of benevolence. But clearly both disinterestedness and benevolence are at odds with a theory that reduces all actions to self-interest. This is a challenge that Godwin is unable to meet, for, despite frequent references in works outside *Political Justice* to the need for altruistic behaviour, his theoretical account in that work follows Helvétius in seeing benevolence as derivative from self-interest.

> The good of my neighbour could not, in the first instance, have been chosen, but as the means of agreeable sensation. His cries, or the spectacle of his distress importune me, and I am irresistibly impelled to adopt means to remove this importunity.[1] . . . Thus the good of our neighbour, like the possession of money, is originally pursued for the sake of its advantage to ourselves. (*Political Justice*, i. 425)

Godwin's account of altruism (which parallels its development to that of avarice) must be profoundly unsatisfying to anyone who really cares about the possibility of benevolence. There is some evidence to suggest that by the date of the *Defence* Shelley could no longer accept Godwin's moral philosophy. Godwin, like Bentham, had a balance-sheet view of morality, according to which an action is evaluated by adding up the pleasures and pains to result from it, considered as plus and minus quantities. The most notorious example of this way of thinking is Bentham's 'felicific calculus', but Shelley would have been more familiar with Godwin's formulation. 'Morality is nothing else but a calculation of consequences, and an adoption of that mode of conduct which, upon the most comprehensive view, appears to be attended with a balance of general pleasure and happiness.' (*Political Justice*, i. 342)[2] Shelley almost certainly has Godwin's position in his sights when he claims that the injustice in English society and the post-war political crisis are the ultimate results of 'an unmitigated exercise of the calculating faculty' (*Works*, vii. 132), to which he refers elsewhere as 'the selfish and calculating

---

[1] Compare Hobbes's explanation of an act of charity: 'Because, sayd he, I was in paine to consider the miserable condition of the old man; and now my almes, giving him some reliefe, doth also ease me.' Hobbes's point was that he did not practise charity because it was 'Christ's command' (*Aubrey's Brief Lives*, edited by Oliver Lawson Dick (1949; Harmondsworth, 1976), p. 317).

[2] John Clark has found the elements of Bentham's 'felicific calculus' in Godwin, arguing that in Godwin the 'qualitative distinction between pleasures really reduces to a quantitative one' (*The Philosophical Anarchism of William Godwin*, pp. 97–8).

principle' (vii. 135). This 'calculating faculty' is the Reason which, as Shelley puts it, '[considers] thoughts, not in their integral unity, but as the algebraical representations which conduct to certain general results' (vii. 109). The Reason that leads Godwin to derive altruism from self-interest could be nothing but a selfish principle. Godwin affirms that our actions must be evaluated 'upon the most comprehensive view', and Shelley would have to reply that the Reason can never take a view that is comprehensive enough.

Shelley was able to free himself from the limitations of Godwin's rationalism at least partly because he had already found a more convincing answer to the urgent question: how is altruism possible? He did not find this answer without some help. I have presented elsewhere[1] the detailed evidence for concluding that in a crucial section of the 'Speculations on Morals' (*Works*, vii. 73–8) Shelley's argument is drawing on Hazlitt's account of the moral imagination, expounded in his *Essay on the Principles of Human Action* (1805). Hazlitt, like Shelley, can be regarded as a disciple of Godwin, and they would have found a good deal in common when they became acquainted through Leigh Hunt, probably in early 1817. On 9 February they joined forces to argue in favour of republicanism, while Hunt and Walter Coulson defended monarchy, the argument continuing until three in the morning.[2] Shelley was impressed enough by Hazlitt to refer to him as a leading writer on the Reform side in *A Philosophical View*. Hazlitt was less pleased with Shelley's politics, to judge from the attack in 'On Paradox and Common-place', though Hunt may have been right to suspect that Hazlitt was paying Shelley back for some fancied slight.[3] If Hazlitt's attack did Shelley's reputation some disserve, against this must be set the help that he gave Shelley in arriving at the theory of the imagination stated in the *Defence*. Hazlitt was very proud of the 'important metaphysical discovery' presented in his *Essay*[4] and as Herschel Baker remarks, he 'lost no chance to publicize its

---

[1] 'Shelley and Hazlitt', to be published as part of the proceedings of the Shelley Conference held at Gregynog in September 1978, edited by Kelvin Everest (forthcoming from the Harvester Press, Hassocks, Sussex).

[2] *Journal*, p. 77; Charles and Mary Cowden Clarke, *Recollections of Writers* (1878), edited by Robert Gittings (Fontwell, Sussex, 1969), p. 26. For other meetings between Shelley and Hazlitt see *Journal*, p. 80, and Godwin's journal (manuscript in the Bodleian Library, Oxford and microfilm in the University Library, Cambridge) for 26 January and 16 February 1817.

[3] *Correspondence of Leigh Hunt*, i. 166. See above, pp. 187–8.

[4] *Complete Works of William Hazlitt*, xvii. 312.

doctrines'.[1] If Shelley ever discussed moral philosophy with Hazlitt (as he is likely enough to have done) he would have been sure to receive a summary of its contents. The *Essay* was in any case available as late as 1819.[2]

The aim of Hazlitt's *Essay* was to provide, in the words of its sub-title, 'an Argument in favour of the Natural Disinterestedness of the Human Mind'. Hazlitt was concerned above all to refute what he called 'the selfish hypothesis',[3] the theory which reduces all actions to self-interest—a theory which even Godwin, however unwillingly, was forced to accept. But arguments like Godwin's derivation of altruism from self-interest only served 'to establish generosity and virtue "lean pensioners" on self-interest', as Hazlitt put it (i. 17). Hazlitt hoped to show that self-love itself was derived from original disinterested benevolence, and the core of his argument is his demonstration that 'the human mind is naturally disinterested, or that it is interested in the welfare of others in the same way, and from the same direct motives, by which we are impelled to the pursuit of our own interest' (i. 1). Hazlitt begins by reminding us that all human actions are directed to the future.

All voluntary action, that is all action proceeding from a will, or effort of the mind to produce a certain event must relate to the future, or to those things, the existence of which is problematical, undetermined, and therefore capable of being affected by the means made use of with a view to their production, or the contrary. But that which is future, which does not yet exist can excite no interest in itself, nor act upon the mind in any way but by means of the imagination. The direct primary motive, or impulse which determines the mind to the volition of any thing must therefore in all cases depend on the *idea* of that thing as conceived by the imagination, and on the idea solely. (i. 8)

The imagination is hence the only link between the present self (who performs an action) and the future self (who is to suffer the consequences). '. . . personal identity neither does, nor can imply any positive communication between a man's future, and present self . . . it does not give him a mechanical interest in his future being' (i. 7). In other words, the pleasure or pain I will feel as a consequence of my actions is not and cannot be an irresistible determining factor in leading me to perform those actions. This

---

[1] *William Hazlitt* (Cambridge, Mass., and London, 1962), p. 142.
[2] *Examiner*, 17 Oct. 1819, p. 665.
[3] *Complete Works of William Hazlitt*, i. 22n.

strikes at the root of the self-interest theory, which depends on a fiction concerning identity; it claims that because the 'same' person both acts and suffers the consequences he must have an interest in the nature of those consequences that will determine the actions. But the idea of personal identity, Hazlitt argues, is derived from our experience of the continuity between our past and present sensations; only by an act of the imagination can the notion of identity be extended into the future.[1] I must, as it were, put myself in my own place, just as I would put myself in the place of another. As Hazlitt puts it, in a brilliant paradox: 'The interests of the being who acts, and of the being who suffers are never one' (i. 11). No one would dispute that benevolence depends on using one's imagination, and Godwin frequently stresses the moral importance of the imagination.[2] Hazlitt's account suggests that the imagination is equally essential to self-love, and in the same way.

The exclusive attachment to the interests of an individual self, conceived of as one and the same in past, present, and future is, then, a product of habit—or, as Shelley would say, of 'Custom'— and of a belief in the truth of the 'selfish hypothesis' itself. It is no necessary condition of voluntary action, for the imagination, now seen to be the central moral faculty, is no respecter of persons. It is not determined by considerations of who is to suffer the imagined future consequences of an action, but by the essential nature of those consequences. 'If there were not something in the very notion of good, or evil which naturally made the one an object of immediate desire and the other of aversion it is not easy to conceive how the mind should ever come to feel an interest in the prospect of obtaining the one or avoiding the other.' (i. 18) Our natural interest is in obtaining good and avoiding evil, defined by Hazlitt as pleasure and pain, but as regards persons the mind is naturally indifferent, that is, disinterested.

If we admit that there is something in the very idea of good, or evil,

---

[1] Ibid. i. 1; that Hazlitt's treatment of the problem of personal identity is central to his account of moral action is emphasized by James Noxon, 'Hazlitt as Moral Philosopher', *Ethics*, lxxiii (1962–3), 279–83.

[2] See *Four Early Pamphlets (1783–1784)*, edited by Burton R. Pollin (Gainesville, Fla., 1966), pp. 195–6; *The Enquirer*, p. 298; C. Kegan Paul, *William Godwin: His Friends and Contemporaries*, ii. 119; *Essay on Sepulchres* (1809), p. 23; *Mandeville. A Tale of the Seventeenth Century in England* (3 vols., Edinburgh, 1817), iii. 45; *Uncollected Writings (1785–1822)*, p. 432; *Thoughts on Man*, pp. 48, 233–4, 273–4.

which naturally excites desire or aversion, which is in itself the proper motive of action, which impels the mind to pursue the one and to avoid the other by a true moral necessity, then it cannot be indifferent to me whether I believe that any being will be made happy or miserable in consequence of my actions, whether this be myself or another. (i. 12)

Hazlitt's theory is in danger of proving too much. If man is naturally disinterested why do most people spend most of their time in performing actions primarily directed to promoting their own personal interests? Hazlitt explains these facts on empirical grounds, in terms of acquired knowledge about the world.

The reason why a child first distinctly wills or pursues his own good is not because it is *his*, but because it is *good*. For the same reason he prefers his own gratification to that of others not because he likes himself better than others, but because he has a more distinct idea of his own wants and pleasures than of theirs. . . . A child is insensible to the good of others not from any want of goodwill towards them, or an exclusive attachment to self, but for want of knowing better. Indeed he can neither be attached to his own interest nor that of others but in consequence of knowing in what it consists. (i. 12)

Before our natural desire to produce pleasure and decrease pain can be directed towards others we must become aware, firstly that others do in fact feel pleasure and pain as we do, and secondly of what causes them pleasure and what pain. Our own pleasures and pains must absorb all our attention so long as they are the only ones we know of. But the natural consequence of our growth in knowledge is for the sphere of our concern to widen, and for benevolence to acquire a correspondingly larger share in directing our actions. There is a continuum linking pure selfishness and pure altruism, and the individual can to some extent determine his position on it.

a sentiment of general benevolence can only arise from an habitual cultivation of the natural disposition of the mind to sympathise with the feelings of others by constantly taking an interest in those which we know, and imagining others that we do not know, as the other feeling of abstract self-interest, that is in the degree in which it generally subsists, must be caused by a long narrowing of the mind to our own particular feelings and interests, and a voluntary insensibility to every thing which does not immediately concern ourselves. (i. 14–15)

Perfect altruism is an artificially cultivated emotion, but so is perfect selfishness; and this makes it worth while debating the issue. To accept the 'selfish hypothesis' as true can only tend to stifle any tendency to benevolence by 'leaving virtue no other basis to rest upon than a principle of refined self-interest'. On the other hand it might be possible to promote 'true generosity' and 'disinterested simplicity of character' by 'shewing to man that his nature is originally and essentially disinterested; that as a voluntary agent, he must be a disinterested one; that he could neither desire, nor will, nor pursue his own happiness but for the possession of faculties which necessarily give him an interest out of himself in the happiness of others' (i. 6–7).

It is not difficult for us to imagine how Hazlitt's theory must have impressed Shelley when he encountered it in the spring of 1817. It cleared up a crux in moral philosophy that would have been of especial concern to Shelley, by showing how human nature could be seen as essentially benevolent, or at least disinterested, rather than selfish. Equally important was the fact that Hazlitt assigned a crucial role to the imagination, which could hardly have failed to excite a poet who also wished to be a moral and political reformer. It is hardly surprising that Shelley laid Hazlitt under contribution in a prose fragment headed 'Chapter one On the [*blank*] of virtue' and printed by Mary Shelley as part of the 'Speculations on Morals'.[1] From a study of the original manuscript Kenneth Cameron concluded that it was written between 10 September 1816 and 10 March 1818.[2] Since Shelley and Hazlitt were in contact between January and May 1817 we would I think be justified, in view of Hazlitt's influence on the work, in making rather more than Professor Cameron felt entitled to do of the fact that part of the manuscript was written on paper similar to that used by Shelley for a letter dated 23 April 1817.[3] In this fragment Shelley follows a traditional classification in dividing virtue into 'benevolence, or the desire to be the author of good' and 'justice, or an apprehension of the manner in which that good is to be done' (*Works*, vii. 73). Justice Shelley interprets in an egalitarian fashion and does not really find it problematical.

[1] *Works*, vii. 73–8. The manuscript is in the Bodleian Library, Oxford (Bodleian MS Shelley adds. c. 4, fos. 190ʳ–193ᵛ) and the Pforzheimer Collection, New York (SC 339). The portion in the Pforzheimer Collection is reproduced and transcribed in *SC* iv. 734–7.

[2] *SC* iv. 740–2.

[3] *SC* iv. 742.

His real task is, like Hazlitt's, to demonstrate the possibility of altruism. There are difficulties here that Shelley does not shirk.

But wherefore should a man be benevolent and just? The immediate emotions of his nature, especially in its most inartificial state, prompt him to inflict pain, and to arrogate dominion. He desires to heap superfluities to his own store, letting others perish with famine. He is propelled to guard against the smallest invasion of his own liberty, though he reduces others to a condition of the most pitiless servitude. He is revengeful, proud, and selfish. Wherefore should he curb these propensities? (*Works*, vii. 73)

Shelley soon finds that he has in fact two problems on his hands. First he must show that benevolence 'will most effectually promote the happiness of mankind' (vii. 74) in order to refute the view of Mandeville, Adam Smith, and others, according to which the general interest is better served by everyone pursuing their own interest rather than by altruism. Anything Shelley may have said on this point was written on a part of the manuscript which was lost between 1817 and 1821. In any case Shelley would be willing to take the utility of benevolence for granted, his most important task being to demonstrate the possibility of altruism, to show 'in what manner the sensations which constitute the basis of virtue originate in the human mind; what are the laws which it receives there; how far the principles of mind allow it to be an attribute of a human being; and, lastly, what is the probability of persuading mankind to adopt it as a universal and systematical motive of conduct' (vii. 74). In the section entitled 'Benevolence' Shelley attempts, with Hazlitt's help, to carry out this task.

Shelley's meaning in this fragment is not always as clear as we might wish, and it is extremely helpful to be able to restore steps in the argument that Shelley elides, from the parallel account given by Hazlitt—this in itself is telling evidence that Shelley was drawing on Hazlitt. At one point Shelley argues that 'Pain or pleasure if subtly analyzed will be found to consist entirely in prospect' (vii. 75). This analysis must appear impossibly subtle, unless we realize that Shelley is referring to pleasure and pain *as motives to action*. He is in fact following Hazlitt's argument to the effect that a future (and therefore as yet non-existent) pleasure or pain can only constitute a motive to action when presented to the mind by the imagination—whose importance Shelley has just been stressing: 'Imagination or mind employed in prophetically delive[ring] its objects is that faculty of human nature on which every gradation of its progress, nay every, the minutest change depends.' (*Works*, vii. 75) In the manuscript '[*illegible*] delive[ring]' is substituted for Shelley's original words, 'imaging forth'. Having attempted in *Queen Mab*, and probably already having begun to attempt in *Laon and Cythna* to 'image forth' an ideal state of society and ideal modes of conduct, Shelley must have found Hazlitt's vindication of the imagination both welcome and exciting, for it provided a link between his own poetic enterprises and permanent principles of human action. Hazlitt's account, by giving the imagination a crucial role in all human action, saved its presentations from being relegated to the status of mere fancies and empty dreams. Shelley follows Hazlitt in using 'ideal' and its cognates to indicate the positive values of imaginative activity.[1] When Shelley refers in the Preface to *Prometheus Unbound* to his own works as presenting 'beautiful idealisms of moral excellence', or mentions 'the loftiest idealisms of passion and of power' represented in the Athenian drama (*Works*, vii. 119), they are thought of as existing in the imagination rather than in the realm of Platonic Ideas.[2]

Shelley follows Hazlitt very closely in considering the problem of man's apparent selfishness, as instanced in the behaviour of children, savages, and the uneducated, who exemplify the 'natural' man. Like Hazlitt, Shelley argues that pain is shunned simply because it is pain, and it is only a contingent fact that it is pain to ourselves personally that is first avoided. 'There is a class of emotions which we instinctively avoid.' (vii. 74) Our apparent indifference to the suffering of others is the result of lack of knowledge; as our knowledge increases, so the circle of our sympathies extends to take in others.

A living being such as is man considered in his origin, a child a month old has a very imperfect consciousness of the existence of other natures resembling itself. All the energies of its being are directed to the extinction of the pains with which it is perpetually assailed. At length it discovers that it is surrounded by natures susceptible of sensation similar to its own. . . . If a child observes without emotion its nurse or

---

[1] See *Complete Works of William Hazlitt*, i. 21.

[2] As Earl Schulze has recognized (*Shelley's Theory of Poetry: A Reappraisal* (The Hague, 1966), p. 19).

its mother suffering acute pain, it is attributable rather to ignorance than insensibility. So soon as the accents and gestures significant of pain are referred to the feelings which they express they awaken in the mind of the beholder a desire that they should cease. Pain is thus apprehended to be evil for its own sake without any other necessary reference to the mind by which its ⟨existence is perceived, than⟩ such as is indispensable to its perception. (*Works*, vii. 74–5)[1]

The difference between selfishness and altruism is one of degree rather than of kind, the differentiating factor being the extent of our knowledge. 'In this sense wisdom and virtue may be said to be inseparables and criteria of each other.' (vii. 75–6) Shelley's argument has brought him round to a favourite maxim of Godwin's: 'In whatever light we consider virtue . . . its degree must be intimately connected with the degree of knowledge.' (*Political Justice*, i. 310) But where Godwin's 'knowledge' is empirical and rationalistic,[2] Shelley's 'wisdom' must be taken to include the knowledge of the existence of other sensitive beings and of their pains and pleasures which is dependent on the imagination.

Shelley distinguishes degrees of benevolence, according to the extent of the individual's knowledge and the scope of his imagination, which are to some extent conditioned by the level of civilization of his society.

The inhabitant of a highly civilized community will more acutely sympathize with the sufferings and enjoyment of others than the inhabitant of a society of a less degree of civilization. He who shall have cultivated his intellectual powers by familiarity with the finest specimens of poetry and philosophy will usually ⟨sympathise more⟩ than one engaged in the less refined functions of manual labour. (*Works*, vii. 75)

Seeing politics as a branch of morals the enlightened Reformer will attempt to cultivate the imagination, on whose scope the capacity for all virtuous action depends. A Reformer who is a poet will also find here the key to the essential unity of all his concerns. Shelley does not in fact follow this up in his fragment, beyond noting that 'disinterested benevolence is the product of a cultivated imagination, and has an intimate connexion with all the arts which add ornament or dignity or power or stability to the social state of man' (vii. 76). It was to be nearly four years before Shelley

---

[1] See *Complete Works of William Hazlitt*, i. 12, quoted above, p. 233.
[2] See J. P. Clark, *The Philosophical Anarchism of William Godwin*, pp. 102–3.

attempted to justify in detail his sense of the 'intimate connexion' between morality and the arts.

Having developed in the spring of 1817 the germ of a highly promising theory of the moral imagination, Shelley seems to have lost it in the welter of his papers and manuscripts. It seems to have come to light again at the beginning of 1821. It was at that time, as Kenneth Cameron has shown,[1] that Shelley drafted a series of fragments printed among the 'Speculations on Morals' and the 'Speculations on Metaphysics' (they should be considered as intended for a single work) in a notebook now in the Bodleian Library (Bodleian MS Shelley d. 1). Cameron suggested that in writing this new work on ethics Shelley 'may have intended to incorporate in it the fragments he had previously written in England', but added that this was 'not certain'.[2] An examination of the manuscript evidence makes it clear that Shelley intended to do just this. Among the 1821 fragments is a note that reads: 'For it is enquired &c. (p. 8)'.[3] This, as Mary Shelley recognized, refers to a passage in the 1817 fragment, beginning: 'It is inquired for what reason a human being should engage in procuring the happiness, or refrain from producing the pain of another?'[4] A little later in the 1821 manuscript we find: 'A common Sophism &c.'.[5] Mary Shelley omitted this note, but Ingpen realized that it was a reference to another passage in the 1817 fragment, beginning: 'A common sophism, which, like many others, depends on the abuse of a metaphorical expression to a literal purpose, has produced much of the confusion which has involved the theory of morals.' This introduces a critique of Paley's account of the notion of 'obligation'. One page or more of the 1817 manuscript is missing, and the critique breaks off with the words: 'But if I observe him returning self-satisfied from the performance of some action, by which he has been the willing author of extensive benefit, I do not infer that the anticipation of hellish agonies, or the hope of heavenly reward, has constrained him to sacrifice'.[6] The sense of this, as Ingpen realized, is continued in a passage omitted by Mary Shelley, beginning: 'his personal advantage to the object previously

[1] *SC* iv. 742–3.
[2] *SC* iv. 743–4.
[3] Bodl. MS Shelley d. 1, fo. 3ʳ (*Works*, vii. 79).
[4] Bodl. MS Shelley adds. c. 4, fo. 191ʳ (*Works*, vii. 73).
[5] Bodl. MS Shelley d. 1, fo. 3ᵛ (*Works*, vii. 344, note to vii. 79, line 18).
[6] Bodl. MS Shelley adds. c. 4, fo. 191ᵛ (*Works*, vii. 74).

proposed'.[1] Now this continuation is part of the 1821 manuscript. Thus we can see that when in 1821 Shelley began to draft a treatise on morals he had before him the fragment he had written on the same topic in 1817, and he twice indicated his intention to copy passages from it into his new treatment of the subject. Moreover he found that at least one sheet of the earlier fragment was missing, and he wrote a new passage to complete the sense of the interrupted sentence. We can also deduce that the composition of a treatise on morals was interrupted by the arrival of Peacock's *The Four Ages of Poetry*, or at least by Shelley's decision to write a reply, for the 1821 fragments on morals are written at the back and front of the notebook in which he went on to draft *A Defence of Poetry*. If the task of refuting Peacock prevented Shelley from developing his speculations on ethics, the theory of the moral activity of the imagination which he had just disinterred was to play a major role in the argument of the *Defence*.

This theory provided an obvious rebuttal to crass utilitarian arguments that poetry was either trivial or even immoral. Such objections rest upon 'a misconception of the manner in which poetry acts to produce the moral improvement of man' (*Works*, vii. 117). Utilitarian moralists demand that art should improve its audience by direct instruction, by enforcing 'admirable doctrines' derived from some external source. Even if poetry could do this effectively it would fail in what Shelley would consider a more important objective, namely the fostering of the moral autonomy of the individual. True morality depends on the activity of the imagination that frees man from the confines of 'the little world of self', and poetry surpasses dogmatic moralizing by arousing this imaginative activity.

The great secret of morals is love; or a going out of our own nature, and an identification of ourselves with the beautiful which exists in thought, action, or person, not our own. A man, to be greatly good, must imagine intensely and comprehensively; he must put himself in the place of another and of many others; the pains and pleasures of his species must become his own. The great instrument of moral good is the imagination; and poetry administers to the effect by acting upon the cause. Poetry enlarges the circumference of the imagination by replenishing it with thoughts of ever new delight, which have the power of attracting and assimilating to their own nature all other thoughts, and which form new

---

[1] Bodl. MS Shelley d. 1, fo. 4ʳ (*Works*, vii. 344, note to vii. 79, line 18).

intervals and interstices whose void for ever craves fresh food. Poetry strengthens that faculty which is the organ of the moral nature of man, in the same manner as exercise strengthens a limb. (*Works*, vii. 118)

Just as Falstaff was both witty himself and the cause of wit in others, so poetry is imaginative and stimulates the imaginations of its readers. To participate in a work of art, to grasp the concepts of the creator through the medium in which they are expressed, is itself an imaginative activity. This is true for the literary arts, at any rate, since a poem or a novel can be said to be something different from the marks on the page which are actually present; simply to make sense out of these marks must involve a synthetic act of the imagination. It would be difficult to claim as much concerning music or the pictorial and plastic arts, and it is evident that Shelley often has 'poetry' in mind when he speaks of 'Poetry'. Nevertheless, it can reasonably be claimed that every work of art possesses formal aspects that can be distinguished from the physical elements of which the work is composed (though the form can hardly be present without them) and which must be grasped imaginatively. Art, by calling on the imaginative resources of its audience, always to some degree and in the greatest art to a very high degree, stimulates their development, and thus prepares its audience for autonomous moral activity. Here we have the magnetic force that binds the 'chain' of minds together.[1]

Shelley's need to repel a utilitarian attack leads him into formulations that could be interpreted in crass utilitarian terms themselves. His claim that 'Poetry strengthens the faculty which is the organ of the moral nature of man in the same manner as exercise strengthens a limb' comes uncomfortably close to justifying art on merely instrumental terms. Peacock asserts that poetry is of no use; Shelley retorts that poetry is very useful for making people more moral. It is clear that Shelley thinks of poetry as more than a means, and he would resist calls to abandon poetry because a more effective means were available for promoting the end of morality. Any such calls would be a contradiction in terms in Shelley's view; the imagination is the key to all moral growth, and what is imaginative is by definition (Shelley's definition at least) 'Poetry'. Poetry is more than useful, it is good, to borrow the

---

[1] Coleridge evolved a rather similar theory, with particular reference to the effect of the drama on its audience (see J. R. de J. Jackson, *Method and Imagination in Coleridge's Criticism* (1969), pp. 131–5).

terms used by Newman, who remarks, ' "Good" indeed means one thing, and "useful" means another; but . . . though the useful is not always good, the good is always useful. Good is not only good, but reproductive of good.'[1] If we look more closely at Shelley's argument we will see that it makes any proposal to subordinate poetry to the interests of morality out of the question, for it implies an *identification* of poetry and morality. The debate on the relation between art and morality is traditionally conducted in terms of two positions which take for granted an essential difference between art and morality. One of these positions, which has been labelled 'moralism', consists in locating 'the importance of art in some moral purpose which it serves'; the other, 'autonomism', holds that 'a decision to concern oneself with art necessarily involves a decision to dissociate oneself from moral concerns'.[2] As John Dewey, one of the few philosophers to take Shelley's aesthetic philosophy seriously, pointed out, both these positions are based on the assumption that 'morals are satisfactory in idea if not in fact, and that the only question is whether and in what ways art should conform to a moral system already developed'.[3] Thus a moralist like Sidney 'would never dream that poetry was teaching or persuading any doctrine which it did not discover in some legislatively competent authority outside itself'.[4] On the other hand Swinburne, from an autonomist position, is unable to think of morality except as a fixed and external orthodoxy. Indeed, his own account of the way in which poets have defied 'established opinion and the incarnate moralities of church and household'[5] would seem to be a demonstration that art is not morally neutral. Both the moralist and the autonomist assume that morality can do without art.

Shelley would find it much harder to make the necessary distinction between the two activities. They are both imaginative activities. If 'Poetry, in a general sense, may be defined to be "the expression of the imagination" ', morality, as we have seen, may be defined by exactly the same predicate. The great poetry of

---

[1] *Newman: Prose and Poetry*, edited by Geoffrey Tillotson (1957), p. 503.

[2] See R. W. Beardsmore, *Art and Morality* (1971), pp. 6, 22.

[3] *Art as Experience* (1934), p. 347.

[4] William K. Wimsatt and Cleanth Brooks, *Literary Criticism: A Short History* (1957; 1970), pp. 422–3.

[5] Algernon Charles Swinburne, *William Blake: A Critical Essay* (1868; 1925), pp. 88–9.

Rome includes the heroic deeds of Camillus, Regulus, and others (*Works*, vii. 125); and Shelley adduced these deeds as examples of disinterestedness in the 1817 fragment on morals, commenting that even the actors' desire for fame 'is allied with all that draws us out of ourselves' (vii. 76). As Earl Schulze comments, 'what ethical science recommends is much the same as the fundamental process of poetry'.[1] In fact Shelley would find it difficult to differentiate between the virtuous man and the poet. 'A man, to be greatly good, must imagine intensely and comprehensively; he must put himself in the place of another and of many others; the pains and pleasures of his species must becomes his own.' (*Works*, vii. 118) This, surely, describes the man who would be a great poet as much as he who would be greatly good; it points to the example of Shakespeare as well as to that of Christ (whose own words 'are all instinct with the most vivid poetry' (vii. 126)). It is hardly surprising that Shelley vigorously repudiates the popular calumnies against poets; if poetry and virtue are synonymous, it is unthinkable that poets could be bad men (vii. 138–9).

Shelley's habit of breathlessly stringing together abstractions, as in 'Life, Joy, Empire and Victory',[2] is at least partly owing to his conviction that all his positive values are virtually different names for the same thing. A jotting in one of his notebooks shows that Shelley himself was aware of this: 'Happiness the end, all other things the means.—Power, Truth, Wisdom, Love—the means convert into the end and the end into the means.'[3] This point may be illustrated with reference to Liberty. True slavery is not so much being overpowered by external force, but rather accepting the limits of a narrow consciousness and a narrow vision. Men only become 'the slaves of the will of others' when they are already the 'slaves' of 'their own will', when, thanks to 'the extinction of the poetical principle', they have become 'insensible and selfish' (*Works*, vii. 126). Poetry frees us from slavery which is really despair of our own powers by demonstrating that we are not eternally bound to what is actual, as Prometheus was bound to his cliff by the belief that Jupiter was omnipotent—poetry 'defeats the curse which binds us to be subjected to the accident of

---

[1] *Shelley's Theory of Poetry*, p. 33.

[2] *Prometheus Unbound*, iv. 578.

[3] Written following 'On Life' in a notebook now in the Pierpont Morgan Library, New York.

surrounding impressions'.[1] We have already seen how poetry frees us from 'the little word of self' by putting us into contact with the beautiful outside us, and poetry is thus the same as love, love itself being identical with liberty in being a 'going out of our own nature'.[2] In the 'Ode to Liberty' Shelley declares that, before Liberty,

> this divinest universe
> Was yet a chaos and a curse.
> (lines 21–2)

Shelley's hypothetical world history is recapitulated in the development of the individual, who can only be redeemed from the general curse by poetry, which makes men 'the inhabitants of a world to which the familiar world is a chaos' (*Works*, vii. 137). Shelley is happy to secularize the concepts of damnation and redemption in order to have yet another way of describing poetry. In the Preface to *The Cenci* he claimed that 'Imagination is as the immortal God which should assume flesh for the redemption of mortal passion'. *Peter Bell the Third* defines 'damnation' as lack of imagination, and sees the poet as the possible agent of redemption, Coleridge being the case in point.

> This was a man who might have turned
>   Hell into Heaven—and so in gladness
> A Heaven unto himself have earned;
> But he in shadows undiscerned
>   Trusted,—and damned himself to madness.
> (v. 383–7)

Not 'earned' in the vulgar Christian sense, for such virtue would be its own reward; the creation of an imaginative Heaven out of the quotidian Hell is, for the poet composing in 'gladness', Heaven in itself. But Coleridge trusted, not in the imagination, but in clerical dogmas and obscure Germanic speculations never apprehended by the imagination—'shadows undiscerned'.

---

[1] *Works*, vii. 137. Some support for the suggestion that Shelley virtually identifies poetry and morality is provided by Daniel Hughes's argument that Act I of *Prometheus Unbound* traces the development of Prometheus as a poet ('Prometheus Made Capable Poet in Act One of *Prometheus Unbound*', *Studies in Romanticism*, xvii (1978), 3–11).

[2] See above, p. 239. I take 'of' here to mean both 'by' and 'from'.

If Shelley sees the imagination as freedom, he also conceives of it as order; it is, of course, natural for an anarchist to insist that true order and true liberty are the same thing. Shelley, of course, would not have chosen to refer to himself as an anarchist, a term that had only negative associations in his day. But his use of words like 'anarchy' does reveal that he makes what we today would see as typically anarchist connections between liberty and order, and between despotism and disorder. Disorder was what Shelley's contemporaries meant by 'anarchy', particularly the disorder resulting from political revolution. Mary Wollstonecraft frequently speaks of 'anarchy' and 'anarchists in condemning the lawlessness of extremists during the French Revolution.[1] In Shelley's political pamphlets 'anarchy' in an unfavourable sense is virtually a synonym for a popular revolution (*Works*, vi. 80–1). In the *Defence* he laments that 'the vessel of the state is driven between the Scylla and Charybdis of anarchy and despotism' (vii. 132). It was a favourite trope in liberal rhetoric to oppose anarchy and despotism, too little order and too much, and then to demand which was the lesser evil. Shelley knew the proper answer to this riddle—'anarchy is better than despotism—for this reason,—that the former is for a season & that the latter is eternal'.[2] In the crisis of 1819 Shelley was willing to take the risk of 'the mischiefs of temporary popular violence' rather than endure 'the mischiefs of permanent tyrannical and fraudulent forms of government' (*Works*, vii 21). Anarchy is preferable because it is temporary and can be expected to yield to a true form of social order; but in their nature anarchy and despotism are very similar. Despotism claims to establish order, but an order of unfreedom imposed on its subjects is just another form of anarchy. In his prose works Shelley is careful to maintain the analytic distinction between anarchy and despotism, and he uses the term 'misrule' to refer to the anarchic aspects of the latter (vii. 25, 26). But he recognizes the way in which anarchy and despotism play into each other's hands. Anarchy in the form of a popular revolution is 'the child and the chastiser of misrule' (vi. 79), and the anarchy of the French Revolution was the result

---

[1] See *An Historical and Moral View . . . of the French Revolution*, pp. 357, 404, 465, 468.

[2] *Letters*, ii. 412. See Burke, *Works*, i. 341; Mackintosh, *Vindiciae Gallicae*, pp. 174–5; John Horne Tooke, quoted in M. W. Patterson, *Sir Francis Burdett*, i. 129; *Political Justice*, i. 13 (misquoting Locke) and ii. 368; *Examiner*, 4 May 1817, p. 275.

of the previous oppression.[1] The process could be seen as working both ways, or as cyclic; Shelley feared, with the example of Napoleon before him, that in the event of a popular revolution 'anarchy will only be the last flash before despotism'.[2] In his poetry Shelley makes even closer connections between disorder and misrule, indeed he virtually identifies them by using the word 'anarchy' to refer to despotism—in doing so he is throwing the oppressors' accusations against the Reformers back in their teeth. The true 'anarchists' are those who worship Anarchy under the names of 'God, and Law, and King', as Shelley describes them in *The Mask of Anarchy* (line 61). Law and Order are Anarchy's favourite disguises, and Shelley strips this mask away by consistently using the coinage 'Anarch' (with ironic allusion to 'Monarch') to describe the agents of the Holy Alliance.

> What anarch wears a crown or mitre,
> Or bears the sword, or grasps the key of gold,
> Whose friends are not thy friends, whose foes thy foes?

Hassan demands of Mahmud.[3] If the only true order springs from self-rule, those who impose their rule on others are directly fostering moral anarchy, and preparing the anarchy of violent revolution.

True order and true liberty are both the result of imaginative activity. It is possible to make at least a theoretical distinction between the actual activities involved. 'The functions of the poetical faculty are two-fold; by one it creates new materials of knowledge, and power and pleasure; by the other it engenders in the mind a desire to reproduce and arrange them according to a certain rhythm and order, which may be called the beautiful and the good.' (*Works*, vii. 134–5) We may see this distinction as one between the moral imagination, which supplies 'new materials' from outside the limits of the self, and the poetic imagination, by which order is discovered in or imposed on experience. This production of order is what Shelley means when he refers to poetry as 'creative'. He always insisted that poetry 'creates, but it

---

[1] See *Works*, v. 264, vii. 13, and Preface to *Laon and Cythna*.
[2] *Letters*, ii. 115.
[3] *Hellas*, lines 318–20. See also 'Ode to Liberty', lines 43, 175; 'Ode to Naples', lines 77, 137–8; *Hellas*, lines 879, 934–9; *The Triumph of Life*, lines 237, 285. Shelley would have found the word 'anarch' in Milton and Pope (D. H. Reiman, *Percy Bysshe Shelley*, p. 168 n.2).

creates by combination and representation'.[1] He remained a utilitarian in ethics, and an empiricist in epistemology.

It is an axiom in mental philosophy, that we can think of nothing which we have not perceived. When it is said we can think of nothing, I mean, we can imagine nothing, we can reason of nothing, we can remember nothing, we can foresee nothing. The most astonishing combinations of poetry, the subtlest deductions of logic and mathematics, are no other than combinations which the intellect makes of sensations, according to its own laws. (*Works*, vii. 59)

We should bear this passage in mind (it dates from 1821) in considering Shelley's comparison of God and the poet as both creators, in a formulation borrowed from Tasso: 'Non merita nome di creatore, se non Iddio ed il Poeta.'[2] The point of the comparison emerges if we realize that Shelley continues to be resolutely opposed to the Christian notion of a God who creates *ex nihilo*. He was far more sympathetic to the Greek hypothesis of a God who created the universe by imposing order on a previously existing chaos; like the poet, this demiurge 'moulded the reluctant and stubborn materials ready to his hand, into the nearest arrangement possible to the perfect archetype existing in his contemplation' (*Works*, vii. 89). This Greek view is, as Elizabeth Sewell points out, 'a deeply human rather than superhuman way of looking at things'.[3] In Shelley's formulation it is a way of conceiving of God on the model of human creativity, rather than the other way around. Such a God would be acceptable to Shelley, though one suspects that it is the human imagination that has priority for him. There is some justification for Ellsworth Barnard's claim that 'Imagination literally *is* "the immortal God"'[4] in view of Shelley's claim in the *Defence* that 'Poetry redeems from decay the visitations of the divinity in man', the crucial phrase being 'the divinity in man' rather than 'the visitations of the divinity'.[5] As Earl Wasserman has shown, the poet, in Shelley's account,

---

[1] Preface to *Prometheus Unbound*.

[2] *Works*, vii. 138; see also *Letters*, ii. 30. It should be noted that Tasso's meaning is that both God and the poet create unity out of diversity (see Curran, *Shelley's Annus Mirabilis*, pp. 203–4).

[3] *The Orphic Voice: Poetry and Natural History* (1960; New York, 1971), p. 389. That Shelley holds such a view of creation is forcefully maintained by E. R. Wasserman, *Shelley: A Critical Reading*, pp. 205n., 207.

[4] *Shelley's Religion*, pp. 255–8.

[5] *Works*, vii. 137. Shelley also refers to 'the divinity in man' at vii. 119.

'[contains] the inspiring force mysteriously within himself but outside the boundaries of his understanding'.[1]

The *Defence* firmly locates the principle of creative order within man. The 'Essay on Christianity' had made human creativity subordinate to a transcendent divine order.

We live and move and think, but we are not the creators of our own origin and existence, we are not the arbiters of every motion of our own complicated nature, we are not the masters of our own imaginations and moods of mental being. There is a power by which we are surrounded, like the atmosphere in which some motionless lyre is suspended, which visits with its breath our silent chords, at will. Our most imperial and stupendous qualities, those on which the majesty and power of humanity is erected, are relatively to the inferior portion of its mechanism indeed active and imperial; but they are the passive slaves of some higher and more omnipresent Power. This power is God. (*Works*, vi. 231)

Closer observation of the poetic faculty convinced Shelley that its operations might be hidden from the conscious mind, without it being necessary to explain them by reference to a transcendent power. By 1821 he uses the language of divine possession to describe the phenomena of poetic inspiration, but only in a qualified and metaphorical way, as in his comments on the *improvvisatore* Sgricci.

l'immaginazione del poeta pareva ch'agiva senza l'agiuto dell'intelletto, ed il appena sembrava conscio, delle parole dittate a lui da qualche superna possa.—

Egli stesso non fu consapevole delle imagine, delle quale l'anima sua fu lo specchio; ed i raigi d'Apolline stesso furono riflettati da quella.— In questo talento, e tutto pur d'Italia – l'immaginazione fa, fra di noi, opra che l'intelletto consomma fra gli altri in lungo tempo, o dopo molte tentative, e questo dono e il [pregio?] del nostro presente destino, ed il pegno del futuro.

it appeared as if the imagination of the poet acted without the assistance of his reason, and he scarcely seemed conscious of the words dictated to him by some superior power.

He himself was not conscious of the images of which his soul was the mirror; and the rays of Apollo himself were reflected therein. In this ability, is the most distinctive characteristic of Italy – among us the imagination performs what among others the reason accomplishes in a

---

[1] *Shelley: A Critical Reading*, p. 206.

long interval of time, or after repeated attempts, and this gift is the [glory?] of our present fate, and the pledge of our future destiny.[1]

But Sgricci's performance, though so astounding that only the language of divine inspiration can do it justice, is after all an exhibition 'della forza della umana mente',[2] rather than an example of divine intervention. When Shelley uses the image of the Aeolian lyre in the *Defence* it is significantly different from the image as used in the 'Essay on Christianity'.

Man is an instrument over which a series of external and internal impressions are driven, like the alternations of an everchanging wind over a Æolian lyre, which move it by their motion to ever-changing melody. But there is a principle within the human being, and perhaps within all sentient beings, which acts otherwise than in the lyre, and produces not melody, alone, but harmony, by an internal adjustment of the sounds or motions thus excited to the impressions which excite them. It is as if the lyre could accommodate its chords to the motions of that which strikes them, in a determined proportion of sound; even as the musician accommodates his voice to the sound of the lyre. (*Works*, vii. 109–10)

Previously the lyre had been a passive instrument, and the principle of order was in the wind that played it; now the wind is no more than the flux of experience, which is ordered by a principle within the lyre. The metaphor as developed in the *Defence* is far from graceful, and this is largely because Shelley is trying to make a familiar trope convey as exactly as possible his sense of what is happening. All man's knowledge comes from his experience of the world, including the inner world, but this experience is a 'chaos' of unorganized impressions which can only receive order from the creative activity of man, who can only create order by imposing it on this original chaos. The ability to create order itself involves an important kind of freedom, for it means that man is not bound to the original order of his impressions. 'Hence men, even in the infancy of society, observe a certain order in their words and actions, distinct from that of the objects and the impressions represented by them, all expression being subject to the laws of that from which it proceeds.' (*Works*, vii. 110)

---

[1] Bodl. MS Shelley adds. e. 17, pp. 12, 18–19. The English translation is by the present author.

[2] Ibid., p. 12: 'of the power of the human mind'.

The ordering activity of the imagination is most evident in its ability to create unity out of diverse and disparate materials. This can easily be given a neo-Platonic turn, as in Wasserman's comment that 'the radical principle of the *Defence of Poetry*—order, arrangement, combination, relation, harmony, or rhythm—is the human means of shaping diversity into an approximation of perfect unity which is truth, beauty, and goodness'.[1] I would strongly disagree with the suggestion that that there is an eternal order to which man must 'approximate'. The really radical thesis of the *Defence* is that there is no order which man does not create. The point of the famous contrast of Reason and Imagination is that Reason keeps all the items of experience separate and distinct, while the Imagination joins them to create unity and order out of diversity. The most appropriate symbol of the imagination is its most characteristic product, poetic metaphor, which 'marks the before unapprehended relations of things, and perpetuates their apprehension', revealing the relations between what was previously thought to be unconnected (*Works*, vii. 111). The Witch of Atlas shows herself to be 'an incarnation of poetry itself'[2] by her remarkable success in harmonizing elements which the Reason would regard as incompatible.

> Then by strange art she kneaded fire and snow
>   Together, tempering the repugnant mass
> With liquid love—all things together grow
>   Through which the harmony of love can pass . . .
> (*The Witch of Atlas* (1820), lines 321–4)

But for poetry, or love—again Shelley's values all tend to merge into each other—experience would be a chaos of detached and conflicting impressions. Every stage of human progress, from perception, through the creation of language itself, up to the greatest products of the arts, consists in reducing this chaos to order. If we argue that Shelley finds such a theory attractive because he wishes to escape from the diversity of the concrete and take refuge in a transcendent One, this is only an *ad hominem* argument and does not dispose of the insight (by no means unique to Shelley) that man possesses values which are not derived from experience but which are used to order and make sense out of

[1] *Shelley: A Critical Reading*, p. 270.
[2] G. W. Knight, *The Starlit Dome*, p. 226.

experience. These are the powers by which he becomes, as Shelley calls him in the 'Ode to Liberty', 'the King of Life' (line 243)—and by whose abdication, as we shall see, Life triumphs over man. Shelley's view of poetry as a principle of order is anticipated by Bacon, who says that 'poesy' 'was ever thought to have some participation of divineness, because it doth raise and erect the mind, by submitting the shews of things to the desires of the mind; whereas reason doth buckle and bow the mind unto the nature of things'.[1] It is possibly because the imaginative activity of poetry enables man to assert his own individuality and impose it on the flux of his experience that Coleridge defines the primary imagination as 'a repetition in the finite mind of the eternal act of creation in the infinite I AM'.[2]

It need cause no surprise that the theory of the imagination expounded in the *Defence* is strongly present in *Adonais*, Shelley's next major work. Since the subject of that poem is the fate of a poet and the perspective in which it is to be viewed, it is rather surprising that few critics have put the imagination at the centre of their readings of it; and the reason no doubt lies in the religious speculations contained in the poem, which beckon in the direction of theology rather than poetics. But they are no more than speculations, which Shelley was emboldened to incorporate into the structure of his poem by the conclusion at which he had arrived in the *Defence*, that poetry's spirit is more operative than its letter. But Shelley's readers must be correspondingly wary of the letter. The religious symbolism of *Adonais* is an imaginative construction, a fiction, which is more important as an index to the activities of the imagination than as theological or philosophical dogma. We are to learn about ourselves, not about an order that transcends the human.

> Who mourns for Adonais? oh come forth
> Fond wretch! and know thyself and him aright.
> Clasp with thy panting soul the pendulous Earth;
> As from a centre, dart thy spirit's light

---

[1] *The Works of Francis Bacon* (5 vols., 1778), i. 50. S. L. Bethell sees a basic similarity between the organic 'Elizabethan reason', to which he sees Bacon as paying 'mere lip-service', and the 'poetic imagination' of Coleridge and Wordsworth, and, of course, Shelley (see *The Cultural Revolution of the Seventeenth Century* (1951; 1963), pp. 104–5, 116).

[2] *Biographia Literaria*, i. 202.

Beyond all worlds, until its spacious might
Satiate the void circumference: then shrink
Even to a point within our day and night:
And keep thy heart light lest it make thee sink
When hope has kindled hope, and lured thee to the brink.
(lines 415–23)[1]

The process of dilation and contraction urged here is the process of imaginative perception, and Reiman and Powers aptly elucidate 'circumference' by adducing a passage fromt the *Defence*: 'Poetry is indeed something divine. It is at once the centre and circumference of knowledge . . .'[2] Hazlitt's moral scheme, in which 'we may consider self-love as bearing the same relation to family affection as this does to the more general love of our neighbour, as the love of our neighbour does to that of our country, or as the love of our country does to that of mankind',[3] can best be visualized as a series of concentric circles, or better spheres, with the 'I' as their common centre. Shelley, who, as Earl Schulze comments, 'thinks consistently in images',[4] does not fail to exploit this one. 'The only distinction between the selfish man, and the virtuous man, is that the imagination of the former is confined within a narrow limit, whilst that of the latter embraces a comprehensive circumference.' (*Works*, vii. 74)[5] One of the grounds of Shelley's defence of poetry is that it 'enlarges the circumference of the imagination' (*Works*, vii. 118). In *Adonais* the fullest scope of this circumference is revealed to be literally cosmic; but the mourner is also urged to 'shrink/Even to a point within our day and night', for the imagination can only order experience by referring it to a common centre, the mathematical point of the individual 'I'. *Adonais* itself follows this dual movement of the imagination. Adonais' death is a cause for grief so long as it absorbs all our attention. and everything else is seen in terms of it; hence the emphatic pathetic fallacies of stanzas 14 to 16, in which the

---

[1] The Reiman and Powers text reads 'world's' in line 419.

[2] *Works*, vii. 135. Shelley is paraphrasing a traditional Hermetic definition of God (see John W. Wright, *Shelley's Myth of Metaphor* (Athens, Ga., 1970), p. 11).

[3] Hazlitt, *Works*, i. 15.

[4] *Shelley's Theory of Poetry*, p. 32.

[5] Wasserman remarks: 'The autonomy of the symbolic sphere that diffuses itself from its mysterious centre and thus embraces itself is radical to all of Shelley's thought and to his rejection of all imposed codes' (*Shelley: A Critical Reading*, p. 331). See also J. W. Wright, op. cit., *passim*.

traditional tropes of elegy are exploited as signs of an imagination overcome by grief. The mourner's imagination must first expand to comprehend the whole scheme within which poets live, die, and live after their death, and within which the earth itself is seen as a body floating in space, and finally contract in order to return to its original situation which is henceforward transformed by being seen in a universal perspective.

In this way the sterile grief of the first movement of the poem is transcended, though the poet finds that he has indeed been 'lured . . . to the brink'.

> The breath whose might I have invoked in song
> Descends on me; my spirit's bark is driven,
> Far from the shore, far from the trembling throng
> Whose sails were never to the tempest given;
> The massy earth and sphered skies are riven!
> I am borne darkly, fearfully, afar:
> Whilst burning through the inmost veil of Heaven,
> The soul of Adonais, like a star,
> Beacons from the abode where the Eternal are.
> (lines 487–95)

But those critics who agree with Ross Woodman, that 'Shelley committed psychic suicide in *Adonais*',[1] are claiming even more than Shelley says. He actually urges no more than 'a readiness for or even willing acquiescence in' death, and death after all is inevitable whether acquiesced in or not.[2] If Shelley welcomes death, it is because death is thought of as bringing immortality. But his attitude is finally ambivalent, because 'immortality' is ambiguous. Woody Allen is reported to have said that he doesn't want to be immortal by making great films, but by living for ever. Artistic immortality is all that Shelley can claim for Keats with any certainty. A poet is never completely dead, because 'the dead live'

> When lofty thought
> Lifts a young heart above its mortal lair,
> And love and life contend in it, for what
> Shall be its earthly doom . . .
> (lines 392–5)

---

[1] *The Apocalyptic Vision in the Poetry of Shelley* (Toronto, 1964), p. 158.
[2] John Holloway, *The Proud Knowledge: Poetry, Insight and the Self, 1620–1920* (London, Henley and Boston, 1977), p. 193.

The 'dazzling immortality' of 'The inheritors of unfulfilled renown' arises from the fact that they are still operative in the living world; their 'transmitted effluence cannot die/So long as fire outlives the parent spark' (lines 397, 407-9). Their literal immortality, Shelley well knows, may be no more than a poetic fiction. What poetic and literal immortality have in common, though, is that it may be necessary to die to achieve either. Donald Reiman has noted that Shelley is obliged to celebrate the values of death 'because Keats died unfulfilled both as a man and a poet'.[1] This unfulfilment is lamented by Urania, who wishes that Keats had 'waited the full cycle, when/Thy spirit should have filled its crescent sphere' (lines 241-2). But complete fulfilment within the natural world over which Urania presides would pre-empt any kind of immortality. Natural things rise and fall in 'cycles', and to fill 'the crescent sphere' is to arrive at the point at which waning must begin. The true symbol for Keats will prove to be, not the moon shining by borrowed light and tied to its repetition of cycles, but a star: 'such as he can lend,—they borrow not/Glory', as Shelley proclaims.[2] But if a poet is not to be fulfilled in life, he must look for fulfilment in death, and for the individual poet this is the hard lesson implied by the generalization that 'no living poet ever arrived at the fulness of his fame; the jury which sits in judgment upon a poet, belonging as he does to all time, must be composed of his peers: it must be impanelled by Time from the selectest of the wise of many generations' (*Works*, vii. 116).

The temptation for Shelley to seek immortality by a renunciation of 'life', seen, in an anticipation of his last poem, as a state of living death, is very strong; but the passion with which he debates the question with himself is in itself proof that he is not yet absolute for death.

What Adonais is, why fear we to become?

Why linger, why turn back, why shrink, my Heart?
(lines 459, 469)

[1] *Percy Bysshe Shelley*, p. 135.
[2] Lines 428-9. Ironically the 'star' that Adonais becomes is in fact the planet Venus, whose light is more constant than the moon's, but still borrowed. That Venus is taken by the earthly observer to be a star suggests that to men the poet is seen as the source of his own light; that it is really a planet hints (as does 'refulgent' in line 43) at the presence of a transcendent source.

To succumb to this temptation is to be 'borne darkly, fearfully, afar' (line 492). Moreover, to claim that 'the moral dimension' of *Adonais* consists of 'a metaphysical defence of suicide'[1] is to imply that Shelley is looking for an answer to the practical question, 'To be or not to be?', whereas he is more concerned with finding a way of seeing and understanding the fact of death. This is a religious problem, but we must recognize that the religious scheme which he evolves in order to answer it is, like his demiurgic conception of God, modelled on the imagination.

Shelley had early accepted the Enlightenment commonplace that the tyrannical God of Judaeo–Christian tradition was a projection of man's own anarchic fears and passions. It was somewhat later that he came to see that the deity might be seen as a projection of man's benevolent and creative impulses, and that while such a deity might be a fiction, it need not be a pernicious or even an unnecessary one. As he remarks in a note to *Hellas*, a poem in which he gives provisional acceptance to a good deal of the Christian scheme, the poet's task is 'to attach himself to those ideas which exalt and ennoble humanity', whether they can be established as philosophically true or not (note to lines 197–238). We saw the importance of such fictions in his view of politics in Chapter III. In the 'Essay on Christianity', where he seems to accept the Deism that he attributes to Christ, he considers it indifferent whether the doctrine of a personal God be 'philosophically true' or 'a metaphor easily understood' (*Works*, vi. 235). If Christ's God is a fiction it is a benignant one.

The perfection of the human and the divine character is thus asserted to be the same: man by resembling God fulfils most accurately the tendencies of his nature, and God comprehends within itself all that constitutes human perfection. Thus God is a model thro which the excellence of man is to be estimated, whilst the *abstract* perfection of the human character is the type of the *actual* perfection of the divine. (*Works*, vi. 239)

To worship this God is to live by the values to which Shelley adheres, and he will not quarrel about names. The last sentence, however, suggests that God is a concept modelled on human ideals, rather than the other way around.[2] As a symbol of a human

---

[1] *Apocalyptic Vision*, p. 172.

[2] But elsewhere in the essay Shelley speaks of God as prior to human creativity (see above, p. 247); the hypothesis of a God may be more than a way of speaking, or a way of speaking that constrains what is said.

perfection that is as yet only potential even a fiction may be of value. In the fragment known as 'The Coliseum' (1818; Shelley's intended title seems to have been 'Diotima') we can see such a fiction in the process of formation, in a passage that makes extended use of the imagery of concentric circles to which attention has already been drawn.

The internal nature of each being is surrounded by a circle not to be surmounted by his fellows; and it is this repulsion which constitutes the misfortune of the condition of life. But there is a circle which comprehends as well as one which mutually excludes all things which feel. And with respect to man, his public and private happiness consists in diminishing the circumference which includes those resembling himself until they become one with him and he with them. It is because we enter into the meditations, designs and destinies of something beyond ourselves, that the contemplation of the ruins of human power excites an elevating sense of awfulness and beauty. It is therefore that the Ocean, the glacier, the cataract, the tempest, the volcano have each a spirit which animates the extremities of our frame with tingling joy. It is therefore that the singing of birds and the motion of leaves, the sensation of the odorous earth beneath and the freshness of the living wind around, is sweet. And this is Love. This is the religion of eternity whose votaries have been exiled from among the multitude of mankind. O Power, said the old man lifting his sightless eyes towards the undazzling sun, thou which interpenetratest all things, and without which this glorious world were a blind and formless chaos, Love, author of good, God, King, Father, Friend of these thy worshippers. . . . (*Works*, vi. 303–4)

The 'spirit' in natural things is in fact a reflux of our own imaginative activity, which animates the deserted or hostile ocean, glacier, cataract, tempest, and volcano. It is no accident that the imagery here recalls 'Mont Blanc', in which Shelley had demanded of the mountain,

> And what wert thou, and earth, and stars, and sea,
> If to the human mind's imaginings
> Silence and solitude were vacancy?
> (lines 142–4)

The old man's speech illustrates from the positive side Coleridge's thesis that

> we receive but what we give,

> And in our life alone does Nature live . . .
> ('Dejection: An Ode' (1802), lines 47–8)

It also reveals that the concept of a deity is derivative from our own imaginative activity. The 'Power' which he invokes as something divine has already been defined in terms which are fully human.

This Power closely anticipates that invoked in *Adonais*, which is also foreshadowed by the old man's address: 'It is thine to unite, to eternize, to make outlive the grave those who have left among the living memorials of thee' (*Works*, vi. 304), where immortality is defined as a presence among the living. The Power in *Adonais* is in effect a deification of the imagination, as Adonais' presence is felt

> Spreading itself where'er that Power may move
> Which has withdrawn his being to its own;
> Which wields the world with never wearied love,
> Sustains it from beneath and kindles it above.
> (lines 375–8)

The analogy is close, for the imagination 'sustains' the human world 'from beneath' as the essential factor in all moral action, and 'kindles it above' as the source of the inspiring creations of art, creations which kindle imaginative activity in their audience. And just as the poetic imagination must strive to impress itself on its artistic medium, so the Power must struggle with the recalcitrance of dead matter.

> . . . the one Spirit's plastic stress
> Sweeps through the dull dense world, compelling there
> All new successions to the forms they wear;
> Torturing th'unwilling dross that checks its flight
> To its own likeness, as each mass may bear;
> And bursting in its beauty and its might
> From trees and beasts and men into the Heaven's light.
> (lines 381–7)

The world is a 'web of being blindly wove/By man and beast and earth and air and sea', through which 'sustaining Love' 'Burns bright or dim, as each are mirrors of/The fire for which all thirst' (lines 481–5). What the Spirit can do is limited by what it has to work with, and something is inevitably lost by its descent into matter. The most glorious phenomena of the physical world are 'weak/The glory they transfuse with fitting truth to speak' (lines 457–8). It is a problem that the poet understands, for Shelley often complains that his words are inadequate to convey his imaginative conceptions.

> The winged words on which my soul would pierce
> Into the height of love's rare Universe,
> Are chains of lead around its flight of fire.—
> (*Epipsychidion* (1821), lines 588–90)

As a poet Shelley knows that, while his words obscure his conceptions, they are also the only means he has of expressing them; as Jerome McGann has shown, he can only 'reveal' them by 'reveiling' them in words and images.[1] The spirit of poetry must incarnate itself in the letter. This spirit is also transmitted through society, losing something in the process, but remaining the only source of value, and forced to accept such compromises if it is to be operative at all. Likewise the divine Spirit or Power loses some of its original perfection in its struggle with matter, but in so doing redeems matter by vivifying it to however great an extent its nature can bear. But the process has its less attractive side. If imagination and the Power redeem life, life corrupts them, and it is tempting to strive to attain them in their uncontaminated purity. This would be to abandon life, but it would also be to abandon poetry, and this is the dark and fearful significance of the last movement of the poem. As Ross Woodman argues, *Adonais* is 'precariously suspended between two kinds of extinction: pure matter and pure spirit. Confronted by both, the poet as poet must preserve for himself an aesthetic ground that commits itself to neither, while partaking of both.'[2] To reject the material world and seek pure Spirit is to move 'beyond the reach of art'.[3] The imagination is unable to present its own transcendence, and at the end of *Adonais* 'A known is yielding to an unknown, and

---

[1] 'Shelley's Veils: A Thousand Images of Loveliness', in *Romantic and Victorian: Studies in Memory of William H. Marshall*, edited by W. P. Elledge and R. L. Hoffman (Rutherford, N. J., 1971), pp. 198–218, especially p. 206. I am not quite sure whether McGann would intend the pun implicit in his argument.

[2] 'Shelley's Urania', *Studies in Romanticism*, xvii (1978), 63.

[3] Woodman, *Apocalyptic Vision*, p. 176.

a vision collapses into mystery'.[1] But even at this point Shelley does not entirely relinquish the imagination, for he is drawn 'where the Eternal are' (line 495), *are*, not *is*—where the poets dwell, rather than the realm of the unknown deity.[2]

[1] Harold Bloom, *The Visionary Company: A Reading of English Romantic Poetry* (1961; rev. edn., Ithaca, N.Y., 1971), pp. 349–50.

[2] The significance of the pluralization at this point has already been indicated by Holloway, *The Proud Knowledge*, p. 193.

CHAPTER VII

The Triumph of Life?

THE TRANSVALUATION of 'Life' that occurs in Shelley's last and greatest poem is anticipated in *Adonais*, where 'love and life contend' to decide 'the earthly doom' of the young (lines 394–5). At the climax of that poem the poet urges himself, 'No more let Life divide what Death can join together' (line 477). Death seen as the reconciler of mortal opposites is at least temporarily welcomed as an ally of the imagination, and 'Life' opposed to 'love' presents one of those disjunctions between existence and value that always appalled Shelley. In the world of *The Triumph of Life* such disjunctions are only too apparent, and the dreamer grieves

>   to think how power and will
> In opposition rule our mortal day—
>
>   And why God made irreconcilable
>   Good and the means of good . . .
>   (lines 228–31)

Such conclusions seem forced on him by the spectacle of human history, Napoleon, the potential liberator turned tyrant, being the case immediately in question; but they need not be the last word. They were certainly not the last word in *Prometheus Unbound*, where one of the Furies taunted Promethus in very similar terms.

> The good want power, but to weep barren tears.
> The powerful goodness want: worse need for them.
> The wise want love, and those who love want wisdom;
> And all best things are thus confused to ill.
> (I. 625–8)

It is a temptation of despair to accept what is as what must be, and to refuse to recognize that 'We might be otherwise'. The dreamer's facile assumption that this state of things is immutably ordained by 'God' is an evasion of the responsibility that man must bear for creating his own world; as Beatrice saw, 'what a world we make,/The oppressor and the oppressed' (*The Cenci*, v. iii. 74–5). In his disgust and despair at the lesson of history the dreamer, like the young Shelley,

> half disdained mine eye's desire to fill

> With the spent vision of the times that were
> And scarce have ceased to be . . .
> (lines 232–4)

However understandable, this is a weakness and one to be deplored, for his vision of human life should be an educative one— he must see the world as it is, in all its horror and absurdity, in order to gain understanding of its condition. His task is to find the answer to his own half-formulated question: 'why . . . is all here amiss?' (lines 178–9). To ascribe this condition to anything external to man is to enslave oneself to the condition that one deplores, as the case of Rousseau reveals.

> if the spark with which Heaven lit my spirit
> Earth had with purer nutriment supplied

> Corruption would not now thus much inherit
> Of what was once Rousseau—nor this disguise
> Stained that within which still disdains to wear it.—
> (lines 201–5)

As Jerome McGann has noted, Rousseau's 'scorn' and 'misery' 'are correlatives'.[1] By blaming his condition on his circumstances and then 'disdaining' it he renounces any hope of changing it, much as Prometheus' belief that Jupiter existed outside himself and his sterile defiance of him worked to keep him enslaved to what he denounced. In refusing to accept the final responsibility for what he has become Rousseau attempts to reject his own being as a 'disguise' which obscures his true inner nature. This distinction between existence and essence is one found elsewhere in Shelley, but which by 1822 he recognizes as a dangerous illusion. In *Prometheus Unbound* the 'loathsome mask' could indeed be cast off to reveal the fair and permanent forms of human nature. In *The Mask of Anarchy* the situation is more complex, in that the mask of social order must be stripped from Anarchy, before men can

---

[1] 'The Secrets of an Elder Day: Shelley after *Hellas*' (1966), in *Shelley: Modern Judgments*, edited by R. B. Woodings, p. 267.

lay aside the masks of Anarchy. But in *The Triumph of Life* it is made clear that, though man can alienate his masks from himself, he cannot dissociate himself from them. It is Rousseau himself who shows us this, though he fails to apply it to his own situation. The climax of his 'new Vision' is the stripping off of 'Mask after mask' (line 536) from those in Life's procession. The fact that there is a succession of masks suggests that there will be no apocalyptic revelation of the true form beneath. Like Peer Gynt's onion, the more layers are removed the less there is left, and those fall 'soonest from whose forms most shadows past' (line 542). Rousseau describes the process from outside as if he were not involved in it, but it is clear that he was, for he admits that those who were weakened in this way 'fell, as I have fallen' (line 541). Men think their words and actions can be divorced from what they truly are, but all they are doing is draining their own imaginative life-blood, and breeding demons that will return to plague them.

The structure of the poem serves to enforce truths that Rousseau has failed to recognize. There is an evident allusion to the scheme of Dante's *Divina Commedia*, with the dreamer adopting Dante's role of questor, and Rousseau fulfilling the role of guide that Dante assigns to Virgil. However, Shelley's revision of the Dantean schema is radical. In the *Commedia* Virgil is, within specified limits, authoritative, his authority being validated by a divine commission, and his function is to prepare Dante for his confrontations with the inhabitants of Hell and Purgatory, and help him to understand the significance of what he learns. These inhabitants function as witnesses, reviewing their mortal careers for Dante's benefit, their assigned place in the next world providing the final placing comment on their activities in this. But the Rousseau of *The Triumph of Life* is both guide and witness.[1] Indeed his function as guide is pre-empted to a large extent by the visionary insight possessed by the dreamer himself. The dreamer knows without being told that the 'banded eyes' of the

[1] John Hodgson has argued that Rousseau's account concerns his post-mortal existence, a reading which is indeed 'radically different from all earlier interpretations' ('The World's Mysterious Doom: Shelley's *The Triumph of Life*', *ELH* xlii (1975), 598). His argument that this reading is supported by the parallel with the *Commedia* is, however, unconvincing, for Dante's interlocutors, though dead, tell him the story of their earthly careers; as, in my opinion, does Rousseau in the *Triumph*.

charioteer could, if unblinded, 'pierce the sphere/Of all that is, has been, or will be done' (lines 103–4); he sees for himself that 'they of Athens and Jerusalem' are neither chained to the chariot nor among the crowd that follows it (lines 128–37); and he can recognize 'the heirs/Of Caesar's crime from him to Constantine' (lines 283–4) without needing Rousseau to identify them. Some of the identifications that Rousseau does make for the dreamer's benefit suggest some irony at Rousseau's expense. This is particularly true of his comments on Napoleon, in view of a remark that Napoleon made concerning Rousseau and Shelley copied in his notebook: 'C'est pourtant lui qui a été la cause de la révolution. Au reste, je ne dois pas m'en plaindre, car j'y ai attrapé le trône'.[1] Shelley considered this 'The sentiment of a rascally Italian domestico di piazza', but he probably agreed that Rousseau was partly responsible for the revolution, and hence for the tyranny of Napoleon. It is thus appropriate that Rousseau should recognize this 'Child of a fierce hour' (line 217), an hour to which he had himself given birth.[2] Immediately following this, Rousseau indicates

> those spoilers spoiled, Voltaire,
>
> Frederic, and Kant, Catherine, and Leopold,
> Chained hoary anarchs, demagogue and sage
> Whose name the fresh world thinks already old—
>
> For in the battle Life and they did wage
> She remained conqueror—I was overcome
> By my own heart alone . . .
> (lines 235–41)

Rousseau's attempt to vindicate himself by condemning others is put in a most ironic light by the fact that he is claiming to dissociate himself from the *philosophes*, the very group with whom he was most closely associated in the public mind.[3] Rousseau himself

---

[1] Bodl. MS Shelley adds. e. 12, p. 62. Shelley found the anecdote in Mme de Staël's *Considérations sur les principaux événemens de la Révolution Françoise* (3 vols., 1818), ii. 379.

[2] See G. M. Matthews, 'On Shelley's "*The Triumph of Life*" ', 127.

[3] One of the best studies of *The Triumph of Life*, unfortunately and inexplicably still unpublished, is Chapter IV of Edward Duffy's 'The Image of Jean-Jacques Rousseau in the Work of Shelley and Other English Romantics' (unpublished Ph.D. thesis, Columbia University, 1971). Duffy attributes Rousseau's fall to an excess of Enlightenment rationalism, a case that he argues with considerable

admits that he cannot answer all the dreamer's questions, nor, like Virgil, direct him to a higher authority; some things a man must find out for himself, and he tells the dreamer,

> follow thou, and from spectator turn
> Actor or victim in this wretchedness,

> And what thou wouldst be taught I then may learn
> From thee.
> (lines 305–8)

These words are truer than Rousseau realizes, for they are meant as a sneer against the dreamer's evident thirst for knowledge. But it is true that each man must learn by participation, and that there is no privileged position from which life can be authoritatively judged. The only testimony that Rousseau has to impart to the dreamer is his account of his own career, and this evidence is not necessarily to be interpreted in the way that Rousseau would choose.

What Shelley achieves in *The Triumph of Life* is a collapsing of the Dantean scheme. He has revised his predecessor's presentation of experience as ordered within a stable conceptual framework, in order to convey his own phenomenalistic vision of existence. For this reason it would be a mistake to think that Shelley intended a separate *Purgatorio* or *Paradiso* to follow the *Inferno* of the *Triumph*, just as it would be a mistake to expect testimony from any other witnesses besides Rousseau. Hell is not a place to which Rousseau has been condemned, it is the condition to which he condemns himself by misusing his own imaginative vision. The premiss of the poem is that 'The mind is its own place, and of itself can make a Heaven of Hell, a Hell of Heaven'.[1] As Jerome McGann says, 'men live in a "valley of perpetual dream" (397) where a man's attitude toward his existence has a good deal to do with the facts of that existence'.[2] This is dramatized in the poem by the contrast between the dreamer's initial vision of the procession of Life and the parallel but far from identical account of it

---

persuasiveness. I am unable to agree, in view of Shelley's explicit distinction between Rousseau and the rest of the *philosophes*, whom he dismisses as 'mere reasoners' while allowing Rousseau to be a poet (*Works*, vii. 133n).

[1] *Works*, vii. 137, quoting *Paradise Lost*, I. 254–5.

[2] Loc. cit. 267.

given by Rousseau.[1] That the two accounts are to be compared is suggested by the similarity of the terms in which they are introduced.

> And then a Vision on my brain was rolled. . . .
> (line 40)

>   on my sight
> Burst a new Vision never seen before.—
> (line 410–11)

Both the dreamer and Rousseau find themselves reminded of the Roman triumphal processions.

> I saw like clouds upon the thunder blast
>
> The million with fierce song and maniac dance
> Raging around; such seemed the jubilee
>   As when to greet some conqueror's advance
>
> Imperial Rome poured forth her living sea
>   From senatehouse and prison and theatre . . .
> (lines 109–14)

>   as if from some dread war
> Triumphantly returning, the loud million
>   Fiercely extolled the fortune of her star.—
> (lines 436–8)

They both recognize the shape in the chariot as female (lines 148, 438), a detail of some significance in view of Rousseau's first vision. The dreamer's account does not minimize the sinister aspects of the chariot, but he is also able to appreciate the impressiveness of its appearance.

> So came a chariot on the silent storm
> Of its own rushing splendour . . .
> (lines 86–7)

The 'cold glare, intenser than the moon/But icy cold' (lines 77–8) is perceived by Rousseau as 'The tempest of the splendour which forbade/Shadow to fall from leaf or stem' (lines 444–5). Here the differences begin to become important. Rousseau does refer to

---

[1] See G. M. Matthews, loc. cit. 110–11, and E. T. Duffy, op. cit., pp. 192–3.

the 'cold bright car' (line 434), but he does not stress the coldness as the dreamer does; indeed Rousseau several times describes the car's light in terms of that of the sun (lines 446, 535), where the dreamer sees a contrast, in that the car's light 'obscured with light/The Sun' (lines 77–8). Rousseau may well be in some danger of confusing the cold radiance of the car with the vital warmth of the sun. While the dreamer perceives the chariot as silent, for Rousseau it is accompanied by 'savage music, stunning music' (line 435). One may remain detached from what one sees, but the hearing is a sense that involves the perceiver far more urgently in what he perceives, and Rousseau is incontinently swept up into the procession.

> I among the multitude
> Was swept . . .
>
>   among
> The thickest billows of the living storm
> I plunged, and bared my bosom to the clime
>   Of that cold light, whose airs too soon deform.—
> (lines 460–1, 465–8)

Now it is too late Rousseau perceives the deathly chill of the chariot's light. There is something rather wistful about his 'too soon', however, as if he would willingly have followed it further had he had the strength, and the poem as it stands ends with him gazing after it 'as if that look must be the last' (line 546).

The vital difference between the two accounts lies in how the participants in the procession are viewed. Rousseau, who was one of them, loathes his own condition, and describes the fate of his erstwhile companions with no more generous feeling than fascinated horror. By participation he has knowledge that no outsider could have; the dreamer sees 'ghastly shadows' (line 171) wheeling round those in the rear of the procession, but it is only in Rousseau's account that their vampiric nature becomes clear. Yet for all its power his description is trapped within the terms of Gothic nightmare and paranoia, 'a world peopled by phantoms, vampire-bats, vultures, and elves'.[1] In his own misery he has little compassion to spare for his fellow-sufferers, and he has lost his ability to conceive that things might be otherwise. He can see

---

[1] J. J. McGann, loc. cit. 268.

that man is the slave of his own evils, but fails to see the possibility of freedom by acting in accord with love, though he himself pays tribute to the power of love in invoking Dante (lines 471–80). Realizing that the elements of man's condition are his own creation, he nevertheless looks for an external source of evil, and imagines that these elements are ordered by 'the car's creative ray' (line 533).

In the dreamer's account the compassion and sense of alternatives so lacking in Rousseau's are strongly present—whether he will be able to retain them if he does 'from spectator turn/Actor or victim in this wretchedness' is a question that cannot be answered. His description of the 'serious folly' (line 73) of the travellers on the dusty road serves to bring out what is absurd and self-contradictory in their conduct.

> Old age and youth, manhood and infancy,
>
> Mixed in one mighty torrent did appear,
> > Some flying from the thing they feared and some
> Seeking the object of another's fear,
>
> > And others as with steps towards the tomb
> Pored on the trodden worms that crawled beneath,
> > And others mournfully within the gloom
>
> Of their own shadow walked, and called it death . . .
> > And some fled from it as it were a ghost,
> Half fainting in the affliction of vain breath.
>
> > But more with motions which each other crost
> Pursued or shunned the shadows the clouds threw
> > Or birds within the noonday ether lost,
>
> Upon that path where flowers never grew . . .
> (lines 52–65)

It is hardly necessary to go to the next world to see this. This is our world, seen through eyes purged of 'the film of familiarity which obscures from us the wonder of our being' (*Works*, vii. 137)—and may also conceal its horror. It is a world of separation and isolation, whose inhabitants are cut off from each other by the repeated 'And . . . And . . .', each 'And' failing to join what has gone to what follows because it serves to introduce a clause which conflicts with what precedes it. Just as everyone contradicts everyone else, so each man contradicts himself as his 'motions' cross 'each other'. All this activity is absurd, but it is not merely condemned or seen as alien, for there is present a lucid understanding of the logic behind these actions—to each man what he does makes sense, however senseless it seems in a wider perspective. This disorder is placed by reference to the natural order to which the travellers are oblivious. The shadows that they incorporate into their own shadow-play are cast by the life-bringing clouds and by birds, symbols of freedom, 'within the noonday ether lost'; lost, that is, to the sight of the travellers, who are, as the epithet reminds us, lost to themselves. They ignore the very things that might be at least a provisional goal for their endeavours.

> And weary with vain toil and faint for thirst
> Heard not the fountains whose melodious dew
>
> Out of their mossy cells forever burst
> Nor felt the breeze which from the forest told
> Of grassy paths, and wood lawns interspersed
>
> With overarching elms and caverns cold,
> And violet banks where sweet dreams brood, but they
> Pursued their serious folly as of old. . . .
> (lines 66–73)

The wakefulness of the dreamer through the night and his falling into a trance just as the natural world awakes is an indication that man is not subject to the natural order so splendidly evoked and celebrated at the beginning of the poem.[1] But if he turns from the natural order it is that he may rise above it and so create an analogous order in which the human imagination will rule the world of man as the sun rules the natural world. The travellers on the dusty road reject nature only to fall below it. Like Rousseau whom 'sweetest flowers delayed not long' (line 461) they neglect what might at least refresh them on their dusty journey.

It is significant that the dreamer sees the travellers before the chariot of Life appears, whereas Rousseau sees the chariot and then its worshippers. The dreamer recognizes that human folly is anterior to the ruling figure of Life, whose triumphal procession is a symbol of human history, that 'record of crimes and miseries' which may seem to be beyond human control. The charioteer

---

[1] See Harold Bloom, *Shelley's Mythmaking* (1959; Ithaca, N.Y., 1969), p. 225.

with his banded eyes recalls 'The world's eyeless charioteer,/ Destiny', as critics have noted,[1] and the point surely is that human history is 'guided' by that necessity which binds good to good and evil to evil. It is blind for it has no power to discriminate and bring good out of evil. And thus history is an all-too-faithful representation of human evil. History is always a terrible burden for the reformer, and it is the apparent lesson of history that brings both Prometheus and the dreamer close to despair. What saves them is the realization that it is not so much history that creates men's condition as men who create both their history and their condition by their own loveless actions. The demonic Life who presides over the pageant of human history is a 'fierce spirit, whose unholy leisure/Was soothed by mischief since the world begun' (lines 145–6); she is a vampire who feeds on human misery, but has no power to create it. Like Anarchy she can only rule by the voluntary subjection of her deluded worshippers. Those who are chained to the chariot subjugated themselves by their refusal of self-rule and their imposition of conquest on others. The 'ribald crowd' (line 136) who dance round the car are not chained to it at all, but have, like Rousseau, made their own decision to worship this destructive Juggernaut. As the dreamer is careful to note, it is possible to refrain from putting oneself in either category. The exceptions are not many, it is true, but they are not limited to Christ and Socrates alone, as is sometimes claimed.

> All but the sacred few who could not tame
> Their spirits to the Conqueror, but as soon
>   As they had touched the world with living flame
>
> Fled back like eagles to their native noon,
>   Or those who put aside the diadem
> Of earthly thrones or gems, till the last one
>
>   Were there; for they of Athens and Jerusalem
> Were neither mid the mighty captives seen
>   Nor mid the ribald crowd that followed them
>
> Or fled before . . .
> (lines 128–37)

---

[1] See A. C. Bradley, 'Notes on Shelley's "Triumph of Life"', *MLR* ix (1914), 447. The phrase quoted is from *Hellas*, lines 711–12, where Destiny is, interestingly, female.

It is clear that two *classes* are being described, of whom the most illustrious members are, respectively, Christ and Socrates. First there are 'the sacred few' who died young and 'Fled back like eagles to their native noon'; these are 'they of . . . Jerusalem', who include Christ and the Keats of *Adonais*. Next come 'those who put aside the diadem/Of earthly thrones or gems, till the last one', men who lived to old age but were strong enough to resist the temptations by which most men allow Life to corrupt them; these are 'they of Athens', like Socrates. Both Christ and Socrates demonstrated their willingness to give up their lives rather than the values by which they lived, but Shelley is not making a virtue of suicide or death; death does not help Rousseau to escape from Life. Christ and Socrates are probably alluded to specifically for the sake of their distinctive teachings. Socrates taught the Delphic maxim, 'Know thyself'—as Rousseau points out, the 'lore' of the great conquerors did not teach them 'to know themselves' (lines 211–12). And Edward Duffy points out that Rousseau himself is decidedly lacking in self-knowledge.[1] Christ preached the doctrine of love and imagination: 'as ye would that men should do to you, do ye also to them likewise' (Luke 6: 31). Those who follow their examples and live by their teachings can escape the slavery of Life. Few are able to do so. Even Plato, the pupil of Socrates, is enslaved, for Life found out his weak spot and 'Conquered the heart by love which gold or pain/Or age or sloth could subdue not—' (lines 258–9). Plato is not necessarily being criticized for loving. It is his association with tyrants like Dionysius II of Syracuse and his brother-in-law Dion that reveals that he sold out to Life;[2] in attributing his original fall to love Rousseau is being relatively charitable.

Shelley regarded both Plato and Rousseau as great poets, and the fact that they are both presented as having succumbed to Life shows how high are the standards by which men are being judged. Or if not all men, certainly poets, humanity's guiding spirits. Shelley is confronting a question of some personal urgency: if the poets should indeed be 'the happiest, the best, the wisest, and the most illustrious of men' (*Works*, vii. 138), how is it that even they may not be unable to resist corruption by Life? The dreamer's vision grows out of the 'thoughts which must remain untold'

[1] Op. cit., p. 216.
[2] This point has been anticipated by Neville Rogers (*Shelley at Work*, p. 304).

(line 21) that he mentions at the beginning of the poem, and the vision itself may be seen as articulating these dark thoughts. One such thought is the fear that 'good' and 'the means of good' are 'irreconcilable'. Rousseau has given up this kind of public anxiety, and, reading the dreamer's mind as Virgil does Dante's, urges him to do the same; had he heard the sound of the stream by which Rousseau awoke, he says,

> Thou wouldst forget thus vainly to deplore
>
> Ills, which if ills, can find no cure from thee,
> The thought of which no other sleep will quell
> Nor other music blot from memory—
> (lines 327–30)

But the dreamer doesn't want to forget the world's troubles, he wants to solve them. This may be a vain hope, but it is preferable to the Lethean oblivion offered by Rousseau. This indifference to the public world on Rousseau's part is connected with the vision he goes on to describe. His account of this experience is directed to another untold thought of the dreamer, the deeper fear that the poet is in danger of being overthrown by something in the nature of the poetic imagination itself.

The crux of any interpretation of this account is agreed to be the 'shape all light' (line 352) and the status she is to be accorded. What one might call the orthodox reading associated her with other female figures in Shelley's poetry, such as Cythna, Asia, and the Witch of Atlas.[1] The 'Hymn to Intellectual Beauty' also tends to get mentioned in this context, for the point of making these comparisons is to establish the Shape as a messenger from a transcendent realm. Kenneth Allott, repelling the heresies of Harold Bloom, was convinced that she 'derives from eternity'.[2] The Witch of Atlas has proved an especially useful term of comparison in that her 'Strange panacea' (*Witch of Atlas*, line 594) can be used to elucidate the Shape's 'bright Nepenthe' (line 359) which seems to have such an unfortunate effect on Rousseau (assuming that he does in fact drink it). Since there is nothing wrong with the Witch's panacea, it follows that if the Nepenthe

[1] A. C. Bradley associates her with the Witch of Atlas (loc. cit. 444), and A. M. D. Hughes with both the Witch and Asia (' "The Triumph of Life" ', *K-SMB* xvi (1965), 16).

[2] 'Bloom on "The Triumph of Life" ', *Essays in Criticism*, x (1960), 224–5.

does not agree with Rousseau the fault lies in him.[1] A rather higher level of ingenuity is needed to establish the credentials of the Shape as heavenly representative when we come to consider these lines.

> All that was seemed as if it had been not,
>   As if the gazer's mind was strewn beneath
> Her feet like embers, and she, thought by thought,
>
>   Trampled its fires into the dust of death,
> As Day upon the threshold of the east
>   Treads out the lamps of night, until the breath
>
> Of darkness reillumines even the least
>   Of heaven's living eyes—
> (lines 385–92)

There is something glib about the assurance that this trampling of thoughts figures 'the effect of a revelation of the ideal in obliterating the modes of thought and feeling habitual before that revelation'.[2] Is this a defence of the Shape or a denunciation of revelations of the ideal? Peter Butter has sought 'a perfectly innocent explanation'[3] (a way of putting it that suggests a measure of embarrassment) by invoking the Witch.

> For she was beautiful—her beauty made
>   The bright world dim, and every thing beside
> Seemed like the fleeting image of a shade:
>   No thought of living spirit could abide—
> Which to her looks had ever been betrayed,
>   On any object in the world so wide,
> On any hopes within the circling skies,
> But on her form, and in her inmost eyes.
> (*The Witch of Atlas*, lines 137–44)

But are the implications of this passage entirely 'innocent'? The 'living spirit' who must renounce all other thoughts and be absorbed by the Witch is said to be 'betrayed'. The Witch in fact has no desire to have any such effect on the beholders, and she weaves for herself 'A shadow for the splendour of her love' (line

---

[1] See A. M. D. Hughes, loc. cit. 16–17, and J. Hodgson, loc. cit. 608–10.
[2] A. C. Bradley, loc. cit. 454.
[3] 'Sun and Shape in Shelley's *The Triumph of Life*', *RES*, n.s. xiii (1962), 49.

152) in order to protect them. No such protection guards those who encounter the Shape, and it is a bold critic who can disregard the sinister implications of the language in which her effect upon Rousseau is described.

It is this passage that provides the strongest support for the interpretation advanced by Harold Bloom and other American critics, according to which the Shape is not benignant at all, but actively malevolent. Bloom triumphantly refuted the readings of Bradley, Carlos Baker, and others, which attempted to show that the Shape tramples (in Baker's words) only 'dark and evil thoughts, not thoughts in general'.[1] Bloom made particularly telling use of the fact that the Shape is said to obliterate the fires of the gazer's mind just as the sun blots out the stars, 'heaven's living eyes'. Now, while it is true that Shelley on occasion uses the sun as a symbol for the imagination,[2] when he contrasts sun and stars elsewhere the stars stand for poets. This is the case in *Adonais*, where the sun is presented as the patron of the hour, while eternal values are in the charge of the stars.

> The sun comes forth, and many reptiles spawn;
> He sets, and each ephemeral insect then
> Is gathered into death without a dawn,
> And the immortal stars awake again;
> So is it in the world of living men:
> A godlike mind soars forth, in its delight
> Making earth bare and veiling heaven, and when
> It sinks, the swarms that dimmed or shared its light
> Leave to its kindred lamps the spirit's awful night.
> (lines 253–61)[3]

In the opening of *The Triumph of Life* the dreamer wakes and sleeps according to the rhythm of 'the stars that gem/The cone of night' (lines 22–3) rather than that of the sun. In the natural world the sun is rightful ruler; in the spiritual world the more distant but eternal stars must be the guides. Here in fact the brightest lights are the most sinister, and the 'cold glare' of the chariot 'obscured with   light/The Sun as he the stars' (lines 77–9) in a

---

[1] *Shelley's Mythmaking*, pp. 268–9.

[2] See G. M. Matthews, loc. cit. 112–13.

[3] Shelley is thinking of Byron, who has just been compared to Apollo, god of the sun (lines 249–50); Byron scattered the critical reptiles, but the mortal parts of his own work have fostered a taste in which poetical ephemera breed.

passage that anticipates the Shape's obliteration of the beholder's thoughts. Later the 'fair shape' is herself obscured by the 'coming light' of Life, and this process is compared to the waning of Lucifer, the morning star, in the sunrise (lines 412–15). It would seem that Bloom does have a strong point, though he rather over-states it when he claims that 'The strength of contending lights and the visions they inform, and the obliteration of one kind of light by another; these are the real themes and the major figures of "The Triumph of Life" ' (p. 227).

By Bloom's reading the Shape is not divine but demonic, 'a diabolic parody of the Witch of Atlas or Dante's Matilda'. Her malevolence is confirmed by 'the fact that Rousseau's draft from the Shape's crystal glass is followed by the sudden appearance of the chariot of Life' (p. 267). The text even hints that the Shape should be identified with Life. When Rousseau refers to Life as 'the new Vision' (line 411) his intention is to distinguish it from his former vision of the Shape, but his words reveal that both are 'visions'. His statement of faith that the beneficent Shape remained with him even when the glare of Life obscured her from him has heavily ironic implications.

> So knew I in that light's severe excess
> The presence of that shape which on the stream
>   Moved, as I moved along the wilderness . . .
> (lines 424–6)

For Rousseau the two visions are as far apart as Heaven and Hell, but the reader may well suspect that there is an intimate if obscure connection between them. The reading advanced by Bloom amounts to seeing the Shape as a mask for Life. James Rieger remarks, 'devils come disguised as angels, as devils always do when they mean to tempt rather than to frighten us'.[1] But put like this the thesis of the Shape's malevolence is as wrong as the previously accepted account of her as divine. To debate whether she be angel or devil is to start from an assumption that is in itself misleading. It is the assumption that Rousseau makes, and it consists in seeing the individual's salvation or damnation as originating outside himself.

Rousseau himself is quick to recognize the Shape as a divine

---

[1] *The Mutiny Within*, p. 207.

messenger, coming from 'the realm without a name' (line 396), and he proceeds to ask her, 'Show whence I came, and where I am, and why—' (line 398). McGann argues that this is a demand for a 'direct confrontation with the Absolute',[1] for knowledge that no man can be given. As Shelley knew even in 1816,

> No voice from some sublimer world hath ever
>   To sage or poet these responses given—
>   Therefore the name of God and ghosts and Heaven,
> Remain the record of their vain endeavour,
> Frail spells . . .
> ('Hymn to Intellectual Beauty', lines 25–9)

By the end of his life he was sure that the wisest course was to be content with our ignorance on such matters: 'My mind is at peace respecting nothing so much as the constitution & mysteries of the great system of things—my curiosity on this point never amounts to solicitude' (*Letters*, ii. 341–2). There are no divine messengers who can satisfy our curiosity on these matters, and Rousseau really has no warrant for the way in which he presents his meeting with the Shape as a kind of parody of Virgil's meeting with Beatrice in Canto II of the *Inferno*. The text is thick with allusions that point to his reading of the situation.

> still before her on the dusky grass
> Iris her many coloured scarf had drawn.—
> (lines 356–7)

Some critics seem to think that Iris is the name of the Shape,[2] but this is to make Rousseau's mistake of confounding metaphor and reality. 'Iris' is a trope for the rainbow, but it is of course a trope that evokes the messenger of Juno in Ovid.

> dixerat: induitur velamina mille colorum
> Iris et arcuato caelum curvamine signans
> tecta petit iussi sub nube latentia regis.
> (*Metamorphoses*, XI. 589–91)

[Juno] finished speaking: Iris assumed her cloak of a thousand colours

---

[1] Loc. cit. 266.
[2] A. M. D. Hughes, loc. cit. 16.

and, marking the sky with its arching curve, made her way to the cloud-hidden palace of the king to whom her errand was.[1]

Just as the rainbow is the result of sunlight and water mist, so the Shape would seem to take its origin from the phenomena of nature.

> And as I looked the bright omnipresence
>   Of morning through the orient cavern flowed,
> And the Sun's image radiantly intense
>
>   Burned on the waters of the well that glowed
> Like gold, and threaded all the forest maze
>   With winding paths of emerald fire—there stood
>
> Amid the sun, as he amid the blaze
>   Of his own glory, on the vibrating
> Floor of the fountain, paved with flashing rays,
>
>   A shape all light . . .
> (lines 343–52)

The rays of the early morning sun reflected from moving water are, as anyone may know from common experience, intensely bright—if there were anything there to see, it would be impossible to see it. What Rousseau has done is to give external reality to a figment of his own dazzled sense. All the elements that compose the Shape are to be found in the description of the scene that precedes her appearance, and it is Rousseau's poetic imagination that has shaped the Shape from these elements. She is, as Rousseau later says, a vision, and, as several critics have pointed out, a beautiful one. Peter Butter, voicing his reservations about Bloom's interpretation, has commented, 'I find it impossible to respond to the descriptions of the sun and the Shape without feeling them as beautiful—with a beauty which may be dangerous, but cannot be evil.'[2] The danger lies in trying to attribute external reality to a poetic idealism. This is what Rousseau does; and this is not the first time that such a situation has occurred in Shelley's poetry.

The visionary maiden encountered by the hero of *Alastor* is quite

---

[1] Text from Loeb Classical Library edition of Ovid, *Metamorphoses*, edited by Frank Justus Miller (1916; 2 vols., 1966), ii. 162. Translation by the present author.

[2] Loc. cit. 47.

explicitly presented as a product of his own imagination.[1] This
maiden appears to him in 'a dream of hopes', and unites in herself
all that he could desire in an object of love.

> He dreamed a veiled maid
> Sate near him, talking in low solemn tones.
> Her voice was like the voice of his own soul
> Heard in the calm of thought; its music long,
> Like woven sounds of streams and breezes, held
> His inmost sense suspended in its web
> Of many-coloured woof and shifting hues.
> Knowledge and truth and virtue were her theme,
> And lofty hopes of divine liberty,
> Thoughts the most dear to him, and poesy,
> Herself a poet.
> (lines 150–61)

The ironies here are palpable. Her voice is 'like the voice of his
own soul' because that is precisely what it is, and it is hardly
surprising that she dwells on 'Thoughts the most dear to him'.
His consummation with this ideal woman is auto-erotic, and
Shelley is fully aware of the physiological basis of the whole
experience in 'the facility with which certain phenomena connected with sleep, at the age of puberty, associate themselves with
those images which are the objects of our waking desires'.[2] To
ascribe this experience to sexual frustration, as a modern might
do, would be unnecessarily reductive; but it is the hero's hitherto
unsatisfied need for love that is revealing itself to him in the form
of what is most worthy to be loved. The Narrator[3] sees the dream
as providential, warning the Poet to seek human contact.

> The spirit of sweet human love has sent
> A vision to the sleep of him who spurned
> Her choicest gifts.
> (lines 203–5)

---

[1] A parallel between *The Triumph of Life* and *Alastor* has been drawn by
Hodgson, loc. cit. 595, 614–15. Duffy associates *Alastor* with the contemporary
image of the historical Rousseau (op. cit., pp. 151–4).

[2] *Shelley's Prose*, p. 222.

[3] I adopt Wasserman's distinction between Shelley, the Narrator, and the
Visionary (*Shelley: A Critical Reading*, p. 11), though I use Shelley's term, the
Poet, for the latter.

In the Narrator's view the dream is a retribution for the Poet's former solipsism, but also a manifestation of natural grace, in that it will serve to redirect him to his fellows, where he will find the appropriate objects of his newly recognized needs and desires. But this optimistic view is not borne out by events. The Poet has no intention of seeking any human substitute for his vision; he will have the ideal itself, and proceeds to seek it in the external world. This quest is doomed to failure, of course, as the Narrator notes with some agitation.

> He eagerly pursues
> Beyond the realms of dream that fleeting shade;
> He overleaps the bounds. Alas! alas!
> Were limbs, and breath, and being intertwined
> Thus treacherously? Lost, lost, for ever lost,
> In the wide pathless desart of dim sleep,
> That beautiful shape!
> (lines 205–11)

If the vision is not to be recovered in this world, the Poet will not be satisfied with anything else it has to offer. He will pursue the vision beyond it, and this can only lead to his death. In this way the alluring vision becomes an Alastor, an avenging demon driving him to destruction. This is the 'fair fiend' of line 297, who, as the Narrator is careful to remind us, has no external existence: 'not a sight/Or sound of awe but in his own deep mind' (lines 297–8). This avenging fiend is, in the words of the sub-title, 'The Spirit of Solitude'. The Poet has refused human love, and his fate is to desire a love that is unattainable, and thus the solipsism which was his crime becomes his punishment, as the vision alienates him from other men and from life itself. Such is the view of the Narrator, and Shelley in the Preface endorses it, though he does not think the problem is as easy of solution as the Narrator would like to believe. To love at all is to love what is most worthy of love, and this must be ideal; but, having conceived an ideal object of love, how is that love to be transferred to any lesser object offered by the real world? Extremes meet, and the ardent idealist is as much cut off from his fellows as the man who is too cold to love or feel at all. There is only a choice of destructions, an alternative described in *The Triumph of Life* as that between 'fire' and 'frost' (line 175).

The Poet's self-centred seclusion was avenged by the furies of an irresistible passion pursuing him to speedy ruin. But that Power which strikes the luminaries of the world with sudden darkness and extinction, by awakening them to too exquisite a perception of its influences, dooms to a slow and poisonous decay those meaner spirits that dare to abjure its dominion. . . . Among those who attempt to exist without human sympathy, the pure and tender-hearted perish through the intensity and passion of their search after its consummation, when the vacancy of their spirit suddenly makes itself felt. All else, selfish, blind, and torpid, are those unforeseeing multitudes who constitute, together with their own, the lasting misery and loneliness of the world. (Preface to *Alastor*)

The three voices distinguished by Wasserman, Poet, Narrator, and Shelley himself, should be seen within the context of Shelley's changing conception of the poem. The original intention seems to have been a demonstration of the dangers of idealism in the example of the Poet, with the Narrator's comments enforcing the lesson. But in the course of the poem Shelley, who must have intended the warning for himself as much as for anyone else, came to feel such sympathy for the Poet, and such scepticism concerning the possibility of avoiding his 'error', that his summary in the Preface has abandoned any attempt to present the Poet's story as a moral warning. According to the Preface, you're damned if you do, and damned if you don't, and at least the Poet is damned nobly and heroically.

The issues treated in *Alastor* were of considerable personal urgency for Shelley, and not only at the period of its composition. They were strongly revived in his mind by the episode of his 'Italian platonics'[1] with Emilia Viviani, that led to the composition of *Epipsychidion*. On reflection he began to see that he himself had been the victim of a confusion between real and ideal, and in June 1822, during or immediately preceding the composition of *The Triumph of Life*, he wrote to John Gisborne:

The 'Epipsychidion' I cannot look at; the person whom it celebrates was a cloud instead of a Juno; and poor Ixion starts from the centaur that was the offspring of his own embrace. . . . I think one is always in love with something or other; the error, and I confess it is not easy for spirits cased in flesh and blood to avoid it, consists in seeking in a mortal image the likeness of what is perhaps eternal. (*Letters*, ii. 434)

---

[1] The phrase is Mary Shelley's; see *The Letters of Mary W. Shelley*, i. 160–1.

A certain Platonic slant can be detected here, as in his earlier remark that 'Some of us have in a prior existence been in love with an Antigone, & that makes us find no full content in any mortal tie' (*Letters*, ii. 364). But the Platonism is invoked consciously as a metaphorical fiction, and deployed with wry humour; Shelley is certainly not committing himself on the subject of post-mortal or antenatal existence. In a more earnest vein he explains the disappointment inherent in all mortal ties by reference to the creative activity of the imagination.

We dimly see within our intellectual nature a miniature as it were of our entire self, yet deprived of all that we condemn or despise, the ideal prototype of every thing excellent or lovely that we are capable of conceiving as belonging to the nature of man. . . . The discovery of its antitype . . . this is the invisible and unattainable point to which Love tends; and to attain which it urges forth the powers of man to arrest the faintest shadow of that without the possession of which there is no rest or respite to the heart over which it rules. . . . So soon as this want or power is dead, man becomes the living sepulchre of himself, and what yet survives is the mere husk of what once he was.— (*Works*, vi. 202)

Shelley is fully aware of the ambivalence of this 'want or power', and the ways in which its possession can be as much of a curse as its lack. McGann has argued that this conception of love as the search for an interior ideal is repudiated in *A Defence of Poetry*, where love is identified with 'a going out of our own nature, and an identification of ourselves with the beautiful which exists in thought, action, or person, *not our own*'.[1] But this need not imply a recantation of 'On Love'; if man must seek beauty outside himself, he must seek it by reference to an ideal (that is, imaginative) concept within his own mind. He must strive to transform the real world to bring it into accord with the idea. Complete success is necessarily impossible, since reality cannot meet all the imagination's demands. There is a danger that the ideal conception will only disillusion us with the real and alienate us from it. Still, in 'On Love' Shelley is rather more optimistic about the idealizing function of the imagination, since, used properly, it prevents us from being enslaved to the reality of our immediate surroundings, and provides the model by which they can be transformed.

The danger that we should be on our guard against consists in

[1] Loc. cit. 257; the emphasis is McGann's.

seeking a complete embodiment of the ideal where it cannot be found, in the mortal world; or, when it cannot be found, of supposing that it must exist in some realm above the mortal—and this is what Rousseau does. He fails to see Life as something 'amiss' (line 179) by reference to his own imaginative vision and therefore to be reformed so far as may be possible in accord with it; he sees it only as the absence of value, as all that is opposed to the ideal Shape and has displaced it. Hence he must believe that the Shape still exists outside himself and will make herself known to him, as it were on the other side of Life.

> And as the presence of that fairest planet
>
> Although unseen is felt by one who hopes
>   That his day's path may end as he began it
> In that star's smile . . .
>
> So knew I in that light's severe excess
> The presence of that shape which on the stream
>   Moved, as I moved along the wilderness,
>
> More dimly than a day appearing dream . . .
>   (lines 416–19, 424–7)

His metaphor shows that he is trusting in a delusion: Venus is indeed both the Morning Star and the Evening Star, but never both on the same day.[1] The individual's imaginative vision is transitory, and when it passes it leaves him subject to the influences of everyday life, as a dream fades in the daylight.[2] But vision comes from within not without, and will not reappear of its own volition or in the natural course of events. The identification of the Shape with Life is a deeper irony than appears at first, for it hints that Rousseau must himself re-create his vision from the materials of common existence if he would ever behold it again.

Life is what it is because men live divorced from all value. Most people, the 'loud million' around the chariot, the 'unforeseeing multitudes' of the Preface to *Alastor*, are simply oblivious to all imaginative values. They must receive vision from the great poets. The danger facing the poets is that of making a divorce between

---

[1] Hodgson, loc. cit. 603–4.

[2] '. . . in the intervals of inspiration, and they may be frequent without being durable, a Poet becomes a man, and is abandoned to the sudden reflux of the influences under which others habitually live' (*Works*, vii. 139).

value and human existence, between 'The Heaven which I imagine' and the 'Hell' of 'this harsh world in which I wake to weep' (lines 333–4). 'We see that we cannot reach the sphere in which we have placed our values; but this does not by any means confer any value on that other sphere in which we live: on the contrary we are *weary* because we have lost the main stimulus.'[1] But it is this divorce between vision and life that makes Life a Hell indeed. *The Triumph of Life* is directed to exposing the dangers inherent in a temptation that Shelley himself was all too familiar with, as is clear from *Adonais*. If Life betrays all the values of the imagination, it is all too easy to reject Life and embrace Death. But, as the post-mortal framework borrowed from Dante serves to show, Death cannot liberate Rousseau from Life. *The Triumph of Life* has often been viewed as implying a recantation on Shelley's part of his optimism concerning human progress. But if it is a recantation of anything it is a palinode to *Adonais*. To argue about the 'pessimism' or 'optimism' of *The Triumph of Life* is to debate in terms that are far too crude to seize the subtle and sceptical quality of what Shelley is saying in it. He sees very well that Life is Hell, and the signs of improvement are all too lacking. But he also sees that there is little point in hoping for a Heaven somewhere else, for Heaven is only known to man through his own imagination. Whether he can create his Heaven on earth cannot be known for certain, but only hoped; and since such faith can alone make itself real it is the only practicable course.

[1] Friedrich Nietzsche, *The Will to Power*, edited by W. Kaufman, translated by W. Kaufman and R. J. Hollingdale (New York, 1968), p. 11. Nietzsche's critique in *The Will to Power* of the concept of the 'true' world is very relevant to the major theme of *The Triumph of Life*.

The Dating of Shelley's Extant Prose Works

Titles in square brackets have been supplied by Shelley's editors. This list does not include Shelley's translations or his notes on his reading.

TITLE	DATE
Zastrozzi. A Romance (*Works*, v. 3–103)	Spring–Summer 1809? (pub. March 1810)
St. Irvyne; or, The Rosicrucian. A Romance (v. 107–99)	Summer 1810 (pub. Dec. 1810)
The Necessity of Atheism (v. 203–9)	Jan.–Feb. 1811
An Address, to the Irish People (v. 213–47)	Jan.–Feb. 1812
Proposals for an Association (v. 251–68)	Feb. 1812
Declaration of Rights (v. 271–5)	Mar. 1812
A Letter to Lord Ellenborough (v. 279–94)	June –July 1812
A Vindication of Natural Diet (vi. 3–20)	Nov.–Dec. 1812 (pub. early 1813)
A Refutation of Deism (vi. 23–57)	late 1813 (pub. early 1814)
'On the Vegetable System of Diet' (vi. 335–44)	June–July 1814
'The Assassins' (vi. 155–71)	Aug.–Sept. 1814
Review of T. J. Hogg's *Memoirs of Alexy Haimatoff* (vi. 175–82)	Nov. 1814 (pub. Dec. 1814)
[Catalogue of the Phenomena of Dreams] (vii. 66–7)	1815
Chancery Declaration (in Edward Dowden, *The Life of Percy Bysshe Shelley* (2 vols., 1886), ii. 86–8)	Jan.–Feb. 1817
A Proposal for putting Reform to the Vote (*Works*, vi. 61–8)	Feb. 1817 (pub. Mar. 1817)
'On the Game Laws' (Clark, *Shelley's Prose*, pp. 341–3)	Feb.–Oct. 1817?
Fragment on Reform (*Works*, vi. 295–6)	Feb.–Oct. 1817?
[Speculations on Metaphysics and on Morals] (vii. 62–5, 73–8, 81–3, 342)	Spring 1817
Preface to Mary Shelley's *Frankenstein* (vi. 259–60)	May 1817

TITLE	DATE
Fragment on God (Clark, *Shelley's Prose*, pp. 138–40)	Sept.–Dec. 1817
[Essay on Christianity] (*Works*, vi. 227–52, vii. 145–6)	Sept.–Dec. 1817
Fragment on Marriage (vii. 149–50)	Sept.–Dec. 1817
An Address to the People on the Death of the Princess Charlotte (vi. 71–82)	Nov. 1817
Review of William Godwin's *Mandeville* (vi. 219–23)	Dec. 1817
Review of Mary Shelley's *Frankenstein* (vi. 263–5)	Jan. 1818
Review of T. L. Peacock's *Rhododaphne* (vi. 273–6)	Feb. 1818
[On Love] (vi. 201–2)	July 1818
'An Essay on Friendship' (vii. 143–4)	July–Aug. 1818
'A Discourse of the Manners of the Antient Greeks' (Clark, *Shelley's Prose*, pp. 216–23)	July–Aug. 1818
'On the Symposium' (*Works*, vii. 161–2)	Aug. 1818
[The Coliseum] (vi. 299–306)	Nov. 1818–? Spring 1819
'A Future State' (vi. 205–9)	Sept.–Dec. 1818
Definition of the term 'atheist' (see Timothy Webb, *Shelley: A voice not understood*, p. 216)	Jan.–Apr. 1819
[The Arch of Titus] (*Works*, vi. 309)	Spring 1819
Notes on Sculptures in Rome and Florence (vi. 310–32)	Mar.–Apr. and Oct.–Nov. 1819
'A Philosophical View of Reform' (vii. 3–55)	Nov.–Dec. 1819
[On Life] (vi. 193–7)	Dec. 1819
[Speculations on Metaphysics] (vii. 61)	Dec. 1819?
Fragment on contraception (see p. 49 above)	Dec. 1819
'Una Favola' (*Works*, vi. 279–82)	1820
'On the Devil, and Devils' (vii. 87–104)	Jan. 1820
'On Polytheism' (vii. 151)	Jan. 1820
'The Elysian Fields' (vi. 269–70)	Feb. 1820–?
'A System of Government by Juries' (vi. 289–92)	Mar.–Apr. 1820?
[On the Punishment of Death] (vi. 185–90)	Aug.–Dec. 1820
Fragment on Reform (vi. 295)	Aug.–Dec. 1820

TITLE	DATE
Review of Tommaso Sgricci's *Morte d'Ettore* (see p. 217 above)	Jan. 1821
[Speculations on Metaphysics and on Morals] (*Works*, vii. 59–61, 71–2, 79–80)	Jan.–Feb. 1821
Fragment on Shelley's philosophy (see Neville Rogers, *Shelley at Work*, pp. 16–17)	Jan.–Feb. 1821
Fragment on Keats's poetry (see Rogers, p. 257)	Jan.–Feb. 1821
Fragment on Reason and Imagination (*Works*, vii. 107)	Jan.–Feb. 1821
A Defence of Poetry (vii. 109–40)	Feb.–Mar. 1821
Two fragments on beauty (vii. 154; the third fragment is by Mary Shelley)	1821
'Cry of war to the Greeks' (see p. 17 above; possibly a joint composition with Mary Shelley)	Apr.–June 1821
Critique of Charles Leslie's *A Short and Easy Method with the Deists* (see Claude Brew, 'A New Shelley Text: Essay on Miracles and Christian Doctrine', *K–SMB* xxviii (1977), 22–5; the fragment in *Works*, vi. 255–6 may be part of this, and was certainly written at the same period)	1822
[On the Revival of Literature] (*Works*, vi. 213–15)	1818–22

Bibliography of Sources Cited

Unless otherwise stated the place of publication of all books and pamphlets is London.

MANUSCRIPT SOURCES

Bodleian Library, Oxford   MS Shelley
MS Shelley adds.
Dep. (temporary classification for material deposited by Lord Abinger)

British Library, London   MS Add. 47569 (Correspondence of Charles James Fox)

Horsham Museum   Albery Collection (Papers of Thomas Charles Medwin)

Library of Congress, Washington   Notebook of Mary Shelley

Pierpont Morgan Library, New York   Part of one of Shelley's notebooks (Containing 'On Life')

PERIODICALS

Published in London unless otherwise stated. The name of the editor is supplied for periodicals where there is a possibility of confusion.
The Annual Biography and Obituary
The Annual Register
The Champion (John Scott)
Cobbett's Weekly Political Register (also published as *Cobbett's Annual Register*, *Cobbett's Political Register*, *Cobbett's Weekly Political Pamphlet*, and *Cobbett's Weekly Register*)
The Dublin Weekly Messenger (Dublin)
The Edinburgh Review (Edinburgh)
The Examiner (James Henry Leigh Hunt)
The Gentleman's Magazine
The Independent Whig (Henry White)
The Morning Chronicle (James Perry, and John Black from 1817)
The New Annual Register
The Reformists' Register (William Hone)
The Republican (Richard Carlile)
The Sussex Weekly Advertiser (Lewes)
The Times

BOOKS, PAMPHLETS, THESES, AND ARTICLES

ABRAMS, M. H., *The Mirror and the Lamp: Romantic Theory and the Critical Tradition* (1953; W. W. Norton, New York, 1958).

—— *Natural Supernaturalism: Tradition and Revolution in Romantic Literature* (Oxford University Press, 1971).

ALBERY, W., *A Parliamentary History of the Ancient Borough of Horsham 1295–1885* (Longmans, 1927).

ALLOTT, K., 'Bloom on "The Triumph of Life" ', *Essays in Criticism*, x (1960), 222–8.

AMIYA-KUMARA Sena, *Studies in Shelley* (University of Calcutta, Calcutta, 1936).

[ANSTER], J., 'Life and Writings of Percy Bysshe Shelley', *North British Review*, viii (1847), 218–57.

ASPINALL, A., *Politics and the Press c. 1780–1850* (Home and Van Thal, 1949).

AUBREY, John, *Aubrey's Brief Lives*, edited by O. L. Dick (1949; Penguin, Harmondsworth, 1976).

BACON, Francis, *The Works of Francis Bacon Baron of Verulam, Viscount St. Albans, and Lord High Chancellor of England* (5 vols., J. Rivington and others, 1778).

BAKER, Carlos, *Shelley's Major Poetry: The Fabric of a Vision* (Princeton University Press, Princeton, N. J., 1948).

BAKER, Herschel, *William Hazlitt* (Harvard University Press, Cambridge, Mass., and Oxford University Press, London, 1962).

BAKER, Joseph E., *Shelley's Platonic Answer to a Platonic Attack on Poetry* (University of Iowa Press, Iowa City, 1965).

BAMFORD, Samuel, *The Autobiography of Samuel Bamford* [1839–41], edited by W. H. Chaloner (2 vols., Cass, 1967). Vol. ii contains a facsimile of his *Passages in the Life of a Radical*.

BARLOW, Joel, *The Works of Joel Barlow* (2 vols., Scholars' Facsimiles and Reprints, Gainesville, Fla., 1970).

BARNARD, E., *Shelley's Religion* (University of Minnesota Press, Minneapolis, 1937).

BARRUEL, A. de, *Memoirs, illustrating the History of Jacobinism*, translated by R. Clifford (4 vols., privately, 1797–8).

BEARDSMORE, R. W., *Art and Morality* (Macmillan, 1971).

BEAVAN, A. H., *James and Horace Smith* (Hurst and Blackett, 1899).

BELCHEM, J. C., 'Henry Hunt and the evolution of the mass platform', *English Historical Review*, xciii (1978), 739–73.

BENTHAM, J., *Plan of Parliamentary Reform, in the form of a Catechism* (R. Hunter, 1817).

BENTLEY, G. E., Jr., *Blake Records* (Clarendon Press, Oxford, 1969).

BERRY, F., *Poets' Grammar: Person, Time and Mood in Poetry* (Routledge and Kegan Paul, 1958).

BETHELL, S. L., *The Cultural Revolution of the Seventeenth Century* (1951; Dennis Dobson, 1963).

BLACK, Eugene C., *The Association: British Extraparliamentary Organization 1769–1793* (Harvard University Press, Cambridge, Mass., 1963).

BLAKE, William, *Complete Writings with variant readings*, edited by Geoffrey Keynes (Oxford University Press, 1969).

BLOOM, H., *Shelley's Mythmaking* (1959; Cornell University Press, Ithaca, N. Y., 1969).

—— *The Visionary Company: A Reading of English Romantic Poetry* (1961; revd. Cornell University Press, Ithaca, N. Y., 1971).

BOAS, L. S., *Harriet Shelley: Five Long Years* (Oxford University Press, 1962).

BRADLEY, A. C., 'Notes on Shelley's "Triumph of Life" ', *MLR* ix (1914), 441–56.

BRAILSFORD, H. N., *Shelley, Godwin and Their Circle* (1913; Oxford University Press, 1949).

BREW, C., 'A New Shelley Text: Essay on Miracles and Christian Doctrine', *K–SMB* xxviii (1977), 10–28.

BREWER, John, *Party ideology and popular politics at the accession of George III* (Cambridge University Press, Cambridge, 1976).

BRINTON, C., *The Political Ideas of the English Romanticists* (1926; University of Michigan Press, Ann Arbor, 1966).

BROCK, M., *The Great Reform Act* (Hutchinson, 1973).

BROWN, Ford K., 'Notes on 41 Skinner Street', *MLN* liv (1939), 326–32.

BROWN, Philip Anthony, *The French Revolution in English History* (1918; Frank Cass, 1965).

BULWER, Edward Lytton, *England and the English* (1833), edited by S. Meacham (University of Chicago Press, Chicago and London, 1970).

BURKE, Edmund, *The Works of the Right Honourable Edmund Burke* (6 vols., Henry G. Bohn, 1854–6).

BURY, J. B., *The Idea of Progress: An Inquiry into its Origin and Growth* (Macmillan, 1920).

BUTTER, P. H., 'Sun and Shape in Shelley's *The Triumph of Life*', *RES*, n.s. xiii (1962), 40–51.

BUTTERFIELD, H., 'Sincerity and Insincerity in Charles James Fox', *Proceedings of the British Academy*, lvii (1971), 237–61.

BUXTON, J., *The Grecian Taste: Literature in the Age of Neo-Classicism 1740–1820* (The Macmillan Press, London and Basingstoke, 1978).

BYRON, Lord, *The Works of Lord Byron. A new, revised and enlarged edition: Poetry*, edited by E. H. Coleridge (7 vols., John Murray, 1898–1904); *Letters and Journals*, edited by R. E. Prothero (6 vols., John Murray, 1898–1901).

CAMERON, K. N., 'A New Source for Shelley's *A Defence of Poetry*', *Studies in Philology*, xxxviii (1941), 629–44.

—— 'The Political Symbolism of *Prometheus Unbound*' (1943), in WOODINGS, R. B. (q.v.), pp. 102–29.

—— 'Shelley, Cobbett, and the National Debt', *JEGP* xlii (1943), 197–209.

—— 'Shelley and the Reformers', *ELH* xii (1945), 62–85.

—— *The Young Shelley: Genesis of a Radical* (Gollancz, 1951).

—— *Shelley: The Golden Years* (Harvard University Press, Cambridge, Mass., 1974).

CAMPBELL, W. R., 'Shelley's Philosophy of History: A Reconsideration', *K-SJ* xxi–xxii (1972-3), 43–63.

CANNON, J., *Parliamentary Reform 1640–1832* (Cambridge University Press, Cambridge, 1973).

CAREY, G., *Shelley* (Evans, 1975).

CARTWRIGHT, John, *Take your choice!* . . . (J. Almon, 1776).

—— *An Appeal, Civil and Military, on the Subject of the English Constitution* (privately, 1799).

—— *A Bill of Rights and Liberties; or, An Act for a Constitutional Reform of Parliament* (1817; T. Dolby, [1821]).

—— *The English Constitution Produced and Illustrated* (T. Cleary, 1823).

—— *The Life and Correspondence of Major Cartwright*, edited by F. D. Cartwright (2 vols., H. Colburn, 1826).

CHARD, L. F., II, *Dissenting Republican: Wordsworth's Early Life and Thought in their Political Context* (Mouton, The Hague, 1972).

CHERNAIK, J., *The Lyrics of Shelley* (The Press of Case Western Reserve University, Cleveland, Ohio, and London, 1972).

CHRISTIE, I. R., *Myth and Reality in Late-Eighteenth-Century Politics and Other Papers* (Macmillan, 1970).

CLARK, John P., 'On Anarchism In An Unreal World: Kramnick's View of Godwin and the Anarchists', *American Political Science Review*, lxix (1975), 162–7.

—— 'Rejoinder to "Comment" by Isaac Kramnick', ibid. 169–70.

—— *The Philosophical Anarchism of William Godwin* (Princeton University Press, Princeton, N.J., 1977).

CLARKE, C. and M. Cowden, *Recollections of Writers* (1878), edited by R. Gittings (Centaur Press, Fontwell, Sussex, 1969).

[CLIFFORD, R.], *Application of Barruel's Memoirs of Jacobinism, to the Secret Societies of Ireland and Great Britain* (E. Booker, 1798).

COBBETT, William, *The Autobiography of William Cobbett*, edited by William Reitzel (1933; Faber, 1947).

COLERIDGE, S. T., *Essays on His Times in* The Morning Post *and* The Courier, edited by D. V. Erdman (3 vols., Routledge and Kegan Paul, 1978).

—— *The Friend*, edited by B. E. Rooke (2 vols., Routledge and Kegan Paul, 1969).

—— *Biographica Literaria* (1817), edited by J. Shawcross (1907; Oxford University Press, 1973).

—— *Specimens of the Table Talk of Samuel Taylor Coleridge*, edited by H. N. Coleridge (1835; John Murray, 1851).

COLTHAM, S., 'The *Bee-Hive* Newspaper: its Origin and Early Struggles', in *Essays in Labour History*, edited by A. Briggs and J. Saville (1960; revd. Macmillan, 1967), pp. 174–204.

CONDORCET, M.–J.–A.–N. Caritat, Marquis de, *Esquisse d'un tableau historique des progrés de l'esprit humain* (1793), edited by M. and F. Hincker (Éditions Sociales, Paris, 1971).

COOKE, Michael G., *The Romantic Will* (Yale University Press, New Haven and London, 1976).

COPPI, A., *Annali d'Italia del 1750 al 1861* (17 vols., Salviucci, Rome, 1848–67).

CRONIN, R., 'Shelley's Language of Dissent', *Essays in Criticism*, xxvii (1977), 203–15.

CURRAN, John Philpot, *Speeches of the Right Honourable John Philpot Curran* (1805; 3rd edn., J. Stockdale, Dublin, 1811).

—— *A New and Enlarged Collection of Speeches, by the Right Honourable John Philpot Curran* (William Hone, 1819).

CURRAN, S., *Shelley's Annus Mirabilis: The Maturing of an Epic Vision* (Huntington Library, San Marino, Calif., 1975).

DANTE ALIGHIERI, *Le Opere di Dante Alighieri*, edited by E. Moore (1894; University Press, Oxford, 1963).

DARVALL, F. O., *Popular Disturbances and Public Order in Regency England* (1934; Oxford University Press, 1969).

DAVIS, H. W. Carless, *The Age of Grey and Peel* (1929; Clarendon Press, Oxford, 1964).

DAWSON, P. M. S., 'Shelley and the Irish Catholics in 1812', *K–SMB* xxix (1978), 18–31.

—— 'Shelley and Hazlit', to be published as part of the proceedings of the Shelley Conference held at Gregynog in September 1978, edited by Kelvin Everest (forthcoming from the Harvester Press, Hassocks, Sussex).

DE BEER, G., 'An "Atheist" in the Alps', *K-SMB* ix (1958), 1–15.

DERRY, J. W., *The Radical Tradition: Tom Paine to Lloyd George* (Macmillan, 1967).

—— *Charles James Fox* (Batsford, 1972).

DEWEY, John, *Art as Experience* (George Allen and Unwin, 1934).

DICKINSON, H. T. (ed.), *Politics and Literature in the Eighteenth Century* (Dent, 1974).

DINWIDDY, J. R., 'Charles James Fox and the People', *History*, lv (1970), 342–59.

DOWDEN, E., *The Life of Percy Bysshe Shelley* (2 vols., Kegan Paul, Trench and Co., 1886).

—— *Transcripts and Studies* (Kegan Paul, Trench and Co., 1888).

DROPMORE MSS, *The Manuscripts of J. B. Fortescue, Esq., preserved at Dropmore* (10 vols., Historical Manuscripts Commission, 1892–1927).

DUFFY, Edward Thomas, 'The Image of Jean-Jacques Rousseau in the Work of Shelley and Other English Romantics' (unpublished Ph. D. thesis, Columbia University, 1971).

EDWARDS, Thomas R., *Imagination and Power: A Study of Poetry on Public Themes* (Chatto and Windus, 1971).

ELSNER, P., *Percy Bysshe Shelleys Abhängigkeit von William Godwins Political Justice* (Mayer, Berlin, 1906).

ERDMAN, D. V., 'Lord Byron and the Genteel Reformers', *PMLA* lvi (1941), 1065–94.

FELL, R., *Memoirs of the Public Life of the late Right Honourable Charles James Fox* (2 vols., J. F. Hughes, 1808).

FLAGG, J. S., Prometheus Unbound *and* Hellas: *An approach to Shelley's lyrical dramas* (Institut für Englische Sprache und Literatur, Salzburg, 1972).

FONER, E., *Tom Paine and Revolutionary America* (Oxford University Press, New York, 1976).

FOOT, Paul, *Red Shelley* (1979).

FORTESCUE, J. B., see DROPMORE MSS.

FULLER, J. O., *Shelley: A Biography* (Jonathan Cape, 1968).

GASH, N., *Politics in the Age of Peel: A study in the Technique of Parliamentary Representation 1830–1850* (1953; 2nd edn., Harvester Press, Hassocks, Sussex, 1977).

GAY, Peter, *The Enlightenment: An Interpretation* (1966–9; 2 vols., Wildwood House, 1967–70).

The Later Correspondence of George III, edited by A. Aspinall (5 vols., Cambridge University Press, Cambridge, 1962–70).

The Correspondence of George, Prince of Wales, 1770–1812, edited by A. Aspinall (8 vols., Cassell, 1963–71).

The Letters of King George IV 1812–1830, edited by A. Aspinall (3 vols., Cambridge University Press, Cambridge, 1938).

GODECHOT, J., *France and the Atlantic Revolution of the Eighteenth Century 1770–1799* (1963), translated by H. H. Rowen (Collier-Macmillan, 1971).

GODWIN, W., *Four Early Pamphlets (1783–1784)*, edited by B. R. Pollin (Scholars' Facsimiles and Reprints, Gainesville, Fla., 1966).

—— *Uncollected Writings (1785–1822)*, edited by J. W. Marken and B. R. Pollin (Scholars' Facsimiles and Reprints, Gainesville, 1968).

—— *Enquiry concerning Political Justice and its Influence on Morals and Happiness* (1793; 3rd edn., 1798), edited by F. E. L. Priestley (3 vols., The University of Toronto Press, Toronto, 1946).

—— *The Enquirer. Reflections on Education, Manners, and Literature* (G. G. and J. Robinson, 1797).

—— *Life of Geoffrey Chaucer, the early English poet* (2nd edn., 4 vols., R. Phillips, 1804).

—— *Essay on Sepulchres* (W. Miller, 1809).

—— *Mandeville. A Tale of the Seventeenth Century in England* (3 vols., Constable, Edinburgh, 1817).

—— *Thoughts on Man, his Nature, Productions, and Discoveries* (E. Wilson, 1831).

[GROTE, G.], *Statement of the Question of Parliamentary Reform* (Baldwin, Cradock and Joy, 1821).

GUINN, J. P., *Shelley's Political Thought* (Mouton, The Hague, 1969).

HALÉVY, É., *England in 1815* (1913), translated by E. I. Watkins and D. A. Barker (1924; Ernest Benn, 1961).

HALL, Walter Phelps, *British Radicalism 1791–1797* (Longmans, Green and Co., New York, 1912).

[HAMILTON, W. H.], *State of the Catholic Cause, from the Issuing of Mr. Pole's Circular Letter, to the Present Day* . . . (H. Fitzpatrick, Dublin, 1812).

HARVEY, A. D., *Britain in the Early Nineteenth Century* (Batsford, 1978).

HAZLITT, William, *The Complete Works of William Hazlitt*, edited by P. P. Howe (21 vols., Dent, 1930–4).

HELVÉTIUS, C. A., *De l'esprit* (1758), edited by F. Châtelet (Éditions Gérard and Co., Verviers, Belgium, 1973).

HENDRIX, R. 'The Necessity of Response: How Shelley's Radical Poetry Works', *K–SJ* xxvii (1978), 45–69.

HILL, B. W., 'Fox and Burke: the Whig party and the question of principles, 1784–1789', *English Historical Review*, lxxxix (1974), 1–24.

HIMES, N. E., *Medical History of Contraception* (George Allen and Unwin, 1936).

HOBSBAWM, E. J., *Primitive Rebels: Studies in Archaic Forms of Social Movement in the 19th and 20th Centuries* (1959; 2nd edn., Manchester University Press, Manchester, 1971).

HODGSON, J. A., 'The World's Mysterious Doom: Shelley's *The Triumph of Life*', *ELH* xlii (1975), 595–622.

HOGG, T. J., *Memoirs of Prince Alexy Haimatoff* (1813), edited by S. Scott (The Folio Society, 1952).

HOLCROFT, Thomas, *The Life of Thomas Holcroft. Written by himself, continued . . . by William Hazlitt* (1816), edited by E. Colby (2 vols., Constable, 1925).

HOLLAND, Lady, *The Journal of Elizabeth Lady Holland (1791–1811)*, edited by the Earl of Ilchester (2 vols., Longmans and Co., 1908).

HOLLAND, Henry Fox, third Lord, *Further Memoirs of the Whig Party 1807–1821*, edited by Lord Stavordale (John Murray, 1905).

HOLLIS, P., *The Pauper Press: A Study in Working-class Radicalism of the 1830s* (Oxford University Press, 1970).

—— (ed.)   *Class and Conflict in Nineteenth-Century England 1815–1850* (Routledge and Kegan Paul, 1973).

HOLLOWAY, J., *The Proud Knowledge: Poetry, Insight and the Self, 1620–1920* (Routledge and Kegan Paul, London, Henley and Boston, 1977).

HOLMES, Richard, *Shelley: the Pursuit* (Weidenfeld and Nicolson, 1974).

[HONE, W.], *Full Report of the Third Spa-Fields Meeting; With the Previous Arrests* (W. Hone, [1817]).

HORNE TOOKE, John, Επεα πτεροεντα *or, the Diversions of Purley* (1786–1805; privately, 1798–1805).

HORSFIELD, T., *The History, Antiquities, and Topography of the County of Sussex* (2 vols., Sussex Press, Lewes, and Nichols and Son, London, 1835).

HUGHES, A. M. D., *The Nascent Mind of Shelley* (1947; Clarendon Press, Oxford, 1971).

—— ' "The Triumph of Life" ', *K–SMB* xvi (1965), 12–20.

HUGHES, D. J., 'Potentiality in *Prometheus Unbound*' (1963), in WOODINGS, R. B. (q.v.), pp. 142–61.

—— 'Prometheus Made Capable Poet in Act One of *Prometheus Unbound*', *Studies in Romanticism*, xvii (1978), 3–11.

HUNT, Henry, *Memoirs of Henry Hunt, Esq. Written by Himself, in His Majesty's Jail at Ilchester, in the County of Somerset* (1820–2; 3 vols., Cedric Chivers, Bath, 1967).

HUNT, J. H. Leigh, *Lord Byron and Some of His Contemporaries; with Recollections of the Author's Life, and of his Visit to Italy* (Henry Colburn, 1828).

—— *The Autobiography of Leigh Hunt* (1858), edited by J. E. Morpurgo (Cresset Press, 1949).

—— *The Correspondence of Leigh Hunt*, edited by T. Hunt (2 vols., Smith, Elder and Co., 1862).

INGPEN, R., *Shelley in England: New facts and letters from the Shelley–Whitton papers* (Kegan Paul and Co., 1917).

JACKSON, J. R. de J., *Method and Imagination in Coleridge's Criticism* (Routledge and Kegan Paul, 1969).

JEAFFRESON, J. C., *The Real Shelley: New Views of the Poet's Life* (2 vols., Hurst and Blackett, 1885).

JONES, F. L., 'Unpublished Fragments by Shelley and Mary', *Studies in Philology*, xlv (1948), 472–6.

JUDD, G. P., *Members of Parliament 1734–1832* (Yale University Press, New Haven, Conn., 1955).

'JUNIUS', *The Letters of Junius*, edited by John Cannon (Clarendon Press, Oxford, 1978).

KANT, Immanuel, *Immanuel Kant's Critique of Pure Reason* (1781; 2nd edn., 1787), translated by N. Kemp Smith (1929; Macmillan, 1970).

—— *On History*, edited by L. W. Beck (The Bobbs–Merrill Company, Indianapolis, 1963).

KEATS, John, *The Letters of John Keats 1814–1821*, edited by H. E. Rollins (2 vols., Cambridge University Press, Cambridge, 1958).

KEMP, Betty, *King and Commons 1660–1832* (Macmillan, 1957).

KNIGHT, G. Wilson, *The Starlit Dome: Studies in the Poetry of Vision* (1941; Oxford University Press, 1971).

KOSZUL, A. H., *La Jeunesse de Shelley* (Foundation Thiers, Paris, 1910).

KRAMNICK, I., 'On Anarchism and the Real World: William Godwin and Radical England', *American Political Science Review*, lxvi (1972), 114–28.

—— 'Comment on Clark's "On Anarchism in an Unreal World" ', ibid. lxix (1975), 168.

LA CASSAGNÈRE, C., *La Mystique du* Prometheus Unbound *de Shelley: Essai d'interprétation* (Minard, Paris, 1970).

LAMB, Charles and Mary, *The Works in Prose and Verse of Charles and Mary Lamb*, edited by T. Hutchinson (2 vols., Henry Frowde, Oxford University Press, 1908).

LANDOR, Walter Savage, *The Complete Works of Walter Savage Landor*, edited by T. E. Welby and S. Wheeler (1927–36; 16 vols., Methuen, 1969).

LAWLESS, John, *A Compendium of the History of Ireland, from the Earliest Period to the Reign of George I* (Graisberry and Campbell, Dublin, 1814).

—— *The Belfast Politics, enlarged; being a Compendium of the Political History of Ireland, for the last Forty Years* (D. Lyons, Belfast, 1818).

LEA, F. A., *Shelley and the Romantic Revolution* (Routledge, 1945).

LEWIS, R. W. B., *The American Adam: Innocence, Tragedy and Tradition in the Nineteenth Century* (The University of Chicago Press, Chicago, 1955).

LIVELY, J. F., 'Ideas of Parliamentary Representation in England 1815–1832' (unpublished M. Litt. thesis, University of Cambridge, 1959).

LOVETT, William, *Life and Struggles of William Lovett* (1876; MacGibbon and Kee, 1967).

MACCARTHY, Denis Florence, *Shelley's Early Life from Original Sources* (J. C. Hotten, 1872).

MACDERMOT, Frank, *Theobald Wolfe Tone: A Biographical Study* (Macmillan, 1939).

McDONALD, Joan, *Rousseau and the French Revolution 1762–1791* (University of London, The Athlone Press, 1965).

MACDONALD, Margaret, 'Natural Rights', in *Philosophy, Politics and Society*, edited by P. Laslett (Basil Blackwell, Oxford, 1956), pp. 35–55.

McDOWELL, R. B., *Irish Public Opinion 1750–1800* (Faber and Faber, 1944).

McELDERRY, B. R., Jr., 'Common Elements in Wordsworth's "Preface" and Shelley's *Defence of Poetry*', *MLQ* v (1944), 175–81.

McGANN, J. J., 'The Secrets of an Elder Day: Shelley after *Hellas*' (1966), in WOODINGS, R. B. (q.v.), pp. 253–71.

—— 'Shelley's Veils: A Thousand Images of Loveliness', in *Romantic and Victorian: Studies in Memory of William H. Marshall*, edited by W. P. Elledge and R. L. Hoffman (Fairleigh Dickinson University Press, Rutherford, N. J., 1971), pp. 198–218.

—— *Don Juan in Context* (John Murray, 1976).

MACK, Mary P., *Jeremy Bentham: An Odyssey of Ideas 1748–1792* (Heinemann, 1962).

MACKINTOSH, James, *Vindiciae Gallicae* (3rd edn., G. G. J. and J. Robinson, 1791).

MACNEVEN, W. J., and EMMET, T., *Pieces of Irish History, illustrative of the Condition of the Catholics of Ireland, of the Origin and Progress of the Political System of the United Irishmen; and of their Transactions with the Anglo–Irish Government* (Bernard Dornin, New York, 1807).

McNIECE, Gerald, 'Shelley's Practical Politics and Philosophical Opinions related to his Vision of Society' (unpublished B. Litt. thesis, University of Oxford, 1951).

—— *Shelley and the Revolutionary Idea* (Harvard University Press, Cambridge, Mass., 1969).

MADDEN, R. R., *The United Irishmen, their Lives and Times* (2 vols., J. Madden and Co., 1842).

MALTHUS, T. R., *An Essay on the Principle of Population* (1798; 5th edn., 3 vols., J. Murray, 1817).

MARKEN, J. W., 'William Godwin's Writing for the *New Annual Register*', *MLN* lxviii (1953), 477–9.

MARSHALL, Mrs Julian, *The Life and Letters of Mary Wollstonecraft Shelley* (2 vols., Bentley and Sons, 1889).

MARSHALL, William H., *Byron, Shelley, Hunt, and* The Liberal (University of Philadelphia Press, Philadelphia, Pa., 1960).

MARX, Karl, *Early Writings*, translated by R. Livingstone and G. Benton (Penguin Books, Harmondsworth, 1975).

MATTHEWS, G. M., 'A Volcano's Voice in Shelley' (1957), in WOODINGS, R. B. (q.v.), pp. 162–95.

—— 'On Shelley's "The Triumph of Life" ', *Studia Neophilologica*, xxxiv (1962), 104–34.

MEDWIN, Thomas, *Medwin's Conversations of Lord Byron* (1824), edited by E. J. Lovell, Jr. (Princeton University Press, Princeton, N.J., 1966).

—— *The Life of Percy Bysshe Shelley* (1847), edited by H. B. Forman (Humphrey Milford, 1913).

'MELVILLE, Lewis' (Lewis S. Benjamin), *The Life and Letters of William Cobbett in England & America. Based upon hitherto unpublished family papers* (2 vols., John Lane, 1913).

[MERLE, Joseph Gibbons], 'A Newspaper Editor's Reminiscences. Chap. IV', *Fraser's Magazine*, xxiii (1841), 699–710.

MIDDLETON, Charles S., *Shelley and his Writings* (2 vols., T. C. Newby, 1858).

MILLER, N. C., 'John Cartwright and radical parliamentary reform, 1808–1819', *English Historical Review*, lxxxiii (1968), 705–28.

—— 'Major John Cartwright and the Founding of the Hampden Club', *English Historical Journal*, xvii (1974), 615–19.

MILLHAUSER, M., 'Shelley: a reference to Ricardo in "Swellfoot the Tyrant" ', *N&Q*, 14 Jan. 1939, pp. 25–6.

MITCHEL, John, *The History of Ireland, from the Treaty of Limerick to the Present Time* (1868; 2 vols., Burns, Oates and Washbourne, no date).

MITCHELL, Austin, *The Whigs in Opposition 1815–1830* (Clarendon Press, Oxford, 1967).

MONRO, D. H., *Godwin's Moral Philosophy: An Interpretation of William Godwin* (Oxford University Press, 1953).

MURRAY, E. B., 'The Trial of Mr. Perry, Lord Eldon, and Shelley's *Address to the Irish*', *Studies in Romanticism*, xvii (1978), 35–49.

MURRY, John Middleton, *Heaven—and Earth* (Jonathan Cape, 1938).

NEWMAN, John Henry, *Prose and Poetry*, edited by G. Tillotson (Rupert Hart-Davis, 1957).

NIETZSCHE, Friedrich, *The Will to Power*, edited by W. Kaufman, translated by W. Kaufman and R. J. Hollingdale (Random House, New York, 1968).

NOXON, J., 'Hazlitt as Moral Philosopher', *Ethics*, lxxiii (1963), 279–83.

NOZICK, R., *Anarchy, State, and Utopia* (Basil Blackwell, Oxford, 1974).

O'CONNELL, Daniel, *The Life and Speeches of Daniel O'Connell, M.P.*, edited by J. O'Connell (2 vols., James Duffy, Dublin, 1846).

O'FAOLAIN, Seán, *King of the Beggars: A Life of Daniel O'Connell, the Irish Liberator, in a Study of the Rise of the Modern Irish Democracy 1775–1847* (1938; Allen Figgis, Dublin, 1970).

OLDFIELD, T. H. B., *The Representative History of Great Britain and Ireland* (6 vols., Baldwin, Cradock and Joy, 1816).

ORSINI, G. N. G., *Coleridge and German Idealism: A Study in the History of Philosophy with Unpublished Materials from Coleridge's Manuscripts* (Feffer and Simons Inc., London and Amsterdam, 1969).

Ó TUATHAIGH, G., *Ireland before the Famine 1789–1848* (Gill and Macmillan, Dublin, 1972).

OVID, *Metamorphoses*, edited by F. J. Miller (1916; 2 vols., Heinemann, 1966).

OWEN, Robert, *A New View of Society and Other Writings*, edited by J. Butt (1927; Dent, 1972).

PACK, Robert Frederick, 'Shelley and History: The Poet as Historian' (unpublished Ph. D. thesis, University of Pittsburgh, 1970).

PAINE, Thomas, *The Complete Writings of Thomas Paine*, edited by P. S. Foner (2 vols., Citadel Press, New York, 1945).

PALMER, R. R., *The Age of the Democratic Revolution: A political history of Europe and America 1760–1800* (2 vols., Princeton University Press, Princeton, N. J., 1959–64).

The Parliamentary History of England, from the earliest period to the year 1803 (36 vols., W. Cobbett, 1806–20).

The Parliamentary Debates from the year 1803 to the present time (41 vols., T. C. Hansard, 1812–20).

PARRINDER, P., *Authors and Authority: A Study of English Literary Criticism and its Relation to Culture 1750–1900* (Routledge and Kegan Paul, London, Henley and Boston, 1977).

PATTERSON, M. W., *Sir Francis Burdett and His Times (1770–1844)* (2 vols., Macmillan, 1931).

PAUL, C. Kegan, *William Godwin: His Friends and Contemporaries* (2 vols., Henry S. King and Co., 1876).

PECK, W. E., *Shelley: His Life and Work* (2 vols., Ernest Benn, 1927).

PERKIN, Harold, *The Origins of Modern English Society 1780–1880* (Routledge and Kegan Paul, 1969).

[PIGOTT, C.], *The Jockey Club; or a Sketch of the Manners of the Age*; Part I (12th edn., H. D. Symonds, 1792), Part II (9th edn., H. D. Symonds, 1792), Part III (H. D. Symonds, 1793).

POLLIN, B. R., *Education and Enlightenment in the Works of William Godwin* (Las Americas Publishing Company, New York, 1962).

PRICKETT, S., *Coleridge and Wordsworth: The Poetry of Growth* (Cambridge University Press, Cambridge, 1970).

Public Characters of 1789–1799 (4th edn., R. Phillips, 1803).

RADER, M. R., 'Shelley's Theory of Evil' (1930), in *Shelley: A Collection of Critical Essays*, edited by G. M. Ridenour (Prentice-Hall, Englewood Cliffs, N.J., 1965), pp. 103–10.

READ, Donald, *Peterloo: The 'Massacre' and its Background* (Manchester University Press, Manchester, 1958).

REID, Loren, *Charles James Fox: A Man for the People* (Longmans, London and Harlow, 1969).

REID, William Hamilton, *The Rise and Dissolution of the Infidel Societies in this Metropolis* (J. Harchard, 1800).

REIMAN, D. H., *Shelley's 'The Triumph of Life': A Critical Study Based on a Text Newly Edited from the Bodleian Manuscript* (University of Illinois Press, Urbana, Ill., 1965).

—— *Percy Bysshe Shelley* (1969; The Macmillan Press, 1976).

RIEGER, J., *The Mutiny Within: The Heresies of Percy Bysshe Shelley* (George Braziller, New York, 1967).

ROBERTS, J. M. (ed.), *French Revolution Documents*, Vol. i (Basil Blackwell, Oxford, 1966).

—— *The Mythology of the Secret Societies* (Secker and Warburg, 1972).

ROBERTS, Michael, *The Whig Party 1807–1812* (1939; 2nd edn., Frank Cass and Co., 1965).

ROBINSON, C. E., 'The Shelley Circle and Coleridge's *The Friend*', *ELN* viii (1971), 269–74.

—— *Shelley and Byron: The Snake and Eagle Wreathed in Fight* (The Johns Hopkins University Press, Baltimore and London, 1976).

ROGERS, N., *Shelley at Work: A Critical Inquiry* (1956; 2nd edn., Clarendon Press, Oxford, 1967).

ROSSETTI, W. M., 'Shelley in 1812–13: An unpublished poem, and other particulars', *Fortnightly Review*, N.S. ix (1871), 67–85.

ROUSSEAU, Jean-Jacques, *Du contrat social* (1762), edited by R. Grimsley (Clarendon Press, Oxford, 1972).

RUDÉ, G., *Revolutionary Europe 1783–1815* (Collins, 1964).

RUSSELL, Lord John, *An Essay on the History of the English Government and Constitution, from the Reign of Henry VII. to the present time* (1821; 2nd edn., Longmans, Hurst, Rees, Orme and Brown, 1823).

SADE, D. A. F. de, *La Philosophie dans le boudoir; ou, Les Instituteurs immoraux* (1795), edited by Y. Belaval (Gallimard, Paris, 1976).

SCHULZE, E. J., *Shelley's Theory of Poetry: A Reappraisal* (Mouton, The Hague, 1966).

SEN, A., see AMIYA-KUMARA Sena.

SEWELL, Elizabeth, *The Orphic Voice: Poetry and Natural History* (1960; Harper and Row, New York, 1971).

SHAKESPEARE, William, *The Complete Works*, edited by P. Alexander (Collins, London and Glasgow, 1965).

SHELLEY, Lady Jane (ed.), *Shelley Memorials: From authentic sources*, (1859; 3rd edn., Henry S. King and Co., 1875).

SHELLEY, Mary Wollstonecraft, *The Letters of Mary W. Shelley*, edited by F. L. Jones (2 vols., University of Oklahoma Press, Norman, 1944).

—— *Mary Shelley's Journal*, edited by F. L. Jones (University of Oklahoma Press, Norman, 1947).

SHELLEY, Percy Bysshe, *A Proposal for putting Reform to the Vote . . . Facsimile of the Holograph Manuscript with an Introduction by H. Buxton Forman* (Reeves and Turner, 1887).

—— *An Address, to the Irish People*, edited by T. J. Wise (Reeves and Turner, 1890).

—— *Shelley's Prose in the Bodleian Manuscripts*, edited by A. H. Koszul (Henry Frowde, 1910).

—— *Note Books of Percy Bysshe Shelley from the Originals in the library of W. K. Bixby*, edited by H. B. Forman (3 vols., For the Bibliophile Society, Boston, 1911).

—— *The Complete Works of Percy Bysshe Shelley*, edited by R. Ingpen and W. E. Peck (1926–30; 10 vols., Ernest Benn, 1965).

—— *The Shelley Notebook in the Harvard College Library*, edited by G. E. Woodberry (John Barnard Associates, Cambridge, Mass., 1929).

—— *Shelley's Prose; or, The Trumpet of a Prophecy*, edited by D. L. Clark (University of New Mexico Press, Albuquerque, 1954).

—— *Shelley's* Prometheus Unbound: *A Variorum Edition*, edited by L. J. Zillman (University of Washington Press, Seattle, Washington, 1959).

—— *Shelley and his Circle 1773–1822*, Vols. i–iv edited by K. N. Cameron (Oxford University Press, 1961–70), Vols. v–vi edited by D. H. Reiman (Harvard University Press, Cambridge, Mass., 1973).

—— *The Esdaile Notebook: A Volume of Early Poems by Percy Bysshe Shelley*, edited by K. N. Cameron (Faber and Faber, 1964).

—— *The Letters of Percy Bysshe Shelley*, edited by F. L. Jones (2 vols., Clarendon Press, Oxford, 1964).

—— *The Complete Poetical Works of Percy Bysshe Shelley*, edited by N. Rogers, Vols. i–ii (Clarendon Press, Oxford, 1972–5).

—— *Shelley's Poetry and Prose*, edited by D. H. Reiman and S. B. Powers (W. W. Norton and Co., New York, 1977).

SOUTHEY, Robert, *Essays, Moral and Political* (1832; 2 vols., Irish University Press, Shannon, 1971).

STAËL, Mme de, *Considérations sur les principaux événemens de la Révolution Françoise* (3 vols., Baldwin, Cradock and Joy, 1818).

SWINBURNE, A. C., *William Blake: A Critical Essay* (1868; Heinemann, 1925).

THOMPSON, A., 'Shelley and "Satire's scourge" ', in *Literature of the Romantic Period 1750–1850*, edited by R. T. Davies and B. G. Beatty (University of Liverpool Press, Liverpool, 1976), pp. 135–50.

THOMPSON, E. P., *The Making of the English Working Class* (1963; Penguin Books, Harmondsworth, Middlesex, 1968).

TODD, F. M., *Politics and the Poet: A Study of Wordsworth* (Methuen and Co., 1957).

TRILLING, L., *Matthew Arnold* (1939; George Allen and Unwin, 1974).

VOLNEY, C. F. C., comte de, *Les Ruines, ou Méditation sur les révolutions des empires* (Desenne and others, Paris, 1791).

WARD, Aileen, 'The forging of Orc: Blake and the idea of revolution', in *Literature in Revolution*, edited by G. A. White and C. Newman (Holt, Rhinehart and Winston, New York, 1972), pp. 204–27.

WASSERMAN, E. R., *Shelley: A Critical Reading* (The Johns Hopkins Press, Baltimore and London, 1971).

WEBB, Timothy, *Shelley: A voice not understood* (Manchester University Press, Manchester, 1977).

—— 'Shelley's Negatives', to be published as part of the proceedings of the Shelley Conference held at Gregynog in September 1978, edited by Kelvin Everest (forthcoming from the Harvester Press, Hassocks, Sussex).

WELLEK, R., *Immanuel Kant in England 1793–1838* (Princeton University Press, Princeton, 1931).

—— *A History of Modern Criticism 1750–1950* (4 vols., Jonathan Cape, 1955–66).

WESTON, Corinne Comstock, *English Constitutional Theory and the House of Lords 1556–1832* (Routledge and Kegan Paul, 1965).

WHITE, Newman Ivey, 'Shelley's *Swell-foot the Tyrant* in Relation to Contemporary Political Satire', *PMLA* xxxvi (1921), 332–46.

—— *The Unextinguished Hearth: Shelley and His Contemporary Critics* (1938; Octagon Books, New York, 1966).

—— *Shelley* (2 vols., Secker and Warburg, 1947).

WHITE, Reginald J., *Waterloo to Peterloo* (1957; Penguin Books, Harmondsworth, 1968).

WHITNEY, L., *Primitivism and the Idea of Progress in English Popular Literature of the Eighteenth Century* (1934; Octagon Books, New York, 1965).

WILLIAMS, Raymond, *Culture and Society 1780–1950* (Chatto and Windus, 1958).

WILSON, Milton, *Shelley's Later Poetry: A Study of his Prophetic Imagination* (Columbia University Press, New York, 1959).

WILTON, R. C., 'Norfolk House: 1746–1815', *Dublin Review*, clxv (1919), 121–40.

WIMSATT, W. K., and BROOKS, Cleanth, *Literary Criticism: A Short History* (1957; Routledge and Kegan Paul, 1970).

WOLFE, Humbert (ed.), *The Life of Percy Bysshe Shelley as comprised in The Life of Shelley by Thomas Jefferson Hogg; The Recollections of Shelley & Byron by Edward John Trelawny; Memoirs of Shelley by Thomas Love Peacock* (2 vols., Dent, 1933)

WOLLSTONECRAFT, Mary, *An Historical and Moral View of the Origin and Progress of the French Revolution; and the Effect it has produced in Europe*, Vol. i (no more published; J. Johnson, 1794).

WOODCOCK, George, *Anarchism: A History of Libertarian Ideas and Movements* (1962; Penguin Books, Harmondsworth, 1971).

WOODINGS, R. B. (ed.), *Shelley: Modern Judgements* (Macmillan, 1968).

WOODMAN, Ross Greig, *The Apocalyptic Vision in the Poetry of Shelley* (University of Toronto Press, Toronto, 1964).

—— 'Shelley's Urania', *Studies in Romanticism*, xvii (1978), 61–75.

WOODRING, C., *Politics in English Romantic Poetry* (Harvard University Press, Cambridge, Mass., 1970).

WORDSWORTH, W., *The Prelude, or Growth of a Poet's Mind*, edited by E. de Selincourt (1926), 2nd edn. revised by H. Darbishire (Clarendon Press, Oxford, 1959).

—— *The Poetical Works of William Wordsworth*, edited by E. de Selincourt and H. Darbishire (1940–9; revised edn., 5 vols., Clarendon Press, Oxford, 1952–9).

—— *The Letters of William and Dorothy Wordsworth: The Middle Years*, edited by E. de Selincourt (1937), revised by M. Moorman and A. G. Hill (2 vols., Clarendon Press, Oxford, 1969–70).

WRAXALL, Nathaniel, *The Historical and the Posthumous Memoirs of Sir Nathaniel William Wraxall 1772–1784*, edited by H. B. Wheatley (5 vols., Bickers and Son, 1884).

WRIGHT, John W., *Shelley's Myth of Metaphor* (University of Georgia Press, Athens, Ga., 1970).

WYSE, Thomas, *Historical Sketch of the late Catholic Association of Ireland* (2 vols., Henry Colburn, 1829).

WYVILL, the Revd Christopher, *Political Papers* (6 vols., privately, York, [1794–1808]).

YOUNG, Art, *Shelley and Nonviolence* (Mouton, The Hague, 1975).

Index